THE OXFORD ILLUSTRATED HISTORY OF
MODERN EUROPE

THE OXFORD
ILLUSTRATED HISTORY OF
MODERN
EUROPE

EDITED BY

T. C. W. BLANNING

OXFORD
UNIVERSITY PRESS

OXFORD

Great Clarendon Street, Oxford OX2 6DP

Oxford University Press is a department of the University of Oxford.
It furthers the University's objective of excellence in research, scholarship,
and education by publishing worldwide in

Oxford New York

Auckland Bangkok Buenos Aires Cape Town Chennai
Dar es Salaam Delhi Hong Kong Istanbul Karachi Kolkata
Kuala Lumpur Madrid Melbourne Mexico City Mumbai
Nairobi São Paulo Shanghai Taipei Tokyo Toronto

Oxford is a registered trade mark of Oxford University Press
in the UK and in certain other countries

First published 1996
Issued as an Oxford University Press paperback 1998
Reissued 2001

British Library Cataloguing in Publication Data

Data available

Library of Congress Cataloging in Publication Data

Data applied for

ISBN 978-0-19-285426-1

7 9 10 8 6

Printed in Great Britain by
Ashford Colour Press Ltd,
Gosport, Hants.

Contents

CONTENTS

List of Colour Plates

List of Maps

List of Contributors

T. C. W. Blanning is Professor of Modern European History at the University of Cambridge and a Fellow of Sidney Sussex College.

John Roberts was Warden of Merton College, Oxford, until his retirement in 1994.

Clive Trebilcock is Lecturer in History at the University of Cambridge and a Fellow of Pembroke College.

Hew Strachan is Professor of Modern History at the University of Glasgow.

Pamela Pilbeam is Professor of History at Royal Holloway and Bedford New College, University of London.

Paul Preston is Professor of International History at the London School of Economics and Poltical Science.

Harold James is Professor of History at Princeton University.

Richard Overy is Professor of History, King's College London.

Richard Bessel is Professor of Twentieth-Century History at the University of York.

David Reynolds is Lecturer in History at the University of Cambridge and a Fellow of Christ's College.

Introduction

In 1914, the French poet Charles Péguy wrote that the world had changed more since he started going to school in the 1880s than during the two previous millennia. If he had not died shortly afterwards but had lived out his full biblical allocation of three score years and ten until 1943, he would have experienced even more dramatic changes. It has been this conviction that the ground is moving beneath their feet which has characterized modern Europeans. Among other things, it has given them a strong dynamism: the world *is* changing, it *can* be changed, and so it *should* be changed. On the eve of the French Revolution, the German playwright Gotthold Ephraim Lessing identified the essence of modern man as follows: 'he often achieves very accurate insights into the future, but he cannot wait for the future to come. He wants to see the future accelerated, and also wants to do the accelerating himself. For what is there in it for him, if what he sees to be desirable is not brought about in his lifetime?'

It is with no sense of triumph, rather the reverse, that one records that modern Europeans have transformed not only their own continent but also the world. What they could not conquer directly, they ensnared in economic, social, and cultural bonds. What is sometimes described as the 'Americanization' of the world has been conducted by the descendants of Europeans who conquered North America and eliminated most of its aboriginal population. The European origin of the culture which was then re-exported with such dazzling success in the twentieth century is revealed not least by the name of its most ubiquitous symbol—the hamburger.

Many explanations for Europe's hegemony have been offered. Was it Europe's special geography, with its deeply indented coastline, profusion of rivers, absence of flood-plains, and its relatively simple flora and fauna deriving from its peculiar mountain pattern? Was it the bracing competition engendered by the plurality of states and churches, saving Europe from stable but stagnant uniformity? Was it

T. C. W.
BLANNING

1

Europe's early embrace of secularization and with it 'the disenchantment of the world', means–ends rationality, and the scientific revolution? Was it Europe's adoption of the division of labour, leading to commercialization, urbanization, and industrialization? Was it the development of new social forms, in which the organic community based on kinship, neighbourhood, or religious belief (*Gemeinschaft*) made way for a society of atomized individuals driven by self-interest and the cash nexus (*Gesellschaft*)? Was it Europe's discovery of the power of the nation-state, combining a sense of national identity with bureaucratic administration and democratic institutions? As we shall discover from this volume, all of these hypotheses—and the many others which have been offered—are more or less persuasive, but none of them is sufficient.

Something which changes is naturally more interesting than something which stays the same. That this banal observation is a truism should not blind us to its importance. A history which presents only changes is a history which tells only half the story: for every value or institution which is modified or disappears altogether, there is another which remains the same. Moreover, not all changes prove to be irreversible. Only predictions as general as 'Europe will never return to a mainly agrarian economy' can be made with any confidence. Such is the 'cunning of history' (Hegel) that the neater the scheme for understanding the past, explaining the present, and predicting the future, the quicker it is undone. 'How many divisions has *he* got?' sneered Joseph Stalin, when dismissing an initiative by Pius XII. Although he lived not a minute too long, it is sad that Stalin did not survive to witness papal authority in eastern Europe eclipsing that of the general secretary of the communist party of the USSR (dec.).

For that reason, this history of modern Europe presents both change and continuity, revolutions and stability. No attempt has been made to work out a definition of 'modern Europe', for that in itself would consume a good-sized volume without yielding an answer likely to command general approval. Indeed, the theory which sees monotheism as the key to modernity would have us begin with the Book of Genesis. The decision was taken to begin this volume at the end of the eighteenth century, for it was then that revolution broke out in France, that the process of industrialization in Britain became visible to the naked eye, that the wars of the French Revolution and Napoleon brought change to every corner of the continent, that the formation of a society of classes rather than orders entered a new and decisive phase, and—last but not least—the great romantic revolution in European culture began.

None of these phenomena began or ended at the same time, it need hardly be said. A date such as 14 July 1789 has little or no meaning for the economic development of Europe. For the political historian, however, it does mark the beginning of a new epoch. As John Roberts shows, in his account of European politics from the French Revolution to the First World War, what happened in 1789 determined much of Europe's history for the next century. By showing that an old regime could be destroyed and a new order created by its own people, the French supplied both the model and the inspiration for generations of revolutionaries to come. They also introduced powerful new sources of political legitimation, obliging their enemies to articulate alternative ideologies. It was during these years that much of the vocabulary of modern politics—'conservative', 'liberal', 'democrat', 'left', and 'right'—was established.

Roberts also shows that once the revolutionary genie was out of the bottle, all the best efforts of the established order could not cram it back in again. Even the period of apparent conservative success after 1815 was punctuated by violent outbreaks of unrest, culminating in the wave of revolutions which spread across the continent in 1848. Their advertisement of the appeal of nationalism led to a renewal of international adventurism, first by Napoleon III and then by Bismarck. When the dust settled, Italy and Germany had been unified and France had finally lost her hegemony on the continent. Another period of calm followed, but nationalism proved to be 'the revolutionary serpent which had still not been scotched in the egg', especially in the Balkans. Between 1871 and 1914, five new nations achieved independence, all of them former provinces of the Turkish empire. So the First World War, or the Great War, could also be called either the War of the Ottoman Succession or the Third German War, for—like its predecessors of 1866 and 1870—it was also about Germany's position in Europe. It was to be the most terrible war Europe had ever seen. It unleashed the Russian revolution, destroyed the Austro-Hungarian and German empires, began the decline and fall of the British empire, and ended Europe's ascendancy in the world. But it did not solve the German question, indeed it only made it worse. So, Roberts concludes, 1789 marked the beginning of an era—but 1918 did not mark its end.

The economic changes of the nineteenth century were not punctuated by precise dates such as 1789, 1815, 1848, 1870, or 1914, but they were at least as profound. In his chapter, Clive Trebilcock identifies three waves of industrialization: from the 1780s to the 1820s, from the 1840s to the 1870s, and during the last two decades before the First World War. In 1780 there was little to choose between the two great powers of western Europe, but the manifold disruption caused by the French Revolution and its wars allowed the British to establish a decisive lead. The continental 'follower economies' had to wait for the second phase to follow suit. It was the railways which proved the key, indeed Britain was the only country to industrialize without them. After this boom had hit the buffers with the recession beginning in the mid-1870s, and known rather grandly as the 'Great Depression', there was another period of rapid expansion, with high-technology electrical, chemical, optical, and automotive sectors coming to the fore. These three phases of industrialization demanded adaptability from governments and entrepreneurs alike. Handicapped by the overconfidence bred by being first in the field, the British began to fall behind. It was the Germans who exploited most successfully the institutional equivalent of steam power—the investment bank. It was also they who proved most adept at generating the science–industry connections which gave them supremacy in high-technology industries.

As Trebilcock shows, although one cannot help but discuss the progress of the European economy in terms of national units, the real context of industrialization is both more international and regional than national. Within any state, there were highly industrialized islands such as northern Britain, the Ruhr, and north-eastern France, but they were floating in agricultural oceans. By 1914 only in Britain did the scale of industrialization make agriculture's contribution to national output seem modest. Everywhere, the social and political power of landed interests was still immense. For most people in most parts of Europe, daily life in the countryside proceeded according to a pace and rhythm that was entirely traditional.

As these first two chapters demonstrate, politics and economics constantly interact. And of the various binding agents, the most direct is war. For example, it was the Revolutionary and Napoleonic wars which put the French economy in lead boots for generations; it was failure in the Crimean war which prompted the Russians to try to modernize their economy; and it was the Franco-Prussian war of 1870–1 which tore from the French economy the two provinces richest in raw materials. In turn, warfare itself was also deeply influenced by industrialization. In his examination of military modernization, Hew Strachan argues that the battlefield of 1918, with its tanks, heavy artillery, machine-guns, flame-throwers, poison gas, ground-attack aircraft, and long-range bombers, was much closer to present-day experience than to the battlefield of Waterloo. The enormous technological advances in weaponry, combined with the speed of mobilization made possible by the railways, had revolutionized warfare. The result was the most intensive blood-letting in the history of mankind—to that point.

Yet it was not the ineluctable forces of economics which determined the course of military history. As Strachan convincingly argues, it was changing *ideas* that mattered most. That is why he devotes a section to the importance of military theory, exemplified by its two greatest nineteenth-century practitioners, Clausewitz and Jomini. The importance of human agency is also revealed in two contrasting ways by the astonishing military success achieved by the Prussians between 1864 and 1871. On the positive side, it was their use of the general staff which gave them a decisive edge over their opponents. On the other hand, their complacent belief in the absolute superiority of their professional army paved the way for eventual disaster in 1918. This is not the only constant feature of European warfare revealed by Strachan's analysis. He also demonstrates, for example, the continuing importance of fortifications and siege warfare. It was the construction programme launched by the French after 1871 which both created the need for the Schlieffen plan and frustrated its execution.

Human material also provides the subject-matter for Pamela Pilbeam's examination of European society in the nineteenth century. There was a rapidly growing amount of it, the population of Europe more than doubling from—in round figures—193 million to 423 million, despite the emigration of 45 million (of whom some 10 million eventually returned). This kind of demographic revolution was bound to put traditional institutions under severe strain. Especially during recessions such as the 'hungry forties', there was an acute awareness of what contemporaries called 'the social question', and a corresponding clamour for state intervention to answer it. Although the masses toiling in the dark satanic mills may have found it difficult to believe, conditions were in fact improving, however erratically and unequally. With more children surviving infancy and the incidence of pandemics declining, average life expectancy was increasing, as was literacy, per capita income, the ability of working people to represent their interests, and, consequently, state provision for social insurance. As a result the class war predicted so confidently by Karl Marx did not materialize.

Of the traditional élites, it was the first estate—the clergy—who suffered most, both relatively and absolutely. Their secular counterparts among the aristocracy proved much better able to adapt to changing conditions. Not only did they retain their grip on the commanding heights of government and society, many of them exploited the opportunities proffered by the industrial era to become rich beyond the dreams of their most avaricious ancestors. As Pilbeam remarks, the aristocratic élite did not perish, it diversified. But the great victors were of course the middle classes, not so much the entrepreneurs among them (despite some spectacular individual success stories) as the landowners, professional men, and state employees. It was they who combined quantity with quality to put their cultural stamp on the period. If most people got richer during the course of the century, the gap between rich and poor widened.

In my own chapter, on the culture of Europe in the nineteenth century, I also examine the impact of modernity on the traditional world. Already under way by the late eighteenth century, the transformation of the representational culture of the old regime was accelerated by the contemporary political, economic, and social changes discussed in previous chapters. In particular, the growth of a literate public eager and able to consume cultural artefacts liberated the artist from dependence on a patron. The simultaneous development of a new expressive aesthetic, which placed the artist at the centre of the creative process, greatly enhanced his self-esteem and—eventually—his status. It also opened the way for him to become the high priest of the sacralized culture which increasingly became a supplement to, or even substitute for, organized religion, as the construction of museums, theatres, opera-houses, and concert-halls in the style of classical temples demonstrated. In the space of less than a century, the artist went from liveried servant to commander of sovereigns: in 1781 Mozart had been brutally ejected from the service of the Archbishop of Salzburg with a kick to his backside; in 1876 the German emperor travelled to Bayreuth to pay homage to Richard Wagner by attending the first performance of *The Ring of the Nibelung*.

But liberation from the patrons of the old regime could also mean enslavement to the new commercial world of the public. All too often it turned out that what the latter wanted to buy was not what the former wished to create and that popularization meant vulgarization. For every Dickens, Delacroix, or Verdi who could satisfy market demand without compromising his—or her—integrity, there were many more who retreated to bohemian garrets, cursing the 'Philistinism' of bourgeois materialism. This sense of alienation from contemporary society could find expression in introspective isolation, but it could equally well erupt in angry *exposés* of the corruption and oppression of the modern world, as it did, for example, in the realist movement of the middle decades of the century. This abrasive relationship between art and society was the grit in the oyster which produced the pearl. Vincent Van Gogh sold only one painting during a career which was a constant struggle with poverty, lack of recognition, alcoholism, and insanity, ending in suicide; his almost exact contemporary, the immeasurably less talented Frederic Leighton, not only made a fortune from his paintings, many of which became best sellers in the form of photogravure reproductions, but was loaded with honours, including a peerage.

The subjectivism of the romantic revolution enjoyed a revival at the end of the century, as part of a more general breakdown of the confident certainties of liberal Europe. With the advantage of hindsight, it is tempting to see this *fin de siècle* decadence as a sultry Indian summer preparing the thunderclap of 1914. In his examination of European politics between 1914 and 1945, however, Paul Preston identifies a wholly material and quite precise cause of the breakdown: the search by German élites to export the problems caused by rapid industrialization, urbanization, and the emergence of the largest and best-organized socialist movement in Europe. It was a 'flight to the front' which ended in disaster, although it might conceivably have succeeded if the Germans had not brought the United States of America into the war. Taking the baton from John Roberts, Preston shows how the conflict begun in 1914 was not to be resolved until 1945, when the great European civil war at long last ended.

The Versailles settlement of 1919 was the peace which made matters worse, leaving Germany not only fiercely revisionist but still strong enough to try another bid for European supremacy once she had recovered. Indeed the creation of a network of feeble states on her eastern frontier made such an attempt almost inevitable. Right across Europe, the political centre fell apart in the 1920s, as the polarizing effects of the war worked themselves out. Mussolini's seizure of power in 1922 was an early example of the corrosive force of disappointed nationalism. Particularly damaging, Preston argues, was the fatal division of the left. Far from seeking an alliance with social democrats against the right, the Soviet-dominated Comintern chose to see them as *the* main obstacle to revolution, attacking them as 'social fascists'. It was only when Hitler's seizure of power in 1933 showed what fascism was really capable of that the divided left began to form alliances known as 'Popular Fronts'. They were too little too late, failing heroically in Spain and cravenly in France. They had their parallel in international politics, where for too long the western democracies saw the fascist regimes not as a threat to themselves but as a weapon to be deployed against Soviet communism.

The unhappy political history of inter-war Europe was married to her equally turbulent economic fortunes. The dynamo of the world economy before the First World War, Europe tottered away from the debris impoverished, depopulated, deeply in debt to her American saviour, and facing sharp new competition from her former dependencies. As Harold James shows in his examination of the European economy in the twentieth century, the attempt to get back to normal proved to be a recipe for disaster. Deflation and unemployment in the west, hyperinflation and unemployment in the east fuelled the political polarization analysed by Preston. After a brief period of stability during the mid-1920s, the depression which began in 1929 became 'the most traumatic economic event of this century'. Indeed, James argues that the story of the subsequent fifty years can be told as a series of attempts to prevent its recurrence. Not all countries, alas, were prepared to try Keynes's benign prescription of demand management. Both the rearmament favoured by Hitler and the forced industrialization chosen by Stalin had consequences so terrible that even the suffering inflicted by the First World War pales by comparison.

The Second World War shifted the world economic balance even more decisively than the First, leaving Europe more impoverished, more depopulated, and more in debt to her American saviour. Fortunately, the Americans had learned from past mistakes and used their power to impose a liberal economic order. The creation of the International Monetary Fund and the World Bank in 1945, the introduction of the Marshall Plan in 1947, and the prevention of a punitive policy towards (West) Germany set Europe on a surprisingly rapid road to recovery. Co-operation not autarky was also on the Europeans' own agenda, as was shown by the formation of the six-member European Coal and Steel Community in 1952 and the creation of the European Economic Community by the Treaty of Rome in 1957. The result was what James terms an 'economic miracle' in the 1950s, with the beginning of democratized mass consumption on the American pattern. Clouded over towards the end of the 1960s by widespread labour unrest and growing inflation, these happy days were brought to a definitive end by the oil crisis of 1973. Subsequent moves towards further European integration, liberalization of world trade, and the promotion of high technology may have ameliorated but have not prevented the continuing structural crisis of European industry and high unemployment. The collapse of the Soviet empire opens up new opportunities, but James ends with the bleak observation that Keynesian remedies can no longer work.

It was not only the economic decisions taken in 1918 which proved to be misguided. In his chapter on European warfare in the twentieth century, Richard Overy shows how what Woodrow Wilson hoped would be 'the final war for human liberty' only paved the way for another and even more terrible conflict. Neither the League of Nations nor the various international peace initiatives of the 1920s and 1930s could persuade the powers not to pursue what they perceived as their legitimate interests. On the contrary, post-war military thinking was transformed by the concept of total war, that blurring of distinction between civilian and combatant which had been signalled during the First World War by German unrestricted submarine warfare, the Allied blockade of German ports, and long-range bombing of German cities. So far as the battlefield of the future was concerned, however, conservatives retained the upper hand, their vested interest in the traditional army and navy blinding them to the potential of air power and massed armour. It was only the Germans and, to a lesser extent, the Russians who correctly learned some of the military lessons from the stalemate of 1914–18. So when war resumed in 1939, the western allies were caught flat-footed, intending to fight a war of attrition from behind the Maginot line. And when the Germans had conquered most of Europe, the British found themselves obliged to continue an indirect strategy, trying to contain their enemies in the Mediterranean while sapping their strength with a combination of blockade and bombing. Meanwhile, in the east, both the Germans and the Soviets fought a mobile war of combat. It was only in 1943 that

7

the British and Americans concluded that they would have to wage war directly on the continent.

Unlike the First, the Second World War did mark a watershed in the history of warfare. So total had war become that it was now doubtful whether it was safer to be a civilian or a soldier. The combination of technological efficiency with ideological absolutism produced in the holocaust what was arguably the greatest horror in human history. The discovery that there existed a weapon with the potential to eliminate life on the planet completed the sobering lesson. So when Europe froze into the rival blocs of the Cold War, both NATO and the Warsaw Pact relied on a strategy of deterrence. By the 1960s both sides had accumulated arsenals of such destructive capability that 'Mutual Assured Destruction' was in prospect. This stalemate prompted a return to the strategy of 'flexible response' with greater emphasis on conventional weapons. So far, so good, but Overy ends with the chilling conclusion: 'The Second World War, not the First, was the war to end all wars, for the moment.'

In 1914, as Richard Bessel writes in his chapter on European society in the twentieth century, Europe provided the model for world societies seeking to modernize, so that Rio de Janeiro, for example, could look to Paris for the best way to organize a city. That status was soon lost, as the European economy was pushed from the centre by the war and its aftermath, as European civilization was tarnished by waves of fratricidal conflict, and as the emigration of Europeans slowed and then stopped. After 1945, indeed, the relationship was reversed, as the post-war labour shortage sucked in migrants from Africa, Asia, and the Caribbean. So the former colonizers are now the colonized and a new English town such as Milton Keynes tries to look not like Paris but Brasilia. As the rest of the world has caught up, European society as a separate identity has disappeared.

It is impossible to judge which of the rich variety of social changes charted and analysed by Bessel has been the most radical. Has it been the separation of sex from reproduction and the plummeting size of families; or the ever-increasing proportion of retired people; or the final emergence of the self-contained 'nuclear family'; or the equally final victory of urbanization; or the disappearance of domestic service and the rise of service industries; or the change in the role of women; or the levelling of income differentials and the rise in the standard of living; or mass ownership of the motor car; or the phenomenal growth of international tourism; or mass literacy and the media revolution; or the increased dependence on the state for social security, housing, and education; or the demystification of the world? As this list suggests, not everything in the twentieth century has been for the worst in the worst of all possible worlds.

Always in a state of flux in the modern period, European society in the twentieth century, Bessel concludes, has become more fragmented and diverse than ever before. That is doubly true of its high culture. In Chapter 10, Martin Jay presents it first in the form of an imaginary mid-century account of the triumphant progress of modernism. First employed in the 1890s, the term was adopted by artists seeking to follow Verlaine's advice to 'twist the neck' of the tired rhetoric of the nineteenth century. Never a coherent movement but an umbrella covering a dozen and more different -isms, from cubism to surrealism, modernism came into its own after the collapse of the old cultural certainties in the First World War. The war may not have made the world safe for democracy, but it certainly made it safe for the avant-garde. By 1939 the modernists had survived assaults from left and right to achieve a supremacy demonstrated most convincingly by the old-master prices paid for their works. On the one hand modernists disdained any causal relationship with the material world, stressing instead their 'absolute self-referentiality and utter disinterestedness'. On the other hand, they liked to see themselves as sacralizing agents, filling the gap left by the demystification of the world in the cause of liberty and internationalism.

This was the kind of triumphalist account which might have been written in the aftermath of the Second World War. But, as Jay explains, during the past thirty years or so a new—post-modernist—critique has challenged this heroic narrative. Modernism has come to seem commercially self-serving, politically suspect, and theoretically flawed. A distinction has been drawn between the modernists who withdrew into the alleged autonomy of art and the true avant-garde who tried to break down barriers between art and life. So once isolated figures such as Marcel Duchamp and Man Ray are celebrated as the true pioneers. In the place of the modernist austere emphasis on form, there has come a return to content, to natural and historical themes, even to architectural ornament. However, post-modernists have not revived the earlier avant-garde's belief that life could and should be aestheticized. On the contrary, they have rejected the missionary impulse of the 'universal intellectual', preferring to operate with the modest local limits of 'weak thought'. Much criticized for its apparent cynicism, rejection of rationalism, deliberate conflation of art and commodity, and willingness to 'learn from Las Vegas', it is too early to say where post-modernism will end. However, that it has disrupted the confident script of the modernists, Jay concludes, is certain.

David Reynolds begins the final chapter, on European politics since 1945, with a timely reminder that historians are poor prophets, quoting the late E. P. Thompson's prediction of 1987 that Europe would be divided into two hostile blocs 'for evermore'. Two years later, the iron curtain was rung down, as the Soviet empire collapsed. Reynolds shows how the Cold War was born out of a new struggle for mastery in Germany. While the Americans believed that German recovery was a precondition for the resurrection of Europe, the Soviets saw it only as a threat. So they countered its promotion by the Marshall Plan of 1947 with a declaration of ideological war, the Berlin blockade, and the formation of a separate state, the grotesquely misnamed 'German Democratic Republic'. Concern to find an answer to the German question was also acute in the West, playing an important role in the formation of NATO (designed 'to keep the Russians out, the Americans in and the Germans down') and the EEC. The division of Europe was then completed in 1955 with West German rearmament and admission to NATO. The intensity of the Cold War could only diminish when Europe recovered and the two superpowers experienced problems of their own. So the Vietnamese war and the short-lived Czech rising of 1968 led to *détente*.

Yet the thaw of the 1970s did not melt the frontiers. On the contrary, mutual recognition only made them more rigid. It was the ending of détente in the wake of the Soviet invasion of Afghanistan in 1979 and the Polish crisis of 1980–1 that precipitated the final crisis of what the new American president, Ronald Reagan, dubbed 'the evil empire'. With their satraps now denied the western loans which had kept their archaic 'heavy metal' economies afloat, the Soviets had to pay the bill themselves. Struggling to keep up with American military technology and demoralized by their failure in Afghanistan, they tried a new way in 1985, with the appointment of a reformer as general secretary of the communist party, Mikhail Gorbachev. As soon as he signalled that he could not and would not supply the force which had supported the Soviet empire since the 1940s, it crumbled so quickly that within a couple of years not even the USSR remained.

This great revolution, no less momentous for being mainly peaceful, began in 1989, exactly two hundred years after our starting-point. As Reynolds observes: 'Like the would-be reformers of the *ancien régime*, Gorbachev had sown the wind and reaped the whirlwind.' Alas, the euphoria of the liberated peoples of eastern Europe was no longer lived than that of their ancestors of 1789. Few areas have escaped impoverishment, social collapse, and civil war. Predicting whether these are the birth-pangs of a new, peaceful, and integrated Europe, or whether they herald a return visit from the four horsemen of the Apocalypse is happily not the brief of the editor or indeed of any of his contributors. Whatever may happen in the future, however, we hope and believe that whoever reads this volume will be in a better position to place events in their historical context and thus achieve a better understanding of their singularity and significance.

Revolution from Above and Below

European Politics from the French Revolution to the First World War

THE hundred and thirty years between 1789 and 1918 have traditionally been, and can still be, sensibly divided into phases with clear chronological markers. They begin with a quarter-century of great upheavals and wars; then, in 1815, there opened a period of peace—at least between the great powers—lasting until 1854, fraying though its fabric begins to look towards the end. There followed two decades of upheaval, war, and state-making, before a second great peace from 1871 to 1914, during which only disputes over the fate of the Ottoman empire seemed likely to bring about war between the European powers (though in 1904 a Russo-Japanese war announced that a new political world was already being born). After that came the descent to 1914, and the beginning of the greatest European war ever. It turned into the First World War and ended (though not quite completely) in 1918. By then European history was no longer a self-contained entity and already could be understood only in a world-wide context. Though 1789 had opened an era, 1918 did not close one.

The Myth of Revolution

What Frenchmen did in 1789, intentionally or willy-nilly, still makes that year memorable. It made later men—and some of their contemporaries—see them as makers of a new age. From that flowed huge consequences, new ways of thinking of what revolution might mean, for good and ill, and a new sense of public possibilities—hopeful or fearful. Whether the French 'Revolution', whose roots lay in a fairly typical eighteenth-century response by privileged élites to an innovating government, was, in essence, simply the logical consequence of a breakdown in

JOHN
ROBERTS

11

the working of an *ancien régime*, or the overflowing of tendencies inherent in French culture and society, or a series of episodes managed or engineered, or an eruption of irrepressible forces, has been long debated and is almost infinitely discussible. What is clear is that, besides furnishing grounds for ever-renewed debate, what happened in 1789 determined much of Europe's history for the next century. It came to be seen as the beginning of an age of revolution *par excellence*. The next few years supplied most of the psychic energy driving European politics for the whole nineteenth century.

That century was haunted by the idea of revolution. Ambiguity explains much of its power over men's minds. Objectively, there were many political events between 1789 and 1918 to which the name 'revolution' could be, and has been, given. Many of them were acknowledged to be changes not only big in consequences, but dramatic enough to appear to be—and sometimes actually to be—true ruptures with the past, even sometimes engineered, rather than organic growths emerging from it. Some of those revolutions could be measured very precisely by, for example, changes in political language and institutions. Democracy, a term of opprobrium in 1789, was by 1918 a shibboleth of the victors in the greatest war in history. Absolute tended to give way to constitutional rule; monarchies turned into republics. Major steps could be calibrated in some countries by the extension of the franchise. Such changes were not always violent; they could be peaceful or at least bloodless, even when coercive. But their scope was always striking.

One conspicuous revolutionary change always tending to violence, none the less, was the emergence of national states. In 1789 Portugal had been the only country in Europe where government and language were more or less coterminous; only two or three monarchies (those of England, Spain, and France) could then plausibly be called national institutions. A hundred and thirty years later, there was not a state in Europe which did not invoke the principle of nationality in its support (while often at the same time vigorously resisting the claims of other nationalities conscious of oppression). Such changes had of course been shaped by others external to politics—in demography, economic development, technology, communications—which were equally revolutionary to those who lived through them. For many little German towns and localities, some of them statelets in 1789, true revolution began not with any of the great dates of German nation-building, but with the arrival of the first railway or the opening of the first steam-powered (or even water-driven) factory. In Russia the final abolition of bonded labour in Europe by the emancipation decree of 1861 at last ended the Middle Ages as a going concern—a revolution, indeed, even if not one in political forms. A general, century-long acceleration of change was continuous and very often upsetting to men and women who found the world of their old age—or even middle life—strangely unlike that into which they had been born.

The sway over the minds of men exercised by the idea of revolution in the nineteenth century is none the less as much a matter of subjective, symbolic, and mythological as of positive facts. In the great French Revolution itself the word 'revolution' first began to be used in new senses. Its connotations were later extended still further and it became one of the great metaphors of the last, mature era of a self-contained European culture. It was a telling symptom that the word soon began to be capitalized in print and used without local qualification. It was hypostasized, and became an abstraction, though its origins lay in very concrete, actual, specific situations. This was easy while there were men about who had lived through the 1790s. Half a century after 1789, Carlyle noted that the French Revolution was still not complete; just over ten years later, Tocqueville thought that the same, continuing revolution was unrolling, still going on, unfinished, though men's fortunes and passions ebbed and flowed. Thiers, the leader of the French opposition at the beginning of the revolutionary year 1848, assured his countrymen that even if it were to pass out of the hands of the moderate revolutionaries, he would never abandon the cause of the revolution. Even much later in the century, John Morley, a politician too moderate to be called a radical anywhere except in England, still felt that 'everywhere we discern the hand and hearken to the tread of the Revolution'.

The myth of revolution probably inspired as many as it frightened. The young authors of *The Communist Manifesto* gloated in 1848 over the spectre of communism haunting Europe; their ideals were rooted in aspirations many felt had been thwarted between 1789 and 1815, and which many believed were still to have their day. The myth was also an intellectual convenience. Whether it was believed that irresistible forces were working to assure that revolution was inevitable, or that propaganda and organization could bring it about—and whether people viewed the outcome as desirable or horrific—the idea that the central issue of politics was to be for or against the revolution was a great simplifier; it provided a way of seeing, understanding, explaining things otherwise difficult or unintelligible. It accommodated other appealing notions too, justifying and provoking the inven-

Almost always nineteenth-century revolutionaries identified themselves with the classical slogan of 1791: Liberty, Equality, Fraternity. These ideals were to have a long mythological life and are here utilized in a German socialist newspaper to depict the ultimate goal of Karl Marx, who in fact viewed 1789 as a bourgeois achievement which was only one step in the revolutionary process.

13

tion of histories, belief in conspiracies, and secret associations. The nineteenth century was the heyday of hidden explanations and plot theories, for there were overt grounds for alarm aplenty. The conscious imitation, invocation, even re-enactment of the events of the 1790s provided the stock-in-trade of French politicians of the left throughout the century. In the greatest urban rising of the age, the Paris Commune of 1871, memory fatally dogged the language and imagination of revolutionaries and conservatives alike. Revolutionary—or self-proclaimed revolutionary—organizations proliferated, from the *Carbonari* to the First International, from the semi-criminal bandits of the Ottoman Balkans to the Serbian Black Hand. The nineteenth century created the international terrorist, though not the ideology of cosmopolitan radicalism which justified him; that, like so much else that was new, had taken shape in the 1790s.

The First Act, 1789–1815

France had been the great power of western Europe, and often the greatest, since the days of Louis XIV. What happened there in 1789 and thereafter was bound to be important elsewhere. A big population gave her great military potential. Whatever changed inside the country, therefore, the outcome was likely to matter in the international struggle for power. In addition, France was a great cultural force. People looked to her to find out what Europe should be thinking about. The eighteenth century was even at the time called the *siècle française*, and more than merely the self-approbation of what Frenchmen came to call 'the great nation' justifies the phrase; French language, manners, style, even fashion, enjoyed an ascendancy never again to be so widespread or so penetrating.

Yet the events of 1789 began in a deceivingly domestic way, and not with innovation but with a deliberate recourse to the past. The spectre that haunted Frenchmen that year was not one of revolution but of national bankruptcy. The monarchy was financially in sad straits. After a long series of failures to deal with a huge deficit, the royal ministers had turned to historical revivalism. The last of several historical *revenants* to be hopefully disinterred for a rerun was the Estates-General. This ancient body had not met since 1614 and was summoned in its historic form, with 'deputies' from the three Estates of the realm, the three great embodiments of the corporate idea of society, clergy, nobles, and commons. They were helped by an unprecedentedly wide consultation of Frenchmen (and a few Frenchwomen) whose views on France's problems had been sought through a system of written commentaries (the *cahiers*). The choice of deputies, though indirect, involved ultimately something like universal male suffrage. A galvanic impulse was thus given to political awareness of an unprecedented kind.

The overwhelming tendency of the *cahiers* and the elections shows that most Frenchmen did not anticipate, far less want, what eventually came about. They believed that the traditional framework could provide what they wanted—though many of their hopes and ambitions were contradictory and incompatible with one another. But when the Estates-General met in May 1789 amid popular excitement heightened by hard times, some quickly saw that in itself it embodied too much history which blocked the way to doing what had been hoped of it. Some of the most vociferous noble deputies saw the Estates-General as one more chance to thwart reforming government. The *roturier* Third-Estate deputies soon discovered that the historic constitution of France might not, after all, allow them to be part of the élite which was to decide the future of France, as they had supposed their wealth, standing, and *lumières* would do. The conflict with the legally privileged which ensued led to the emergence of a political idea new to France and a crucial revolutionary engine, the doctrine of the sovereignty of the nation.

So began for Europe a new political age and a new legitimation for authority. Instead of quasi-judicial debate about vested interests, law, conventions, and chartered rights, political life was to be about will: what did the nation want? The bishop who preached at the mass which formally opened the sessions of the Estates-General had himself said 'France, ta volonté suffit'. The separate Estates turned themselves into a National Assembly to write a new constitution, an incarnation of national sovereignty. Inevitably, a host of questions was for the moment ignored or postponed. Who were the true representatives and interpreters of the national will? Was there really nothing that lay outside the scope of that will? For what were the claims of the individual to count? Were they to be those of possessors of historic rights (soon stigmatized as 'privilege') or those of morally autonomous beings? What of the claims of God—or at least of his Church, whose 'eldest daughter' was France? These questions (and others) were to provide the stuff of political struggle for the rest of the Revolution. They would ensure a decade of upheaval in France and abroad, dominate the rhetoric of French politics until well into the twentieth century, and set new terms for Europe's political thinking. In 1789 few could have guessed that. Once the conservatives (a word not yet invented) and the Crown had caved in, surely it would be simple to agree on what that will was? Plausibly, barely a month after the Estates-General first met, an English observer commented that 'the whole business now seems over, and the revolution complete'.

New Landmarks, New Rules

Almost every revolutionary change in French institutions which was to endure came about by the end of 1791. The constitution approved in that year, though not long to survive, set several markers for the future. It embodied a special declaration of the rights of individuals, and abolished many old institutions (sovereign courts, ancient provincial divisions, privileged corporations) which had stood in the way of truly national government. Entrenched privileges of birth and status disappeared along with the old legal immunities and judicial protections. For the first time France became a unified state, explicitly based on the people (the new title of the monarch was not 'king of France', but 'king of the French'). One of the deepest changes it wrought was the incorporation in the constitutional community of all Frenchmen as citizens. It implied the politicization of groups not hitherto involved in public life.

The outstanding example of political struggles driving Frenchmen far beyond

anything they had asked for in the *cahiers* arose over religion. National community conflicted with old confessional ties. A question of allegiance was soon posed
for Catholics; were they to look to Rome or the National Assembly (in which sat
Protestants and Jews) for final authority in the government of the Church? For the
clergy the issue of Church and State was crystallized by the imposition of oaths of
civic loyalty. Almost incidentally, there followed toleration for all religions and,
even, for disbelief. The magnitude of this step emerged almost unnoticed from a
guarantee to individuals of freedom in the expression of their opinions—'même
réligieuses'. Anticlericalism and anti-papalism thus re-entered the political
agenda, but now in a new way, allied to a new phenomenon, political liberalism.
Church and State would be a European issue throughout the next century—in
Germany, Belgium, Spain, and Italy, as well as in France.

Ideological strife sometimes reflected ideas and ambitions born of the
advanced thought of the Enlightenment. So did the ending of what was referred to
comprehensively and confusingly as 'feudalism' (*féodalité*) in August 1789 when
suddenly and in a few days the National Assembly transformed the land law of
France and the working arrangements of thousands of communities. The huge
complex of privileges, tenures, customs, and practice which regulated rural
France was swept away (at least in theory). Status gave way to contract. Effectively,
land became only another commodity, and French agriculture and rural society
were to be left to the market and the law of freehold. This happened principally
because of the fears aroused in the summer of 1789 by rural disorder. Its widespread nature and frightening violence made it one of those external motors
which were to radicalize the Revolution, driving it forward, jerkily and erratically,
but always faster than many of those we may now call 'politicians' wished. The
main radicalizing centre of the Revolution, though, was Paris, whose crowds were
easier to manipulate or manage than the peasants. Its excited population intimi-
dated first the monarchy (after the king was moved there in October 1789) and then
successive National Assemblies. But neither peasants nor Parisians did so much to
drive France towards extremism and division as did war.

For all the optimism of 1789, France experienced something like a suspension of
national government that year and it lasted well into 1790. Among other things, the
fiscal system virtually broke down. One consequence was that a way out of
national bankruptcy was sought by seizing the lands of the Church. This further
defined views of the Revolution. It gave a stake in its success to those investing in
the ecclesiastical property sold off to back the government's credit. But land sales
and a paper currency based on the credit they provided offered only a temporary
respite. They could not suffice when France went to war with Austria and Prussia
in 1792.

The origins of the war were complex and reflected new ideological forces in
international affairs. To many Frenchmen the issue was one of preserving the Revolution—not only from foreigners but from a king and court increasingly distrusted as covert enemies of what had been done. To a few, it was also an issue of
spreading the universal Rights of Man. The great nation should assert them for the
good of mankind, they thought. More immediately, war suddenly and hugely

enhanced the pressures on self-appointed trustees of the nation's will. The politicians had to meet their countrymen's demands for bread, for lower prices in a period of rocketing inflation and currency depreciation, for the hot pursuit of enemies at home, where profiteers and hoarders as well as political dissidents were stigmatized as traitors, for victory in the field, or, at the very least, for defence against the return of those who would destroy what the Revolution had achieved. In responding to such pressures, the politicians fought one another for survival, and slid or were forced into the extra-legal and extraordinary measures summed up as Terror or 'revolutionary government'. Attempts more radical than any of the *ancien régime* were made to control the economy. A universal conscription hitherto unthinkable became possible. What was done helped France to survive a great crisis, created counter-revolution, and in the end wore out the Parisian revolutionaries, driving them under, in 1795, for over thirty years.

The king became a scapegoat for disaster in the first months of the war. The monarchy was overthrown in August 1792 and he was tried and executed the fol-

The Directory (the new regime set up in France in 1795) was widely seen and much promoted as the defender of the Revolution from, on one side, reaction and, on the other, from anarchy—as in this print, occasioned by the thwarting of the 'Conspiracy of Equals', led by Gracchus Babeuf. His failure none the less assured him a place in the martyrology of nineteenth-century socialism.

lowing year. One set of politicians was swept aside and a 'Convention' was elected to draw up a constitution for a republic. Another important change was that France again began to act as a great power. Revolution mobilized the nation's strength as never before. The demonstration of what state power might become was noted by rulers elsewhere. From a crisis of self-preservation France emerged to drive Prussia and Austria to terms in 1795 and 1796. At one moment she may have had armies of 800,000 men in the field; numbers such as these were to be the foundation of the regime of an adventurer, Napoleon Bonaparte, a general who seized power in a *coup d'état* in 1799. The restoration of France's international standing can be added to the legislation and ideological achievements of 1789–91 as one of the major results of the Revolution in France.

On the other hand, the extreme aspirations of the revolutionaries in the end went unfulfilled. A new Calendar replaced the Christian one (1792 becoming Year One) but even in the offices of the bureaucracy it lasted only a few years. A 'de-Christianization' programme, the first to be mounted in a great state since the days of Julian the Apostate, was only briefly vigorous, though it added new venom to France's internal quarrels and stimulated the resurgence of Catholicism. Meanwhile, the great institutional changes of 1789–91 were further entrenched and developed by Napoleon. He formally endorsed the sovereignty of the people by using plebiscites to legitimize major constitutional change (such as the inauguration in 1804 of a short-lived French empire) but also pushed centralization further. Though 1815 brought his final defeat and the restoration of a Bourbon king to France, much that was revolutionary survived. Louis XVIII's was a parliamentary monarchy, run by bureaucrats, freed from the restraints the *ancien régime* had placed on their predecessors, and working through a machinery of departments and prefects still in place today.

Europe after the First Revolutionary Age

The Revolution had also rolled outwards under Napoleon. The map of 1815 showed a Europe politically recast. Restoration of the frontiers of 1789 was not a realistic goal. The changes registered and made at Vienna in 1814–15 confirmed radical breaks already made, and added to them. This was clearest on France's borders. The search for effective barriers against any renewal of French imperialism led to the establishment of a Prussian glacis for Germany on the lower Rhine, the addition of new territories to the kingdom of Sardinia, and the creation of a new kingdom of the Netherlands embracing both Belgium and the Dutch provinces. Elsewhere, the quest for security brought new roles for the major continental monarchies. Austria became the policeman of Italy, her own territories enlarged by those of the former Venetian republic, with garrisons in the Duchies and Papal States. A new Germany of thirty-nine states was loosely tied together in a new form (and, soon, in a customs union) which left Austria and Prussia dominating it. The simplification was dramatic; most of the three hundred or so old small sovereign entities did not re-emerge. Further east, the *status quo ante* was restored with slight modifications. After three Partitions (between Prussia, Russia, and Austria)

Facing: **In 1792 Parisian National Guard battalions** (which had played an important role as counterweight to the royal army in the survival of the Revolution in its early years) were sent to the front after the fall of the monarchy to be amalgamated with units of the regular army. The new formations turned back the Prussian invasion of that year.

Poland had disappeared in 1797. This had been another indirect consequence of events in France which had allowed her three powerful neighbours to get on with their crimes undisturbed. Napoleonic hints of a recovered independence for the country were forgotten in 1815, which left Russia controlling most of a nominal 'kingdom of Poland', and Cracow with the status of a 'Free City' and a fig leaf of independence.

Prussia, Austria, and Russia all ruled many subjects who owed nothing historically to the Hohenzollern, Habsburg, and Romanov dynasties. The struggle of dynasticism and nationality was to be for the last two a crippling and major theme of their history for over a century. But, in 1815, dynasticism seemed firmly in the saddle, its strength newly recruited by the impetus given to a consolidation over a quarter of a century of state power such as eighteenth-century 'enlightened despots' could only have dreamed of. The state was stronger because of technical changes (which would continue to evolve, and would make it stronger still) and because of irreversible changes in ideas and institutions. The example of France, sometimes *in terrorem*, had shown what could be done by state power untrammelled by the privileges or 'intermediate bodies' of old-fashioned corporate society. Sometimes there was inspiration in defeat, such as in Prussia after Jena, the crushing blow of 1806. Modernization in such circumstances was undertaken with one eye on the need to mobilize the strength needed to offset Napoleonic superiority, and this did not mean only administrative and military reform, but the abolition of hereditary serfdom and the removal of medieval restrictions on industry and trade. In some places (the Rhineland and Italy, for example) the actual arrival of French occupation forces, followed or not, as the case might be, by French law and bureaucracy, had swept away many obstacles to a new level of intensity in government. Intelligent conservatives could see after 1815 that they had a new

MANCHESTER HEROES

Peterloo was the mocking name given to the blunder of the local Yeomanry and magistrates at St Peter's Fields, Manchester, on 16 August 1819 when a peaceable and unarmed crowd assembled to hear speeches about parliamentary reform. The crowd was charged by the cavalry. Eleven were killed and hundreds wounded.

armoury of resources to employ in defence of conservative interests—and widespread fear of revolution did much to make even extreme conservatism tolerable to frightened peoples.

There were few countries, too, which did not in some measure show that, at the most fundamental level, the Revolution had invented (or released) and generalized a new political life. The central idea of modern politics—that legitimacy for government is to be sought in some kind of debate and competition for the support of a public, however narrowly defined—struck at the root of the traditional order everywhere. It was impossible to resist a new drift in public affairs once the Revolution had coloured the issues of power with the key oppositions of old versus new, tradition versus will and reason, and history versus the future. All of these were implicit in the power exercised everywhere over the political imagination by the Revolution itself and the assumption (held by opponents and supporters alike) that he who was not for it must be against it.

On this new politicization was built a new world of ideas and institutions, expressed in a new public language. 'Conservatism' and 'conservative' were new words from France. 'Liberal', from Spain, acquired a new currency as a noun, and, in English at least, a new application as an adjective. 'Democrat' and 'democracy' began for the first time to be used by at least some in a favourable way. Above all, the great contrast of 'left' and 'right', originating in the distribution of seats in the first French National Assembly, began to mask division, consolidate political groupings, and simplify (sometimes misleadingly) political discussion in a manner which persists even today. On such abstractions, politicians built new institutions. 'Party' was one, though it was an idea hated by the great Jacobin leaders of France, who could not reconcile the integrity of national will and adherence to it with the practice of opposition. Even in 1830 it could only be clearly distinguished from 'faction' in the United Kingdom, where the idea of constitutional opposition was by then established. 'Patriotism' was another old idea reshaped; it became a revolutionary creed in the multinational empires. Patriotism and nationalism were to be inseparably attached to revolution in Italy, Germany, and Ottoman Europe, as, by 1815, they already were in Poland and Ireland.

The Conservative Success, 1815–1848

The inheritance of the Revolution took time to mature and reveal its full strength. From 1815 to 1848, in spite of alarms and excursions, Europe enjoyed her longest period of peace between major powers for centuries. At first, this owed much to the management, by diplomacy, of the machine of security set up by the victorious powers, a concert whose operation was saved from diversion into excesses of frightened conservatism (such as a 'Holy Alliance' of Russia, Austria, and Prussia seemed for a time to threaten) by the rapid incorporation into its working of a restored, constitutional France and the existence of a British sea power unchallengeable by any continental state.

Notwithstanding the successful maintenance of peace between the great powers, the years down to 1848 were years of heightening revolutionary aspiration. A wave of incidents in Germany, Italy, Spain, and Russia—and even the language of some English radicals—showed until the early 1820s that flames kindled in the revolutionary and Napoleonic years were still alive in the Europe of Stendhal's young Julien Sorel. But there were distinctions to be made. Some of the disturbances of these years were strongly marked by the participation of soldiers and ex-soldiers frustrated by the onset of peace; essentially these upheavals were not so very different from what much of South America and Africa were to undergo in the next two centuries, and perhaps signified little except that there were men about whose experience and abilities gave them special opportunities to act decisively whatever their ideological orientation. Others made more deliberately political efforts to exploit both the economic hard times of the early 1820s and exasperation with what one Italian historian has called 'the mingled atmosphere of police station and sacristy'. Michelangelo Buonarroti, who has some claim to be recognized as the first career revolutionary, wished to keep alive the most socially radical traditions of the 1790s and turned to international secret societies to do so; he failed utterly for they proved at best evanescent, and usually of little substance. Yet their supposed ramifications caused much alarm. A more ambitious conspirator still, the Genoan Giuseppe Mazzini, looked more specifically to youth, not a bad bet in an age of rapid population growth. 'Young Italy' and 'Young Europe' were both launched by him in the 1830s.

Real revolutionary turmoil arose from sources other than conspiracy. Chronologically speaking, the first fuse to be lit led to the ethnic powder barrels of Ottoman Europe. A revolt against local misrule in Serbia in 1804 demonstrated that, to the pressure of great powers which had long threatened the Ottoman empire, was now to be added that of insurrection. Both came together in the Greek revolt of 1821 which opened a decade of bloodshed and international crisis. Further to inflame an issue born of the opposition of disloyal pashas and the aspirations of levantine merchants there now were added new ideas of nationality and political liberalism, the propaganda appeal of religious fervour, and the threat of great power interest. Much was archaic—some Greeks consciously invoked memories of the Byzantine empire—while the final emergence of a formally constitutional and national Greek monarchy under a king chosen by outsiders was a portent. It looked forward not only to the collapse of the Ottoman empire itself in the next century, but to the spreading into some of the most barbarous and backward parts of geographical Europe of western politics and institutions, with all their disruptive potential. It also left a Turco-Greek quarrel behind, which was still to trouble Europe in our own day.

Poland was another enduring source of disturbance. Polish revolution in 1830 found the dynastic powers united; force could contain the Poles so long as Russia, Prussia, and Austria made common cause. They managed to do so over Poland until 1914, even if Austria wobbled a little when another unsuccessful Polish revolution broke out in 1863. But wobbles were inevitable. Russia's role in Greece, after all, had not been unambiguously conservative, and the most consistent support for the crumbling Ottoman empire came from Britain, a 'liberal', even 'revolutionary', influence in South America and the Iberian peninsula.

Left: **Grievously ill and in despair,** Napoleon III vainly sought death on the battlefield of Sedan where, instead, defeat by the Prussians led to his capitulation (2 September 1870), the end of his dreams of a Europe dominated by France, and of his dynasty's empire; two days later the republic was proclaimed in Paris, and he was a prisoner of war.

Below: **One of many symbolic acts** common during the French Revolution: in hundreds of towns and villages 'trees of liberty' were planted to encourage enthusiasm and fan patriotic feelings to the accompaniment of speeches by local activists.

XII · XXIII · XXIV · FÈVRIER · M·DCCCXLVIII

By the end of 1830, however, a crude and oversimple ideological categorization could be made between constitutional states, 'liberal' in their external sympathies and policies, and the despotisms of eastern Europe, the would-be policemen of international order. That year gave such a characterization more substance. A successful revolution took place in France (though some of its supporters almost at once denied that any such event had occurred) and another began in Belgium. Unsurprisingly, every government in Europe, including the British, was terrified by the prospect that revolution in France might lead to new great wars (the Tsar helped to provoke Polish revolution by proposing to use the Polish army against the revolutionaries in Paris and Brussels). It looked as if revolution might again roll outwards from a country which it had taken the united efforts of all Europe to subdue. But in the end it turned out that in France little had changed except the dynasty (Belgium, by contrast, became an independent nation—a radical change). Though some important constitutional innovations were to follow, the enlarged French electorate of the July Monarchy was still smaller than the unenlarged British electorate before the Great Reform Bill of 1832 changed the nature of the constitution there—and France had twice the population of Britain. France continued to be a great power, but a peaceable one. Her dominant social interests

Poor relief became a major concern for governments in many countries in the nineteenth century. In Restoration Paris, inadequate official provision was supplemented by privately organized doles—of wine, in the instance shown in this unsympathetic painting of 1822.

Facing: **a French allegory of the Republic** surrounded by appropriate symbols. The date on the plinth commemorates the start of the Second Republic. It was to last for five years (1848–52) in a formal sense until (like its predecessor of 1792–1804) it was replaced by a Bonapartist empire on (again like the earlier republic) 2 December.

23

The July Revolution. The union of all classes in 1830 in defence of the constitution provides the central theme of this representation of a barricade in the Rue Dauphine. Such obstacles were a feature of urban insurrection in many countries in the nineteenth century until improvements in artillery and small arms made them increasingly ineffective.

remained the same and her slow economic development towards a more industrial order went on as before. The idea that France was likely to stand beside Britain on the liberal side of the division from the eastern empires was, none the less, confirmed and made a little more plausible.

1848

Nearly two decades later, in 1848, France sneezed again, and most of continental Europe caught cold. There followed a complex, continent-wide crisis. All that is easily discerned is the strength of the hopes and fears aroused by one revolution after another. It is much harder to decide where to begin even a description, let alone analysis. Hard times had stimulated *jacqueries* and risings in the 1840s. As early as 1846 the Galician peasants had set to work with a will butchering their Polish landlords, believing, it seems, that their Austrian emperor wanted them to do so. The connection with a simultaneous rising in Cracow is obscure but these events may have had the paradoxical effect of ensuring that Poland, one of the most turbulent countries in Europe, kept relatively quiet in 1848. Well before that, Germany was smouldering in an anticipatory glow of revolution: 'we lived', wrote one German, 'like people who feel under their feet the pressures of an earthquake'.

The year began with a revolt in Palermo in January, a protest against what was seen as misgovernment by the mainland Neapolitan Bourbon monarchy of the

24

Two Sicilies. But this was little more than a formal precedence. The first real alarm came on 24 February; an almost bloodless overthrow of the July Monarchy set up in 1830 and the proclamation of a republic in Paris then startled liberals and conservatives alike. It was a signal to Europe. True, the new regime did little that could be called revolutionary beyond recognizing a 'right to work'—which had a socialist sound to it—unless the abolition of the death penalty or a proclamation of sympathy for the Poles is to be considered such. But there were soon signs that government in Paris was slipping towards a powerlessness like that which had released the violence and radicalism of 1793 and the Revolutionary wars. Meanwhile, a system of doles to the unemployed of Paris accumulated an army of discontent in the capital.

Memory (there were men alive in 1848 who had seen Robespierre in the flesh) was the source of inspiration as well as of fear. Besides haunting the thinking and shaping the style of the Paris politicians, it speeded revolution elsewhere. The wave swept through scores of German cities. All could unite against the powers that were. Constitutions were suddenly conceded and the paralysis and sometimes the overthrow of the existing order throughout Germany was soon complete; by the end of March, the Vienna government, too, was helpless. Within the Habsburg dominions revolution spread to Milan, Prague, and Budapest; there were risings in Dalmatia and Transylvania. Habsburg control of Italy crumbled as Venice followed Milan into rebellion. As much in fear as in favour of revolution, the Sardinian monarchy sent its army into Austrian Lombardy on the side of what some Italians saw as a patriotic and national, and some as a constitutional and liberal, cause—some saw it as both. When a hitherto idolized Pope remembered his position as Supreme Pontiff of the universal Catholic Church and said his forces could not fight Catholic Austria, it caused consternation.

Though two of the three members of the old Holy Alliance had their backs to the wall for most of 1848, everything in the end went wrong for the revolutionaries. They were everywhere divided: liberals and radicals moved apart, to left and to right; both came to fear the peasants whose destabilizing of the German and central European countryside had done so much to paralyse the old order's power of resistance. The French liberals and their peasant countrymen came together in alarm at the rise of what they saw as socialism. The republic was only saved by an appalling week of street-fighting in Paris, the 'June Days' which Tocqueville called the 'greatest slave-war in history' and cost 20,000 dead. After that, order reigned in Paris as it had done in Warsaw since the 1830s. Meanwhile, the third reactionary power, Russia, like Britain almost untroubled in 1848, re-emerged as the policeman of eastern and central Europe. As the Vienna radicals contemplated with dismay events in Prague and Budapest—it had not occurred to them that the paralysis of the government might mean that Germans would no longer run the empire—the Habsburgs' Croat soldiers and, in 1849, the Tsar's army gradually cut the ground from under them.

Bohemia and Lombardy were again under control by the end of 1848, and the following year opened with the Habsburg forces' reoccupation of Budapest. In the summer, the last Hungarian revolutionaries were overwhelmed; they were by then

25

facing Serb revolutionaries and risings by Romanians in Transylvania, as well as the Austro-Russian armies. The interplay and conflict of nationality was even more marked in Germany. There, liberals who sought German national unity found indispensable the protection of a Prussian monarchy which was the epitome of conservatism. When, in 1849, the Prussian king contemptuously refused an imperial crown offered by the German constitutional assembly, it was clear that the German revolution was over.

The legacy of the upheaval was immense. It deprived Germany, through emigration, of much of her radical political leadership and it took the country a further stage towards a Prussian hegemony. Elsewhere, the shock of 1848 left the French middle class distrusting Paris, republican forms, and even the 'career open to talent'. Italy was more securely than ever under the heel of Austria; hopes that the Papacy might lead her to national unity and political reform had been exposed as daydreams. But 1848 had also shown that enthusiasm could be aroused for the cause of nationality which might be used by conservatives to promote their ends as well as by the liberals who had so long been seen as its foremost standard-bearers. Finally, and perhaps most importantly, revolution had extended to much of central and eastern Europe changes that had been brought to other countries by French occupation and example before 1815. Notably, peasants had been liberated from serfdom, bond-labour services, and much else summed up as 'feudalism'. This was true, above all, in the Habsburg empire, where the peasant deputies in revolutionary Vienna had turned into staunch supporters of the dynasty once their demands for land and freedom from bond-labour had been met.

The Great Age of Revolutionary Wars

The 1850s and 1860s were dominated and transformed by a renewal of warfare between the great powers. This owed much to the establishment of a new regime in France. The democratic election of a president for the Second Republic, in December 1848, was followed by a *coup d'état* and his assumption of unrestricted power in 1851. This was endorsed by plebiscites which turned the president into an emperor a year later. So came into being the French Second Empire under Louis Napoleon Bonaparte. There was much about this which was alarming, not least his name. He was the first democratic dictator, endorsed by popular vote. Liberals despaired. More important, if Napoleon III (as he called himself) had a consistent policy stance, or at least an outlook to which he tended to return, it was directed towards overturning the 1815 settlement and promoting the cause of nationality. Mazzini thought him a sham both as a democrat and as a nationalist. But his hold on power remained firm while many of his countrymen could see him as the guardian of social order and others could believe he had progressive ideas about the working class.

Paradoxically, he first took France to war in a seemingly conservative cause. Great Britain and France fought Russia in 1854 to protect the Ottoman empire. Russian armies had invaded the Danubian provinces of Moldavia and Wallachia. This had opened a new phase of the Eastern Question—what was to be the fate of

the Ottoman empire in Europe?—which released further revolutionary wars after the Crimean war, and shaped the history of Europe not only until 1918 but well beyond. Any decision about what should be done with the territories of the Ottoman empire when it fell apart, and about what should be done to speed or delay that falling apart, was bound to affect the balance of power set up in 1815. In 1854 that balance was upset and the Holy Alliance powers divided. Dynasticism and partnership in the Polish crime were huge conservative forces, but Austria could not ignore Russian encroachment in the Danube valley; though she did not go to war with Russia, she mobilized her own armies and sent them into the Danubian principalities.

The main conservative goal of the war, the safeguarding of the Ottoman empire, was achieved, but at the Congress of Paris, which met to settle the war in 1856, there were representatives of the smallest of the victorious allies, Sardinia. Her prime minister, Cavour, used the Congress to bring forward an Italian question—was Italy to remain disunited and under Austrian domination?—though he got nothing immediately for his pains. A more obviously revolutionary result of 1856 was the eventual emergence of an independent Romania (finally acknowledged in 1881). Finally, it became clear, the war brought revolution to Russia, but it did so from above. Russia had always escaped it from below, and contained it successfully in her Polish provinces even if her countryside was often turbulent. But defeat in the Crimea showed that Russia could not regain her standing as a great power without modernization. That meant at least one major change. So, in 1863, the Tsar decreed the emancipation of the Russian serfs, the largest single piece of social engineering to be attempted by any European state down to that time. Bond-labour, an institution which lay at the root of all European history hitherto,

The Italian *Risorgimento* tapped patriotic enthusiasm among the better-off, above all in the recruitment of Garibaldi's 'Thousand' (actually 1089) volunteers with whom he landed in Sicily in May 1860. Among them were a boy of eleven, veterans of the Napoleonic Wars, and one woman—the mistress of a future prime minister of united Italy.

27

The possibilities of the plebiscite as a major device for the legitimizing of aggression and despoliation were discovered by practising politicians in the nineteenth century. In 1860 it had launched the new Italian state. Ten years later it sanctioned the seizure of Rome, here celebrated in a painting of a Roman woman in traditional dress casting her affirmative vote under the inspiring influence of the bust of King Victor Emmanuel II.

was now abolished—and, it may be noted, before it was abolished in the United States.

Russia's eclipse as a European policeman was also assured for some years. This opened the way to revolution further west, but in ways importantly different from those envisaged in the first half of the century. Assured of Napoleon III's benevolence towards changes in the map at the expense of the Habsburgs, two able conservative statesmen managed a series of rearrangements which rebuilt international order in the interests both of the vested interests they wished to uphold and, paradoxically, of the cause of nationalism. Each sought to assure the survival and, if possible, preponderance of the states they represented (Sardinia and Prussia) within larger national units (Italy and Germany). One was Cavour, the Sardinian who built on an alliance with France a policy of provocation towards Austria which enabled him to retain the support of Italian liberals disappointed in 1849. Ten years later, France went to war with Austria in support of Sardinia. Napoleon did not exact from a defeated Austria all that Cavour wanted, but the peace gave his king Lombardy, and opened the way to the unification of the rest of the peninsula. That unification was part political manipulation, part revolution, part conquest: Sardinian forces invaded the kingdom of Naples, ostensibly in support of a filibustering campaign by the radical Garibaldi, whose revolutionary language alarmed conservatives everywhere, but in reality as a way of containing what Cavour feared might be a democratic revolution threatening the Papacy and provoking a new war—this time, with France. When he died in 1861 a united Italy was in existence, formerly sanctioned by plebiscites—as was the transfer to France of Nice and Savoy, the *douceur* exacted by Napoleon III—under the former king of Sardinia. Garibaldi and Mazzini lived on, unhappy and disillusioned by the outcome; Rome and Venetia remained 'unredeemed' outside the new nation-state.

Bismarck, Prussia's conservative revolutionary, began, like Cavour, with the acquiescence of France but ended fighting her. His was a much more important impact on Europe than Cavour's, because

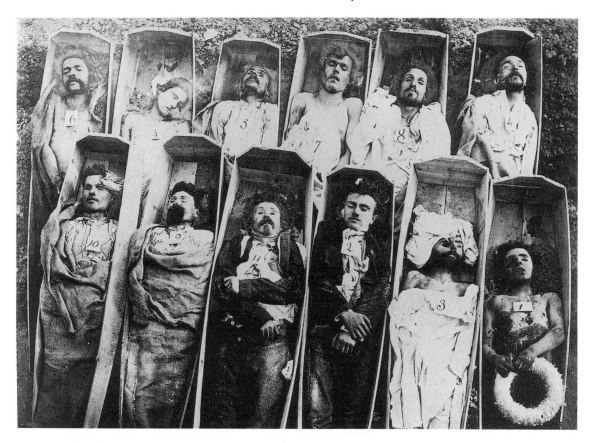

the demographic and economic might of a united Germany was much greater than that of a united Italy could ever be. Yet his starting-point and fundamental ambition were limited: the preservation of Prussia and the interest of its ruling class, the *Junker* nobility and squirearchy to which he belonged. This meant Prussian predominance in Germany, which was achieved in three wars—one with Denmark in 1864, one with Austria in 1866, and the last with France in 1870. The first began the successful evolution of Bismarck's policy towards a bid for the leadership of German nationalist opinion; the second excluded Austria from any share in the internal affairs of Germany; the third announced that France was at last displaced from her long ascendancy as western Europe's great power. Bismarck coupled the peace he imposed in 1871 with the creation of a new German empire, a second *Reich* which appealed to national sentiment, seduced German liberals, and had a formally federal structure which saved the faces—and the palaces—of the German princes. But the king of Prussia was the emperor.

Defeat in 1866 had other consequences for Austria than exclusion from German affairs. She surrendered Venetia to Prussia's ally, Italy—her only cession of territory—but this was less important than an internal change, the remodelling of the Habsburg empire into a Dual Monarchy. This, too, had its roots in the decline of Ottoman power. The Ottoman retreat and the consequent extension of Habsburg

Some of the dead supporters of the Commune. Ferocious repression and reprisal killed more Frenchmen and Frenchwomen in a few weeks than perished in the Great Terror of 1793–4—until then a benchmark for political ruthlessness.

Above: **Over a hundred thousand Russians** gathered in St Petersburg on 22 January 1905 to bring their grievances to the notice of the Tsar. They were fired upon, hundreds died, and the crowd fled. 'Bloody Sunday' was soon seen as the moment at which popular faith in the monarchy was lost and the revolution of that year became inevitable.

Right: **Liverpool 1911**. A year of unusual industrial unrest and strikes in the United Kingdom led at times to the deployment of soldiers in support of the police. On one occasion in Liverpool troops opened fire and two people were killed. Disputes continued well into mid-1912.

Facing: **International socialist solidarity** in 1909. A well-policed demonstration, escorted by cavalry, protesting against the execution in Spain of a revolutionary politician, Francisco Ferrer.

territory would mean new subjects, sometimes of national groups not hitherto represented in the empire, sometimes of groups which were and whose relations with it might therefore change. Yet, as 1848 showed, the most troublesome of the 'subject peoples' were the Magyars, the dominant people of the old kingdom of Hungary. Like the Germans of Bohemia and Austria, they were increasingly self-conscious as a people anxious to protect both a much-touted historical culture and their real advantages over other peoples—mainly Slav—of the historic Hungarian lands. They had long resisted a centralizing monarchy. Austria's weakness in Germany was the Magyars' opportunity. After defeat by the Prussians, the Habsburgs had to concede to them the historic 'Compromise' (*Ausgleich*) of 1867 which set up a Dual Monarchy, Austria-Hungary. The emperor Francis Joseph was emperor in Vienna and king in Budapest. Though negotiated, this was a revolutionary change. It produced a Hungary—territorially including Croatia, Transylvania, and much else—independent in virtually all internal matters but, because of the Magyars' own need to ensure that the Monarchy retained its international weight, locked into an often uncomfortable common management of foreign affairs. The Magyar response to necessity was to try to ensure that the making of foreign policy was dominated by Magyar interests. Unfortunately for Europe, they were sometimes successful in doing so.

The Great Peace, 1871–1914

In 1871 the French provisional government suppressed a movement in Paris led by a radical Commune or city council, and did so with great severity. The bloodshed was unprecedented. The damage done to Europe's city of pleasure by street-fighting and incendiarism was striking. For a moment it seemed to some that social revolution had come again. It had not, however, nor in spite of many fears did it come in other developed nations in the decades that followed. True, there were dangerous moments in some places. Defeat in war forced concessions to revolution out of the Tsarist autocracy in 1905. In Spain, traditionally a land of revolt and rebellion, the government for a time lost control of the great city of Barcelona in the 'Tragic Week' of 1909. Italy seemed for a moment at the edge of breakdown in 1913. Yet what the Paris Commune had demonstrated was that there was little chance of popular insurrection overthrowing society when a government had control of its armed forces and the will to use them. Nevertheless, the fear of revolution did not diminish after 1871. It was even enhanced by new bogies. Socialism and communism—words vaguely and widely used about ideologies and aspirations implying a more equal distribution of material benefits and social power—appeared as open, organized threats. Trade unions were their most obvious manifestation. Two socialist 'Internationals' of working-class organizations appeared to have international substance. Yet the second, and much more important, though embodying an unprecedented degree of

Above: **Rosa Luxemburg** was a Polish Jewess who emerged as a leading combatant in the struggle for the ideological soul of the German SPD. Here she addresses a meeting in 1907 flanked by the portraits of the founding fathers, Marx and Lassalle, whose different legacies marked the party from the outset. She was to be murdered in 1919 by right-wing soldiers fighting the revolutionary Spartacist movement.

Right: **Deep feelings and a sense of outrage** were easily provoked among the supporters as well as among the opponents of the movement to assert women's rights in the pre-1914 years. English suffragettes were particularly vigorous and provocative and were often removed by force by the police from the places where they chose to protest.

international organization for the working classes, had become by 1914 a far from revolutionary body, as its acts in that year showed.

The virtual disappearance of violent revolution from European history is a complex story. One element in it may be the long-term—though uneven—rise in material wealth in the half-century that followed 1860. Another was the increasing—if by 1914 still far from complete—integration of mass societies, and the more effective government they enjoyed: popular education and rising literacy; at least formal participation in representative systems by larger numbers; the conscious extension of what would now be called 'welfare' legislation; better communications; the use of conscription to create national armies—these were some of the many changes silently transforming the relations of government and governed. This transformation was neither even nor uniform in its advance. Germany, with a wider franchise, had a government more firmly under the thumb of traditional privilege than England in 1914. By then Englishmen were entitled to old age pensions, such as Frenchmen were not to receive until after the First World War—and Russians not until after the Second—and, again unlike the French, were used to paying income tax. But the tendency is notable, and is probably one reason why the threat of violent revolution receded. Not all liberals, as the twentieth century began, remained optimistic about the spread of constitutionalism, far less democracy—but by 1914 there was not a major European state—except, of course, the United Kingdom—without a written constitution; most gave some formal protection to the citizen against arbitrary interference, whatever the practical realities of the way it worked. Conscious political reform—sometimes conceded only reluctantly, and occasionally only cosmetic—had led everywhere to a prevailing set of ideas and institutions unthinkable a hundred years earlier.

The revolutionary serpent which had still not been scotched in the egg was nationalism. Social revolution was still a real threat where it coincided with nationalist resentment. Irish national leaders looked with admiration to Magyars who, they believed, had fought the good fight against national oppression from the Hofburg while they were fighting against the same threat from Dublin Castle. But to the Romanian peasant of Transylvania, to the Croat or the Slovene, Magyars looked—and often were—both rapacious landlords and alien tyrants; they hoped independent nationhood would give them what Magyars had got in 1867. Elsewhere, there were still Italians in 'unredeemed' Habsburg territory, the British had a national problem in Ireland, and Norway and Sweden parted company (peaceably) in 1905. But it was in the great eastern empires that the real revolutionary potential lay. Poland could be managed, but Russia faced greater difficulty; her Poles and Jews were only two of the scores of non-Russian peoples she ruled. Above all, tension was greatest in Austria-Hungary and Ottoman Europe.

WHO SAID WE'RE TO HAVE HOME RULE?

COME TO BELFAST AND WE'LL SHEW 'EM.

A postcard from Belfast at the height of the Ulster crisis of 1914, when competing nationalisms appeared to be bringing the United Kingdom to the brink of civil war.

33

Revolution and the Approach to Disaster

By the end of the century, as neighbours of the decaying Ottoman empire, Austria and Russia were openly concerned about what was to take its place. France and Britain, too, were always acutely sensitive to any prospect of changes anywhere in the empire and, indeed, over its capacity to survive at all. Broadly speaking, the eighteenth-century solution had been the direct extension of Habsburg and Romanov power into former Ottoman lands. In the nineteenth century, that became more difficult to accept, and other solutions were sought. One sometimes welcomed was the emergence of new national states in south-eastern Europe. Thus emerged Serbia during the Napoleonic wars and a Greek national state in 1830; so crystallized Romania after the Crimean war.

In any particular instance the powers were tugged in different directions by different impulses and interests. Russia always found it somewhat tempting to stand up for Christian populations alleged to be oppressed by Turkish misrule—of which much more was heard as the nineteenth century went on. Her rulers also grew increasingly susceptible after 1870 to the blandishments of a supranational 'Slavophilism', popular among many Russians, which linked the protection of the Orthodox Christian Churches to that of the Slav peoples (although one of those peoples, the Polish, was embarrassingly Roman Catholic). This encouraged Russian diplomacy to cultivate potential satellites as new states appeared in the Balkans. In its turn, this was likely to favour other elements in Russian policy: ambitions to dominate the lower Danubian lands and to control the Straits of Constantinople—an artery which grew in importance with the sea-borne export trade in grain from Odessa.

The Austrian position was normally more conservative and reactive. No such domestic influences as in Russia urged the Roman Catholic Habsburgs towards interference to protect the Balkan Christian peoples. Vienna was more concerned over its own interests in the Danube valley, the Monarchy's major outlet for water-borne commerce other than Trieste, and for the maintenance of stability in the Ottoman territories so that other powers would have no excuse to interfere in the region. As the nineteenth century progressed, another concern loomed larger in Austrian calculations. Whether or not Russian power was extended overtly and formally in the Danube

Free Bulgaria was one of the new nations to emerge in the last decades of the nineteenth century. But in 1878 Bulgarian patriots were granted only a portion of what they saw as historic Bulgarian territory to form an autonomous principality under nominal Ottoman suzerainty, with a German prince as ruler, and Russia, briefly, as its patron.

valley and the Balkans, would not the Monarchy's strength be weakened by the appearance there of new Slav nations? They might seek not only to exploit their shared Slavdom so as to reduce the Monarchy's influence beyond its borders, but perhaps also to attempt to turn its own Slav subjects against it. This prospect increasingly troubled Magyar politicians, aware as they were of the huge Slav population of their half of the Monarchy. And, if the 'South' Slavs, as those peoples increasingly came to be called, won concessions, what would then happen with others: the Romanians of Transylvania, the Ruthenes of the Polish Ukraine, the Poles themselves?

Between 1871 and 1914 five new nations emerged into full independence and sovereign status in south-eastern Europe. All were in formerly Ottoman lands, all were poor and largely barbarous, but they were also Christian, talked the language of nationalism, and were governed by what purported to be constitutional regimes. Serbia, Montenegro, and Bulgaria were Slav; Romania and Albania were not. They were the final monuments of over a century of effective diplomacy which, except in 1854, avoided direct conflict between the great European powers in south-east Europe by building up such states at the expense of the subsiding Ottoman empire (of which by 1914 there was very little left north of the Bosphorus). In 1913 some of these states, along with Greece, showed that this solution to the Eastern Question had bought success at the cost of creating new problems: in the second of two Balkan wars—the first, a year earlier, had been with the Turks—they fought one another over the division of the Ottoman spoil.

A Revolutionary War

The exhaustion of diplomatic solutions in the Balkans, the persistence there of problems, such as Macedonia, which could not be solved at the expense of the Ottoman empire, and the bungling of Austro-Russian relations all contributed to the descent into the abyss in 1914. To that extent, it would be fair to call the struggle which began then the Third Balkan War, or another of the Wars of the Ottoman Succession. But with no less appropriateness it could be called the Third German War, for it was fought, as those of 1866 and 1870 had been fought—and as a fourth, still greater, was to be fought in the future—to settle questions about Germany's weight in Europe. Some, Germans among them, would even have said it was about Germany's place in the world, but historians have tended to agree that extra-European, and specifically colonial, issues did not play a major part in the outbreak of war. The long resentment of Frenchmen over the loss in 1871 of Alsace and Lorraine, their government's alliance with Russia and understandings with Britain, and the provision of the British government with a cast-iron legal excuse for entry to war when Germany invaded Belgium were all much more important. Some of Germany's rulers were haunted by the fear that their moment of effective supremacy might pass if they did not fight then. Germany was a huge mass of demographic, economic, and therefore military power. They felt that, while there was still time, they should demonstrate and exploit that fact, before a modernizing, stronger Russia could throw her full weight into the scale.

The Macedonian Question has over a century's history. In 1903 it erupted in a rising instigated by the Internal Macedonian Revolutionary Organization (IMRO) which sought autonomy for the province within the Ottoman empire. Sympathetic pictorial journalism in the west provided imaginative representations of the discomfiture of the Turks. But the rising failed.

The narrative of the war which began in 1914, though fascinating for its own sake and important for the explanation of its nature, cannot be set out here. In that story, in any case, it is easy to lose sight of the revolution—or revolutions—which made the war unique in more than its huge scale and extent. Nothing like it had happened since the struggles of 1792–1815, which were also, like those of 1914–18, referred to long after they were over simply as 'the Great War'. Much of this revolutionary effect was a matter of the intensification of processes already long under way. The war demonstrated the immense strength of the national state which had become the dominant political institution in Europe since 1789. Military police were not needed to force conscripts aboard the troop trains which took them in millions to the fronts in 1914. Until 1916, the huge British army in France could still rely on volunteers to fill its ranks. Perhaps even more impressive evidence of the power the state could now mobilize was wartime management of economic life. It was carried further than ever before, and though Russia's starving cities in 1917, and those of Austria and Germany in the following year, presaged the closeness of breakdown and surrender, for years bureaucrats succeeded in warding off famine by the exercise of administrative controls and the exploitation of technical resources on an unprecedented scale. Paradoxically the war made the central direction of the economy advocated by socialists a reality over much of Europe.

War aims developed as the struggle continued and combined with deep-rooted facts and long-evolving trends to make it a revolutionary war. Poland's hour came at last, as the combatants began to look round for new allies. Their concessions to her were implicitly revolutionary—the Germans had helped to set up an 'independent' Polish state as early as 1916—but revolution had already been unleashed by the British outside Europe in their support for Arab revolt in the Ottoman empire. Promises with revolutionary implications were also made; Italy's entry to the war in 1915 could be read as the opening of the last war of the *Risorgimento* because the Allies offered her the 'unredeemed' lands in Dalmatia and the Trentino. Most extraordinary of all, France and Britain had secretly conceded the great aim of Tsarist foreign policy for a century and perhaps more—the promise of acquiescence in the Russian occupation of Constantinople after victory.

These were perhaps only indicators of revolution. Two great events in 1917 changed world history. The major precipitating agency in each was the same small group of men. They were not, as revolutionaries had long hoped and conservatives long feared, the self-designated successors of Robespierre, Mazzini, Nechaev, and so many other devoted disturbers of the *status quo*. The revolutionizing of world affairs in 1917 was the work of the German general staff. By the beginning of that year its soldiers had at last worn out even Russia's huge strength. Though her armies were then still in the field and still capable of great feats of arms, Russia's cities were starving, her transport system was wrecked, and her government had lost its moral authority. The regime was mortally wounded. A revolution in February (March in the older calendar) brought it down and installed a republican provisional government. It recognized Poland's independence and gave autonomy within a Russian state to Finland and Estonia. Unhappily, it did not give Russians what they longed for above all: peace. War-weariness and the tireless exploitation of its political weakness by the Marxist socialists called Bolsheviks, whose leader had been sent back to Russia by the Germans, in the hope that some advantage might come of it, enabled them to thrust aside the provisional government in a *coup d'état* in October. Soon, Russia was out of the war and a new state had appeared, the Union of Soviet Socialist Republics (USSR).

These events took time to demonstrate their full revolutionary consequences. But some were very quickly apparent. The Bolshevik regime inaugurated a new foreign policy by a dramatic (and ineffective) appeal over the heads of governments to the peoples whom they were supposed to oppress. This symbolized the new regime's rejection of traditional assumptions of international life and diplomacy. It was a signal sent by a government which wished to show that it was essentially subversive of any other which did not share its ideological position. Soon, gestures of support—acts were later to follow—towards revolutionary movements in other countries confirmed that. A new instability was thus injected into international life.

The other great revolutionary event of 1917 had been the entry to the war of the United States. This too was the work of Germany's military leaders. The proximate cause was their decision to launch unrestricted submarine warfare against the Allies, which meant trying to sink all ships, whether under combatant or neutral flags, approaching Allied ports. The ships were often American, so this assured America's entry into the war on the Allied side. Soon it was clear that, since Germany was not winning the maritime battle, the Allies were therefore bound to win the land struggle, even after they had lost their Russian ally, since American numbers and industrial strength more than made up the loss. Win they did, and Germany sued for peace in October 1918.

By then, the American entry to the war had transformed the struggle and had implicitly settled much of the character of the peace which was to follow. Other events helped. In the spring of 1918, the full military weight of the United States had still to be deployed in Europe. The French and British faced the last great German onslaught without much support in the field from their new associate. In the crisis, they looked around for new resources. Among them were some which might be brought to bear through revolutionary and subversive means, both by propa-

A mural in the parliament building of Prague designed by a Czech artist, Mucha, in the first decade of this century. For all its tragic drama, and in spite of the inscription speaking of the humiliation and torture of the Czech nation, the Habsburg tyranny in retrospect seems mild by comparison with what the century was later to bring.

ganda and diplomacy. The Allies began to recognize and encourage those who spoke for the 'subject peoples' of the Austro-Hungarian empire. This fitted, more or less, the rhetorical diplomacy of the American president, whose commitment to a break with the self-interested war aims of the Allies—significantly, the United States government did not accept that it was their 'ally', but described itself as an 'associated power'—was made evident in assertions that the coming peace was to be based on the principle of self-determining nationality; six of the 'Fourteen Points' the President announced as the basis for a peace settlement expressed this.

America's entry to the war initiated the final evolution of the wars which had sprung from 1914. They had turned into the greatest revolutionary war in history. The old Europe was gone. On the eve of the armistice which ended fighting in the west, a German republic replaced Bismarck's Reich. The Polish republic emerged again as an independent state. Long before the peace conference began, two great dynastic empires crumbled away, both in revolution. The Dual Monarchy dissolved into Austria, Hungary, and Czechoslovakia, while others of its former lands were now part of a new 'Yugoslavia' which also swallowed Serbia and Montenegro. Soon, the new Russian state was desperately fighting a civil war to hold itself together. The peace treaties when they came endorsed and furthered the triumphs of nationalism and the collapse of dynasticism and briefly brought about an unprecedented extension of formal democracy. They also registered the other and still vaster revolutionary change denoted by the American army's presence in France. The New World had been called in to settle the problems Europe could not herself solve—and, it was to appear in due course, failed in turn to solve them. Symbolically, the majority of the countries whose representatives signed the Treaty of Versailles lay outside Europe. The age of European ascendancy was over.

The Treaty of Versailles was not signed until 1919 and was only one of several which settled the terms of the new order. Some were not signed for years, and 1918 is not, therefore, a good date to break Europe's political story. Her German problem had not been solved and 1918 was to that extent only a pause in a new Thirty

Years' War. Even as hostilities ended, there were either established, or fighting strongly for existence, nine independent sovereign states which had not been there in 1914—Finland, Estonia, Latvia, Lithuania, Poland, Czechoslovakia, Austria, Hungary, Yugoslavia (a name not officially adopted until 1929; in the Treaty of Versailles it was referred to as 'The Serb-Croat-Slovene State'). Like the new Germany, all of them were constitutional in form. Seven of them were republics. Above all they witnessed the triumph of the principle of national sovereignty announced in the French Revolution. It was still double-edged, implying at once a new way of authenticating authority and a huge revolutionary potential, as minorities in the new Europe quickly grasped.

Other facts also registered sweeping change. At Vienna in 1815 the Papacy had been officially represented; there was to be no nuncio signing the Treaty of Versailles, for since 1870, when the Italians occupied Rome, the Papacy had ceased to enjoy its temporal power. Rome had retreated on other fronts too. For all the Papacy's claims, even states with large Roman Catholic populations had already made concessions to a creeping secularism. European political life since 1789 was influenced by innovation in science, philosophical ideas, social assumptions, and much else which redefined the role of religion. Élites which had once rested on unquestioned foundations dissolved, or abandoned themselves to the opportunities of industrial and commercial society. There were doubts, even about ideas which seemed to triumph; not all nineteenth-century liberals viewed the onset of democratic society with complacency. In 1918 new, illiberal principles were already abroad, and were being solidly entrenched in Russia, a country which was bound one day to be a great state again. Such reflections lead back to the conclusion that the Europe of 1918 had not reached a new resting-place. She was only a little way into the phase of world revolution in which we still live, and which Europe's global supremacy had launched. The cannonade at the Bastille was in the end to be heard round the world, however astonishing the transformations, compromises, and distortions away from their ideal origins the principles and ideas of Europe were to undergo.

2

The Industrialization of Modern Europe

1750–1914

The Three Waves of Industrialization

BETWEEN 1750 and 1914, Europe experienced three major waves of industrialization. One peaked in the period between the 1780s and the 1820s; a second crest appeared in the decades between 1840 and 1870; and a third rolled through in the last two decades before the First World War. Each was associated with a particular region and with a particular type of technology.

The process began in Britain, the world's first industrial economy, accelerated during the second half of the eighteenth century, and was centred upon relatively simple and cheap innovations in two leading sectors, cotton textiles and iron-making.

This pioneer industrial revolution defined the requirements for its successors: that new sources of power should be applied to production; that manufacturing should increasingly be organized in large-scale units or factories; that there should be structural change within the economy as the share of national wealth contributed by agriculture dropped back and that derived from industry and trade moved into the lead. Clearly, there are other identifying features—such as innovations in process technology and new levels, and types, of investment; but these three requirements are central.

Parts of continental Europe began to emulate the British example quite early. France, though beset by an antiquated and fiscally inept state administration, possessed economic capabilities in the private sector which, even around 1780, were not so far behind the British. Her output of coal, ships, and cottons was less than Britain's, but she turned out more woollens, silks, linens, and even iron. French total industrial output was ahead of the British, but French industrial out-

CLIVE
TREBILCOCK

40

put per head well behind. This promising attempt at early parity was frustrated by the political upheavals of the French Revolution and the subsequent Revolutionary and Napoleonic wars. These non-economic interruptions cost France some thirty years of industrial growth, decimated French overseas trade, and left the economy stranded in a European market dominated, throughout the 1810s and 1820s, by British manufactured exports. But skills and structures remained, and, even during the war period, there was notable regional development in the French north and east.

Similarly, some areas of the German states—Silesia, Saxony, Rhineland-Westphalia—were able to exploit the opportunities opened up by the first generation of factory technology between 1780 and 1820. In the first case, the Prussian appetite for weaponry promoted an interest in the new metal processes; in the others, market shifts created by Bonaparte's expansionism, and especially by his attempt to exclude British goods from Europe by the Continental System of 1806, allowed the growth of regional specialisms in textile production. But these areas too suffered from British industrial supremacy after the French defeat at Waterloo. The only other economy, apart from Britain, to achieve a sufficient combination of new technology, large-scale production, and structural transformation in this first wave of industrialization, was, logically enough, a small one: Belgium in the 1810s

Shipbuilding before the Industrial Revolution. A French yard constructs a timber merchantman around 1770. Specialization of labour is marked; but so is the absence of 'plant'.

41

The Le Creusot ironworks in the mid-nineteenth century. Le Creusot, perhaps the premier metallurgical works in France, was one of only two French foundries equipped to use modern coke-smelting around 1800. Its progress was most marked from the 1830s, when it was taken over by the Schneider brothers.

and 1820s. Here the centres were Ghent for cotton, Verviers for wool, Liège and Charleroi for metals.

But follower economies of any scale had to await the second wave, which may be located roughly in the period 1840–70. This period saw the industrial take-off of France, the German states, not unified into the German empire until 1871, and, across the Atlantic, the United States. By this time, the detailed qualifications for full industrial status had advanced: technology becomes more sophisticated and expensive with time and new entrants need new tools and products to break into markets already occupied by their predecessors. The three central requirements regarding power, scale, and structure will stand, but the means of achieving them will alter. Britain had begun with canals, cotton spinneries, and the iron puddling process. By the 1840s and 1850s, new entrants needed railways, engineering works, and steel mills.

Above all, they needed railways. Britain was the only major economy to industrialize without them. For every successor economy, they were basic equipment. They were the central innovation of the second industrial wave and their influence was huge. They could integrate disparate economic regions, which is what most nations or pre-nations consisted of at this time, into reasonably articulated markets. They could link production sites with distant raw materials. States were interested in them for their capacity to move troops rapidly, and, in some places, promoted them for this reason. They required unprecedented amounts of investment to concentrate in a single venture, and, in a whole range of countries, from France to Austria, from Italy to Russia, they forced a wholly new type of investment

Facing: **British engineering in France.** A very early locomotive built at Rouen in 1843 by the great British rail construction and engineering concern Allcard, Buddicom & Co. Named 'Buddicom', the engine was still running in the 1950s, and appeared as a distinguished visitor at the Festival of Britain in 1951.

42

bank into being in order to provide this capital. Their construction required support from key technologies such as engineering, iron and steel, and coal, the classic heavy industries, and they could become dominant customers—in the German states, for instance, the rail sector accounted for nearly 25 per cent of domestic pig-iron consumption over the years 1850–4—for these industries.

Of course, it is not satisfactory to pin the development of many economic sectors on a single transport industry; for it says nothing about first causes. While the rail sector provided services and markets for manufacturers, it required on its own account inputs of capital, labour, and enterprise from other quarters. Nevertheless, it is striking that, in economies such as France and the German states in the mid-nineteenth century, the curve of railway construction also traces the curve of industrial take-off.

Just as the first and second industrial waves were separated by a quarter-century of continental recession after 1815, so a further hiatus occurred after the railway-based upswing of 1840–70. This was the world-wide Great Depression of 1873–96. Ironically, this phenomenon was itself a result of improving levels of

Above: **The opening of the Potsdam–Magdeburg line,** 1846. The first railway in the German states was constructed between Nuremberg and Fürth in Bavaria in 1835. The Potsdam–Magdeburg connection, an important early Prussian line to the southwest of Berlin, consisted of some 75 miles of track.

economic integration in the world, and indeed directly of the transport revolution in both railways and steel ships which affected so many countries, both in Europe and outside it, after 1850. For that revolution allowed the increasingly developed areas of Europe to connect up with those areas of the globe which produced foodstuffs and raw materials at the lowest cost. Wheat could be had from the Dakotas, from Canada, from Russia, from Hungary, or from Latin America; by the 1890s it was cheaper in Liverpool than at any time since the reign of Charles II. This was good for the consumer, and, on the face of it, cheap raw materials of all kinds were good for the industrialist. But, of course, western Europe itself contained producers of foodstuffs and raw materials. Cheap grain from the New World was not good for the large farmers of France or the new German empire; cheap tin from Malaya was not good for the miners of Cornwall.

Moreover, the downward pressure on prices, which was sufficient to trigger a general deflation, exerted a squeeze on profits in these countries which were not able to adjust *all* costs downwards. Older industrial producers, such as Britain, proved to be less flexible in this respect than newer ones such as Germany. Britain's performance throughout the period 1870–1914 was lacklustre; Germany experienced tribulations during the 1870s but recovered rapidly.

Improved transportation also raised competition levels *between* industrial producers. By the 1870s and 1880s, some of the second-wave industrial producers, such as Germany and the United States, were more than competent industrial exporters in their own right. Older industrial producers, such as Britain, again had trouble in responding flexibly to this competitive challenge.

Even before the 1890s, the stronger industrial economies, such as imperial Germany and the United States, were casting off the restrictions of the Great Depression. What disposed of it in a more general way, and brought about a recovery in world price levels, was an upsurge in economic activity from a third wave of new industrial economies during the two decades preceding 1914. This group included Italy, Japan, Sweden, the Austrian section of the Habsburg empire, and Russia. A less extensive form of economic modernization could be argued for Spain and Hungary. Among the larger subset, there must be doubts as to whether Austria had achieved sufficient structural transformation for industrial take-off by 1914, and, despite the fact that it was the fifth largest industrial producer in the world by that date, there is a special difficulty about Russia.

The technologies with which this surge of world industrialization is associated are those of chemicals, electrical engineering, bicycles, and automobiles. These were scarcely suitable to form the central foundations for newly industrializing economies largely because of the demanding scientific content of many of them. They were more conspicuous in promoting further structural change among the second-wave follower economies: France, the United States, and, above all, Germany became the leading exponents of these high-technology manufactures, while Britain once again was slow to promote the 'new industries' of the years before 1914. By the early 1900s, Germany produced 80 per cent of the world's output of artificial dyestuffs, was by 1907 the world's largest producer of chemicals, and by 1913 controlled over half the world's trade in electrical products.

It is definitely significant, however, that these new technology sectors were rarely entirely unrepresented even within the third-wave industrializers of the pre-1914 world. By the 1900s Italy numbered among her industrial products automobiles, typewriters, and chemical fertilizers; Japan was involved in joint ventures with western firms in explosives and electrical engineering; Hungary was producing switchgear for the London Underground system. These third-wave industrial economies needed railway systems, shipyards, and steel mills for their basic manufacturing equipment, but the full range of their technologies was wider and richer than that displayed by the classic follower economies of the 1840s and 1850s.

Industrialization as Evolution

By 1914, therefore, industrialization was an established presence in many of the nations of Europe. It is particularly difficult to convey the realities of this in illustrated form. A picture of a seven-storey textile factory in Lancashire in the 1800s does not look so very different from a picture of the blast furnaces at Königshütte, Silesia, in the 1830s, and a picture of a steel mill in the Ruhr in 1890 would not look much different from one in the Donbas in 1910. All will be huge, grimy, and emitting large quantities of smoke. The illustrations give no clues to the relative measures or spread of industrialization in the various locations at the time. They cannot tell the observer how representative these formidable institutions were of the national economy. And they give no indication of what is not in the picture:

The great Silesian ironworks at Königshütte. This perspective, from about 1830, clearly shows the blast furnaces in the foreground.

how much of the country in question does *not* look like this. Perhaps they do indicate that industrialization is a very capital-intensive process: the monsters of Le Creusot or Königshütte clearly consumed a great deal of investment. And they do flag the fact that some parts of Silesia or of southern Russia, amongst many other places, contained some plant that looks quite advanced for the dates which the pictures bear.

This, in turn, connects to the vital point that industrialization is a long drawn out process; it is not achieved in a rush. Professor Rostow, in a famous work, *The Stages of Economic Growth,* once argued that the achievement of industrial take-off required the doubling of the percentage of national income devoted to investment within thirty years. But this was not believed for long: in most countries, the doubling process appears to take closer to between five and eight decades than to three, and, in the British case, nearer to ten, from the 1750s to the railway boom of the 1840s. If individual factories were capital intensive, and the process of industrialization expensive in the aggregate, it was still not necessary to shift large slices of national wealth across the economy in a hurry: it was indeed better if the transfer was conducted in an accumulative, sequenced manner.

Industrialization is thus not a revolution in the sense of a violent, sudden upheaval compressed into a short period of time. One of the silliest things ever written about it was Charles Beard's melodramatic remark that it fell upon the agricultural economy 'like a thunderbolt from a clear blue sky'. Instead, in one measure or another, it is a process of evolution, covering many decades. Modern research now insists that Britain's pace of advance before 1830 was distinctly relaxed, at less than 2 per cent per annum in GNP growth, scarcely better than the pace associated in later times with periods of Britain's decline. Britain's industrial growth, it appears, has always been slow. So, the structural transformation which had occurred in Britain by the 1850s—when agriculture supplied only 21 per cent of total national product, against 35 per cent for industry and 19 per cent for transport and commerce—had been achieved by an extended period of adjustment. Similarly, the most persuasive description of French industrial development in the period 1815–1914 combines slow growth throughout the century with occasional spurts of accelerated development in the 1850s and 1860s and again after 1905. Even in the case of Germany, the continent's strongest economy by the 1900s, the notable growth of 1850–70 and 1885–1914 was constructed upon foundations first laid well back in the eighteenth century. The nineteenth-century growth in net national product—from 0.5 per cent per annum in 1830–50, to 2.4 per cent in 1850–70, and 3.1 per cent in 1870–1900—displays a fairly orderly progression. Indeed, F. B. Tipton has found, from yearly estimates, a 'nearly constant long-term growth rate' on both sides of 1870.

Industrialization as Great Spurt

There is, however, an expectation that very late developers will develop at a significantly more rapid rate. This is the 'great spurt' out of backwardness, proposed by Alexander Gerschenkron. The hypothesis here is that development elsewhere

places the backward economy in a critical situation: economic inferiority imposes political and military perils, yet the industrial might of the advanced powers defines a method of escaping the dangers of underdevelopment. A tension between actuality and potential encourages the state authorities in the backward country to gather scarce resources for a concerted drive for development. Advanced technology will be available because the powerful economies already have it. Growth cannot be gradual because the backward state cannot afford the time, and, anyway, its starting level for industrial growth is so low that the application of new technology will automatically produce high percentage growth rates.

If this model is to resemble reality, it should apply best to the third-wave economies which industrialized after 1890. Some of these, notably Russia and Sweden, did achieve very high rates of industrial growth. Under the prompting of Count Witte's Ministry of Finance, Russian industrial output achieved an annual growth rate close to 8 per cent during the 1890s, one of the highest experienced anywhere in the pre-1914 world, and possibly exceeded only by Sweden with about 12 per cent for the period 1888–96. The Tsarist empire, Europe's largest economy, had by 1900 ousted France from fourth place in world iron production and had taken fifth place in steel output. Its railway system, a vital component of modern-

Russian oil. Early drilling towers in the Baku oil fields, on the Caspian Sea, around 1900. Some of the reserves were very near the surface. They made Russia briefly the world's biggest producer of oil around the century's turn.

47

First train to Irkutsk.
This remote township in the Russian east, lies close to the southern end of Lake Baykal, and very nearly 3,000 miles by rail from Moscow. The railway, and this train, only reached it in 1898, as an important stage in Count Witte's huge trans-Siberian project. Irkutsk was a station on the high-priority Central Siberian stretch of the line; building had begun in 1893. The warm-water port of Vladivostock which was the terminus, and target, of this construction lay a further 2,000 miles and more to the south-east. The isolation of Irkutsk gives a special edge to the celebratory mood of the crowd.

ization in such a vast land mass, increased in mileage by 87 per cent between 1892 and 1903, while oil extraction more than tripled between 1887 and 1898. Indeed, around 1900, Russia became, briefly, the biggest producer of oil in the world.

There are two major reservations to be made about this interpretation. First, even the Russian surge of the 1890s had a prehistory. Between 1861 and 1885, industrial output growth had managed a very respectable average annual advance of about 6 per cent and the 'railway ukaz' of the Tsar Liberator, Alexander II—which had recognized that 'our fatherland, equipped by nature with abundant gifts, but divided by huge spaces, especially needs suitable communications'—had been passed in 1857. Even before the serf emancipation of 1861, which is conventionally taken as the benchmark for Tsarist modernization, an 'autonomous stream' of Russian enterprise was discernible in such industries as cotton textiles, sugar-refining, and distilling. Not even Witte's drive for growth in the heavy industries lacked a pedigree. Secondly, the other member of the third-wave economies for which Gerschenkron tried to find a 'great spurt'—Italy—resolutely refuses to supply one. This latecomer contained very significant areas of underdevelopment, particularly in the south, and meets most of the criteria for backwardness. Yet its industrial take-off, which Gerschenkron locates in the years 1896–1914, proceeded, on his own measurement, at average rates of manufacturing output growth no higher than 5.4 per cent per annum. This is actually somewhat slower than the much more mature German economy was managing during its high-technology expansion of the 1890s. It is difficult to escape the conclusion that the Ger-

48

schenkron perspective on the rapid escape from backwardness is overly dependent on the experience of the single Russian case.

The Strength of the Old Economic Order

If in most cases industrialization was a gradual and accumulative process, it was in no case before 1914 a complete process. When we talk of an industrial economy, it is easy to forget that the economy is not entirely occupied by industry, let alone by factory industry. Traditional sectors composed of agriculture and non-factory craft manufactures survived in all European economies down to 1914; and in some they retained considerable social and political power. Even in Britain the factory did not become the dominant form of industrial organization until beyond 1830; before that, workshop production was the most common type of industrial organization. France remained a country of market-town economies and widespread rural industry until late in the century; a genuinely national and urban market probably did not come into existence before the 1890s. Even in Germany, where the rise of cartels in the 1870s and 1880s helped to carry large-scale industrial organization further than anywhere else on the continent, traditional methods of production were by no means extinguished: as late as 1882 one-third of all German textile workers were still employed within the domestic system of manufacturing. In Italy, the early application of electric power gave an extended lease of life to small-scale workshop methods of production. And, in Russia, the physical separation between modern factories and village markets allowed peasant craft manufacturing to survive *en masse* to the end of the Tsarist period and beyond: in 1914 some 30 per cent of all manufacturing output derived from these *kustar* industries in the countryside. So, although a transition towards large-scale forms of organization is an essential feature of modern economic growth, it is not a sweeping transition. Traditional technologies and modes of work proved durable well into this century and most industrial economies were characterized around 1914, to one degree or another, by technological dualism, by the coexistence of modern processes and corporations alongside much older methods and types of venture.

Rarely, however, did small-scale industry or craft production do much to impede the progress of the modern sector. It either coexisted or it was crushed. But in agricultural production proper, matters could be quite otherwise. This was because

Cottage industry: a complete knitwear workshop, late eighteenth century. The spinning wheel on the left is generating the yarn; the machine in the centre is spooling it; and the loom on the right is producing the cloth.

interests existed in this sphere which were both large-scale *and* traditionalist. Often the aristocratic or gentry exponents of cultivation on large estates, they possessed good access to political power. Indeed, it is an irony of nineteenth-century economic history that, in many states undergoing industrial modernization, the political or administrative leadership lay in the hands of an agrarian ascendancy, or its relatives. Sometimes, usually in the early stages of the growth process, this ascendancy would perceive a utility—normally a military one—in industrial activity and would not seek to constrain it. But other aspects of industrial growth—loss of labour from the countryside, encroaching urbanization, a leaning towards free trade—could easily cut across the interests of this group. When this happened, its members possessed the means to extract a particular price for the inconvenience of living in an industrial society.

Table I gives a measure of the amount of economic muscle remaining in agriculture around 1910; and this in turn, of course, provides a very rough measure of its political muscle. Only in Britain had the process of industrial change reduced the agricultural share in national output to truly modest dimensions. And Britain, of course, maintained agricultural (and all other forms of) free trade between 1846 and 1914. Another notable measure of modernity in the British case is the size of the services sector. All mature economies undergo a shift in this direction, but only one case displays it convincingly in this sample from the pre-1914 world. At the other end of the scale, it is striking that in three countries which had clearly achieved industrial take-off by 1910—France, Germany, and Italy—the traditional sector still accounted for at least 25 per cent of national output. In Russia, agriculture was still massively predominant, which highlights the central conundrum of the late Tsarist economy: despite its high growth rates and its world-ranking industrial sector, how can it be said to have achieved modern economic growth if the traditional sector still covered 60 per cent of the economy?

The event of the pre-1914 decades which most irritated the large agricultural interests who lived in these large agricultural sectors, particularly those of France, Germany, and Russia, was the pressure on grain prices which built up after 1870. Their response was to demand tariff protection in order to defend their domestic prices from the inroads of extra-European cargoes infiltrated into the home market by newfangled locomotives and cargo ships. Some industrialists, worried by rising competition levels, also perceived

The face of economic conservatism: a Prussian *Junker* in 1910. The neo-feudal estate owners of trans-Elbean Germany insisted on growing outmoded grain crops, such as rye, and used their political power to secure the tariff protection needed to sustain this uneconomic endeavour.

50

Chancellorial stunts. Fürst von Bülow (Reichschancellor 1900–9) performs the European Balancing Act, hoping that, should he fall, he would be whisked to safety by the Prussian eagle. His balancing act between naval expenditure for the middle class and agricultural tariffs for the *Junker* aristocracy was another of his routines.

virtue in tariffs at this point. This convergence of interests permitted alliances like that in Germany in the late 1870s, the famous 'compact between iron and rye', aimed at securing tariff aid for the great producers of both. But the convergence did not last long. The industrial depression, especially in Germany, was not as extended as the agricultural price crisis. As markets recovered, industrialists wanted to get back into the export business and realized that freer, not more restricted, trade was the correct recipe for this. Even worse, tariffs on food crops meant higher living costs and thus upward pressure on the wages industrialists had to pay.

Nevertheless, the grain lobbies of France, Germany, and Russia fought for their tariffs and got them, whatever the true developmental interest of the economy concerned. Probably, this interest was most heavily compromised in Germany. The east Elbean plains of Prussia contained some of the most unblushing and unbridled agrarian conservatives to be found anywhere in Europe. These *Junkers* did not like democracy, industry, cities, foreigners, and many other things besides;

TABLE 1. *Shares of National Output by Sector around 1850 and 1910*

	1850			1910		
	Agriculture	Industry	Transport/ Commerce	Agriculture	Industry	Transport/ Commerce
Britain	21	35	19	6	34	29
France	45	29	7	35	36	7
Germany	47	21	8	25	43	15
Russia	75	10	12	60	29	12
Italy	57	19	17	42	22	23

yet their families provided much of the civil service, officer corps, and court of the new Reich. They had a tune to call; and they roared it out. In the tariff revisions of 1879–87, the industrialists sang along, although the *Junkers* got by far the larger share of the takings. When German Chancellors of the 1890s—most notably Caprivi—tried to relax the tariff system and trim it more in favour of the modern sector, the *Junkers* erupted. These pillars of conservatism threatened to withhold taxes from the treasury, block recruits for the army, or obstruct the much-prized naval programmes of the fledgling empire. They forced Chancellors into resignation or ransom. In 1902, Prince Bülow chose the latter, and, in order to get the latest naval scheme through, consented to another enormous round of protection for the grain estates. This was clearly contrary to the interests of the modern sector and converted German arable farming into the biggest agricultural hothouse maintained by any of the advanced economies. That the most powerful industrial system in Europe could be so constrained is powerful testimony to the enduring strength of pre-industrial forces. It is important to recall that economic modernization did not proceed to unanimous applause.

Industrialization as a Regional Experience

It follows from this distribution of industrialization within, rather than throughout, economies that it was *both* an international and a regional experience. It was international because it travelled in an important sense: later developing countries could copy technologies and methods or borrow capital from earlier ones, while early developers could act as customers for the raw materials and foodstuffs produced by later ones. It was regional because the modern industrial sectors took shape as particular area concentrations within individual economies, which were more like similar concentrations, lying across the waters or the frontiers, than they were like their own rural and craft-based hinterlands. The main industrial pockets by 1914 were situated in northern Britain, northern and eastern France, the Rhine–Ruhr triangle of Germany, northern Italy around Milan, southern Russia and the Baltic strip, the region around Vienna, and the Basque coast of Spain. Certainly, Tyneside at this time would have had more in common with Rhine–Ruhr than the former would have had with Cornwall or the latter with East Prussia. This type of observation is the basis of Professor Pollard's insight that industrialization was less a national circumstance than a regional event.

Still more to the point, these regions interacted with one another. Thus, in the early nineteenth century, cotton yarn spun in Lancashire could be purchased as an input by the cotton weavers of the Rhineland. Later, Krupp of Essen would secure iron ore from wholly owned mines in Spain and Thyssen would cultivate parallel connections in Normandy and French Lorraine. By 1914, about one-half of all German iron-ore supplies came from industrial regions outside Germany, mainly Sweden and French Lorraine. Similarly, the Bilbao–Cardiff axis formed a famous mutual trade in iron ore and coal between the industrialists of the Basque and South Welsh economic regions. This axis had even *replaced* the earlier Bilbao–Gijon connection through which the Basque metal-makers had tapped the coal of the neighbouring Spanish mines of Asturias. In eastern France, the notoriously disputed frontier of Alsace-Lorraine ran through what was in reality a single integrated complex of mining and manufacturing, bisecting trading partners, and even individual firms, with sporadically disastrous political consequences.

After victory in the Franco-Prussian war in 1871, in which Germany's rapidly advancing capacity in high-quality steel manufacture and gun-making was a not insignificant variable, the Germans drew the new frontier in Alsace to what appeared the maximum economic advantage of the moment. But the iron-ore field of Longwy-Briey, the richest in Europe, was not discovered until the 1880s and it lay on the French side of the border. It became a German war aim in the disturbed years leading up to the next confrontation between these two, and many other, powers in 1914.

But this last case should be a warning against an overenthusiastic commitment to international regionalism in our perspective of the pre-1914 era of industrialization. Frontiers were clearly more than merely lines on a map, across which economic impulses cheerfully and freely flowed. Rather, as Professor Supple has correctly observed, 'they frequently defined quite distinctive systems of thought and action'. Frontiers allowed individual governments to move the economic goalposts by tax, tariff, or territorial acquisition, and such tactics certainly altered the prospects for industrialists of one country *vis-à-vis* those of another. Even the cotton-spinner in *laissez-faire* Lancashire lived under a markedly different fiscal and administrative regime from his weaving colleague in the early nineteenth-century Rhineland. So, if regions matter, so do regimes.

The Institutions of Development from Backwardness

In one powerful view of industrialization during this period, what lies inside the political frontier—the economic power, intent, and will of a particular state—matters a very great deal. It is clear that the various waves of industrialization were associated not only with different places and technology but with notably different institutional patterns. By institutions we mean private firms, educational systems, financial agencies, and government ministries. Alexander Gerschenkron, though he talked least of the pioneering British model and too much perhaps of the late developing Russian one, produced the most orderly arrangement of thoughts on this subject.

In the British experience—which was spontaneous, individualistic, open-market, and gradual—institutions above the level of the private firm played little part. The private firm was itself characteristically small—the largest class of cotton mill in late eighteenth-century Britain boasted a fixed capital of no more than £10,000—and its finances were provided by the informal sources of family, congregational, local, or partnership funds. The long-running alienation between finance capital and industrial capital in Britain derives from this formative growth stage: since banks were asked to provide little in the way of (fixed) capital for plant or buildings, they readily accepted the lower-risk, and arms-length, strategy of providing (working) capital for the purchase of materials or payment of wages.

53

These short-run transactions, quickly repaid, allowed the bankers to maintain a distance from industrial risks. Similarly, since technology levels at this point in world industrialization, like capital levels, were relatively modest, and there were no external competitors to push them upwards, the early British industrialists were under little pressure to employ scientific discovery or theoretical break-through to achieve innovation. Rather, this tended to be supplied by the crafts-man's observation or adjustment at the bench, the famous 'practical tinkering' of the first industrial revolution. Unlike those that followed, this pioneer movement owed little to the scientists.

Consequently, little connection was perceived between educational effort and industrial outcome: technology appeared to be self-generated. Of course, this would hold true only of a limited stretch of world industrialization. But because this approach created the world's first and richest industrial state, it seemed in Britain to be truer than that. Indeed this misperception, as it turned out to be, exercised a recognizable influence upon British educational practice until 1914 and beyond.

Modest requirements in capital and technology in early industrial Britain per-mitted many small ventures to enter the market. These were often family firms and they created a tradition of atomistic competition and a suspicion of modern large-scale corporate enterprise that was long lasting. Between 1750 and 1870, British governments had little incentive to do much about this; and after 1870 old habits died hard and old principles succumbed only slowly to new realities. This is scarcely surprising. Open markets, self-directed capitalists, and gentle govern-ment had combined to produce huge industrial and imperial pre-eminence. Before 1870 no convincing competitors emerged to provoke official anxiety. And when they did emerge, they were met only with official complacency; they were seen for too long as industrial also-rans who required newfangled devices and dubious policies merely to approach the starting-line in the industrial race. British methods were tried and trusted. And set, it seemed, in gold; only later did this sub-stance turn out to be stone; and porous.

Early institutional 'imprinting' of this kind has featured in some powerful recent explanations of Britain's inability to adjust to the competitive markets and new technological prospects of the late nineteenth century. However, Gerschenkron had more to say about the follower economies, whose situation around 1850 or 1860 was not the soon-to-be-threatened industrial prosperity of Britain, but the relative deprivation of economic backwardness. How were they to escape from it? Particularly now that the threshold for entry to industrial status was steeper: the railways, engineering shops, and steel mills of this technology band would not yield to the institutional equipment of small firms, aloof banks, non-technical education, and lordly restraint by governments. If the follower economies were to react positively to the dangers and examples proffered by the industrial leaders something more in the way of affirmative action was needed.

Gerschenkron's achievement was to propose that a certain kind of institutional action was associated with particular levels of backwardness. Chronic backward-ness required a full programme of development spearheaded by an intervention-

Facing: **The Ironforge,** by Joseph Wright 'of Derby' (1734–97). A handsome, if somewhat idealized evocation of ironworking in the early stages of the British Industrial Revolution, before such processes were mostly absorbed into large-scale plants of the type shown on p. 42. Nevertheless, heavy equipment was employed even at the workshop level of enterprise by the 1770s and is accurately portrayed here. Wright pioneered the depiction of scientific and industrial subjects and had close ties with men of science and manufacture such as Erasmus Darwin, Josiah Wedgwood, and Richard Arkwright.

54

Steelmaking at Krupp of Essen (*above*) around 1900. Here a Bessemer converter is being readied for tilting so as to disgorge its contents of molten steel. Krupp made some of the highest-quality steel of the day.

Right: **The Silesian industrial revolution at work.** The great ironworks at Königshütte (now Królewska Huta) in Chorzow, Poland. The coke store is in the foreground, the iron foundries beyond. Modern coke-burning furnaces were installed as early as 1802, but are here shown in action around 1850.

ist state. Medium backwardness was best managed, and growth extracted from it, by the use of specialized investment banks. Suppressed backwardness, or, put another way, economic maturity, could be left in the capable hands of the modern large-scale corporation. Any given country could pass through all these institutional stages as backwardness was confronted and beaten back.

The logic is quite simple. The developed status of other powers poses a threat to the chronically backward society. By definition, that society lacks sufficient capitalists, markets, or investment for modern economic growth. The economy contains so many gaps that the state is the only agency with sufficient power, reach, and resources to fill them. It can use its own officials as substitute capitalists or as mentors to what capitalists there are. It can use its own custom—often for weapons or railways—to create markets for manufactured goods. It can use its own exchequer—for the state is always potentially rich, however poor the country—to finance the necessary capital formation. Military inferiority will often be a sufficient motive for even very conservative states to undertake these tasks.

In the context of medium backwardness, some gaps have been filled. The easiest are filled first, and thus some markets and some capitalists will exist. The major residual bottleneck will be in capital supply. Breaking it will require the institutional innovation of the investment bank. British-style, short-term credit provision will be no use amidst the problems of medium backwardness. Here capital is not plentiful but scarce, technology thresholds are not low but high. Some method has to be found of concentrating scarce capital within large-scale financial institutions which will then confront the dangerous task of lending it on a long-term basis to railways and factories. This was the method discovered in the mid-nineteenth century in the shape of the investment bank. Outside Britain, it was used throughout Europe; but most intensively in Berlin and Cologne. The investment bank was to institutional innovation what the steam engine was to technological innovation—and it was just as important to industrialization in the last century. Many steam engines would never have run without it; the investment bank was the financial engine of nineteenth-century development. Its wide spread also indicates how many economies experienced medium backwardness in the period preceding 1914.

If the investment bank was the premier institution of medium backwardness, it was not the only one. It revolutionized the flow of industrial capital in the high-cost development process of the mid-century. But this process contained high thresholds in areas other than finance; one also certainly existed in skills. The supply of human capital, as well as the supply of finance capital, had to be improved. And for this polytechnics, technical high schools, and scientific universities were needed. These too were institutions of the mediumly backward economy.

In the context of suppressed backwardness, or economic maturity, the problems of development are past. The issue is now how most equitably to distribute the fruits of development—a new welfare role for the state at the other end of the growth process—and how to maintain momentum amidst maturity. In this connection, the job of the large-scale corporation is to maximize throughput, organize markets, and, through research, to sustain technological fertility. Institutions

Brunel's Great Eastern.
She weighed in, at her launch in 1858, at 27,400 tonnes, and was for many years the largest vessel ever constructed. Her double-skin iron hull and mixed propulsion system (steam-powered paddle wheels and propellers) emphasize the technological advance upon the wooden merchantman shown on page 41. Though a miracle of engineering, she was a white elephant of finance. She failed to pay her way as an ocean liner on the England–India run and was relegated to cable laying in the North Atlantic. She laid the trans-Atlantic cable from Ireland to Newfoundland in 1866 and was broken up in 1889.

able to do this, some of them multinational corporations, certainly existed in the United States and Germany, and even in Britain, before 1914; but their heyday was to be somewhat later.

Classic European cases of growth out of medium backwardness are those of France and Germany in the period 1840–70; with traces of similar patterns occurring in Italy from the 1890s and in Austria and even Russia from the 1900s. Classic cases of growth out of chronic backwardness are those of Prussia, 1780–1820, and Russia in the 1890s; with some echoes occurring in Hungary around the turn of the century.

The Investment Bank and Medium Backwardness

Until the 1850s, France lacked the markets and the governments suitable for industrial acceleration. Her markets had been compromised by the destruction of French overseas trade in the wartime years before 1815 and by the British export domination of Europe in the peacetime years after Waterloo. French governments between 1815 and 1848 consisted of restored monarchies afraid of every socio-economic shadow. These regimes saw in the preceding Revolutionary and Bona-partist phases sufficient social change to last many lifetimes and they were deeply averse to any more. This encouraged them to regard any attempt at financial inno-vation as an unprovoked assault on the Bastille of the Bank of France and any rail-way project of economical scale as the spawning ground of monster capitalism. At mid-century, the main constraints on revived industrial activity in France were capital shortage and the lack of a sensible transport policy.

The Second Empire of Napoleon III (1850–71), authoritarian in its domestic pol-icy and vainglorious in its foreign policy, was not the most obvious source of eco-nomic reform. But whatever his shortcomings in diplomatic vision and political substance, this Bonaparte had a clear view of what France needed for greater industrial prowess. A firm push from imperial government was required to achieve it: Napoleon III's autocratic regime did more to promote economic advance in nineteenth-century France than the weak monarchies that preceded it or the weak republic that succeeded it. However, this was achieved less by the active gap-filling policies which are associated with state campaigns against chronic backwardness than by the removal of the bureaucratic obstacles to eco-nomic capabilities that already existed.

Rationalization of the railway policy owed much to imperial initiative. Rejecting the cautious concessions and nit-picking administrative controls of the previous two decades, the new government advocated operation by network or by region and threw itself 'full-steam into long concessions'. Plenty of capitalist interests were ready to respond. Trunk-line construction in the three decades after 1855–64 exceeded the building of the previous three decades by 700 per cent and of the succeeding three by over 20 per cent. The decade after 1855 saw the peak of French rail construction in the nineteenth century, at 7.2 per cent of gross industrial prod-uct. This boom saw the construction of many important lines, from Paris to Mar-seilles and to the German, Spanish, and Italian frontiers, from Bordeaux on the Atlantic to Sète on the Mediterranean.

However, willing as the private sector was to respond to these new transport opportunities, it needed capital to do so. Railway ventures of the scale of the Chemin de Fer du Nord had taxed the limited French market before 1848, and the vast requirements of the Midi line outran the resources of the merchant bankers and even of the Rothschilds. Yet France had been allowed to develop few financial institutions which could do the job. Once more, the key innovation which made good this deficiency, the Crédit Mobilier of 1852, was launched under the personal imprimatur of Louis Napoleon. Designed as a counterbalance to the Bank of France, and the next largest financial institution in the country, the Crédit pro-vided a real alternative to the restrictive investment policies of the preceding three decades. It became a European exemplar for the growth-conscious bank, stocking its coffers with scarce investment resources and opening them to adventurous capitalists, although pre-eminently to railway capitalists. By the mid-1860s, *mobilier*-type institutions had been established in French provincial centres such as Lille, Lyons, and Marseilles and large-scale metropolitan banks like the Crédit

Sir Henry Bessemer: the view from *Vanity Fair*. Bessemer's process for burning off excess carbon revolutionized the economy of steelmaking. Around 1850 Britain could make only 60,000 tonnes of steel in a year. By 1870 a single Bessemer converter could produce one tonne every minute. After Bessemer, steel was as cheap as cast iron.

Industriel et Commercial (1859), the Crédit Lyonnais (1863), and the Société Générale (1864) had followed the lead set by the innovating Crédit Mobilier. Although it was eventually driven under by an unforgiving Bank of France in the financial crisis of 1867, it had—with a little help from the emperor—achieved the necessary liberation of French finance.

The effect upon heavy industry of these major adjustments in transport and banking was profound. The three decades from 1840 saw the replacement in France of the textile industries by a new leading sector of capital-intensive industries such as iron and steel manufacture, metal fabrication, and coalmining. Steel was a rare metal in 1850 but an industrial staple by 1870, and French advances here were nicely timed for the development of the Bessemer process. This, the first method for mass-producing steel, was invented in 1856 by Henry Bessemer, resident in Britain but the son of a French engineer, and became available just as the French metal industries entered their phase of modern growth.

The France of the Second Empire did thus exploit the opportunities and institutions of medium backwardness, but not to the same extent as the German states. The French borrowed, or borrowed back, the Bessemer process from the industrial leader, Britain. The Germans initiated little but they devised highly original ways of borrowing from all other initiators, including the French. The French used investment banks well in the 1850s and 1860s, but, noticeably, they did not utilize them far beyond the railway tracks. No major financial institution specializing in credit for manufacturing was created until the foundation of the Banque de Paris et de Pays Bas in 1872 and the establishment of the Banque de l'Union Parisienne even later in 1904. The big bank flotations of the 1860s, especially the Crédit Lyonnais and the Société Générale, summed up French financial inclinations during the last third of the century by drifting away from domestic lending altogether into huge foreign investment operations. By contrast, the German states from 1850, and the Kaiserreich from 1871, became the classic exponents of bank-led industrial growth, and the masters of good practice for those who wished to imitate them.

After its mid-century growth surge, the French economy of 1871–1905 was both prone to accident and wasteful of opportunity. Defeat by the Prussians in 1871 cost France the province of Alsace-Lorraine. This was more than a matter of pride and territory. The region contained France's most important textile centres, most of her machine-building industry, and 80 per cent of the country's known iron-ore reserves, with their attendant blast furnaces and steelworks. While war savaged

French industry, disease blighted French agriculture. From the late 1860s to the 1890s, the most unsporting of all pests, the corpulent aphid, *phylloxera vastatrix*, munched its way through the vines of France. Government was scarecely more helpful. Within the unstable democracy of the Third Republic, law-making proceeded by faction fight and lacked the economic resolve of the Second Empire. The bankers preferred to cast their nets overseas. And the industrial bureaucracy of the Corps des Mines made worse what was already bad: the ironmasters trying to exploit the Briey basin were subjected to an unremitting stream of discouraging advice. Some of this was pure bad luck. Some of the rest makes the point that institutional devices, just like any items of technology, are only as good as the people who direct them.

Those who directed the German investment banks were more determined. As in France, the capital requirement for railway construction in Saxony, Silesia, and, above all, the Rhineland, drove the bankers of Leipzig, Breslau, and pre-eminently Cologne, into new forms of lending from the 1830s and 1840s onwards. The first German investment bank, the Schaaffhausen'scher Bankverein, was founded in Cologne in 1848, and, between that year and 1856, a tight cohort of institutions, which were to become known as the German great banks, were launched into the railway and industrial markets.

Differences with French experience were twofold. From the beginning, these German banks not only floated share issues for their railway clients; they also bought packets of these shares for themselves; built up an equity interest; and placed their officials as directors on the boards of railway companies. When railway demand for capital waned from the late 1860s, the German bankers did not go in search of foreign pastures; they went in search of German industrial flotations. They purchased slices of these for themselves; they pursued the industrial equity interest; and they infiltrated their directors on to the boards of industrial companies.

In one sense this was simple prudence. The bankers were being asked, or were choosing, to extend long-term credit to risky ventures; one way of controlling the risk was an ownership interest and a voice in the management. In another sense, it gave the bankers a remarkable perspective across, and influence over, the industrial sector. By 1914, a mere sixteen of Germany's top bankers controlled between them 437 industrial directorships. Between 1885 and 1900 the leading banks, and mainly the Big Six, placed some £1,200 million worth of industrial securities in the market.

These bank–industry connections could be used for a variety of purposes. Bankers could push industrial clients towards best-practice technologies, thus influencing the demand as well as the supply for capital. Industrial debtors, afraid for their overdrafts, could be bullied by bank managers into joining cartel associations—where prices were fixed, profits more secure, and the debt safer. Or, as in the great mining–industrial region of Rhine–Ruhr in the 1890s, industrialists in one industry, such as coal, could find themselves led by a financial hand into marriage with industrialists in related fields, such as iron or steel. The very high levels of such vertical integration in German industry by 1914 derived in many cases from pressure applied by the bankers. From the bank manager's viewpoint, a coalmine with a guaranteed outlet for its coal, or a steel mill with an assured supply of cheap fuel, was a safer coalmine or a safer steel mill.

It is clear then that the German banks, unlike their British, or even French, counterparts, were a central design influence upon the German industrial economy. They financed its new technology; by promoting cartellization, they helped select its market context; by fostering vertical integration, they influenced its patterns of ownership and control. It was only with a small measure of exaggeration that W. F. Bruck concluded that 'These banks created the German industrial state'. Fittingly, the term used to describe this kind of financial entrepreneurship is German: *Bankinitiative*.

If high-pressure capital formation, pumped into heavy industry, was one dominant characteristic of German industrialization, it was not the only one. Perhaps the next most striking feature, especially after 1885, was the organized incorporation of scientific knowledge into industrial practice. This was not only a matter of technical education, although that process was conspicuously well handled in Germany. Some German states, notably Saxony, had possessed advanced educational systems from the eighteenth century, but the second third of the nineteenth century saw widespread adjustments across many states. By 1905, the Kaiserreich could offer a system of education which matched a technical-school capability to virtually every rung of the conventional educational ladder. Between 1872 and 1914 educational expenditure added as much to the national budget as the imperial army and navy.

The saloon on wheels: the 1899 model Renault. This was the world's first 'inside drive' car. The notion that the motor car might offer mobile comfort as well as mobile excitement began here.

This commitment produced a useful array of carefully designed human capital but it did not ensure that the relevant science got into industry. Of course, few other countries ensured this. The British lacked both the human capital and the science-industry connections. The French made successful initiatives in theoretical science but could not master the business of application. Their industrialists were the first to introduce trained chemists into factories but they could not persuade managers to take any notice of them. The French

defined many of the ground rules for chemical manufacturing, yet made the poorest explosives in Europe.

Nevertheless, French science and engineering won some notable rosettes. Precocious discoveries in dyestuffs, particularly artificial fuschine, came from French laboratories; the first recognizably modern 'inside drive' automobile was the 1899 Renault; and electrical engineering and specialist metal industries were prominent in the French industrial revival after 1900. Indeed, in the key sector of motor cars, the French dominated the European trade of the pre-1914 years. Car factories, which were huge by average French industrial standards, generated continental exports which outstripped American exports to Europe in 1911 and 1912, and produced a total output more than twice that of the British car industry.

Yet it remained a hit-and-miss matter whether a French technological breakthrough ever penetrated as far as the production line, and, if it did, in which country the production line might be. By contrast, in Germany very little from anywhere went to waste. Many of the country's industrial achievements followed less from initial discovery than from the rapid application of methods pioneered elsewhere. Processes central to Germany's late nineteenth-century successes—aniline dye manufacture, the generation and conveyance of electrical power, the Gilchrist–Thomas process in steel production—were French and British, not Ger-

High technology in the gunshops: Krupp of Essen in 1890. The large weapon at centre-right is a breech-loading rifled artillery piece of recognizably modern design. The 1890 weapon would require much precise attention from a variety of advanced machine-tools. It would take several months of unbroken machining to inscribe the rifling in a weapon of this size.

61

man, discoveries. The essential link in Germany between discovery, wherever it took place, and application was an institution: the research team. Whereas French industry was the first to receive trained chemists, German industry was the first to incorporate entire laboratories.

Aniline dyes came from Britain, fuschine from France, but it was the industrial laboratories of Frankfurt and Mannheim which perfected them for mass manufacture and converted them into world-leading exports. By 1900, German chemical firms were deploying research teams of up to fifty to seventy scientists, allowing them to follow their noses, and expecting to discard 90 per cent of the results. But the outcome could be, as it was at BASF's Ludwigshafen factory after seventeen years of research, the priceless reward of artificial indigo. In industries like metals and engineering, the pattern was the same. The Westphalian steelmasters made none of the new process discoveries but were quicker than any foreign rivals in applying them. Again, the research laboratory stole the march. At Essen, behind Krupp's excellence in armament manufacture, there lay, in the words of a British competitor, 'an immense physical and chemical laboratory . . . such as is possessed by no university in the world'.

Germany's onslaught on the automobile industry, which *was* a pioneering initiative, began in the same way. The Swabian gunsmith Gottlieb Daimler set up a research laboratory with Wilhelm Maybach in 1883, before developing his lightweight petrol engine the following year. Daimler first used his engine in a car in 1886, while his rival, Karl Benz, produced the world's first standard production model in 1894. By 1896 Daimler was promoting the Daimler Wagonette in the British market and in 1901 offered the first technically advanced Mercedes to an

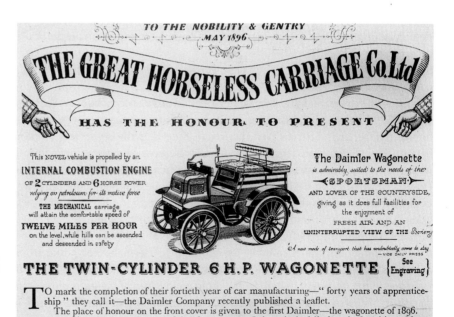

Made in Germany: Daimler's advertising for the British market, 1896. The Wagonette—still very much a 'horseless carriage'— was one of the first imports offered to the British motorist. A wave of German imports caused an economic panic in Britain during the 1890s.

appreciative world. By 1914, the Mercedes Grand Prix racer had shaken off the dust of its pottering antecedents of the 1880s and 1890s: it could reach 112 m.p.h.

The German approach to science-in-industry did not spread especially widely outside Germany before 1914. But the German *Bankinitiative* was copied by others in the last decades of peace. In the 1890s, the Italian economy turned away from French-style *mobilier* banking and deliberately adopted German-style investment banks, as well as attracting German overseas investment and German bank officials to help run them. Similarly, when the Russian economy emerged from the state-dominated growth phase of the 1890s, and sought relevant institutions for the next era of growth, it found that the traditional English-style banks of Moscow were not adequate for the purpose. Instead, in the 1900s, St Petersburg was developed as an investment banking centre modelled closely on German prototypes. In these countries, and in its homeland, the investment bank proved itself one of the most powerful development aids of the pre-1914 world.

The State and Severe Backwardness

European experience offers perhaps two outstanding examples of economies which drew significant measures of industrialization out of severe backwardness by means of concerted state action. These are Prussia in the late eighteenth century and Russia in the late nineteenth century. In each, as in many instances where old-regime states bring themselves to contemplate the ambiguous delights of modernization, the motive was military advantage.

The importance of Silesia to its Prussian rulers was its location, jutting out like a battering-ram towards the rival empires of Russia and Austria. It was precisely the place to contrive and foster the first major heavy industries on German soil. The first blast furnace anywhere in Germany was installed at Silesia's Malapane Hütte during the reign of Frederick the Great in 1753. But it was in the period 1780–1820 that the state did most to raise the industrial capacity of this sparsely cultivated and thinly populated province. In the 1780s and 1790s, a formidable industrial bureaucracy led by von Heinitz, head of the Prussian industrial and mining agency, and von Reden, the industrial commissar for Silesia, scoured Europe for techniques and technologists. The result was that by 1802 the government foundries at Königshütte and Gleiwitz boasted furnaces of best-practice quality, that the first British steam engine in Germany was erected at the great Silesian lead works of Friedrichsgrübe, and that the iron-puddling process was commissioned in Silesia only shortly after Britain had developed it. The British ironmaster, William Wilkinson, was brought over to manage the Malapane Hütte and the Scot, John Baildon, to look after the blast furnaces.

Around 1800 Silesia possessed some of the most active mining concerns and efficient ironworks to be found in Europe. By 1842 one observer could claim that Silesia was 'the equal of England and the foremost on the Continent'. This, of course, was an exaggeration. One Silesia did not make a German industrial revolution. The province lacked any genuine market outside the state. Its economic rationale lay in its proximity not to consumers but to battlefields. Nevertheless, if

Reading the emancipation decree, Prozorov estate, 1861. Former serfs receiving the news of liberation are seen at left. However, the emancipation was a hollow one, conferring a new legal status while economic, social, and fiscal suppression of the rural community persisted.

the first industrial nation had, by the 1840s, encountered a proficient Germanic imitator, this was almost wholly a function of induced growth—of state interest in the task of development.

In Russia, the commencement of economic modernization conventionally dates from the emancipation of the serfs in 1861. This is a misattribution. Alexander II, the Tsar Liberator, although himself humanitarian and liberal in outlook, did not free 'the baptized chattels' of Russian feudalism because he thought that reform would do anything for the economy. He did so because serfdom was already collapsing under its own weight, because the countryside consequently was in ferment, and because he feared the onset of reform from below if the regime did not rapidly pre-empt it with reform from above.

Instead, emancipation became a covert exercise in social control. The peasants who had the liberating decrees read to them in the 1860s merely exchanged one kind of overlordship for another. They were removed from the domination of the gentry and aristocracy who had previously owned them and set, in the majority of cases, under the control of the village commune. The regime used the commune to keep the vast horde of the Russian peasantry where social control dictated: in the countryside, in poverty, and under taxation. The commune controlled all land supplies and distributed them to households according to family size. Most got less than they had farmed under feudalism. Taxation was collectively assessed. So if an individual left the village or the household, the burden fell more heavily on those who remained. An internal passport system reinforced these constraints on mobility. Any improvement in cultivation required a two-thirds majority vote in the village assembly. So there were few changes in cultivation. For the privilege of living inside this system of 'liberation', the peasant household paid through the nose, in forty-nine annual instalments of 'redemption'. Freedom within this structure was merely a matter of legal definition. Reality, for those bequeathed it, was oppression by another name. The peasantry had too little land, too much taxation, almost no cultivatory technique, and very little prospect of getting out of the countryside. Genuine emancipation came not in 1861 but in the Stolypin reforms after 1905.

The true stimulus for economic modernization was not the emancipation of the serfs but defeat in the Crimean war of 1854–6. Backward Russia was trounced by the two most advanced industrial powers in the world at that time, Britain and France. This made a point of devastating force. If conservative, old-regime Russia wished to remain a great power, she needed to attain a measure of advanced, new-regime industry. Tsardom was committed to an active international role; if it did not pursue the industrial means to sustain this, it would fail in its own terms. It was this which made the Romanov dynasty the least likely, and least comfortable, contender for industrial status in late nineteenth-century Europe.

But Tsardom was also committed to the maintenance of autocratic power at home. It saw industrialism as a threat to that power. Where Tsardom required social control, industrialism brought social mobility, urban expansion, disaffected workers, and upheaval. So if industry was to be pursued in Tsarist Russia, it

Social control in action. Soldiers protect the residence of the Director of Factories from strikes, 1895. The threat of violent strike action became much more intense in Russia between 1900 and 1905.

would have to be within a particularly rigid, two-sector strategy of development. In one sector, the state would build up the core of heavy industry needed for strategic viability. In the other, the village commune would keep the mass of the population isolated from the contagion of factory and town. The circle would be squared: both internal security and external security would be attained. Industrial capitalism would be safely confined within a technological *gulag*.

Between 1856 and 1900, the Russian ministers of finance, the state officials responsible for pursuing the minimum of industrialization which the regime deemed acceptable, worked within the terms of this equation. Growth based on railway construction, selective importation of western technology, and the recruitment of European industrialists proceeded at a respectable rate until 1890. But before the advent of Count Witte to the ministry, it also proceeded on the assumption that Russia was primarily an agricultural society. Witte changed the emphasis: although he had no choice but to accept the regime's particularly limited concept of capitalistic development, especially in regard to the veto on agricultural reform, he was the first finance minister to make a full programme of industrialization his first priority.

Some have read too much into this and have mistaken a programme for a 'system' or a 'plan'. Von Laue, famously and risibly, saw Witte as 'a forerunner of Stalin rather than a contemporary of Nicholas II' and attributed the record growth rates of the 1890s to the economic hero at the finance ministry. In fact, of course, Witte was no time traveller and could not invent the economics of planning thirty years before the theoreticians at Gosplan had worked them out. His achievements, though considerable, were simpler than this. He saw railway construction as a priority, nearly doubling transport capacity, but also providing a major market for the steel, engineering, and coal industries. These heavy manufactures were those most needed for the purposes of both defence and rapid industrial growth. They were also expensive in capital and demanding in technology.

The true liberator: Prime Minister Stolypin and his wife. The provisions of the Stolypin reforms, in the wake of the 1905 Revolution, brought a measure of genuine freedom and, briefly, prosperity to the Russian countryside.

Witte confronted these difficulties not with an anachronistic plan but with the pragmatism of the broker. He did everything possible to make Russia attractive to the foreign investor, bringing in huge amounts of French, German, and British capital in the late 1890s. And if financial capital could be imported, so could knowledge capital. All manner of inducements were provided to lure western industrialists to set up shop within, and set examples to, the late Tsarist economy. All this lay

Countrymen on the move. Russian peasants seek factory work about 1910. One of the consequences of the Stolypin reforms was that the poorest peasants used their new freedom to sell their land and rush to the towns. The stampede was concentrated between 1907 and 1910. Ironically, this helped create precisely the volatile proletariat that the Tsarist regime had always feared.

within the range of financial diplomacy around the turn of the century; it did not require Witte to anticipate Stalin. And, significantly, the growth surge of the 1890s came to an end when bad harvests interrupted the fiscal tribute from the country-side and international financial crises cut Witte's credit line to the European exchanges.

It was significant too that the subsequent economic recession of 1900–5 did not bring a halt to the Tsarist industrial experiment. Foundations by now were firmly established. Industrial output growth resumed healthily after 1907, even though the finance ministry now pursued a more orthodox, and lower-profile, style of pol-icy. Indeed, the supervision of industry in the final pre-war decade lay with invest-ment banks and large industrial trusts rather than with government agencies. Where Witte had concentrated on heavy industries, growth was more evenly spread across the sectors. This was due not least to the Stolypin reforms which, at long last, brought a measure of genuine reform to the Russian countryside. Stolypin ended the redemption system and allowed the individual peasant house-hold to withdraw from the commune into independent cultivation.

Cultivation levels, harvests, and prosperity in the Russian countryside im-proved between 1905 and 1914. *Kustar*, or village craft industry, tapped this market and extended the consumer side of Russian manufacturing. Poor peasants, at last able to escape the commune, provided labour for these crafts, or ranged further afield, seeking jobs in factories and towns. With its large-scale industrial concerns,

Mother Russia. The village community about 1910. Amidst industrialization and agrarian reform, more than 80 per cent of Russia's population continued in traditional settlements, which had looked very much like this for centuries.

its investment banks, and its freer agricultural regime, the Russia of late Tsardom displayed signs of economic westernization, indications that it was becoming more like the industrial systems on the other side of the continent.

It is salutary, however, to end with a different perspective on Russian growth before 1914. For the Russian case defines what economic modernization could not do. Even the Stolypin reforms touched only a minority of the villages: two-thirds of households remained in the worst-practice sector and used the most primitive agricultural methods. Even after the industrial growth of the 1890s and 1900s, over 85 per cent of the population remained in the countryside. And those who moved from country to town were the most rootless and hopeless, the dispossessed who would help form the revolutionary proletariat that the regime had so long feared. But the enduring feature was village life. In the world's fifth biggest industrial economy, the vast majority of Russians would never have seen a factory. The figures who peer into the camera from the village street of the 1900s look, and lived, like their forebears of the 1800s. Had the camera been available then, the image would have been the same.

Military Modernization

1789–1918

Industrialization and War

THE landscape of the western front in 1918 would have looked familiar to soldiers of the late twentieth century. Scarred and fissured by war, its features, or rather the lack of them, bore testimony to the destructiveness of modern military technology. Tanks, heavy artillery, machine-guns, flame-throwers, gas, ground-attack aircraft, long-range bombers—all had reached a level of high performance and remarkably robust reliability within a few years. Their effect was to clear the surface of the battlefield, at least by day: men dug deep or flew overhead, but only pressing necessity caused them to stride over that pock-marked ground.

The same comparison could not be made between the soldiers of 1918 and those of the battle of Valmy in 1792, or even of Waterloo in 1815. The weaponry with which the latter fought, and its effects, would have seemed extraordinarily primitive to their successors. Indeed the smooth-bore flintlock musket, the grapeshot, and canister of the artillery had evolved little during the twenty years of the Revolutionary and Napoleonic wars; they had not even changed much since the wars of Louis XIV. For all their destructive impact, their limited accuracy, short range, and slow rate of fire did not compel dispersion for the sake of survival. The battlefield was not empty but congested; men and horses were tightly packed and clearly visible to their foes. Nothing symbolized more succinctly the contrast between the warfare of the French Revolution and that of the First World War than the change in dress. The scarlet- or blue-coated infantrymen of Napoleon's age, advancing into action with colours streaming and bands playing, were popinjays, at least in outward form; the combatants of 1918, clad in khaki or field grey, their faces

HEW
STRACHAN

obscured by steel helmets and gas masks, had lost their humanity and their individualities to the self-protective necessities of industrialized warfare.

The dramatic and rapid nature of the change in the contours and characteristics of warfare in Europe can clearly be linked, in the first place, to national economic development, and in the second to its concomitant, technological innovation. Between 1815 and 1914, to take the most dramatic example, Germany's production of coal increased two hundred fold and of pig-iron eighteen times. From these raw materials were fashioned the steel and then the guns and rifles whose

quantity and quality effected a revolution in fire-power. The broad equation between Europe's industrialization and its military modernization seems to provide a simple explanation for change, a linking of cause and result which is hard to resist. But such determinism must be rejected. The story is more complicated. In particular, it must make greater allowance for the role of ideas.

Economics and War

A history of Europe's military modernization which is shaped by technological and economic development leaves far too much out of account. Comparative advantage in the process of industrialization did not necessarily transfer into comparative advantage on the battlefield. During the Napoleonic wars the trend-setter in military affairs on the continent was France. And yet Britain, not France, led the way in the process of economic growth.

A similar point could be made of the next major European conflict, the First World War. The machinery of war stood at an apex of technological development; it required the mobilization of all a nation's resources. At the war's hub stood Britain's successor as Europe's industrial leader, Germany. But the capacity to sustain continued fighting in 1914–18 was not confined to the economic giants of Europe. Russia, the most backward of the great powers in 1914, maintained the war on one of her major land fronts for three years. Furthermore she did so single-handedly, and without ever fully mobilizing the manpower she had available. Bulgaria did not enter the war until September 1915, but, like Russia, also fought on for three years. And, most remarkable of all, the Ottoman empire, whose demise as a European power in the two Balkan wars of 1912 and 1913 had been a precipitant of the First World War, maintained activity on three and sometimes four fronts between 1914 and 1918. Thus, just as economic forwardness had not been translated into conventional military superiority in the case of Britain a hundred years earlier, so in the Great War backwardness did not necessarily correlate with military ineffectiveness.

The Germans were the first to make effective use of gas, at Ypres in April 1915. But its reputation for awfulness far exceeded its lethality. What worried soldiers was its contribution to the dehumanization of warfare: insidious and unspecific in its effects, it demanded protective gear that robbed men of their individuality.

Facing, above: **Sauerweid's painting of Waterloo** captures the density of troops on the battlefield and the directness of command in the Napoleonic era. Being brought up behind Wellington, who is in the centre, are the two French eagles taken by the heavy cavalry in the charge of the Union Brigade.

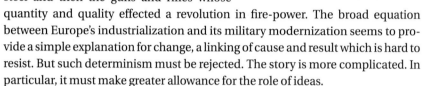

Below: **The pattern of ordered and deep trenches** could not sustain the punishing effects of artillery bombardment in the later battles of the First World War. At Ypres in 1917 or—as here—at Verdun in 1916, infantry took up positions in shell-holes, fighting a more fluid battle, and evading the predicted fire of the guns.

Above: **The growth of Krupp,** the German arms manufacturer based at Essen, was associated with the unification and rise of Germany. But, although the firm's reputation rested on its production of artillery, it had—like all others in the arms business—to diversify in peace into other business in order to be viable.

Right: **Women entered munitions work** in the First World War more easily than many other occupations as the newly created factories were less subject to restrictive practices. Women were also regarded as more sensitive in their handling of delicate explosives. The woman shown here is making shell cases at a Vickers plant in 1915.

States still had choices to make in terms of military priorities. In the eighteenth century, Frederick the Great's Prussia had 'punched above its weight' by giving priority to the army and its organization. By the twentieth century, economic development made it harder for the backward nation to counter the more advanced. But it was not impossible. Resource allocations were the products of political decisions. In 1914 Russia and Italy were appropriating, respectively, 35 per cent and 30 per cent of total government expenditure for military needs: despite smaller gross national products and smaller taxable bases, they opted to spend proportionately more on defence than more advanced nations. In gross terms Britain, although now ranking third in the world behind the United States and Germany as an industrial power, still disbursed more on her armed services than either of them. Between 1900 and 1913 average defence spending in Britain was £2.04 per head per year, as opposed to £0.77 in Germany and £0.85 in France. But her outlay did not translate into military hegemony on the continent. The strategic priorities which confronted Britain were those of maritime power and of imperial defence: by European standards her army remained diminutive.

So topsy-turvy was the logic imposed by the cost of war and of preparing for it that many observers before 1914 concluded that economic sophistication—rather than advancing military effectiveness—was contributing to the inutility of war as

Although artillery, and particularly heavy artillery, was the dominant weapon of the First World War, monster guns remained the exception rather than the rule. The Germans used a 420 mm to suppress the defences of Liège in 1914; the illustration is of a French 400 mm on the Somme in 1916; and in 1918 the German 'Big Bertha' ranged on Paris itself.

an instrument of policy. I. S. Bloch, a Polish banker, whose six-volume study of future war, published in 1898, rested on a careful examination of its technology as well as its financing, contended that war might become impossible. Production depended on an urban workforce and international credit; the onset of war in Europe would therefore halt industry by drawing off its manpower and by disrupting normal financial relations. On this basis the more advanced the economy became, the more difficult was the waging of war. The corollary of such arguments was that economic backwardness could be an advantage. In 1914, some Russians reckoned that their agrarian economy and its relative lack of dependence on trade would make them more resilient in protracted warfare. For all the impressiveness of new technology, the prime resource required by armies in the First World War remained, as in the Napoleonic wars, manpower. The Balkan states were able to fight so continuously, and so ferociously, between 1912 and 1918, partly because they had men in abundance, not yet absorbed by the demands of industry.

So the significance of national economic development for the making of war was confused. The picture is little clearer with regard to technological innovation.

Technology and the Arms Race

Neither of the industrial leaders cited above, Britain nor Germany, enjoyed any decisive technical superiority in weaponry as a consequence of its forwardness. In

Christian Sell's triumphant portrayal of Prussia's victory at Königgrätz belongs to a genre of battle painting that is traditional and even Napoleonic. But conspicuous in the foreground are the guns of the Austrian artillery, that almost forestalled the victory, and a Prussian infantryman with the Dreyse rifle that was given the credit for it.

the main, armies in Europe, regardless of the economic development of their parent nations, were comparably equipped. Backward states put a premium on competing with the standards set by those with more sophisticated technologies. The magazine-fed, breech-loading rifle, firing smokeless powder, was adopted by Germany in 1884, France in 1886, Austria-Hungary and Britain in 1889, and Russia in 1891. Thus lags in the procurement of new weaponry tended to be short lived. Even if this was not the case, an inadequacy in one weapons system might well be compensated for by a superiority in another.

Therefore, surprisingly few explanations for ultimate victory rest, in the years between 1789 and 1918, on a marginal technological advantage. Prussia's defeat of Austria at Königgrätz in 1866 was popularly attributed to the Dreyse needle-gun, the first breech-loading rifle in regular military use. But the Dreyse, although pioneering in its day, was hardly a revolutionary weapon by 1866; it was adopted in 1840, and issued on a regular basis in 1851; its principles had been examined and rejected (principally because of the delicacy of the needle-fire mechanism and the escape of gas at the breech) by a number of European armies; and the Austrians enjoyed a superiority in artillery sufficient it seemed to compensate for any inferiority in small arms. Four years later at Sedan, the Prussians' victory over the French was ascribed to the steel breech-loading guns which they had adopted in the intervening period. But in 1870, as in 1866, the sources of triumph could be more satisfactorily sought in explanations that were operational and organizational than tactical or technological. Inferior tactics based on the poor application of new technology did not prevent their practitioners from achieving victory—as the Prussians found at Gravelotte-St Privat in 1870 and as the French showed when themselves defeating the Austrians at Solferino in 1859.

In two major areas only did European practice in war in the nineteenth century not display this ambiguity concerning the relationship between technological innovation and battlefield success. But both concerned war on the periphery of Europe, and not at its core.

First, Europe's domination of the world through the growth of empire reflected the ability of sophisticated technology and advanced techniques to overcome the inherent advantages of native populations. The latter were inured to the climate and its diseases, knew the terrain, and were masters of the local logistical infrastructure. But the gap between local technologies and those of Europe widened in the second half of the nineteenth century. The machine-gun was only the most concrete military expression of the tactical superiority enjoyed by European armies in Africa or Asia. As important were improvements in cartography and in medicine. But, since the latter were not military in any narrow definition of the term, they helped confuse the significance for war in Europe of war in the colonies. Britain was only the most obvious of the European powers in the frequency of her wars beyond the continent: France and Russia, and latterly Germany, Belgium, Italy, and Portugal, also gained more regular—if less intense—direct experience of war overseas than they did closer to their own European frontiers. But the very technological inferiority of the enemy made it hard to see what was relevant in a European context and what was not. Even Britain, the

75

Austria's defeat of the Italian fleet at Lissa in 1866 was overshadowed by its own humiliation on land at Königgrätz. Although the tactics would have been recognizable to Nelson, both ironclad wooden ships and ships constructed of iron were used. Proving impermeable to gunfire, their greatest threats proved to be fire and the ram.

power best poised to cull tactical benefits from hard-won conquests in India or South Africa, remained in the thrall of France or Germany, and looked to the continental precepts of those nations' armies rather than to her own first-hand knowledge.

The second arena in which technological advantage proved less ambiguous was also one in which Britain played a major part. War at sea required a navy to master not only the technology that would enable its ships to survive in a hostile environment. The move from sail and wooden ships to steam and iron integrated for the sailor both the complexities of navigation and the necessities of combat. One interacted with the other. But naval battle was rare. The world's pre-eminent navy, Britain's, did not fight a fleet action against a comparable opponent between 1805, the battle of Trafalgar, and 1916, the battle of Jutland. Ironically, the former was the more decisive, although only in the latter was significant new technology employed. Jutland was as sure an illustration as were the land battles on the western front that comparable levels of enhanced technological sophistication cancelled each other out. But, in the years before Jutland, Europe's navies had had a forceful and recent prod to innovation. At Tsushima in 1905 a marginal technological advantage had enabled the Japanese navy to send the bulk of the Russian Baltic fleet to the bottom. Arms races, particularly those between Britain and France in the middle years of the nineteenth century, and between Britain and Germany in the decade before the First World War, were contested with far more urgency at sea than on land.

The response to Tsushima reflected its scarcity value. The last major fleet action between European navies, Austria's defeat of the Italian navy at Lissa, had been fought in 1866. In the Crimean war the Russian navy had deemed discretion the better part of valour and had not come out to face the British and French fleets. Thus the period of most sustained industrial and technological advance, and the period in which those developments were applied to warfare—the forty years between the end of the Franco-Prussian war and the outbreak of the First World

War—remained remarkably devoid of battles. Without combat, fleets were deprived of the best laboratory for assessing the tactical impact of the devices with which they were equipped. The point was just as true for land forces as for navies. With colonial wars at a discount, and with continental wars confined to the Balkans, armies could not readily take on board the full implications of industrialization for the business of fighting.

The Military Theorists

The contrast with the preceding two hundred years is striking. Since the Thirty Years' War, European armies had fought each other with a regularity bordering on obsessiveness. But at least until 1850 the changes in weaponry were small, gradual, and incremental. It was during those two centuries, however, that standing armies were shaped; it was during the course of them that officers acquired professional self-regard, and it was as a consequence of these institutional developments that military academies were established. The groundwork of military doctrine was therefore done during the course of the eighteenth century, not during that of the nineteenth: it was the fruit of the age of the Enlightenment, not of that of industrialization. Military theorists, like Turpin de Crissé or the comte de Guibert, responded to the influences of the *philosophes*: they believed that in war, as in other human activities, durable principles of universal application could be

The campaigns of the 1790s were characterized by the adoption of skirmishing tactics. This may have been a reflection of the French Revolution on military thinking. But for France it was also a consequence of the improvisation of mass armies, and for Britain (whose light dragoons are here engaging French infantry in 1799) of experience gained in the American War of Independence.

formulated. Technology did not for them represent a variable which would challenge military thought with constantly shifting foundations.

For the military theorists of the eighteenth century Frederick the Great represented the embodiment of the art of war. Indeed Frederick, like other eighteenth-century despots, himself made significant contributions to theory through his own writings. For the writers of the nineteenth century, however, Frederick's throne was usurped by Napoleon. Unlike Frederick, Napoleon did not expatiate on his own experiences; his achievements as a practitioner of war were never balanced by his own contributions to its understanding. What he had wrought was therefore left to the interpretations of others. Napoleonic warfare became the repository of the universal principles of war, but what constituted Napoleonic warfare was itself never capable of succinct definition. Both the principal interpreters of modern war, Antoine Henri Jomini and Carl von Clausewitz, based their analyses on their experiences in Napoleonic warfare. From them flowed most of the leading ideas associated with the conduct of war; for neither was economic development or technological innovation an important consideration.

The differences of opinion over the nature of war between Jomini and Clausewitz (prompted by the acerbic and in many respects unwarranted attacks of the latter in *On War* (1832)) reflected in part the fact that warfare did not remain constant and unchanged between 1792 and 1815. Napoleon himself, for all his obscuring of his intellectual origins, had almost certainly drunk at the well of three far-sighted, eighteenth-century French writers—not only Guibert, the prophet of the citizen army, but also Pierre de Bourcet, who described how to manœuvre a large force in separate components, and J. P. du Teil, who advocated the mobility and concentration of artillery. Napoleon's early campaigns, in Italy in 1796 and 1797, were compatible with much that was Frederickian. His armies were small, never more than 30,000: this was traditional. His ability to dispense with supply arrangements—which seemed more novel—was fortuitous, depending in part on the fertility and wealth of Lombardy. The interaction of these phenomena created the opportunity to manœuvre with speed. When Jomini began writing his *Traité des grandes opérations militaires* (the first volume was published in 1804), it was Napoleon's ability to fuse mobility with battle—so clearly expressed not only in his first Italian campaign but also at Marengo in 1800—which preoccupied him. Jomini had been deeply impressed by Frederick's defeat of the Austrians at the battle of Leuthen in 1757. In the course of that action Frederick, who was outnumbered almost two to one by the Austrians, had managed, through marching in echelon against the Austrian flank, to bring his main concentration against the decisive point. Jomini's study of Napoleon elevated the direction of masses on the decisive point to a universal principle in operations: his claim to have subsumed Frederick and Napoleon within one tradition was not totally at variance with the truth.

For Clausewitz, the dominant experiences of Napoleonic war were very different, principally because they were later. He was a member of the Prussian army smashed on the same day in 1806 at Jena and Auerstadt. The trauma of that event confirmed the irrelevance to the Prussian army of its past. He fought with the

Russian army in the 1812 campaign, and was restored to the Prussian army for Waterloo. The forces engaged in these later Napoleonic battles were massive: at Leipzig in 1813, Napoleon deployed 195,000 men, but he was none the less outnumbered by the three allies opposing him (Russia, Austria, and Prussia) who fielded 365,000. Battles could still be decisive, but the interaction of manœuvre with combat was less evident. Indeed Napoleon's operational superiority in the campaigns of both 1814 and 1815 did not lead to victory. What struck Clausewitz more forcefully than Jomini was the nature of fighting—continuous, bloody, confused, and fearful.

Clausewitz is best remembered today for his formulation that war is an instrument of politics. In attacking Jomini for endeavouring to establish the principles of war, Clausewitz was therefore being less than fair. The German was not opposing all principles: he wished in fact to elevate one principle above all others, because he belatedly recognized that only thus could he give his writings on war a universal validity that extended beyond the ambit of his own experiences of Napoleonic warfare. The fact that his central idea is only fully incorporated in two out of the eight books of *On War* means that the dominant considerations of the text as a whole remain the late Napoleonic battle and its nature. For many of his nineteenth-century readers what he had to say about war and politics was either a statement of the obvious or out of date. At many points in his writings Clausewitz is a romantic, a child of the era of revolution and nationalism. But in his formulation of the relationship between war and politics he is a rationalist, a disciple of the Enlightenment. Napoleon had united supreme political and military control but so too had many eighteenth-century monarchs. During the nineteenth century their separation and even antagonism became more obvious than their coordination. Even in Prussia and then (after 1871) in Germany, where the king remained the nominal supreme commander, political and military direction divided. In 1870–1 Bismarck, as Minister President of Prussia, had to struggle to subordinate Helmuth von Moltke, the chief of the general staff, to his political objectives; in 1916–17 his successor as Chancellor of Germany, Theobald von Bethmann Hollweg, lost the fight to Hindenburg and Ludendorff. The First World War seemed only fitfully to be fulfilling the needs of policy. Clausewitz's universal principle was an ideal: it was what should happen, not a description of what always happened. War frequently followed its own grammar, not its own logic. Clausewitz's analyses of Napoleonic battles were more recognizable to nineteenth-century generals than his account of the relationship between war and politics.

For principles of operational utility they turned to Jomini. Jomini was not as prescriptive as his detractors, or as his diagrams in *Précis de l'art de la guerre* (1838) suggested. Like Clausewitz, Jomini recognized that the conduct of war should be subordinate to the objective to be achieved through war; unlike Clausewitz, Jomini did not elevate this to the status of a pervasive theme. Operations were therefore treated separately, and this gave his account a thrust more akin to the actual experience of most commanders. Again like Clausewitz, Jomini appreciated that war was 'a terrible and impassioned drama', which was 'dependent upon a number of moral and physical complications'. Clausewitz elevated these themes to the level of abstraction, describing the inbuilt tendency of war to drive towards extremes, to 'absolute war'—a drift moderated in practice only by the inherent difficulties of conducting war, what he called 'friction'. By contrast, Jomini emphasized—in accordance with his own experience as a staff officer—the ability of the commander to master and direct war for the achievement of clear operational ends. Jomini's immediate influence cannot be exaggerated; Clausewitz's can. Jomini gave his contemporaries the intellectual tools with which to understand what they took to be Napoleon's art of war—the importance of the line of communications, the need to protect one's own, the aim of mastering the enemy's, and so forcing him to battle. When Jomini's own texts were not read, they were assimilated in the plagiarisms, adaptations, reinterpretations, and popularizations of others, through men such as W. von Willisen in Germany and E. B. Hamley in Britain.

Jomini's focus was on operations or 'grand tactics'. He said little about what we would now call grand strategy, the level at which the relationship between war and politics assumed greatest relevance; he also wrote only briefly on tactics, on the business of fighting at lower unit levels. In this he faithfully reflected Napoleon's own strengths and innovations. The emperor's forte was the ability to see a theatre of operations as a whole, and to combine the conduct of marches within that theatre in order to achieve decisive success on the battlefield. This—an idealized concept of Napoleonic warfare—became itself the ideal form of war.

The Impact of the Railway

Attention to the operational level of war, embodied in Napoleon, interpreted by Jomini, and perpetuated by general staffs until 1914, put the weight of military theory firmly on the influence of ideas, not of technology. Tactics were shaped and challenged far more profoundly by technology than were operations. But if the focus of operations lay in communications, in the organization of marches, and in the concentration of masses on the decisive point, they could not fail to be influenced by one major innovation, the railway. Under the guidance of Alfred von Schlieffen, the chief of the general staff from 1891 to 1905, railway planning became the prime motor of Germany's military preparations for war. Its chosen theatre of operations, north-west Europe, possessed the greatest concentration of track in the world. The task of the German military travel plan in 1914 was to move over 3 million men and 600,000 horses in 11,000 trains during a period of 312 hours.

During the period 1914–18 the railway contributed to the indecisiveness of war. It enabled large armies to be moved rapidly across great distances. But beyond the railhead, the supply of such large armies slowed to the pace of the slowest horse and of the marching man. Ease of communication to the rear made for abundance, and therefore for congestion at the front. Operationally, the railway probably conveyed greater advantages to the defence than to the attack. Rapid reinforcement of potential weakness prevented the exploitation of offensive opportunities.

But this was not the view prevalent before 1914. In two European wars in the nineteenth century, the railway played a dominant operational role. In 1866, Prussia defeated Austria by using five available railway lines, so concentrating its armies from convergent directions on the battlefield itself. In 1870, speed of mobilization and superior exploitation of the available track again paid dividends in Prussia's defeat of France. The popular conclusion, therefore, was that the railway had made the Napoleonic ideal more achievable, not less. The prime architect of the Prussian victories, Helmuth von Moltke, was not so carried away by his own success. He appreciated that strategy must be flexible and adaptable; in his old age he anticipated that the next European war would last seven or even thirty years. But his successors in office pushed aside such forebodings. Professional pride and political necessity meant that the ideal remained the short campaign crowned with total victory on the battlefield; for this, manœuvre, an operational concept, was the key, fighting the mere instrument.

The Rise of the General Staff

The combination of Jominian principles and railway planning produced systematization. Foreign observers in the wars of German unification were impressed by the role of the Prussian general staff. All armies had staff officers serving with troops in the field, but in 1866 Prussia was the only major power in Europe to possess a central general staff, entrusted with the development of war plans in time of peace. It also had responsibility for doctrine, whose implementation relied on the staff officers serving with troops in the field, and with corps and divisional commanders. After the Prussian victories, these two aspects of command and staff work were emulated elsewhere. Austria-Hungary reformed its staff organization in 1871 and 1881; France opened its staff corps to rotation with line officers in 1883 and appointed its first chief of the general staff in 1890; Britain created a general staff in 1906. Without these bodies, the armies of the First World War could never have been deployed or controlled. But they created a sense that war was a matter of management. Attention to the railway as the linchpin of operations put the weight on timetabling and routine. A perceptive and important British observer, Frederick Maurice, writing in 1891, reckoned that the great change in modern war was the perfection of army organization. British soldiers tended to attribute the misfortunes of the Crimean war to administrative incompetence; the Prussian victories were thus the reverse of the same coin.

Nor did the First World War demolish the ideal as conclusively as the clichés of attrition and stalemate might suggest. The opening campaign in the west embodied all the hallmarks of Napoleonic operations. Conceived on a grand scale, embracing an entire theatre of operations, its sweeping movements gave it a unity and comprehensibility absent from subsequent battles in France and Flanders. Moreover, its denouement was a decisive battle, albeit not in the sense envisaged by the German general staff. The French and British victory on the Marne in September 1914 destroyed Germany's hopes of rapid victory. The expectation that such manœuvres could be repeated, if not on the western front itself, then at least elsewhere, thus found some reinforcement from the campaign of the Marne. It could find even more in East Prussia, where operational manœuvre produced a great German victory over the Russians at Tannenberg by the end of August 1914. The authors of that triumph—or at least its putative authors, as claims to its paternity continue to multiply—were Hindenburg and Ludendorff. For the next two years on the eastern front, they would conduct campaigns characterized by manœuvre and mobility—even if the expectations generated in their planning exceeded their execution. Under other commanders, the German army in 1915 and 1916 overran Poland, Serbia, and Romania: the Napoleonic concept of rapid wars culminating in decisive victories continued to find confirmation within the First World War itself.

But planning and system had put a blight on imagination. Significantly, Tannenberg was a victory that was improvised out of desperation, not one that was programmed. The perpetuation of the Napoleonic ideal through Moltke's victories (if not teaching) and through Schlieffen's teaching (if not victories) had shut out the consideration of wars which did not fit the accepted model. Soldiers throughout Europe in 1914 aimed to fight a broadly similar sort of war; different general staffs did not formulate radically different conclusions; they were imitative; and the war could become protracted and indecisive partly because the ideas that governed its operational conduct were not sufficiently distinct to prevent congruence.

Siege Warfare

When observing the failure to anticipate the true nature of the First World War, critics comment on the reluctance to derive lessons from the American Civil War. This was a long war, which drew on the total resources of both belligerents, and deployed at least some advanced technology. But the neglect of the American Civil War seems comprehensible when it is recognized that the contending armies were characterized by a lack of professionalism and a tendency themselves to want to emulate European practice. Furthermore, the dazzling German victories came after the end of the American Civil War, and naturally, therefore, seemed more relevant to the immediate issues of the conduct of war in Europe. More surprising than the neglect of a war outside Europe was the selective appreciation and analysis of wars within Europe.

Napoleon's campaigns had been rapid partly because he had eschewed the business of sieges. His eighteenth-century predecessors, tied by the exigencies of supply to set lines of communication, were deemed to have become fixated on fortifications. The fashion after 1815 was to condemn the technicalities of Vauban and his successors as self-important and deliberate mystifications. Military engineers continued to develop systems of attack and defence, conditioned in part by the progress and development of artillery. Here was an area of war clearly determined by technological progress, as masonry gave way to reinforced concrete, and as longer-range heavy artillery forced the defence to create detached forts at some distance outside the perimeter to be held. But siege warfare became detached from the mainstream of operational thought. The great commander

concerned himself with manœuvre and battle, not with the sedentary and slow processes of sapping and mining.

The result was an extraordinary blindness to a potentially dominant form of war. In 1849 Colonel T. P. Thompson told the British House of Commons 'of the superannuated notions of the effect of fortifications, which the experience of modern wars had entirely exploded'. But the first major conflict to erupt in north-west Europe after 1815, the Belgian war of independence of 1830–2, pivoted around the bombardment and siege of Antwerp. Five years after Thompson gave vent to his feelings, the British army, in conjunction with the French, laid siege to Sebastopol, the site of the Russian naval installations in the Black Sea. Posterity has chosen to remember the battles of the Alma, Balaclava, and Inkerman, the charge of the Light Brigade, and the thin red line; it has neglected the conditioning characteristic of the Crimean war as a whole. The siege of Sebastopol lasted eleven months, and drained the Russian army of its strength. But for many observers the siege was evidence of the war's irrelevance to the theory of war, of the failure of its participating armies to reform, not of its modernity.

Two factors made the science of fortification and of its suppression by heavy artillery increasingly important. The first, evident at Sebastopol, and also at Plevna in the Russian invasion of Ottoman Bulgaria in 1877, was tactical. To dig

The Crimean war was one of the last European wars in which supply by sea enjoyed an advantage over communication by land. It was, however, one of the first to be extensively photographed, principally by Roger Fenton, responsible for this view of the crowded harbour at Balaclava.

The Malakoff, a key element in the Russian defences at Sebastopol, was captured by the French in a surprise attack on 8 September 1855. Pictured here by Doré, the French success triggered the Russian abandonment of the southern part of the town.

trenches and to erect field defences was a logical response to the growth in fire-power in the second half of the nineteenth century. An attacking army insufficiently endowed with artillery and failing to anticipate protracted operations would find itself considerably embarrassed. The Russians were held at Plevna for five months.

The second was strategic. Napoleonic warfare still assumed, as eighteenth-century commanders had been able to assume, that the principal focus of a nation's wealth and identity was its army: if the army was defeated in the field, then political consequences followed. But the growth of the nation-state, the integration of a nation's resources with its military effort, meant that the defeat of the national army in the field might not in itself prove decisive. The capture of the capital was required in order to master the nation's administrative and industrial life, the fountain-head of its army.

This was not the lesson which was drawn from the wars of German unification, but it might have been. In 1866, the Austrian army was defeated at Königgrätz, but not routed. The fact that the Prussian army did not then advance and lay siege to Vienna was a product not of the military circumstances but of political intervention—of Bismarck's anxiety to conciliate rather than to humiliate the Habsburg monarchy. In 1870 Bismarck's attitude to the French was more bellicose, and the

84

French response proved equally disobliging. The defeat of the French army in the field, at Sedan on 1 September, was far more comprehensive than that inflicted on the Austrians. But a popular uprising in Paris, a city ringed with fortifications, compelled the Germans to lay siege to the French capital until January 1871. A six weeks' war lasted six months.

The immediate response of the Third Republic to its experience of the Franco-Prussian war was to create a new system of fortifications for the defence of its frontiers. Between 1874 and 1884 Séré de Rivières masterminded the construction of 166 forts, 43 secondary works, and 250 batteries at a cost of 660 million francs. Typically the forts were six kilometres apart, designed to give each other supporting fire and to catch an enemy attack in enfilade; the French were ready to check the next German attack with defence in depth and with indirect artillery fire. So robust did this defence look, Schlieffen eschewed all thought of confronting it, and instead planned to direct Germany's armies through the Low Countries, thereby outflanking it in its entirety. Thus he embraced operational manœuvre, on Napoleonic lines, rather than the tactical conundrums of modern war. Indeed, to justify his plan for envelopment he cited historical examples that were tactical rather than operational in design, and whose outcomes had depended on weaponry totally different from that in use by 1900. The importance for Schlieffen's thought of Leuthen and of Hannibal's victory over the Romans at Cannae in 216 BC shows how much more significant in shaping military attitudes were continuously operating concepts than ever-shifting technology.

Fort Douaumont, here pictured before the Germans opened the battle of Verdun in February 1916, became both the symbol and the heart of French resistance. First captured by the Germans on 25 February 1916, it was finally retaken by the French on 24 October.

But what was even more surprising than Schlieffen's dodging of the issue of fortification was France's effective abandonment of its own strengths. The development of a delayed action fuse in 1885–6 meant that artillery shells penetrated
masonry before exploding. Thus, almost as soon as they had been completed,
Séré de Rivières's forts had to be remodelled. They were brought closer to the
ground, and the concrete was reinforced with steel. But the expense was dispirit-
ing and the overall conception was lost. France increasingly put its weight into
men, not material. It abandoned the idea of a defensive strategy, followed by a
counter-attack, in favour of an initial offensive designed to deprive Germany of
the initiative. Although forts and field fortifications played a not inconsiderable
role in slowing the German advance in 1914, their importance was still not recognized. The German army on the Marne was weakened by its need to detach two
corps to cover Antwerp and one for Maubeuge. The drama of the battle itself pivoted around Paris; but these manœuvres were themselves contingent on the
French armies holding steady along a fortified line from Verdun to Belfort,
through Toul, Nancy, and Epinal. Thus both Séré de Rivières's conception and his
achievements played a vital role in saving France. But the orthodoxy that down-
graded fortification persisted. In 1915 the French army concluded that it would not
hold Verdun, a network of twenty major forts, in the event of its being attacked; by
October forty-three heavy batteries and eleven field batteries had been moved out
of that sector of the front. But when the Germans did attack in February 1916, it was
the forts which provided the spine as well as the soul of the French defence.

The Professionalization of Warfare

Equally important in the German intellectual suppression of the second phase of
the Franco-Prussian war was its denial of the *levée en masse* and of the nation in
arms. After the fall of the Second Empire in 1870, Léon Gambetta masterminded a
campaign of national resistance of which the defence of Paris was but a part. The
operations of *francs tireurs* on the Germans' rear and communications confronted Moltke's armies with guerrilla warfare—a style of fighting for which operational manœuvres and decisive battles were inappropriate concepts. The
Germans' reply was terror. Confronted with the unfamiliar, they responded with
the unreasonable. Determination to avoid a repeat of this experience was evident
in 1914, when the German army displayed a harshness towards the civilian populations of Belgium and north-east France that was far more brutal than anything
meted out to the soldiers of the opposing armies: international law was used as an
edifice to demarcate and render as self-contained the conventional operations of
professional armies.

The Germans' reaction, at least at an intellectual level, was not atypical. Guerrilla warfare was seen as the resort of the weak, not an alternative strategy possessed of its own strength and validity. The word 'guerrilla' itself derived from the
Spanish response to Napoleon's invasion of the peninsula in 1807. But the clothing
of popular passions and, at worst, of brigandage in the vocabulary of national
resistance was not something that came naturally to the Spanish government or to

The studied informality (*left*) of the singer Chenard, a *sans culotte* painted in 1792, contrasts with the powdered queues and the white gaiters of France's soldiers three years earlier. His dress reflects the poverty of the new state; as the heroic lighting makes clear, it also embodies the new army's image of itself.

Despite appearances to the contrary, neither all France nor all Napoleon's former soldiers rallied to Napoleon when he escaped from Elba. But Steuben's picture (*below*), painted in 1818, demonstrates how effectively the emperor exploited his personal allure with his troops, and how little Waterloo dented his aura of invincibility. Here is the idea of war as the path to glory.

Of all the British war artists of the First World War, Paul Nash best expressed the destructive effects of modern war on the landscape. Apparently empty during the day, it became active under cover of night, as here in the Ypres salient.

its British allies. Spain only embraced guerrilla war in the face of its army's continuing incompetence in conventional operations. The French, dispersed in order to feed, became vulnerable to attack by the guerrillas; thus the ability of their army to concentrate became weakened by the need to protect their lines of communications. In battle, the British met portions of the French army rather than its entirety. But neither Wellington nor William Napier, the first and most important (for British military thought) historian of the Peninsular war, acknowledged the importance of the guerrillas. Their neglect was not simply a national prejudice, a way of elevating Britain's own achievements; it was also the standard response of the professional soldier. Jomini too expressed in graphic phrases his own distaste for what had happened.

In the aftermath of Waterloo it was the small professional army, its soldiers committed to relatively long periods of service, which prevailed as the norm. The notion of a people in arms carried a double indemnity: first, it smacked of democracy or even of revolution, and secondly it betokened a form of war that in its frenzy would become unlimited both in its methods and in its length. By belittling the efforts of Gambetta and the *francs tireurs*, Moltke ensured that the conventional pattern of military organization remained unchallenged. In 1870 Prussia conscripted men for a shorter period, and rotated them into a more effective reserve, but the dominant ethos was royal, regimental, and professional.

In his latter years William I of Germany had to conduct the annual Kaiser manœuvres from his carriage, as here in 1884. In order to inject greater realism into the proceedings, Moltke the younger insisted in 1906 that his grandson, William II, forfeit his right to command on these occasions.

So powerful was this idea that not even the necessities generated by successive manpower crises in 1917–18 could shift the attitudes of the German high command. Before the outbreak of the First World War, Germany called up 57 per cent of its available adult males; it could therefore spurn urban and industrial workers, possibly tainted with socialism, in favour of its preferred recruits, those from agricultural and rural backgrounds. By January 1918, however, known socialists and radical trade unionists were being drafted; the army as a whole was described by its commanders as little better than a 'militia'. But their solution was to continue to inculcate the old values, not reshape the army in the light of its changed composition. Amidst the preparations for the March 1918 offensives, the Germans still found time to consider giving instruction in the goose step.

The crowning evidence of this continuing commitment to the prevailing patterns of organization and consequently also of fighting came in October 1918. The allied counter-offensives, begun in mid-July 1918, were running out of steam; their communications were lengthening; the roads were turning to mud as winter approached. Walther Rathenau, a German businessman on the fringes of government, proposed the initiation of a *levée en masse*. Citing the example of Gambetta, he wanted a defence minister with far-reaching powers. A number of soldiers were supportive: with good defensive positions, Germany could hold out some months longer, and so force the *entente* to accept a negotiated settlement. But Ludendorff's opposition was categorical. He preferred to precipitate Germany headlong into an armistice that amounted to total defeat, rather than preside over a revolution in the character and ethos of the army.

The ideas which were most powerful were those hallowed by success: weaker powers tried to catch up with stronger powers by competing in the same terms rather than by exploiting new methods. Thus the Germans' victories in 1866 and 1870 reaped dividends long after their immediate objectives had been achieved. For by handing them the palm of military superiority, other nations condemned themselves to continuing inferiority, preferring to dog the Germans' footsteps rather than branch out on their own. In 1918 this success rebounded, for by then the Germans were inferior, but they also were too wedded to their own conventions to be able to change.

The British pulled off a comparable trick at sea. In this they relied not only on the precepts of their own history, but also on the writings of Alfred Thayer Mahan, and especially his book, *The Influence of Sea Power on History* (1890).

Mahan's writings constituted a case for the possession of a fleet of battleships. Maritime power might be exercised through trade and commerce, and through the control of the 'narrow' seas. But ultimately suzerainty would be achieved through the clash of navies in fleet actions. As on land, the evidence for these propositions was historical—and reliant on the wars of the eighteenth century and of the French Revolution. In the years between 1871 and 1918 both Britain's major challengers at sea, first France and then Germany, preferred in the last resort to follow the British (and Mahanian) example rather than try a different solution.

The Challenge to the Battleship

France came closest to the adoption of a radical alternative. In 1878–9 the naval commission of the chamber of deputies cast doubts on the wisdom of pursuing the expensive solution of battleship construction, when battleships might prove vulnerable to torpedoes. By the early 1880s the so-called *jeune école* had rejected a balance between torpedo boats for coastal defence and battleships for offensive action in favour of something more extreme. It advocated a *guerre de course*, which Mahan was to condemn as the weaker form of naval war. A war fought without restrictions against merchant vessels, and eschewing fleet action, was the maritime equivalent of a guerrilla campaign or a *levée en masse*. But in this case

the concept rested on more than an idea; it depended also on new technology—on the torpedo, and in due course on the submarine.

After 1905 and Tsushima, the ideas of the *jeune école* fell into decline. Moreover, the ship of the line restated its ability to counter the torpedo boat or destroyer. The big guns of the Dreadnought, ranging 20,000 yards, and her speed of 24 knots, enabled her to stay beyond torpedo range, and to outmanœuvre her smaller opponents. The French 1912 naval law set a target of constructing 2.5 capital ships each year until 1920.

The elevation of the attack on merchant shipping to the prime role for navies was shelved amidst cold war notions of conventional naval equivalence. Such policies played into British hands. Provided the Royal Navy maintained its own technical lead and its rate of building, British maritime hegemony was assured. Britain's vulnerability at sea lay along her trade routes and in her possession of the world's largest single merchant marine. If her opponents built only battle fleets, they disqualified themselves from exploiting their one possible advantage in a war at sea.

The Germans before 1914 never even seriously entertained alternatives to the battleship. The Kaiser briefly argued the case for a fleet of ocean-going cruisers, but Tirpitz, the secretary of state for the naval armaments office, concentrated on matching British warship construction with capital ships designed specifically for

At the end of June 1914, when the news of Archduke Franz Ferdinand's assassination at Sarajevo broke, the British fleet was visiting its German counterpart at Kiel. Flying over the ships of the Royal Navy is an airship, which the Germans planned to use for naval reconnaissance.

89

battle in the North Sea. On the outbreak of war, Germany had too few submarines for their effects to be of any consequence. Moreover, like the British, the Germans considered the submarine in the context of fleet action and not in that of economic warfare. In reality, after some early and well-publicized successes against British warships which were being negligent in adopting precautionary routines, the U-boats posed only minor threats to warships. However, when they adopted the philosophy of the *jeune école*—when, in other words, they were directed against weaker targets and specifically against merchant vessels—they achieved dramatic successes. It was ironic indeed that in February 1917, Germany, the major land power of the continent, embraced a maritime method of achieving all-out victory—unrestricted U-boat warfare. She did so belatedly—and not just because of diplomatic fears of repercussions in the United States. Naval attitudes had produced an over-investment in the wrong types of vessels. As a result, Germany did not have sufficient submarines for a major U-boat campaign until 1917. Moreover, handing responsibility down the chain of command to junior submarine captains carried profound implications for a conventional naval hierarchy based on a large surface fleet. Thus, to enable the exploitation of new technology, changed concepts were required. Similar points could be made about the Allied response. In this struggle, the Dreadnoughts of the British Grand Fleet proved redundant. The ultimate response to the U-boat rested not on any technical innovation but on organizational change—the adoption of the convoy.

The Origins of Change

Therefore, even in the First World War itself, what mattered as much as new technology were new ideas to enable the effective exploitation of the technology

What made the submarine a viable weapon for oceanic warfare was the diesel engine. By 1914 all the most modern submarines were so powered, and the increase in range and size was demonstrated in 1916 when the cargo vessel, *U-Deutschland*, arrived in New York. The illustration is of U-boats at sea in June 1917.

already available. Of course new weapons systems were evolved between 1914 and 1918, especially in land warfare. The tank was developed *ab initio* under the pressure of the trenches; the fixed-wing aircraft, although its military applications had been glimpsed before 1914, moved from infancy to maturity within the war itself. But the dominant arm of the war was artillery, and the next most important the machine-gun. Neither was novel in 1914. What changed was their application, and above all the methods by which they achieved effective co-ordination with the infantry. Demand-led technical improvements played their part in the evolution of this relationship: sound-ranging, flash-spotting, and aerial reconnaissance all enabled guns to fire from the map with greater accuracy and without preliminary registration. But even here the idea—the notion of what was militarily desirable in order to improve battlefield performance—proved a more fertile agent of change than undirected scientific progress.

The great tactical conundrum of the First World War was the reintegration of fire and movement. The tendency to rain down a preliminary bombardment, for the artillery then to stop, and for the infantry to advance across no man's land, split fire and movement into two successive phases. In March 1918 the Germans showed that it was possible to reintegrate the two, to use fire to enable movement, and to move the better to deliver fire. To achieve this they kept the artillery bombardment short, they had the infantry moving close to its protective curtain, and they gave the infantry its own fire-power in the shape of mortars, light machine-guns, and flame-throwers. But, although the Germans seemed to have solved the tactical difficulties of trench war, the advance had no strategic outcome. In order to enable

Grandiose schemes for bomber offensives in 1917–18 delivered much less than they promised. The trade-off between sufficient range and the weight of bombs was never satisfactorily resolved. But the German attacks on London in 1917 helped foster the growth of an independent British air force, and for France (whose aircraft are shown here) bombers were a way of taking the war into Germany.

the momentum of the attack to be sustained, command was delegated forward—direction came from the front. But the effect was to carry the attack where the tactical opportunities arose rather than where the strategic advantage lay.

The Rise of the Mass Army

What the ultimate failure of the 1918 offensives demonstrated was that the cause of the stalemate on the western front was not primarily the consequence of technological dominance, of a fire-swept no man's land. Again and again, the battles of the First World War showed that fire-power could be as powerful an aid to the offensive as to the defensive. The problem was one of command, and of the difficulty of effective leadership in a mass army.

The determining characteristic of land warfare in the period from 1789 to 1918 was the growth in the size of armies without a comparable increment in the means of directing those armies. When Revolutionary France set about the re-creation of the French army in 1790 and 1791 her instincts were not particularly radical; her tendency was to call for volunteers. However, the failure of sufficient men to come forward and the transformation in the power of the state through the Revolution made conscription both a practical necessity and a legitimate tool. In the 1790s the French revolutionary armies were not individually particularly big, but they could fight more battles successively than their opponents. By the closing stages of the Napoleonic war, France fielded individually big armies. In 1812 Napoleon led 614,000 men into Russia. The problem of gigantism was co-ordination. How could one man deploy and direct armies whose component corps were a day's march or more from each other?

By 1917 the use of gas shells by artillery was one of the more effective methods of counter-battery fire. The opposing gun crews were forced to don their gas masks, which exacerbated the strenuous effort of loading and firing a gun such as the one shown here, a German heavy howitzer.

The development of doctrine and of general staffs was a partial solution to this problem. But they created the means to manage the mass army, not the methods by which to lead it. Both Wellington and Napoleon, despite the growth in the size of armies, were visible on the battlefield itself. For supreme command in the First World War forward presence was incompatible with rational direction. But the heroic expectations of the leader persisted. They were met by junior officers. So management and command became divorced, without anybody fully appreciating what was happening. Tactics in the First World War were developed at lower unit levels, and became separated from the operational thinking of general headquarters. The two could only be harmonized when operational direction shaped itself according to tactical practicalities. But to do this was to risk abdicating operational direction itself.

The problem became one of ideas and attitudes. Senior commanders needed to recognize that practical leadership had to be exercised at lower levels, that aspects of the battle were now beyond their control. But the fact that tactics did assume their own momentum was at least in part the consequence of technological change. And thus the domination of ideas in effecting military change was being undermined. Moreover, the solution to the problem of operational command and the reintegration of the vertical lines of communication through the command hierarchy were both dependent on technological innovation. With the advent of the man-portable radio on the battlefield the divide between tactics and operations would be bridged, and the harmonization of ideas and technology rendered more realizable.

In the studious appearance of Helmuth von Moltke, chief of the Prussian general staff in 1866 and 1870, can be seen the changing role of the military commander. His task was to provide overall direction rather than to issue orders for immediate execution: the desk-bound general had begun to replace the heroic warrior on horseback.

4

From Orders to Classes

European Society in the Nineteenth Century

> While there is thus a progressive diminution in the number of capitalist magnates . . . there occurs a corresponding increase in the mass of poverty, oppression, enslavement, degeneration and exploitation; but at the same time there is a steady intensification of the wrath of the working class—a class which grows ever more numerous, and is disciplined, unified, and organized by the very mechanism of the capitalist method of production.

MARX writing thus in *Das Kapital* echoed the view of many of his contemporaries, of all political persuasions, that industrialization brought social conflict. Unlike most, he welcomed it as a necessary prerequisite for a future socialist revolution. The demise of Soviet communism in the later twentieth century, and the current emphasis on gender, colour, and nationality as determinants of social relationships, make Marx's prediction of class war seem simplistic to us.

What was important to his contemporaries? Working people worried about the influx of foreigners or the departure of their loved ones overseas to find work. They were terrified of the prospects of sickness, old age, or the possibility that technical innovations or short-term crises would put them on the scrap heap. The better off deplored expanding and unhealthy cities, baby abandonment, prostitution, the erosion of family values—all rolled up as the 'social question' for journalists, novelists, and politicians. They tended to write in the language of class, or even in an older vocabulary of orders. These terms were used quite loosely, but their lack of specificity does not mean that we can dismiss them.

The Numbers Game

PAMELA
PILBEAM

Before the first censuses in 1801, population statistics were guesswork. The estimate for pre-census France has recently jumped from 26 to 28 million. There was a totally unprecedented population explosion in nineteenth-century Europe from around 193 million to about 423 million, but with considerable variations between countries and regions. Another 45 million left for overseas, of whom perhaps 10 million returned. In 1800 the French population was the biggest in Europe after Russia. It was still the largest at mid-century with around 36 million, but in the 1850s it levelled out at around 39 million and hovered there until the 1930s. The British population was the first to rise quickly, standing at 16 million in 1800, 31 million in 1870, and then slowing down to reach 44 million in 1900. In 1800 the total population of the German states was 24 million, reaching 40 million at unification in 1871 and soaring to be the largest in Europe, after Russia, with 60 million by 1900. The growth in the Russian population was the most dramatic, though the least well documented. Apparently around 70 million in the 1870s it had leapt to 170 million in 1914, of whom all but 30 million lived in European Russia.

The Europe-wide increase in numbers appears to have been closely related to a falling death rate (precise figures are scanty for the years before 1850), and in Britain to a reduction in the age of marriage from around 30 to about 22, which would have led to a telescoping of generations, and possibly healthier stock. Apparently couples continued to produce at least nine children at roughly twenty-month intervals throughout most of their reproductive life. What made the difference was that from the 1730s more infants survived birth, the vulnerable first year, and the years between 1 and 5. We do not know the full story of why the infant death rate fell. The most significant factor seems to have been a reduction in the pandemics which had eliminated whole communities in past centuries. Can this be attributable to a greater awareness of hygiene and health care? More soap was used and cotton clothing worn, but by whom? More hospitals offered free care to the poor. But until the introduction of anaesthesia in the 1840s and antiseptics in the 1860s, mortality rates after surgery remained high. Hospitals were rightly thought of as merely places of death for the poor. Public health actually deteriorated badly with the increasing size and insanitary conditions of industrial towns and the municipal clean-up operation did not begin until around 1880.

Smallpox vaccination reached nearly 80 per cent of children in France by the mid-nineteenth century and was made compulsory in England in 1852. By then smallpox mortality rates in England had tumbled from 16.5 per cent of all deaths to 1–2 per cent. Vaccination against diphtheria, introduced in France in 1894, was another instant, and to the uneducated, magical cure. These successes were exceptional, but they had a huge psychological impact, giving bourgeois medicine a new status in comparison with the much cheaper treatment available from popular healers, who only charged if the patient recovered. Although the cause of infections was not properly understood until towards the end of the century, the growing practice of isolation, and the accompanying increased attention to cleanliness, had a marked, though unquantified, effect on death rates from TB and other ailments. Unfortunately for our investigations, such improvements came after the period of most rapid population increase.

There were epidemics at intervals during the nineteenth century, spectacularly cholera, which arrived in Europe for the first time in 1816–17, reached France and

Britain in the early 1830s, and did not begin to diminish until after the Hamburg epidemic of 1892. Contemporaries were inclined to ascribe cholera to the moral as well as the sanitary evils of the new industrial society. The disease was terrifying. Its cause and treatment were unfathomed; death was rapid and indiscriminate, in contrast to earlier killer diseases. Healthy prosperous adults were as likely to be affected as the obviously vulnerable young and elderly. However, cholera did not reduce numbers on the scale of earlier plagues.

How far were improved chances of survival related to better nourishment? We know that food production rose during the eighteenth century, but harvest failures and ineffective transport systems led to serious shortages until the 1860s. Food adulteration continued throughout the nineteenth century and until pasteurization was developed an increased availability of cows' milk would not have contributed to the decline in infant mortality. However, it would seem perverse to see no connection between more food and more babies surviving. Recent research on the birth weight of children born in a number of hospitals (therefore to poor mothers) in different European countries shows a modest increase in birth weight, although there was a downturn in the later years of the nineteenth century.

Romanticized mother-and-child portraits emphasized the close maternal relationship urged by Enlightened writers. Labille-Guiard painted one of the first studies of an upper-class mother breast-feeding her own child—a novel experience for the wealthy at the time.

The increase in live births and surviving babies must, in part, be due to social factors, especially parental care. The way in which children were represented in paintings might be said to indicate that childhood and individual children were more valued. Enlightened theoreticians like Rousseau in *Emile* urged mothers to breast-feed their own children. Wet-nursing was well established among all social classes in some countries, especially France. Church-run hospitals and parish priests often acted as wet-nursing agencies and provided moral sanction for a practice which was little more than infanticide. Even in 1869 only 59 per cent of babies were nursed by their own mothers and concern that this was in part responsible for an excess of deaths over births led to legislation which put wet-nurses under the supervision of the local doctor, an arrangement which neither enjoyed. However, wet-nursing had a limited geographical appeal. Most English mothers, particularly the less well off, apparently had always fed their own children.

Since the early eighteenth century French noble families had practised birth control. The fuss made by the Church of England in the eighteenth century and the Catholic Church in the nineteenth century in condemning coitus interruptus indicates that such primitive methods of contraception quickly reached poorer families. Popular medicine put faith in a variety of herbs and primitive douches. Barrier and interventionist methods of birth control were little developed until the 1880s and remained the playthings of the better off until 1914.

Contemporaries tended to assume that population growth was a consequence of industrialization. However, numbers grew fastest in poorer rural areas such as southern Italy, southern Germany, and Russia. Some, like Malthus, predicted uncontrolled growth and starvation. Did war decimate European populations less than at other times? The Revolutionary and Napoleonic wars (1792–1815) killed 1.5 million Frenchmen, the same number as in the First World War. Some French observers, including Zola in his hair-raising tale of family murder, *Earth*, were inclined to believe that the Napoleonic Civil Code was a potent contraception, because it replaced primogeniture with equal subdivision among heirs. But equal subdivision was the norm in southern Germany.

Boy and dog. Photography made family albums a must with their posed studio studies of each child who survived early infancy, ranging from the stark images of the almost-poor, stiff in 'Sunday' togs, to the over-elaborate chocolate-box pictures of the rich.

The Lure of New Worlds

Young adults migrated to towns in search of jobs. Novels such as Mrs Gaskell's *Mary Barton* deplored the living conditions they endured in Lancashire cotton towns. In 1842 Edwin Chadwick, in a seminal report, revealed that in Manchester the average age at death of mechanics was 17 compared with 38 in rural Rutland. Urbanization was relatively slow. Although by 1850 more than half the population of Britain lived in towns, it was not until the mid-1930s that the same was true in France. Migration was not new. Traditionally, men from poor areas such as the Limousin worked part of the year in Lyons or Paris in the building trades and returned to their families during the cold months when there was no work. Whole districts in London and Paris still bear the imprint in café, shop, and street names of such movements. What made the nineteenth century different was that migration grew in scale and became permanent. By 1907 50 per cent of Germans lived a substantial distance from their birthplace. Middle-class observers were alarmed at the rootlessness, alienation, and godlessness of migrant towns. Their answer was to build cavernous churches.

Many left their own country, some for Europe, especially for France, but more frequently for North, later for South, America and Australasia. In the 1850s over

1 million Germans left for the Prairies, a quarter of a million in one year alone. A nucleus, 'pushed' by economic and/or political desperation, tended to encourage neighbours and family to join them later. Overseas migration was probably the biggest single factor controlling European population growth. France, in contrast, kept her numbers steady with over 3 million resident foreigners by 1914. Belgians worked in mines and mills in the north-east, Italians, Spaniards, and Portuguese worked on southern farms, deserted by the younger generations.

Social Effects of Industrial Growth

There was a decline in the proportion of the population engaged in agriculture over the century in almost all European countries, but the actual numbers involved and the activities themselves generally continued to increase until around 1914. In England in the 1850s agriculture was the largest single employer (1.8 million), followed by domestic service (1 million). During the first half of the century, the most significant change in industry everywhere was the expansion of the rural sector. Cotton-weaving was put-out from the new spinning factories until large-scale weaving machines were developed. In England at mid-century the cotton industry employed 800,000, but one-third were still working in small workshops or in their own home.

Merchants encouraged the growth of rural production in traditionally organized craft industries such as silk to undercut urban prices and controls, until technical innovations like the Jacquard loom allowed merchants to control the urban craftsman more directly by loaning him the cost of his equipment. A Jacquard loom cost 1,000 francs, a very considerable outlay for a master weaver whose daily earnings might be less than 3 francs, from which he had to pay assistants. At the beginning of the century, agrarian and industrial activities were often interdependent. Iron foundries were set up within the extensive forests of large landowners because charcoal was used for smelting. An increasing proportion of country dwellers sustained life by a mixture of craft industry and agriculture. For many rural communities the century was one of diversified growth and opportunity, followed by shrinkage, migration, and depopulation.

Facing, above: **Emigration— a solution to poverty?** En route from Cork to Boston, 1851.

Facing, below: **Young and old queue** in the Despatch Hall, Hamburg Harbour, in 1900, hoping that the Hamburg– America Line's motto 'The world is my field' will prove true for them.

Artisan industry was often home-based. This photograph shows a weaver in the one room which answered for work and home.

The Myth of Orders—and Classes

Did nineteenth-century industrial change transform independent craftsmen into dependent proletarians? Socialists were convinced it did; conservatives were scared that it had or would, while liberals hoped that the social corrosion of poverty would eventually disappear. In other words, the language of class helped to define political polemic.

Eighteenth-century Europeans imagined themselves part of a society of orders or estates. For practical purposes the concept was anachronistic, intersected with more dominant ideas of class, and was soon to be romanticized by novelists such as Sir Walter Scott. Whereas class distinctions were and still are, at least in part, based on the type and scale of economic activity, the concept of orders rested initially on social duty. Class divides society into mutually dependent, but competing, elements. The notion of orders rested on a belief in a static society. The first order was the clergy because they kept the devil at bay. The second order, the nobility, were responsible for organizing the defence of the community from more visible enemies. The third order, which included everyone else, provided for the bodily needs of society. During the medieval and early modern periods the wealthier members within each order acquired privileges, the most desirable of which were fiscal. By the eighteenth century the tail wagged the dog. Privilege, limited to a small, wealthy subsection of each order, came to be a definition of the order itself, while their original duties were performed by the poorer elements of each group. Financial standing and perceived status, the basis of a modern notion of class, emerged within the vertical subsections of the society of orders.

By the second half of the eighteenth century, writers, most memorably British economists such as Adam Smith, used class terms as subdivisions of orders. Some wrote with fear and nostalgia, some with hope, not just of a Europe in which monetary values had replaced a sense of duty and of a society polarized between rich and poor, familiar themes at all times, but of a change in the nature of wealth and of a new emerging entrepreneurial element.

The events of the French Revolution contributed to the hardening and politicization of the notion of class. In his influential pamphlet 'What is the Third Estate?', published on the eve of the calling of the Estates-General in France in 1789, the abbé Sieyès appeared to speak on behalf of the Third Estate, which he defined in the traditional way as the vast majority and described as the true nation. But for the practical purpose of the election to the assembly, he addressed the wealthy bourgeois educated élite only; in other words, he was speaking a language of class with an old-fashioned accent.

Key episodes contributing to concepts of class were the cascading abolition of all privileged institutions on the night of 4 August 1789 and the Declaration of the Rights of Man and Citizen later that month. The remnants of the spectre of privileged orders was legislated away in France with the abolition of feudal rights, clerical privilege, particularly the right to collect the tithe, and the elimination of all privileged corporations of all kinds within the state, from the *parlements*, or courts of appeal, to the guilds.

Resistance to the dismantling of privilege helped to fuel a counter-revolution and, with it, not only class definition, but also class conflict. The noisy and belligerent emigration of opponents of the Revolution quickly transformed liberal definitions of citizenship into intolerant exclusions based on rough-and-ready class-type distinctions. The Revolution became anti-'aristo', even, for a time, anti-bourgeois. Ultimately, however, it was the traditional professional, official, and landowning bourgeoisie who gained most.

The Revolutionary and Napoleonic wars, 1792–1814/15, ensured that the social conflicts experienced in France reverberated in conquered territories. As in France, the purchase of land and office by members of the old Third Estate, as well as gradual economic change, contributed to social stratification. In much of western Europe, professional, official, and landowning and entrepreneurial bourgeois groups advanced their claims during the Revolutionary years, aided by French territorial ambitions. Ironically, in the Russian empire the Romanovs were struggling to strengthen an aristocratic warrior element, midway between an order and a class, to reinforce their own power over an enormous and growing state.

What did it mean to be part of a society of classes? In France the Church was dismantled as the first order by the sale of its land. For a time in the 1790s it was denied the right to celebrate ceremonies to register births, marriages, and deaths. Its role in administering hospitals and schools was halted, although in the latter area only temporarily. In Spain, Portugal, and Italy (until the 1860s) the Catholic Church remained a major landowner as well as a powerful political, social, and spiritual force, although leading noble families were decreasingly interested in bishoprics for younger sons. In Protestant and Orthodox countries the Church owned no land, but senior clergy were drawn from leading families and exercised a strong moral influence. In Britain the bishops of the Established Church of England were automatically members of the House of Lords.

The second order, the nobility or aristocracy, was regarded as the leading element in the upper class. It included very rich aristocrats, who had a powerful national voice, and less wealthy gentry, whose influence was more local. The

Society was a pyramid. This is Cruickshank in 1867, but similar representations of society were drawn throughout Europe. Many believed that social hierarchies were part of the 'survival of the fittest' and the better-off were anxious to keep it so.

A PENNY POLITICAL PICTURE FOR THE PEOPLE, WITH A FEW WORDS UPON PARLIAMENTARY REFORM.

base of their power and influence was land, but they habitually had many other varied financial and economic interests, especially the top families. They formed a tight network, intermarrying carefully to preserve their economic position.

Next in the hierarchy of classes was the top slice of the old Third Estate, the bourgeoisie or middle classes. The term meant little, beyond the assumption of a certain prosperity, freedom from manual labour, and the possibility that, while the husband enjoyed good health, the wife and daughters would not have to work outside the home. Observers often added upper, middle or middling, and lower to their definitions in a search for precision. The middle classes included members of the professions, state servants, and men with financial, commercial, or industrial interests. Many were landowners and the richer elements intermarried with complaisant, usually impecunious, noble families. The most wealthy would certainly have included themselves within the upper class, but acceptance was limited. While the number of noble families remained fairly stable in the nineteenth century, apart from a sprinkling of invented titles, there was an astronomic growth in the numbers of those who called themselves middle class. Contemporary observers were most aware of the expansion of the entrepreneurial element, but there was a dramatic growth in the professions and especially in state service.

Finally, the largest element in any society remained those with the least economic security, who survived by the labour of their hands. Middle-class contemporary observers, at their most complimentary, would have referred to the 'lower orders', using old terms sloppily, or a 'lower' class or classes. Such terms defined little more than the ignorance and sense of superiority of the observer. Definition necessitates further subdivisions, sometimes based on levels of taxation, sometimes on lifestyle, often on geography. The rural community included everyone from small farmers, who might own or rent land, to landless labourers. They ranged from the formally free in Britain and France, where feudal institutions, run merely as commercial operations, were abolished in the 1790s, to Russia, where a form of serfdom survived until the 1860s. Outside Britain the term peasant is often used for this, the numerically most substantial element in most European societies, but the word does not tell us much. Contemporaries would always subdivide the rural population according to the amount of land they

The advent of photography and the awareness that lifestyles were changing encouraged many studies of people at work. Our first shows a smallholding near Berlin (1897) devoted to pig-rearing.

Spanish rural workers on their lunch-break, 1894.

farmed, frequently judged by land tax payments, since one family would habitually own or rent several scattered parcels of land. France had the highest proportion of country people owning some land, about 6 million; Russia, until the 1860s, the least. It must also be remembered that many country dwellers combined rural and artisan activities.

The largest group of urban workers, particularly among the 30 per cent females in the labour force, were often those in 'service', usually living in; their numbers did not begin to decline until about 1900. Urban industrial workers might be artisans who owned and ran their own workshops, ran a workshop wholly or partly financed by a merchant, or one which was part of a putting-out operation. They could be journeymen or apprentices within any of these. They might be highly skilled factory workers, the 'labour aristocracy' as they have been called by historians of Britain, less skilled and lower-paid factory workers, or unskilled labourers. In town and country this worker element lost some economic independence during the century, although there was a distinct tendency to exaggerate lost freedom. The industrial sector became both larger and more urban, particularly towards the end of the century, but tidy, continent-wide statistics should be regarded with scepticism. An 1848 report on Parisian industry, intent on proving that unemployment had fallen, tried the ageless but unconvincing trick of calling unemployed

103

journeymen self-employed or small employers. People grasped what work they could, where they could. What is absolutely certain is that working people did not think of themselves as a single united class in the sense used by Marx.

The Consequences of Class: A Stalled Society?

Marx assumed that the proletariat would only become class conscious when the entrepreneurial sections of the bourgeoisie had taken over economic, social, and political power. The high profile of cotton and railways kings encouraged the view that this was happening. Publicists like Samuel Smiles eagerly created the idea that entrepreneurial growth liberated society from old bonds, offering new opportunities for the self-made man. In the mid-eighteenth century the brewer, Whitbread, bought big estates and a seat in Parliament. In 1830–1 successively, two bankers, Laffitte and Périer, were chief ministers in France. Marx assumed that their elevation showed that the 1830 revolution had replaced the nobility with a financial aristocracy.

Social change was far less rapid. The revolutionaries in France in the 1790s may have raged about 'aristos', and heads of families, many of them noble, who emigrated during the Revolution lost some land, but the proportion of noble-owned land fell by only 5 per cent to 20 per cent. Recent research has shown that the nobility were still the richest group in France during the first half of the nineteenth century. The revolutionaries abolished nobility as an order, but Napoleon created new titles, and in 1814 an hereditary Chamber of Peers shared legislative power with an elected Chamber. From 1831 no new hereditary titles were created, but families continued to luxuriate in the social snobbery of the plethora which survived, and to invent new ones. Both before and after 1789 French nobles shared political and economic power with the wealthier elements in the bourgeoisie. In Prussia nobles retained control of the top jobs in the state and army throughout the century, alongside some newer bourgeois families whose fortunes had been made in industry.

In Britain the power and wealth of the aristocracy increased. Between the Glorious Revolution of 1688 and the 1780s the number of such families had stayed constant at about 200, but their wealth had grown immeasurably. Some, like the Bedfords and Devonshires, were richer than some German princes. Land was the basis of their wealth; there were the considerable rewards of patronage and government office; the richest owned very prosperous mines. All built, or 'improved' large houses on country estates. Investment in trade and in innovative transport developments completed a portfolio more varied than that of most other European aristocrats. The emergence of a money market at the end of the seventeenth century offered the large landowner alternative investments in property development and as directors of joint-stock companies. Britain was supremely an aristocratic entrepreneurial society.

The Russian Tsars tried to strengthen their noble élite, but the apparent static nature of Russian society concealed more rapid social change than elsewhere. The extravagant lifestyle of the nobility and their decreasing willingness to engage in trade and industry led to the rapid decline of some families. Some serfs, who made their fortunes in cotton, bought their freedom and a few were later ennobled. While never regarded as equal, they directed the civic life of Moscow.

What of the middle classes? The entrepreneurial element were rarely self-made Cinderellas; most business and industrial enterprises were created by established families. Nor were entrepreneurs as numerous or as dominant in political life as the short-lived elevation of Laffitte and Périer might indicate (Périer died in the 1832 cholera epidemic). It was the landed and professional middle classes, already established in state service, whose numbers and influence increased rapidly during the century.

Lawyers and doctors profited from the increased role of the state and were often in the lead in criticizing established rulers. Before 1789 the French appeal courts, the *parlements*, constantly blocked monarchist reform projects and led demands for the calling of an Estates-General. Lawyers from a less exalted social milieu were leading figures in the revolutionary politics of the 1790s. Such individuals represented the corporate interests both of professional and traditional craft organizations. In the later years of the eighteenth century they condemned what they defined as the advance of absolutism and tried to defend their own corporate interests in the name of popular sovereignty under attack by rapacious rulers. In France in 1789 they were granted compensation when their venal privileges were abolished. Although reform went far beyond the self-absorbed demands of the members of the old *parlements*, lawyers successfully defended their own professional corporate identity in the name of national sovereignty and the separation of powers within the state.

Notions of self-selection, self-administration, and restricted entry were turned from detestable monopolistic privilege into the triumph of the freedom of the individual. Educational prerequisites, professional qualifications, and the role of the professions came increasingly under the scrutiny of the state. In Prussia degree courses were officially validated and no one could practise as a lawyer without a state appointment. In the early nineteenth century changes in the Prussian legal system made it the norm that after ten to twelve years of expensive legal training, a man had to spend nearly as long again working unpaid within the courts before he could hope to secure an official post, and even then his prospects for promotion were less than a generation earlier. In France, although lawyers could practise without an official post, they complained that the rationalization, standardization, and centralization involved in creating a single legal system for France in the 1790s reduced the autonomy of their profession. However, a glance at personnel dossiers reveals that many senior court officials in the nineteenth century would put high on their CV the fact that members of their family had occupied similar posts since the fifteenth century.

The professions responded to increased centralization and state initiative by trying to establish more specific educational prerequisites for acolytes and to standardize training under their corporate control, which they hoped would develop a new sense of professional identity. The huge expansion of education during the century was the product of middle-class initiative. Secondary and tertiary education was strictly confined to the élite by cost and content. Primary schooling was developed to define and discipline the less well off. Secondary school-leaving certificates, rarely completed by pupils from poorer families, became prerequisites for professional training. Professional associations were formed to replace old corporate interest. The professions reinforced their social élitism, but ironically they continued to be drawn into an expanding state bureaucracy—doctors vaccinating children against smallpox, taking part in state health insurance schemes, and so on.

Vocal sections of the leading professions remained critics of the state in the years up to 1848, and not entirely for selfish reasons. In Prussia members of the judiciary were prominent in demands for a constitutional regime and took the lead in the 1848 revolution. But partly because of the fear which the scale of popular support for their protest engendered, lawyers were subsequently mostly transformed into faithful and obedient servants of autocracy. Their reward was employment; job opportunities in the German bureaucracy were increased and from the early 1880s growth was rapid as lawyers were allowed to practise privately.

Doctors had key roles in movements for social reform and in the 1848 republic in France. Their politicization was ethical and altruistic. A generation of European doctors was appalled at the social effects of industrial and urban change. In England in 1830 Dr Kay drew attention to the plight of women and children cotton operatives. In France Drs Villermé and Buret wrote influential commentaries, the first detailing conditions among workers, especially women and children, in all of the textile industries, the second comparing their circumstances in England and France. Villermé, although sympathetic to capitalism, drew up the first French legislation restricting child labour. Republican socialist doctors like Guépin in Nantes and Raspail in Paris set up free clinics to help the poor.

Observers believed fervently that education was a crucial social cement and that it would reinforce social hierarchies. The provision of institutions like the Workingmen's Reading Room, Carlisle, provided access to modest learning for men and—to judge by this illustration—women.

Traditional middle-class groups used the opportunities of modernization. The experience of the guilds is revealing. Some were substantial property-owners and developed massive financial interests in the capitalist economy. They used their resources to retain privileges for their members, long after their original significance as industrial leaders had passed. Their significance can best be gauged by the power and standing of the guild companies in the City of London, which became the financial centre of the world in this period. They became more élitist in the process and comprised distinct and powerful pressure groups within the state, both facilitating and moulding centralization. The term 'stalled society' has been used in recent years to describe the problems created by the impact of the varied transformed corporate interests on the modern state. On the other hand, nineteenth-century reforming liberals such as Alexis de Tocqueville believed they represented 'liberty'.

The professional middle classes were not part of a class, but a series of powerful corporate interest groups. They came to dominate the elected institutions which developed, largely due to their own demands. The extent of their privilege is masked when they are labelled a 'class' and particularly when they are lumped together with the numerically much more numerous lower middle classes, the white-collar workers, who took up minor posts in the massive bureaucratic expansion of the second half of the century.

The privilege of wealth dominated the society of classes, just as it had dissected the society of orders. Money, whatever its source, bought access to power. The nineteenth century set store by education and everywhere attempts were made to provide primary education, eventually free, for all. But access to secondary education, which became institutionalized as a vital prerequisite to higher education and the professions, was often increasingly reserved for the rich. Education was used to reinforce existing hierarchies, to define the self-perpetuating professions, and thereby strengthen a sense of class barriers. More than ever, wealth controlled access to, and advance within, state service and the professions. Venality and patronage were gradually replaced by professional hurdles for state service and entry into the professions, but the net result was to limit the best jobs and access to the professions to the rich, if anything even more than under the old regime.

Class Consciousness—Class Conflict

To what extent did individuals perceive themselves as members of mutually conflicting social classes? While liberals such as Guizot defended class divisions as open, equal, fair, and rational, critics on the right and left presented a very different interpretation. On the right, ultras such as Bonald and de Maistre and liberal Catholics such as Villeneuve-Bargemont lashed the bourgeois élite for their selfish disregard of higher values. Radicals and socialists condemned capitalist competition. Socialists refused to acknowledge that class divisions were part of the natural order in the same way as species of butterflies and geological formations.

Before Marx, with a few exceptions, socialists hoped to transform class conflict into harmony by peacefully replacing capitalist competition with co-operation.

They proposed a variety of strategies ranging from Utopian experiments to government-primed co-operative workshops. The philanthropic British industrialist Robert Owen initiated experimental Utopian communities and artisan associations. For Proudhon a classless society would emerge when everyone took a hand at a variety of trades and skills. Cabet thought it would need the elimination (by persuasion) of private property and total equality and sameness in everything, including housing. Marx claimed that capitalist exploitation and class consciousness were unavoidable stages in economic development. A final revolution by a class-conscious proletariat would eliminate class and exploitation alike.

The first half of the nineteenth century was a time of popular unrest and protest. The impact of economic change and repeated economic crises like that of 1816–18 made rural areas as well as towns the scene of repeated violent upheaval. Popular unrest became endemic: at Peterloo in 1819, in the Captain Swing riots of 1830–1, among silk weavers in Lyons in 1831 and 1834, among tailors and printers in Paris, Berlin, and other cities in 1830, culminating in Chartism in Britain, and in the revolutions of 1848. The target of protesters was 'government', which, they claimed, was responsible for iniquitous taxes and tariffs and decreasingly willing, evidenced by recent legislation dismantling guilds and attacking freedom of association, to protect the traditional (rosily romanticized) moral economy.

Rioters were almost never committed to the overthrow of neglectful governments; they wanted government help to check damaging innovations. Grievances were specific and limited, involving attacks on property, especially new machines, forced grain sales, threats, but very little serious physical assault and almost no theft. The immediate target was often other workers, sometimes foreigners, sometimes women. Journeymen tailors complained that the growth in 'ready-made' production methods using cheap female labour reduced their income and belittled their trade. Printers were Luddites and rebels because they feared that new machinery would threaten both their skills and jobs. Silk weavers resented their increasing financial dependence on merchants. Poorer peasants protested about the erosion of communal rights, the better off that the vagaries of the market left them dependent on money-lenders, or that tariffs on imported manufac-

La Barricade, by J. L. Meissonier, 1848. This tragic study of dead artisans—men, women, young, and old—who had fought to the end in their own narrow street of the Marais behind the collapsed cobblestones of their barricade was exhibited in 1850 as 'a memory of Civil War'. It was a very unusual product by a man who became Napoleon III's favourite painter, the microscopic detail of whose work was considered 'value for money' by his patrons.

tures blocked their foreign wine market—and that was just in France. Factory workers were seldom involved in protest. There was no concerted class consciousness, but a series of particular, often regionally limited, issues which sometimes coincided in depression years. The rhetoric of class conflict was aired in the cheaper, sometimes worker-run, newspapers of the day, but it only had a wide audience when food prices soared and work was scarce.

Governments responded to popular protest with violent repression. Real and mythical recollections of the Terror of the 1790s in France convinced all governments of the need to repress disorder before it could escalate. Socialists had far more success in convincing ruling élites of the imminence of class war than they had in converting and uniting working people. In 1843 Flora Tristan complained of artisan indifference and hostility to her idealistic plan for a single Union of all Workers. Military repression at Peterloo, Lyons, Paris, Milan, and St Petersburg did far more to create a sense of lower-class solidarity than the writings of the socialists or the inequities of the capitalist economy.

Class Organization

Rioting was one way of drawing attention to problems in crisis years. During more ordinary times in the eighteenth century prosperous workers had formed insurance schemes to provide death and other benefits. Journeymen formed defensive, sometimes violent, groups. In the nineteenth century a variety of worker associations for mutual aid among groups of producers, employees, or consumers became more numerous. Popular associations, whether peaceful or violent, were feared by ruling élites. In France the liberal claims of the Declaration of Rights of 1789 were gainsaid by the Civil Code which put any association larger than twenty under the scrutiny of the prefect. Craft and the mutual-aid insurance associations might be tolerated, but a vague whiff of politics or violent action brought in the army. In 1834 even associations of under twenty were banned.

In Britain the right of workers to negotiate wages was denied in 1799, although from 1825 they were permitted to associate and collect funds. Robert Owen attracted considerable artisan support for the co-operative ideal in the 1820s and by 1830 500 societies with 20,000 members had been formed. In Britain, France, and the German states mutual-aid insurance associations and producer and especially retail co-operative associations took off, often harmonizing existing craft formations with the ideas of socialists such as Buchez, Blanc, and Proudhon as well as Owen. In these years small artisan formations did best. They usually began, like the Rochdale Pioneers, as self-sufficient primitive communist communities and, if they became successful, developed into profit-making concerns. By 1872 in Britain there were nearly one thousand groups with 300,000 members and sales of £10 million a year.

Specific trade unions, distinct from producer or consumer co-operatives, developed from earlier artisan trade associations. In Britain Owen planned a Grand National Consolidated Union in 1834, which very briefly attracted support among tailors and shoemakers. Unions were the self-defence schemes of the

Below: **Around the turn of the century** in Germany photographers were engaged to 'snap' families in their homes to record social trends. This study reveals that a family of nine children *could* live respectably. All are well-fed, dressed, and shod. Signs of strain show in aspects of their living-room—and perhaps on the mother's face!

Facing, below: **The next home in Berlin** has all the essentials—and some of the decorative niceties such as lace curtains—but there are no rug or curtains, the family are living in an attic, and—a threat for the future—the two tiny children are about to gain a sibling.

Facing, above: **Descending the poverty ladder** further, this 1910 study shows a truly poor family living in their tiny—and only—room. Shoeless—but the father has a bowler: perhaps he has a clerical job?

better-paid crafts, the 'labour aristocracy' as they were regarded by less skilled workers. Individual trades organized many tiny local unions. In 1842 over 100,000 men belonged to separate small mining unions in Britain. In return for a small weekly fee members obtained death and limited unemployment benefits, but unlike mutual-aid or friendly societies, unions also tried to impose collective bargaining on merchants or, in a factory situation, on employers.

Strikes could result. The French silk weavers' strikes of 1831 and 1834 were crushed by government troops, but in north-east England miners organized large-scale strikes in 1844 and 1863 and Lancashire cotton weavers were active in 1878. Large unions were also successful in collective bargaining; in 1853 a 20,000-strong strike of Preston weavers settled rates of pay and won middle-class support and cash donations. In the 1860s Boards of Arbitration emerged in England and in 1868 a Trades Union Congress was formed. In 1871 unions were recognized and four years later the peaceful negotiation of trade disputes permitted. In France in 1864 the right of unions to engage in peaceable bargaining was acknowledged.

Despite the formation of unions and socialist parties, worker organization remained embryonic compared with that of the landed, commercial, and industrial élites, who were associated by education, marriage, and common economic interests. They could operate in formal and informal pressure groups in and out of parliaments and through institutionally powerful industrial cartels and money markets, both to control and to override government policy.

The Family under Threat?

The family was honoured as the basic unit of society by all nineteenth-century observers, apart from a tiny number of socialists and the occasional satirist. The family home, even of the poor, was changed from a functional dwelling, shared

with animals in rural areas, to an idealized, plush, aspidistra'd temple, complete with thick curtains, drawn almost together in poorer homes, which did not sport the required 'best' room furniture and piano. In the later years of the century the catalogues of the burgeoning 'palaces of purchasing', the department stores, shaped the standards of a new middle-class consumer society. Poorer families in their 'two-up, two-down' terrace house or rooms in a tenement imitated the norm of 'respectability' to the limits of their wages.

Reformers raised the alarm that poor families were threatened by urbanization and factory development. They argued that omnipresent poverty, prostitution, and illegitimacy were on the increase. Although child abandonment, then as now, was often seen as a touchstone of moral decline, it peaked only in times of economic crisis.

It was female and child employment in cotton mills and mines, in the former of which small children filled a technological gap for a couple of generations, which appalled educated reformers, shocked at the regimentation and publicly displayed inhumanity of hard manual labour and apparently unaware that women and children inevitably always contributed to the artisan family economy. At mid-century in France about 40 per

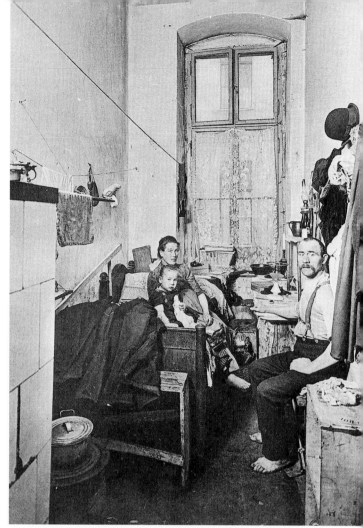

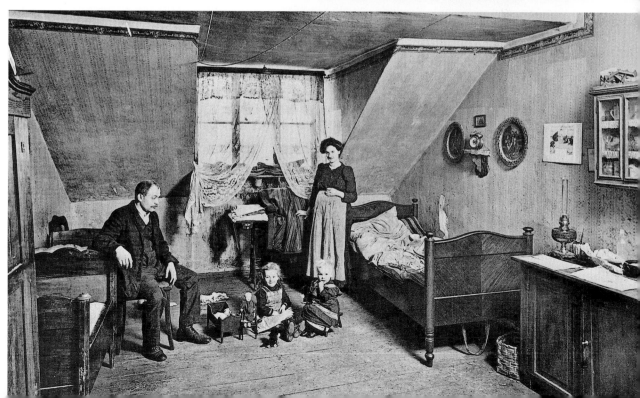

Right: **Home-based work** would often utilize children as well as men and women. This family busy making Christmas crackers also live, sleep, and eat all in this one room.

Below: **The siege of Paris** is over—but the washing still has to be done! From the innocent young beauty to the mature laundry-thumper the women are hard at work—and talk—with the National Guardsmen in attendance (are they only waiting for the shirts?).

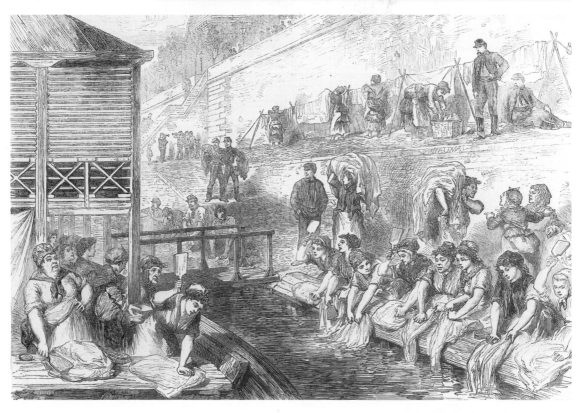

cent of cotton workers were women, 12 per cent were children under 16. By the 1870s the figure for child labour had fallen to about 7 per cent because technical advances made them redundant. In Britain most female cotton operatives were unmarried, so the anticipated deleterious effect on family welfare presumably did not occur. In France, however, women artisans in Paris and Lyons, in particular, sent their babies to rural wetnurses.

In many large-scale industries, such as mining and potbanks, teams of workers were paid as a unit and family groups traditionally worked together, imitating earlier artisan practices. In France unmarried female workers were habitually lodged in hostels run by nuns to protect their virtue and their fathers' authority, for their wages were sent directly to him. From the 1860s the new department stores also ran hostels for unmarried workers, often on the top floor of the shop, carefully segregating the sexes and trying to encourage uplifting cultural experiences for their leisure time. Their workers, at least, received their own wages.

Factories did not, of their essence, affect family relationships. But the culture of

Factory industry was often organized on artisanal lines with family groups employed as teams. Wedgwood built a model factory by the canal in Etruria in the Potteries. His family work teams were housed nearby in tolerably comfortable terrace houses, most with long narrow gardens where vegetables, chickens, etc. could be tended.

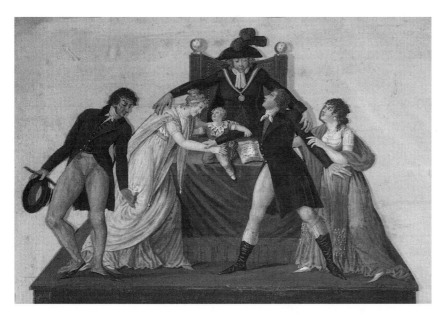

Le Divorce, by Le Sueur. The French revolutionaries introduced a civil process permitting divorce in 1792 as one prong of their attack on the social role of the Catholic Church. In quick succession civil registration of births, marriages, and deaths compulsorily (and temporarily) replaced the religious ceremonies. Some men used the exigencies of civil and foreign war to escape unwelcome marriages; and in Rouen 75 per cent of divorce petitioners were women. Divorce legislation fell into disuse during the Empire and was overturned in 1814.

the family meant that it was assumed that everyone lived in a mutually supportive nuclear, or in southern Europe more extended, family, and rates of pay for women (and of course children) were adjusted downwards accordingly. Single mothers, who had fled to a town to escape family condemnation, or who were widowed, found it impossible to sustain life by honest means. The greater visibility of prostitution in nineteenth-century towns was not the direct result of a collapse in morals, but because honest labour often paid a woman only 25 per cent of a man's wage.

In rural and artisan economies women had a chance of respect and authority based on their interlocking work and family responsibilities and the mutual support of a small community. In the factory, both sexes were merely labour and the status of cheaper, less strong and skilled female workers dropped accordingly. Their position within the family would depend on personal circumstances, although traditional norms might prevail. Some men brought

Above: **The nineteenth century** invented both the traditions of the family Christmas and the annual seaside holiday. The railway and economic change meant that the very rich no longer monopolized expanding seaside and spa resorts. The passion for sea-bathing was also a sign of increased liberation for women. This Nordeney shot of 1910 reveals what perhaps was better hidden!

Right: **The working class** would have to make do with a day-trip with the Boys' Brigade to a local lake. There would also be annual outings for master craftsmen and their team to the 'great house' of the Wedgwoods—complete with formal invitation cards.

A much larger section of the female population than ever before was privileged to live a life free from paid employment and a complete progression of rituals to fill that existence grew up. 'Unsere Backfischlein' (our little girl) shows the stages in the life of such a girl, from bookworm, ritually entertaining her girl-friends to tea and cake, day-dreaming, fighting with her brother (an important training ritual!), the little housewife, the 'Icebirds', and the three stages of attendance at the high point of the social calendar, the Ball.

home their wage packet unopened to their wives, some only reluctantly con-tributed to food for the family, but was that new? In Rouen in the 1790s, when divorce was available, 75 per cent of petitioners were wives, many of whom had been deserted by their spouses. The effectiveness of family structures was closely related to the size of, and degree of anonymity within, the community.

While some feared that the poverty and drudgery of industrialization threat-ened the social fabric, others became concerned that better-off women might snatch the chance of education and economic independence to challenge male dominance. From time to time female writers alarmed men with the prospect of a 'world turned upside down'. Cartoonists mocked the 'liberated' woman. But the reality was hardly a threat. Secondary and tertiary education for women was several generations behind provision for men; in Catholic countries the female orders were considered the most suitable educators for girls. The development of large-scale retail, commercial, and industrial organizations tended to reduce the role of wives in family firms, although widowhood might still demand their business acumen. Greater affluence for growing middle-class groups offered women an accentuated role in the family. Paid employment came later.

Elected Assemblies and the Biggest Myth

The social problems created by growing numbers, urbanization, and economic change, which at times brought violent confrontation, led to what was to be an even more pervasive alteration in social organization, the interventionist bureaucratic state. The pressure from middle-class reformers and popular unrest in the first half of the century ensured that institutional reform came to be seen as the panacea to the social problem. The state became the agency to legislate on industrial relations, town-planning, public health and the medical services, female and child labour, education, railway construction, etc. In France Napoleon III dreamt of turning worker insurance schemes into a national plan. In the newly united Germany, Bismarck, appalled by the growth of the Socialist Party, co-ordinated self-help mutual-aid sickness and pensions' schemes into a state-run system in the 1880s.

Institutional reform was a peaceful route usually embarked upon by defensive ruling élites who feared both cholera and social unrest, but its results were revolutionary. At a positive level the nineteenth-century reformers constructed a cleaner, safer (less revolutionary), more harmonious social environment, and the transport revolution and urban building programme they generated sustained unprecedented economic expansion. However, it also risked transforming the state into the anonymous, bureaucratic omnivore depicted by Kafka—and a monopoly capitalist into the bargain as the biggest single employer in each country.

Radical reformers tried to ensure that the interventionist state did not become a massive, expensive, uncontrollable leviathan. Elected institutions were seen as the antidote to both popular unrest and a brake on the expansion of the role and cost of the state. The French revolutionaries of the 1790s campaigned unsuccessfully for representative institutions and acquired a dictatorial emperor at the head of their modernized state. After the Napoleonic wars British radicals demanded reform of the House of Commons and the French argued over voting rights within a constitution modelled to some degree on that of Britain. Campaigns for suffrage reform were mainly, but not entirely, the initiative of middle-class reformers. In Britain the Chartist movement of the 1830s and 1840s, backed by some members of the lower middle classes, artisans, and better-off factory workers, pressed for a democratic electorate as did societies like the mainly middle-class Friends of the People in France. The French enfranchised all adult males after the 1848 revolution

and in 1867 all male householders got the vote in Britain. Elected assemblies at all levels, municipal to national, gradually became the norm in all countries, although none rivalled the French until 1919 and few worried that 50 per cent of adults had no vote.

The extension of the right to vote tended to perpetuate traditional élites. In Britain the Reform Act of 1832 had no impact on the composition of Parliament. In 1840 80 per cent of members still represented the landed interest and the proportion of bourgeois entrepreneurs, 97 : 658, was the same as at the end of the eighteenth century. Perhaps this was unsurprising, given the limited nature of the legislation. However, the same was true in France, even after the introduction of universal male suffrage in 1848. In 1861 the new united Italy adopted a 40 lira tax qualification for voters, which produced an electorate comparable to that of France before 1848. The Italian ruling élite was not only wealthy, it was almost exclusively northern. Universal male suffrage had to wait until 1919. Frederick

Over London by Rail, by Gustave Doré, 1872. Railway-building, like motorway construction today, spawned pockets of housing alongside the track, whose front-view privacy was often belied by the view from the train of a less tidy and prosperous lifestyle.

117

William IV of Prussia established a graded suffrage for the elected Landtag in 1849 which allowed the richest 18 per cent of taxpayers to elect two-thirds of the new legislative assembly he created. This system was retained for the assemblies of the individual states after unification. The Reichstag, the representative assembly for the whole German empire created in 1871, was elected by all adult males, but it exercised little power. When elected local councils, *Zemstvos*, were set up in Russia in the 1860s and an imperial parliament, or Duma, after the 1905 revolution, an even narrower hierarchical voting system was inaugurated. Elected assemblies only began to find a role for themselves in Russia during the First World War. Unsurprisingly, in an age of unpaid MPs, assemblies tended to represent the interests of wealthy élites. However, by 1914 the socialists were the largest single group in both the German Reichstag and the French assembly, and a growing, though a very divided, number in Italy. Socialist voters were mostly workers, but, significantly, their leaders and MPs tended to be members of the professional middle class, especially lawyers.

Social tensions were prominent in nineteenth-century Europe but conflict was reduced and fudged by social insurance schemes, private and state run, by the legalization of trade unions, by the provision of state-organized education, by the development of parliamentary institutions which created the illusion of consultation and democracy, and by the promotion of nationalist and imperialistic sentiments. Class war had never been on the cards, for working people at least. The Socialist International's demand for international proletarian solidarity in 1914 went unheard. Yet, although society may not have become polarized quite in the way socialists including Marx had predicted, the gap between rich and poor had widened since 1789.

This was most visible at the top. In Britain in 1803 the top 2 per cent owned 20 per cent of the wealth of the country; by 1867 they owned 40 per cent. The aristocratic élite had not perished, they had merely diversified. The French revolutionaries in the 1790s and liberal, mainly middle-class reformers in the following century set their sights on the elimination of irrational privilege. But property rights were applauded and became the basic legitimation of nineteenth-century society. Guizot and many others maintained that a man's independence and sense of social responsibility could be measured by his wealth.

Wealth had always corresponded pretty closely to power; the nineteenth century merely institutionalized the equation, while appearing to do the reverse. Hierarchically structured education systems, professions, and assemblies of all sorts reinforced improved policing, military control, and the monitoring and managing of public opinion. The wealthy made the mistake for much of the century of not recognizing that, while considerable wealth might protect political leaders from temptation and corruption (though this belief in the altruism of the wealthy was, and is, not borne out by experience), the less well off, and even, perish the thought, females, were also capable of participating in electoral politics, without wanting to turn the world upside down.

It was not the entrepreneur who visibly triumphed, but the aristocracy, assisted by traditional professional and official middle-class elements which by 1914 had

Facing: **This Belgian study** depicts the harshness of peasant life, showing not only the resignation and ageing of the group of peasant children, but also how quickly death took a high proportion of them.

gained considerable ground, both in state service and in elected assemblies. On the eve of the First World War the aristocratic section of the society of orders remained powerful; but the society of classes and class rivalries which the nineteenth century had anticipated, some in hope, most in fear, had not emerged. However, the idea of class was a powerful myth, as the Bolshevik revolution and the fascist dictatorships were to show. The absence of trust between middle- and working-class elements was crucial to the polarization of politics in the twentieth century, especially when laced with the most destructive demon to emerge from Pandora's box, nationalism.

Facing: **La Famille Heureuse**, by André-Henri Dargelas. A charming, if sentimental, depiction of the comforts of middle-class childhood. Note that the parents are not included; 'happy' families involved even greater distance between parents and children and even less 'quality' time than today.

5

The Commercialization and Sacralization of European Culture in the Nineteenth Century

T. C. W.
BLANNING

The End of the Old Regime

THE high culture of nineteenth-century Europe was shaped by a tension between two opposing concepts of art: between art as consumerism and art as redemption. What should take priority: making money or saving mankind? This was not a new dilemma, but it was given added urgency around 1800 by the cumulative effect of long-term social and intellectual changes. The rise in population, the growth in the size and number of towns, expanding literacy, and improved physical communications had combined to create a market for culture which could already be dubbed 'popular' and was well on the way to becoming 'mass'. The culture of a century earlier had been essentially representational, with the primary function of re-presenting (in the sense of 'making present' or giving visual or aural expression to) the power and the glory of the royal, aristocratic, or ecclesiastical patron. The palace of Versailles, where all the various arts combined to sing the praises of Louis XIV, was the most complete example. This peacock world of gorgeous display by the favoured few before a passive audience was challenged in the

course of the eighteenth century by quite a different culture: the culture of the public sphere. In the place of flamboyance it brought sobriety, in the place of the senses it brought the intellect, in the place of the image it brought the concept, in the place of hierarchy it brought 'a republic of letters' open to talent. Above all, it substituted criticism among equals for passive acceptance by the subordinate spectator.

For the creative artist, this development of a public seemed to offer the chance of emancipation. In the place of the over-mighty individual patron—famously defined by Samuel Johnson (1709–84) as someone who watches with indifference a man struggling for his life in the water, only to encumber him with assistance when he reaches shore—came the anonymous public, to whom the German playwright Friedrich Schiller (1759–1805) dedicated himself in 1784: 'I write as a citizen of the world who serves no prince . . . From now on all my ties are dissolved. The public is now everything to me—my preoccupation, my sovereign and my friend.' Unfortunately, Schiller then found that his high opinion of the public was not reciprocated and was obliged to seek employment as a professor of history (a menial position if ever there were one) from the duke of Weimar. The public was not yet large enough or rich enough to sustain an independent artist—but it was growing all the time.

The Festival of the Supreme Being held on the Champs-de-Mars, 8 June 1794. This was the greatest of the revolutionary festivals, the climax of Robespierre's attempt to replace Christianity with a state religion based on reason. Neither the message nor its medium proved to be durable.

The transformation of the people from passive recipients into active participants was dramatized by the rapid development of a democratic political culture in France after 1789. The elaborate revolutionary festivals turned spectators into actors, with mass processions, mass demonstrations, mass bands, and mass singing. At the great Festival of the Supreme Being in Paris on 8 June 1794, delegations from each of the city's forty-eight sections paraded from the Tuileries to the Champs-de-Mars, where a great artificial 'mountain' had been constructed, decorated with such 'accidents of nature' as rocky outcrops, grottoes, and undergrowth, and crowned by a symbolic tree of liberty. To the accompaniment of an immense band of brass and woodwind (stringed instruments were of little use in the open air), revolutionary hymns were sung, interposed between two speeches by Robespierre. That the latter's windy rhetoric was inaudible to the great majority present, in the absence of electronic amplification, did not matter one jot: this was not a culture based on the word; rather it relied on open-air spectacle, visual symbol, the singing of simple verses to simple music, and the special excitement which comes from being part of a crowd.

In the excited atmosphere of Revolutionary France, the ephemeral nature of the poetry, painting, or music produced for such occasions could be overlooked. Three of the country's leading artists collaborated on the Festival of the Supreme Being: the painter Jacques-Louis David (1748–1825), who supervised the whole affair and was indeed the great 'pageant-master' of the Republic, the composer François Joseph Gossec (1734–1829), and the poet Marie-Joseph de Chénier (1764–1811). Yet their work for the revolutionary masses survives only as historical curios. The exception which proves the rule is David's deeply felt *Homage to Marat*, which depicts the assassinated radical bleeding to death in his bath, a personal statement of outrage and grief. It may well be the case that in public life 'the festivals inaugurated a new era because they made sacred the values of a modern, secular, liberal world', as Lynn Hunt has suggested, but for the creative artists of Europe the culture of the French Revolution proved to be a blind alley.

The Romantic Revolution

Disillusionment had been prepared by an ever-strengthening movement in favour of individualism. Just as the French Revolution erupted with a liberationist message deriving from the Enlightenment—a message which was universal, abstract, and rational, the most powerful minds in Europe were travelling in the opposite direction. This was the romantic movement, a cultural revolution so momentous that we continue to share many of its main axioms today. The word 'romantic' first appeared in English in the middle of the seventeenth century, used in a pejorative sense to denote something exaggerated or fantastic 'as in the old romances'. By the end of the eighteenth century, however, the fabulous and the irrational had begun to exert an increasingly powerful appeal. From pioneers such as Jean-Jacques Rousseau (1712–78) and Johann Gottfried Herder (1744–1803), the romantics built a world-view which opposed emotion to reason, faith to scepticism, intuition to logic, subjectivity to objectivity, historicism to natural law, and poetry to prose. In their view, the Enlightenment and its scientific method had analysed and analysed until the world lay around them in a dismantled, atomized, and meaningless heap. So it was a common accusation that the Enlightenment 'could explain everything, but understand nothing'. It was in this spirit that Heinrich von Kleist (1777–1811) sneered that Sir Isaac Newton (1642–1727), the personification of the scientific revolution, would see in a girl's breast only a crooked line and in her heart nothing more interesting than its cubic capacity, while William Blake (1757–1827) proclaimed that 'Art is the Tree of Life . . . Science is the Tree of Death'.

In the place of the arid abstractions of rationalism, the romantics called for a remystification of the world. To gain access to what really mattered, reason and its main instrument—the word—were not so much inadequate as misleading, instilling a false sense of precision and clarity. If nature was not an inert mass, governed by the blind, mechanical Newtonian laws, but a vibrant organism pulsating with life, then it could be understood only by allowing the other human faculties to resume their rightful place. It was an indication of their rejection of the Enlightenment's rationalism that they turned its central metaphor—light—on its head. 'The cold light of day' was rejected as superficial and in its place was enthroned 'the wonder-world of the night'. From Novalis (the *nom de plume* of Friedrich von Hardenberg, 1772–1801) and his *Hymns to the Night* to Richard Wagner (1813–83) and *Tristan and Isolde*, the night was celebrated as 'the mother of all that is true and beautiful'. It is at night, in our dreams, that we leave the false world of appearances and enter the only true world—the world of the spirit. In Wagner's *The Mastersingers of Nuremberg*, the young knight Walther von Stolzing tells his host, the cobbler Hans Sachs, that he has had such a beautiful dream that he is reluctant to recount it, lest it should vanish. To this Hans Sachs replies that it is just the task of the poet to depict and interpret dreams, for it is in dreams that our truest feelings are revealed. This maxim was drawn from Wagner's own experience: on 3 September 1853 at Spezia on the Ligurian coast of Italy, suffering from the cumulative effects of exhaustion, dysentery, seasickness, and self-pity:

The Sleep of Reason Begets Monsters (1799), by Goya. Is this a monster to be feared, or is it not rather the Owl of Minerva, the symbol of wisdom, who—as Hegel observed—'flies only at dusk'. The romantics preferred the dark side of the moon.

123

I sank into a kind of somnambulistic state, in which I suddenly had the feeling of being immersed in rapidly flowing water. Its rushing soon resolved itself for me into the musical sound of the chord of E flat major . . . I recognized at once that the orchestral prelude to *The Rhinegold* [the first part of *The Ring of the Nibelung*], long dormant within me but up to that moment inchoate, had at last been revealed; and at once I saw precisely how it was with me: the vital flood would come from within me, and not from without.

'From within me, and not from without'—there could be no better summary of the essence of romanticism, unless it is Hegel's even more pithy '*absolute Innerlichkeit*', which can be translated as 'absolute inwardness' or 'absolute subjectivity'. From being the agent who strives to give the natural laws of beauty visible, aural, or verbal form, the artist raises *himself* to become the prime point of reference. In other words, mimesis (art in relation to nature) was replaced by an *expressive* aesthetic (art in relation to the artist). In the new scale of values thus created, the premium is placed on inspiration, originality, and authenticity, as the artist turns from the models provided by the classical tradition to draw on his own experiences and his own psyche. This was the meaning of the advice given by the most original of all romantic painters, Caspar David Friedrich (1774–1840): 'The artist should not only paint what he sees in front of him, but also what he sees inside himself. If, however, he sees nothing inside himself, then he should also stop painting what he sees in front of him. Otherwise his pictures will look like those folding screens behind which one expects to find only the sick or even the dead.' Significantly, Friedrich never felt the need to travel to Italy to study classical civilization ('No one can give the law to everyone else, everyone must be a law only unto himself'). His paintings are usually religious and always deeply introspective, almost to the point of abstraction. This stress on authenticity was retained even by artists of later generations who rejected much of the rest of romanticism— by Edouard Manet (1832–83), for example, who wrote in 1867: 'The artist does not say today "Come and see faultless work", but "Come and see sincere work".' And still, today, the most damning accusation a critic can level at a new work is 'derivative'.

Commercialization and Alienation

The egocentric aesthetics of the romantic artist made the yoke of patronage seem intolerable, however gilded the bars of the cage. Summoned back to the Berlin Academy after overstaying his sabbatical leave in Rome, the painter Asmus Jacob Carstens (1754–98), a classicist by style but a romantic by temperament, replied with sublime self-confidence: 'If nature produces a genius (which after all is a rare event) and if that genius manages to overcome a thousand obstacles and achieve recognition, then what he deserves is encouragement. A monarch wins just as much honour from posterity by supporting a genius as from winning a battle or conquering a province.' But it was not only the old regime (which in fact had treated Carstens with considerable generosity) which seemed oppressive. The growing power and pretension of the modern state, dramatized by the terrorist atrocities of the French Revolution, brought only ever greater alienation of artist from establishment. The optimistic Prussian aristocrat Novalis hoped for a state which was a work of art, ruled by a king who was 'the artist of artists'; only an early death from consumption prevented inevitable disillusionment.

Nor could the alienated artist seek refuge in civil society, for the agenda set by ever-accelerating modernization gave priority not to the aesthetics of an artistic élite but to commerce and the greatest pleasure of the greatest number. The fate of the piano is an object-lesson in how problematic material progress could be for the creative artist. Probably invented by Bartolomeo Cristofori (1655–1731) at Florence in the first decade of the eighteenth century, the piano took a long time to get established, not appearing at a public concert until 1768 (in Paris). Its advantages were such, however, that its eventual victory over other keyboard instruments was inevitable, for it is much louder than the clavichord, much less bulky than the organ and both much more versatile and resilient than the harpsichord. In particular, its dynamic range was such that it was the ideal instrument for the new music of feeling. As a French manual of 1785 put it: 'The amount of pressure by the finger determines the strength or weakness of the sound. It lends itself, consequently, to *expression*.' The twenty-seven piano concertos of Mozart (1756–91) were both symptom and cause of the instrument's arrival as a major musical force.

What then followed was a striking example of how music and technology can interact. Ever larger and more robust pianos were constructed for ever more demanding and ambitious composers, notably Beethoven (1770–1827), whose 'Hammerklavier' sonata of 1818 required a piano with six and a half octaves and the ability to withstand the pressure exerted by 20,000 notes, many of them marked *fortissimo*. Even that paled by comparison with the onslaught launched by Franz Liszt (1811–86), the greatest pianist of the century, whose amazing virtuosity and

Piano recital by Franz Liszt (1842). Larger and louder pianos and the new railway network allowed Liszt to exploit his wonderful talents to the full. His tours across the length and breadth of Europe aroused tremendous enthusiasm—and earned him huge sums of money.

demands on his instruments won for him from the French critic François Danjou the title of 'the Alexander, the Napoleon, the Caesar of pianists—and the Attila of pianos'. No wonder that by the middle of the nineteenth century pianos had come to be equipped with iron frames. The range also increased: from the four octaves of Cristofori to the five and a half of the English manufacturer Broadwood in 1790 to the six and a half required by the 'Hammerklavier' to the seven of the Erard used by Liszt to the seven and a quarter or even eight of the twentieth century.

With quality went quantity. The application of modern techniques of manufacturing based on the division of labour, together with commercial marketing, transformed the piano from a rare luxury item into a cheap article of mass consumption. From an annual output of about 130 in 1790, production in France soared to 8,000 by 1830 and 21,000 by 1860. Even that figure was eclipsed by the German manufacturers who were producing 60,000–70,000 pianos each year by the 1880s. In other words, by the middle of the nineteenth century the piano industry was big business, giving employment to tens of thousands of production workers and teachers across Europe (and North America). At the Great Exhibition held at the Crystal Palace in 1851, 101 exhibitors from 10 countries presented 173 different pianos. As economies of scale brought prices tumbling down, the piano found its way into every middle-class household with pretensions to culture: 'it has become so essential, so indispensable that even those who are not musicians buy a piano as furniture for their sitting-rooms' recorded a French musical periodical in 1850. Satires on its ubiquity were common:

—Oh! My dear chap, what a delightful person Miss Clarisse Filandor is!
—I know her: eighteen years old, a blonde and pretty.
—Yes, with blue eyes and dark eye-lashes.
—And she has a dowry of 200,000 francs.
—Exactly, and what is more, she is the sole heir of a rich uncle who is terminally ill.
—But her crowning glory is that *she doesn't play the piano.*
—I was just going to say that. So she is not a woman like any other, this one—she is an angel sent from heaven!

This example supplied by the piano could be replicated in other branches of the arts. Everywhere, commercialization and industrialization brought democratization: but, in the eyes of Europe's cultural élites, popularization had become synonymous with vulgarization. When a musical instrument was reduced to a piece of furniture and musical skills were acquired for social prestige—or when paintings were reproduced lithographically in thousands of copies and hung on suburban walls—the aesthete turned away in disgust. Of all the cultural stereotypes created by the romantics of the early nineteenth century, the most durable has been the bourgeois Philistine. The modern (as opposed to the biblical) use of the word 'Philistine' was invented by German students as a term of abuse to describe the town burghers they both envied—for their wealth—and despised—for their materialism. That contribution of two powerful if unattractive emotions led to the intelligentsia distancing itself from the rest of the population, fleeing an increasingly commercialized society for the austere purity of the bohemian garret. This

The Poor Poet, by Carl Spitzweg. Painted in 1837, this is an ironic comment on the retreat to a bohemian life in a garret by intellectuals too sensitive for the crass materialism of the bourgeois world. The poet is inspecting an flea he has just caught.

internalization of the creative process demanded by the romantic aesthetic could certainly lead to originality but could equally certainly lead to incomprehensibility on the part of the audience. When culture was conducted according to classical models, everyone spoke the same language, but the romantic revolution proved to be the tower of Babel. If Mozart pleased everyone, Beethoven puzzled many; if Wagner outraged many, Arnold Schoenberg (1874–1951) baffled everyone. Most artists professed indifference to public response, and many of them even meant it. One such was certainly John Constable, who told his biographer when asked whether he painted a picture for 'any particular person': 'Yes, Sir, it is painted for a *very particular* person, the person for whom I have all my life painted.'

As the creative artist seized the centre of the cultural stage, his or her own life came to provide the main material for the dramas performed on it. If the romantics did not invent the autobiography, they certainly raised it from exception to rule. Taking their cue from Rousseau's *Confessions*, not just writers but creative artists of every genre felt the urge to recount their lives and explain their innermost feelings. Very little is known about the personal life of Johann Sebastian Bach (1685–1750); much more about Mozart, thanks to his substantial correspondence; more still about Beethoven, who left not only letters but diaries and 'conversation books'; and a very great deal about composers such as Berlioz and Wagner, whose autobiographies ran to around 270,000 and 370,000 words respectively. Even when not formally autobiographical, the subjective element was very strong. It is a cliché that all first novels are autobiographical, but a growing number of writers came to follow Goethe (1749–1832) in seeing their entire œuvre (voluminous in his case—the standard edition of his collected works runs to 133 volumes) as 'fragments of a great confession', most notably Fyodor Dostoevsky (1821–81) and Marcel Proust (1871–1922). Much of the work of composers as diverse as Berlioz, Tchaikovsky (1840–93), and Mahler (1860–1911) had an autobiographical reference, while Bedřich Smetana marked his first string quartet 'from my life'.

Sacralization

In theory, the follower of 'absolute inwardness' could devise an expressive language so personal as to be comprehensible only to himself. This tendency was counterbalanced, however, partly by the need to make a living and partly by art's new sacral status. The culture of the old regime had had three purposes: to represent the power of the sovereign, to assist the Church in saving souls, and to provide recreation for the élites. All three functions had been undermined by eighteenth-century developments. The deification of monarchs by multi-media extravaganzas such as Versailles was no longer in fashion. In the place of the 'Sun King' (Louis XIV) came the king as first servant of the state (Frederick the Great) or the king as

Right: **Emperor Francis I of Austria** (1832), by Friedrich von Amerling. The pathetic discrepancy between the symbols of authority and the shrunken figure of the genial, popular but undistinguished sovereign signalled that traditional forms of representation had lost their validity. This life-size portrait is more likely to excite mirth or pity than awe.

Far right: **Emperor Francis I of Austria and his Family** (1826), by Leopold Fertbauer. A new style of portraiture for a modern bourgeois sovereign. This presentation of simplicity, economy, and the family virtues pointed the way to a fresh legitimation of monarchy.

family man and simple farmer (George III). Representational portraits of monarchs swathed in ermine and dripping with jewellery continued to be painted, but now seemed anachronistic—what the nineteenth century needed was the royal family portrayed as good solid bourgeois, as in the scenes of a dowdy Queen Victoria and her exemplary Prince Consort surrounded by their ever-growing brood. The Church as a patron declined sharply in relative importance, its authority eroded by creeping secularization and its material resources destroyed in many parts of Europe by expropriation during the Revolutionary–Napoleonic period. Although still formidable, the élites' control of culture was being weakened progressively by the ever-expanding public sphere.

From this crisis—which can reasonably be described as a 'crisis of modernization'—culture emerged as an autonomous force. It was not only liberated by the decline or collapse of its old political, religious, or social masters, it was strengthened by the need of the growing intelligentsia to find a secular substitute for—or supplement to—revealed religion. The solution offered by the French Revolution—political activism—was discredited by the excesses it inspired and the degeneration of liberty into despotism. Especially in German-speaking Europe,

The Rijksmuseum, Amsterdam. Designed by P. J. H. Cuijpers and built between 1877 and 1885, this was only one of a host of grand museums constructed in every European city in the course of the nineteenth century. Witnesses to the sacralization of art, they are the cathedrals of the modern age.

there was a flight from the mob and the guillotine to the unsullied world of the spirit. In his *Letters on the Aesthetic Education of Mankind* (1795) Schiller argued that true emancipation could be found only through aesthetics—through beauty to freedom. Four years later the less rigorous but more evocative Novalis gave the definitive version of what many might regard as escapism: 'Whoever feels unhappy in this world, whoever fails to find what he seeks—then let him enter the world of books, the arts and nature, this eternal domain which is both ancient and modern simultaneously, and let him live there in this secret church of a better world. There he will surely find a lover and a friend, a fatherland and a God.'

In other words, secularization, in which revealed religion and the churches lost their dominant position, was accompanied by sacralization, in which art rose above its old handmaiden status to full autonomy and in the process acquired a new sense of self-importance and seriousness. Visual evidence can be found in the scores of museums which sprang up across Europe, built to resemble temples or churches. The first state museum ('founded by the authority of Parliament') was the British Museum, deriving from the bequest by the Irish doctor Sir Hans Sloane in 1753, although it was first housed in a converted mansion and did not move to its present location until a century later. Commensurate with its new importance, Sir Robert Smirke's majestic structure in Bloomsbury, with its great Ionic colonnades, took almost a quarter of a century to build (1823–47). The first custom-built museum in Europe was the *Museum Fridericianum* at Kassel (1769–

130

79), but it was not until the following century that its example was followed generally: by the Rijksmuseum in Amsterdam (founded 1800, present buildings 1877–85), the Glyptothek in Munich (1816–30), the Prado in Madrid (1819), the Old Museum in Berlin (1823–30), the National Gallery in London (founded 1824, present buildings 1833–8), the Alte Pinakothek in Munich (1824–36), the Fitzwilliam Museum in Cambridge (1837–47), and the Historical Museum in Moscow (1874–83), just to mention a few of the major foundations. Of course not all great collections acquired their own purpose-built shrines, obvious exceptions being the Louvre and the Vatican. The Hermitage in St Petersburg falls somewhere in between, being housed partly in the Winter Palace but acquiring an adjoining temple-like structure from Leo von Klenze (1784–1864) in 1838–52; this structure was also Russia's first purpose-built gallery. Whatever the original function of the building, the sacral nature of a pilgrimage to the galleries was heightened by leading the visitor to the exhibits via carefully arranged steps, portico, hall, staircase, landing, and ante-chamber—in just the same way that subjects had once approached the throne-room. But now it was not the sovereign but Art which was the object to be venerated.

The same trend can also be observed in the construction of theatres. Traditionally, they formed part of the palace, often gorgeously decorated to be sure, but externally only one part of a greater representational whole. Even municipal theatres were usually incorporated in a continuous street façade. The first free-standing theatre in France, for example, was Soufflot's Grand-Théâtre at Lyons (1753–6), built to look like a noble palace. By the early nineteenth century, theatres

The Festival Theatre at Bayreuth. Seen here soon after completion in 1876, it stands on a green hill outside the town. Intended by Wagner to be a place of pilgrimage for the redemption of mankind, it remains the scene of the most important musical festival in the world.

were becoming more like temples, the most striking examples being the San Carlo Opera House at Naples (1810–12) of Antonio Niccolini (1772–1850), or the theatre on the Gendarmenmarkt in Berlin (1818–26) of Karl Friedrich Schinkel (1781–1841), or the Alexandrinsky theatre in St Petersburg (1827–32) of Karl Ivanovich Rossi (1775–1849). It was a trend taken to a characteristic extreme by Richard Wagner's Festival Theatre at Bayreuth (1872–6), placed in splendid isolation on a green hill overlooking the small town of Bayreuth ('without a city wall') in Franconia. To attend the annual festival there was as little like 'going to the opera' as it is possible to imagine. The visitors were not paying customers but pilgrims (Wagner's original intention had been not to charge for admission), joining with the best singers and instrumentalists (who were expected to give their services free) in a common redemptive exercise. This austerity was thrown into sharper relief by the flamboyance of the almost exactly simultaneous construction of the Paris Opéra (1860–75), whose neo-baroque exterior was mirrored by equally sumptuous decoration inside. It was no accident that the relatively small auditorium was overshadowed by the grand staircase and *salles de promenade*, for the building's main function was not musical but social—to allow members of the Parisian élite to parade in front of each other.

Wealth and Status

The juxtaposition of the Paris Opéra and Bayreuth well demonstrates the artist's two means of social advancement—making money or becoming a high priest of the sacralized secular culture. The opportunities for getting rich multiplied during the nineteenth century, interrupted only by periodic revolutions or slumps. Increasing literacy, a growing population, urbanization, more leisure time, improved technology (especially in paper-making and printing), new retailing techniques (the railway station bookstall, for example), more secure copyright, and faster communications all combined to create a vastly expanded market for the consumption of cultural artefacts. Successful British novelists such as Sir Walter Scott (1771–1832), William Thackeray (1811–63), Charles Dickens (1812– 70), Anthony Trollope (1815–82), and George Eliot (the *nom de plume* of Mary Ann Evans, 1819–80) became rich

Facing: **The Paris Opéra**. This painting by Edouard Detaille shows the grand staircase during the opening ceremony on 5 January 1875. Providing the starkest possible contrast with the Bayreuth Festival Theatre, the Opéra was designed as a framework within which Parisian high society could dazzle and be dazzled.

Sir Walter Scott, by Sir Francis Grant (1810–78). The adoring greyhounds symbolize Scott's status as a country gentleman and his devotion to field sports. Yet it had been his eye for the market opportunities presented by urbanization and growing literacy which enabled him to win, lose, and recoup a great fortune.

beyond the dreams of avarice of earlier generations. Trollope was quite frank about his motivation: 'I write for money. Of course I do. It is for money that we all work, lawyers, publishers, authors and the rest.' Literature became a profession. In his novel *New Grub Street*, George Gissing (1857–1903) proclaimed through one of his characters: 'Literature nowadays is a trade . . . your successful man of letters is your skilful tradesman. He thinks first and foremost of markets; when one kind of goods begins to go off slackly, he is ready with something new.'

In this respect, an instructive comparison can be made between the careers of Mozart, who travelled infrequently and in great discomfort across western Europe, giving concerts to small audiences for modest returns, with that of Liszt, who swept from the Pyrenees to the Urals, performing before thousands of people at a time and accumulating great wealth in the process. It has been estimated that he appeared in public well over a thousand times between 1838 and 1846. At a recital in Milan he was asked to improvise on 'the railway', the wonderful new invention which had allowed him to travel from Venice in six hours: undaunted, he responded with a dazzling sequence of *glissandi*. The railway became a potent symbol of progress: in the words of the German industrialist Friedrich Harkort, writing in 1840: 'The locomotive is the hearse which will carry absolutism and feudalism to the graveyard.' Reproduced in visual images without number, the railway station provided the opening setting for works as diverse as Tolstoy's *Anna Karenina* and Offenbach's *La Vie Parisienne*. It was appropriate that in this commercialized age of the railway, touring musicians could become famous just for being rich: Johann Strauss the elder, for example, about whom *The Musical World* wrote in 1838: 'Who has not heard of Strauss, the *Crœsus* of waltz composers,—him who scours round the world and returns home ten thousand pounds the richer man? We were not a little anxious to meet this *modern Midas*.'

Commercialization and the communications revolution together brought the democratization of culture. In the eighteenth century, very few newspapers enjoyed a circulation of 20,000; the *Petit Journal* of Paris, thriving on a diet of scandal and sensation, passed the 1 million mark in 1887. In the eighteenth century, theatres were few and socially exclusive; by the 1880s, at least half a million Parisians were going to the theatre once a week, with a million going once a month. In the eighteenth century, concerts were mainly confined to aristocratic salons or associations of connoisseurs, although in London in the 1790s the entrepreneur Johann Peter Salomon showed the way forward with his subscription concerts at the Hanover Square Rooms. By 1880 Parisians could choose between three series of popular concerts at the cavernous Cirque d'Hivers, the Cirque d'Été, and the Châtelet, where among other things they could join in the brawls which erupted when Wagner's music was played. In the eighteenth century, only those who lived in the great capitals of Europe might hope to see a painting outside church, and then only very infrequently; by the late nineteenth century, developments in printing and photography allowed every home to hang reproductions of masters great and small, ancient and modern, on the wall.

Mass participation in culture was not confined to purchasing upright pianos, 'penny dreadful' novels, or reproductions of Landseer's *The Monarch of the Glen*.

Facing, above: **The Monk by the Sea.** Painted in 1809 by Caspar David Friedrich, the greatest of the German romantic artists, it was bought by King Frederick William III of Prussia for his fifteen-year-old son. This intensely introspective and near-abstract study of death exemplifies Friedrich's characteristically German combination of expressive aesthetics with deep religiosity.

Facing, below: **Romans of the Decadence,** by Thomas Couture. This enormous canvas (4.75 × 7.9 metres) was a richly deserved sensation when exhibited at the Paris Salon in 1847, brilliantly combining a moral message with visual titillation. The two Germanic 'barbarians' solemnly observing the scene at the far right of the picture represent the virile invaders from beyond the Rhine who were soon to put an end to Roman civilization (and whose successors were to conquer Couture's own country in 1870).

It was often mediated through a voluntary association. It had been through organizations such as masonic lodges, reading clubs, and literary societies that the public sphere had first emerged, but it was not until the nineteenth century that associations for almost every imaginable form of cultural activity were formed. 'We live today in the epoch of associations!' trumpeted a reporter covering the great choral festival held at Mainz in 1835 to raise money for a memorial to the city's most famous son, the inventor of printing Johannes Gutenberg (1400–68), and he went on to stress their variety: 'from the great stock companies for steam-driven ships, locomotives and railways, to the confederations of tailors' journeymen, from the gigantic assemblies of natural scientists to the reading circles organized by the village barber, from the monster music-festivals in England to the equally earnest singing clubs of our beloved German fatherland, everywhere everyone seems to venerate the old principle: *Concordia parvae res crescunt* [it is by co-operation that small things grow]!' All over Europe, greater prosperity and improved communications allowed very large numbers of people from many different regions to come together in great cultural festivals. Here again, the English were in the van with the Three Choirs Festival, which dates back to 1715, and the great Handel Commemorations, beginning in 1784; it was not until the French Revolution and beyond that the more fragmented continental countries began to follow.

Never mind the width, feel the quality, lamented the artists, as they watched the grubby hands of the masses soiling their sacred culture: 'The musical fever which has gripped our age will be the ruin of art, for popularity is very close to vulgarity' was a characteristic complaint from a French periodical in 1846. Nor does this élitism seem so unreasonable when one discovers that at just this time at popular concerts the movements of a Beethoven symphony had to be sandwiched between sessions of dance-music; or that Beethoven's Septet was arranged by an Italian music-publisher for accordion and piano; or that sacred music was rewritten for the dancehall (the '*Stabat Mater* Quadrilles', for example); or that, at the Promenade Concerts at the Royal Adelaide Gallery in the Strand, selections from the latest Meyerbeer opera were accompanied by 'the real Scotch Quadrilles, introducing the Highland pipes . . . followed by the performances of the Infant Thalia, Experiments with the Colossal Burning Lens and the new Oxyhydrogen Microscope, Popular Lectures, and The Laughing Gas every Tuesday, Thursday and Saturday evenings'.

So it was not just a question of money. To achieve celebrity unstained with contempt, the artist had to be successful *on his or her own terms*, not by following popular fashion. For all the arts, the great role-model for the nineteenth century was Beethoven, whose very appearance proclaimed rugged integrity and independence. Recalling his feelings on hearing a Beethoven symphony for the first time, Wagner wrote: 'Its effect on me was indescribable. On top of this came the added impact of Beethoven's physiognomy, as shown by lithographs of the time, as well as the knowledge of his deafness and his solitary and withdrawn life. There soon arose in me an image of the most sublime, supernatural originality, beyond comparison with anything.' So powerful was Beethoven's influence that it lasted into

Facing: **Louis XVI in his Coronation Robes**, by Joseph Siffrein Duplessis. A quintessentially representational portrait of the old regime. The gorgeous robes, attributes of kingship (the crown and sceptre), and suitably commanding expression are all designed to create an aura of authority. The revolutionaries were not impressed.

the following century, reaching its apotheosis in 1902 when the artists of the Vienna Secession decided to transform their entire building into a temple to receive the statue of Beethoven by the Leipzig sculptor Max Klinger. Among the contributions was a frieze painted by Gustav Klimt (1862–1918), the last panel of which was inspired by 'This kiss to the whole world' from Schiller's *Ode to Joy* (and thus Beethoven's Ninth Symphony) and bore the legend 'the longing for happiness finds its surcease in poetry'. The accompanying catalogue suggested that 'here art leads us into the ideal realm, wherein alone we can find pure joy, pure happiness, pure love'.

Following Beethoven's example was not always easy, but it was something an increasing number of artists liked to boast about in their autobiographies. The composer and violinist Louis Spohr (1784–1859), for example, recorded with pride that he had resolutely refused to play at the court of the king of Württemberg unless the royal card-playing ceased during his performance. Such gestures had a necessarily limited impact. What was really needed were artists who could reach out beyond the court and make an impact on the general public. The artist best equipped for this task was the musician, thanks to his ability to appeal to a large number of people through their emotions simultaneously and collectively. Operating in a medium which speaks to the psyche directly, without any mediat-

At the Railway, by Vasily Grigorievich Perov. Painted in 1868, just as the railway age was beginning—rather belatedly—in Russia, this is an unsurpassed visual representation of the confrontation between traditional and modern culture. As the iron locomotive thunders by on its undeviating tracks, the humans left in its wake are torn between curiosity, wonder, amusement, and fear.

136

ing word or image, the musician is the quintessentially charismatic artist. The painter, architect, dramatist, novelist, or even poet can never generate such excitement. So it was during the early decades of the nineteenth century that music began its relentless march from subordinate artistic genre to its present-day hegemony.

This development was greatly assisted by the fortuitous coincidence of three great musicians—Niccolo Paganini (1782–1840), Gioacchino Rossini (1792–1868), and Franz Liszt, whose impact on European audiences was without precedent. Significantly, the fame of the three men owed as much to their carefully nurtured image as it did to their superlative musical skills. Paganini was widely believed to be in league with the devil, having sold his soul to acquire superhuman ability, and would never remove his boots lest he reveal his cloven hoof. As he did not begin to tour until 1828, it was rumoured that he had spent the previous twenty years in prison for the murder of his mistress, whose intestines he had converted into strings for his violin and whose soul he had imprisoned in its sound-box. His jet-black hair, deathly pallor, and ugly-handsome saturnine features, ravaged by the mercury with which he vainly tried to arrest syphilis, made an unforgettable impression on all who saw him. He was also a master-showman, playing up his secrecy and supposed diabolism—coming on stage, for example, with three strings dangling uselessly from his instrument, then dazzling the audience with a virtuoso performance on the survivor. His fame was best summed up by a verse

The 1859 Crystal Palace Handel Festival (2 July 1859). To commemorate the centenary of Handel's death, an orchestra of 450 and a choir of 2,700 performed *The Messiah* before an audience of tens of thousands. Only the invention of electronic amplification and reproduction could democratize music further.

137

left on the score of his second concerto by an adoring musician at the Academy in Paris after a performance:

> Nature wished to show in our century
>   her infinite power;
> So, to astonish the world, she created two men:
>   Bonaparte and Paganini!

Both Rossini and Liszt were also compared to Napoleon, the former by no less a person than Stendhal (the *nom de plume* of Henri Beyle, 1783–1842): 'Napoleon is dead; but a new conqueror has already shown himself to the world; and from Moscow to Naples, from London to Vienna, from Paris to Calcutta, his name is constantly on every tongue. The fame of this hero knows no bounds save those of civilization itself—and he is not yet thirty-two!' Liszt combined the raffishness of Paganini with the sobriety of Rossini and added to both a dignity and intellectualism which raised the status of the musician to heights unknown. He was the man who could be rude to kings, was rumoured to be engaged to the queen of Spain, coined the phrase '*génie oblige*', and demonstrated his equality with aristocrats by seducing their wives and sleeping with their daughters. He paved the way for the apotheosis of the musician in the shape of his even more imperious son-in-law, Richard Wagner, to whose Festival Theatre at Bayreuth for the opening night in 1876 came the sovereign of the most powerful state on earth—William I, German emperor. How things had changed since that day in June 1781 when Mozart had been thrown out of the room by his employer's chamberlain, Count Arco, and given a kick to his backside to boot! If Mozart's notorious burial in a mass grave was less unusual than some have supposed, his obsequies were certainly less impressive than those devoted to Beethoven, whose coffin was followed by an immense crowd estimated at between 10,000 and 30,000, with a school holiday proclaimed by the emperor and the funeral oration written by Austria's greatest playwright, Franz Grillparzer (1791–1872).

The artists also enhanced their status by playing a leading role in the great public issues of the day. Romantics may have given priority to the inner world of the spirit in theory, but in practice most found it impossible to avoid being carried along with the rest of society. In the process, they created quite a new kind of topical art. It was no longer the monopoly of official artists recording only their patron's triumphs, it became much more spontaneous, individual, passionate—and memorable. Among the images which impressed both contemporaries and posterity more powerfully than—say—any great fresco by one of Louis XIV's court painters were Goya's *The Third of May 1808*, recording the terrible reprisals exacted by the French occupying force in Madrid after the insurrection of the previous day; or Caspar David Friedrich's *Chasseur in the Forest* (1814), utterly different in style and mood, yet on the same theme, depicting a French soldier standing alone and lost in the snow-covered clearing of a German forest, as a raven on a tree-stump croaks out his doom; or Delacroix's *Scenes from the Massacres at Chios* (1824), the greatest visual statement of the European intelligentsia's support for the Greek struggle for independence from the Turks; or the same artist's *July 28th: Liberty Leading the People*, painted after the revolution of 1830, in which a bare-breasted woman carrying

Kaiser William I arrives at Bayreuth railway station, 12 August 1876. That the ruler of the most powerful state on the continent of Europe should travel all the way from Berlin to a small Franconian town to attend the first cycle of Wagner's *Ring* was conclusive evidence of the rise in the creative artist's status.

the tricolour storms with irresistible élan through gun-smoke, over a barricade and a pile of dead bodies towards the viewer, supported by a worker, a student, and a child. Less direct in their allusions but no less topical were Théodore Géricault's *The Raft of the Medusa* of 1819, which attacked the aristocratic corruption of the Bourbon restoration, and Thomas Couture's *Romans of the Decadence*, exhibited at the last Salon before the revolutions of 1848.

Although all these paintings were critical of the *status quo*, there is no clear political direction to be inferred. When Lucien Chardon, the central character in Balzac's novel *Lost Illusions* (written 1837–43 but set in 1821–2), arrives in Paris, he is told firmly that 'the royalists are romantics, the liberals are classicists'. Given the French Revolution's preference for neo-classicism, that seems entirely plausible. However, in 1826 the famous slogan '*le romanticisme est le libéralisme en littérature*' (romanticism is liberalism in literature) first appeared and in the following year the critic Auguste Jal defined romantic painting as 'the cannon shot of 1789', which seems just as plausible when one looks at Delacroix's *Liberty Leading the People*. The safe but bland conclusion must be that even an identifiable movement such as romanticism can be assigned no clear location on the left–right spectrum.

Facing: **Beethoven,** by Max Klinger (1902). Not only for musicians was Beethoven the great Promethean figure. All the artists of the Vienna Secession co-operated to create a setting worthy of their hero: 'Having been prepared by every available means for reverence, one arrives before [the statue] in a kind of hypnosis', reported a local art critic.

Nationalism

In any case, that horizontal axis was being increasingly confused by a vertical scale of loyalties determined by nationality. The culture of the eighteenth-century

Enlightenment had been self-consciously cosmopolitan, a position neatly summarized by Voltaire: 'I prefer my family to myself, my fatherland to my family, and the human race to my fatherland.' Following the trail blazed by Rousseau and Herder, the romantics rejected the universal natural law on which this cosmopolitanism was based. In their view, human beings differed from one epoch to another and from one country to another. The natural unit was not the abstract individual but the concrete community, identified by a common culture, of which the most important element was language. Each national group had its own special identity, deriving from a complex interaction of historical, geographical, political, and cultural forces, which it should seek to protect and develop. In the words of Friedrich Schleiermacher (1768–1834), the Prussian philosopher and theologian: 'every language constitutes a particular mode of thought, and what is thought in one language can never be repeated in the same way in another.' Two kinds of nationalism developed: first a cultural form, which identified the nation as the most important point of reference in human affairs, the supreme source of value and focus for loyalty; and later a political form, which sought to make the political and cultural boundaries of a state coincide. The latter was, of course, especially prevalent among national minorities in multinational empires (the Habsburg and Russian empires being the prime examples) or among national groups divided among more than one state (such as the Italians and the Germans before unification).

The extraordinary power exerted by nationalism during the nineteenth (and indeed the twentieth) century was due to the depth and variety of its sources. In part it stemmed from the need to find a secular alternative to religion (as, for example, in the invocation of the French nationalist historian Jules Michelet (1798–1874): 'Oh glorious mother of France! You who are not only our own, but who are destined to carry liberty to every nation, teach us to love one another in you'); in part from a more general process of social modernization which was destroying old landmarks and transforming a network of particularist communities (*Gemeinschaft*) into a single atomized society (*Gesellschaft*); in part from the awesome power unleashed by the French Revolution and its principle of national sovereignty; and in part from the reaction against the conquest and exploitation of the rest of Europe which that power made possible. Nationalism influenced the creative artist in two distinct ways. On the one hand, it encouraged the creation of work with a nationalist message, as in many of the early operas of Giuseppe Verdi (1813–1902), 'the musical Garibaldi' as one French critic called him, whose *La Battaglia di Legnano* (1849) begins with the following chorus:

> Long live Italy!
> A holy pact
>   binds all her sons together.
> At last it has made of so many
>   a single people of heroes!

Although the work ostensibly deals with the Lombard League's defeat of the German emperor Frederick Barbarossa's army in 1176, audiences had no difficulty in reading the topical message. At the opening night in Rome in January 1849, the excitement was such that the last act was encored *in its entirety*. When revived eleven years later during the eventual unification of Italy, it was actually renamed *The Defeat of the Austrians*. Examples of this kind could be repeated *ad infinitum*, from every artistic genre. In particular, just a glance at public buildings in every European capital will reveal a plethora of nationalist images.

Nationalism also influenced European culture in a more subtle way, by making its creators aware of their national identity and encouraging them to find a national voice. This too stemmed from the proto-romantic theorists of the eighteenth century, especially Herder, who found the social location of true cultural value not among the classically trained élites with their elegant but superficial Frenchified sophistication but among the common people—*Das Volk*. It was through their folk-songs, folk-poetry, and folk-dances that the authentic spirit of the nation was made manifest. A growing number of artists turned from studying classical models in pursuit of ideal beauty to their own native traditions, seeking to reproduce the images, styles, rhythms, or melodies they found there in their own work. The result was a prolifera-

This title-page of a piano arrangement of *From Bohemia's Fields and Groves*, the fourth movement of Bedřich Smetana's tone-poem *Má Vlast* [My Fatherland], presents Czech nationality in an idyllically rural setting. Yet it was rapid urbanization which created the demand for an authentically Czech voice.

tion of self-consciously national styles. For most of the eighteenth century, an equally self-conscious international style had ruled the various arts, making it both impossible and pointless to identify the nationality of any particular work. But no one would suppose that Delacroix was anything but a Frenchman or Friedrich anything but a German, while one need only hear a bar or two of Gaetano Donizetti (1797–1848) to know that he was Italian or an equally short snatch of Mikhail Ivanovich Glinka (1804–57) to know that he was Russian (notwithstanding G. B. Shaw's acerbic comment on Edvard Grieg (1843–1907): 'his music does not remind me of Norway, perhaps because I have never been there').

The arts returned the compliment by expressing—and in large measure creating—the common culture without which no nation-state can survive. Indeed, the 'submerged nations' of eastern Europe owe their existence to the efforts of diligent (and often inventive) philologists, historians, and poets. Even such well-established peoples as

the Czechs, with a long if chequered history, found it essential in the nineteenth century to rediscover their own culture. For them, the long campaign to build a National Theatre at Prague, financed entirely by public subscription, and to perform there historical dramas such as Smetana's opera *Libuše* (1881) on a stage whose proscenium arch bore the legend '*Národ sobě*' (The nation to itself), was a powerful integrating force in the face of what they believed to be German oppression. It was also culture which allowed another oppressed nation—the Jews—to celebrate their formal emancipation from the ghetto with truly spectacular achievements. In the previous eighteen hundred years, the only Jew to have made a major impact on European culture had been the philosopher Baruch de Spinoza (1632–77). Yet artists of Jewish origin formed perhaps the most distinguished single group in nineteenth- (and twentieth-)century Europe, especially in music. The explanation for this extraordinary burst of creative energy has been sought in European Jewry's simultaneous liberation from the physical ghettoes of central Europe and the intellectual constraints of orthodox Judaism. For once, a simple list of names *is* helpful: Giacomo Meyerbeer (1791–1864), Heinrich Heine (1797–1856), Jacques Halévy (1799–1862), Felix Mendelssohn (1809–47), Karl Marx (1818–83), Jacques Offenbach (1819–80), Joseph Joachim (1831–1907), Max Bruch (1838–1920), Sigmund Freud (1856–1939), Gustav Mahler (1860–1911), Arnold Schoenberg (1874–1951), Albert Einstein (1880–1952), Franz Kafka (1883–1924)—just to name the most prominent.

Nationalism also built a bridge between state and artist. Slowly, fitfully but surely, governments came to realize that culture is power, and not only in the obvious sense that educated citizens are more useful than illiterate subjects. It was also realized, especially after 1789, that in a secularized age national symbols and cultural institutions were needed to bind state and society. Hence the proliferation of academies, museums, galleries, public memorials, festivals, and so on, all of which provided commissions. One need only contemplate the marble memorials crammed into Westminster Abbey, or Valhalla, the German Pantheon built by Klenze for King Ludwig I of Bavaria outside Regensburg, to appreciate how much sculptors, for example, owed to the new need to sacralize the nation's past. When the amiable if indiscreet Ludwig was obliged to abdicate in 1848 due to his affair with 'Lola Montez' (the stage name of the Irish dancer Maria Gilbert), the artists of Bavaria were quite right to issue a statement lamenting his departure as an 'unmitigated disaster'. At a time when even railway stations were being made to look like Gothic castles (St Pancras), renaissance palaces (the Gare de l'Est), or Greek temples (Euston), and were being decorated accordingly, the demand for artists had never been greater.

This natural alliance between intelligentsia and the state was more obvious to some contemporaries than to others. As early as 1833 the great German historian Leopold von Ranke (1795–1886) could write: 'If the main event of the hundred years before the French Revolution was the rise of the great powers in defence of European independence, so the main event of the period since then is the fact that nationalities were rejuvenated, revived, and developed anew. They became a part of the state, for it was realized that without them the state could not exist.' The gov-

ernments of Europe were not yet listening: in the 1830s nationalism was still too closely associated with the French Revolution to be welcomed into the establishment. So the repression of the Restoration period after 1815 drove nationalism into an unnatural alliance with liberalism and sent nationalist intellectuals into prison or exile. It was not until the later part of the century that more acute statesmen such as Bismarck grasped the ideology's integrative potential. By 1900 colossal national memorials such as the Memorial to Victor Emmanuel in Rome and the Memorial to the Battle of the Nations at Leipzig (which attracted 600,000 visitors even during construction) were rising to proclaim the unity of state and society under the aegis of the sacralization of the nation. Most artists nestled snugly into the opulent welcoming embrace of the state, many took the money with a mental reservation and guilty conscience, some resolutely ploughed a lone furrow. Perhaps the best metaphor for this problematic relationship was Friedrich Dahlmann's phallic description of the Prussian state as 'the magic spear which heals as well as wounds'.

The monument to Victor Emmanuel II, Rome. New nations felt they needed triumphalist structures to legitimate their creation. None was more pompous than this vast pile, begun in 1885 to the designs of Count Giuseppe Sacconi but not completed until 1922—the year that Mussolini came to power.

Realism

The uneasy relationship between state and intelligentsia over nationalism had been accompanied by a crisis over the 'social question'. The various forms of dislocation caused by industrialization and urbanization convinced many observers that the poor were becoming both more wretched, more numerous, and more dangerous. This did not mean that all artists became socialists, but it did mean that a growing number of them chose the material conditions of the here and now as their central concern. By the 1840s, a reaction against romanticism and its introspective spirituality was due anyway. It was no accident that the literary genre best suited to the new direction, first known as 'realism' and later as 'naturalism', was the novel, for the world of the modern city was prosaic rather than poetic. In works such as Dickens's *Oliver Twist* (1837–9), Gustav Freytag's *Profit and Loss* (1855), Dostoevsky's *Crime and Punishment* (1866), or the twenty volumes of Émile Zola's 'Rougon-Macquart' cycle (1870–93), the wonderful variety of commercialized urban society was usually less apparent than its attendant squalor and tension. This was the realm of anomie, that sense of moral rootlessness which the French sociologist Émile Durkheim (1858–1917) identified as the essence of the human condition in the industrialized world.

Also naturally suited for capturing contemporary reality was painting, which found an articulate spokesman for the new approach in Gustave Courbet (1819–77), as well as a wonderfully gifted practitioner. Among his trenchant observations on the nature of his art were 'painting is an essentially *concrete* art and can only consist of the presentation of *real and existing things*', and the quintessentially anti-romantic jibe: 'show me an angel and I'll paint it!' Although never a propagandist, Courbet was very much a man of the left, a republican and supporter of the revolutionary Commune of 1871, who paid for his beliefs by spending two years in prison and the rest of his life in exile. Together with Jean François Millet (1814–75) and Edouard Manet (1832–83) he represented, as it were, the 'heroic' phase of realism, all funerals, firing-squads, hunched peasant women, and horny-handed sons of toil. Shown the way forward by Manet, in the 1870s a younger generation of painters lightened both the mood and their palettes. The 'impressionists', notably

The Stone-breakers,
by Gustave Courbet. Although the original was destroyed by bombing in the Second World War, this remains the quintessential realist painting. First exhibited in Paris in 1850, its bleak depiction of the labouring poor at work struck contemporaries as the artistic equivalent of the 1848 revolution.

Camille Pissarro (1830–1903), Edgar Degas (1834–1917), Alfred Sisley (1839–99), Claude Monet (1840–1926), Pierre-Auguste Renoir (1841–1919), and Georges Seurat (1859–91) moved from the place of work to the place of recreation—to the garden, seaside, racetrack, dancehall, or theatre. Their dazzling explorations of light in every conceivable shape and form were to become *the* great artistic success story of the following century, in both auction-rooms and on chocolate boxes. This realist trend was underpinned by a positivist belief in the natural sciences; as Zola wrote of the Salon of 1866 'The wind blows in the direction of science. Despite ourselves, we are

Iron and Coal, by William Bell Scott. Painted in 1861 as part of a series of eight murals describing the history of Northumberland, this presentation of the workplace packs less of a punch than Courbet's bleak vision. Yet ultimately its optimistic picture of the potential of industrialization proved more accurate.

pushed towards the exact study of facts and things.' So it seemed almost as if the wheel had turned full circle and the sunlit, superficial days of the Enlightenment had returned.

Fin De Siècle

Realism triumphed after 1850 with what appeared to be the forces of progress—liberalism, nationalism, and industrialization. This was the period when Italy and Germany were unified, when liberals took control in one state after another (even in the multinational Habsburg empire), and when in just a few years villages could become towns, towns cities, and cities metropolises. As is the way with progress, disillusionment was not long delayed. The social tensions created by the long recession beginning in 1873 and the eruption of new mass political forces, with socialism, clericalism, and anti-semitism to the fore, ensured that this bourgeois liberal culture did not reign for long. Once again the 'grandfather law' asserted itself, as a younger generation reverted to earlier models and discovered the wheel again. In 1888 the 20-year-old French painter Émile Bernard repeated Friedrich's maxim of sixty years before when he stated that the artist should not paint what he

Medicine, by Gustav Klimt, captures perfectly the *fin de siècle* mood. Completed in 1901 as one of three paintings commissioned for the University of Vienna, this erotic phantasmagoria not surprisingly aroused fierce controversy. Behind the figure of Hygeia, the Greek goddess of health, lurk more interesting phenomena than physical fitness and wholesome hygiene, notably sex and death.

sees in front of him but the idea of the thing he sees in his imagination. Similarly, the central tenet of what became known as 'symbolism', as expressed by its main organ *Symbolist*—'Objectivity is nothing but vain appearance, that I may vary or transform as I wish'—could have been said by any romantic two or three generations earlier. The old romantic obsessions with death, the night, and sex were all back in favour again, nowhere more powerfully than in Gustav Klimt's notorious ceiling paintings for the University of Vienna. What the academics had wanted and expected was a portrayal of the victory of reason, knowledge, and enlightenment; what they got was a world turned upside down, in which 'Philosophy' is subconscious instinct, 'Medicine' is overshadowed by death, and justice in 'Jurisprudence' is a cowed and helpless victim of the law.

By the time Klimt came to create these wonderful paintings (1898–1904), art was fragmenting into stylistic anarchy: the decadent movement, symbolism, synthetism, neo-impressionism, post-impressionism, constructivism, fauvism, expressionism, cubism, futurism, constructivism, orphism, neo-plasticism, vorticism, suprematicism, and so on. The disintegration of Europe's classical vocabulary, which had begun with the romantic revolution a century earlier, was now complete. Even this multiplicity of -isms cannot accommodate an isolated genius such as Vincent Van Gogh (1853–90), who belongs in a category of one and who can yet serve as an appropriate symbol for the fate of the creative artist in the postromantic age. In the course of his life, which was a constant struggle with poverty, lack of recognition, alcoholism, and insanity, ending in suicide, he sold just one of his 850-odd paintings—*Red Orchard* for 400 francs to a Belgian artist. At the time of writing, his *Portrait of Dr Gachet* holds the record for the most expensive painting ever sold at public auction, having been sold in 1990 to a Japanese papermanufacturer for $82,500,000.

With the avant-garde thrusting into the new century and untold wealth (the ultimate accolade in a commercialized society but, alas, very often only awarded posthumously), it is time to stop. There are many ways of finding patterns in the infinite diversity of nineteenth-century European culture, most of them valid and none of them sufficient. To approach it by tracing the abrasive relationship between sacralization and commercialization at least has the merit of linking cultural artefacts to the society which produced them without reducing them to 'superstructure'. The friction generated between spirit and matter also helps to explain the extraordinary vitality of a culture which colonized the world. As Kant observed (and theorists as diverse as Grillparzer and T. S. Eliot repeated in their different ways): 'man wishes concord, but nature, knowing better what is good for his species, wishes discord.'

6

The Great Civil War

European Politics, 1914–1945

PAUL
PRESTON

THE long peace from Bismarck's triumphs to the outbreak of war in 1914 was a period of optimistic belief in progress, economic and technological. This confidence was sustained by the growing prosperity of capitalist economies and the self-adjusting mechanisms of the balance of power. However, the disproportionate growth of one of those economies would soon throw the balance of power out of kilter. This was not just because the burgeoning economic and military strength of Germany was to become increasingly difficult to contain. Rather it was a consequence of the fact that Germany's ruling classes chose to cope with the domestic problems arising from industrialization, urbanization, and the emergence of a powerful socialist movement by a process of what has come to be known as 'negative integration'. This essentially meant that rather than adjust to domestic challenges, the German ruling classes chose to submerge, or indeed export, them by uniting the nation against the spectre of foreign enemies. To a lesser extent, other states also tried to sidestep their domestic problems by similar means. With stark differences of emphasis and with dramatically different consequences in each case, a recognizably similar story can be told for Germany, Austria-Hungary, Russia, Italy, France, and Britain.

The collective consequence was that, between 1914 and 1945, the energies of Europe were to be consumed in a long intermittent war whose economic and human costs would see world pre-eminence pass from the great European empires to the United States and the Soviet Union. The internal pressures of industrialization—internal migration, urbanization, the emergence of a new working class, and its creation in self-defence of societies, unions, and political parties—constituted a challenge to the existing order. Addressed flexibly, this challenge might have been resolved to the benefit of European society. In fact,

148

Death in winter. A view of the battlefield after Russian troops were defeated by the Germans at Naroczsee in northern Poland at the end of March 1916.

only in Scandinavia, the Low Countries, France, and Britain, and then only partially, did this happen. Elsewhere, in the most restless of the advanced industrial states—Germany—and in several of the more prominent developing ones—Russia, Italy, Spain—the response was repression and a consequent intensification of class confrontation. In addition, there was an equally potent challenge to the established order arising from nationalism—both the small-scale nationalisms threatening to break up the balance of power in eastern Europe and the large-scale nationalist ambitions of Russia, Italy, and above all Germany.

In the midst of this cauldron of instability, there were, in the broadest terms, two sorts of state: those which were sufficiently flexible, open to popular pressure, more or less democratic, and with the safety-valve of colonial empires, such as Britain and France; and those with rigid, authoritarian (if apparently democratic) systems uneasily presiding over highly unstable societies, such as Germany, Austria-Hungary, Italy, Russia, and Spain. To a large extent, the fate of Europe hinged, between 1914 and 1945, as indeed it does now, on the comportment of the state with the largest and most dynamic economy—Germany.

The First World War

It was a savage irony that a war fought in large part to anaesthetize the great problems of the day, social conflict and nationalism, should send them spiralling out of control. Once war was declared, German war aims developed ambitiously. Whereas, before the war, socialist pressure for domestic social spending had been

149

deflected by means of militaristic propaganda, in war there emerged a plan for the permanent resolution of the problem. To put it crudely, socialist demands for a redistribution of national wealth would be rendered obsolete by the plunder of other nations' wealth. The plan was essentially directed at the annexation of the industrialized parts of northern France and Belgium and of Luxembourg, the creation of a central European customs union (*Mitteleuropa*), colonization of the food-producing areas of eastern Europe after the removal of unwanted local populations, and all this as the basis for seizures of British colonies elsewhere. It was to gamble the very survival of the German establishment on victory in war. Had victory been secured, the *Junker* system would have been consolidated on a basis of world mastery.

It quickly became apparent that such triumph would be elusive. There would be none of the swift victories anticipated by General Alfred von Schlieffen. The early defensive victories achieved at the Marne by the French and at Ypres by the British Expeditionary Force ensured a long slogging war. In the first five months of the war, nearly 2 million men were either killed or wounded. Thereafter, there would be little significant movement of the front despite bloody offensives. After initial disasters, the Germans fared better on the eastern front where General Paul von Hindenburg and his chief-of-staff General Erich von Ludendorff masterminded the defeat of the Russians at Tannenberg. Nevertheless, on the western front, railways allowed huge armies to be transported to long defensive fronts. Thereafter, the lack of light armoured transport condemned further advance to the walking pace of the infantry. Alerted to offensive threats by air reconnaissance and radio, reinforcements could always be brought up faster than attackers could break through enemy lines.

It was a war that would be won in the last resort by industrial might, population resources, access to raw materials, and geographical position. The Central Powers had the advantage that troops could be moved from the eastern to the western front as tactics dictated while the western Allies could help Russia only with the greatest difficulty. On the other hand, British command of the sea permitted the blockade of Germany and enabled Britain and France to go on importing food and strategic raw materials from their colonies and from the United States. None the less, given the poor quality of Allied leadership, it is likely that Germany would have won had she not gone to war with the United States in 1917.

From 1915, there developed a war of attrition in which suicidal British and French offensives were broken, at enormous costs on both sides, by the well-dug-in German defensive forces. This was the story at Neuve Chappelle and Loos, in Artois and Champagne. In that one year, the French lost 1,500,000 dead and wounded, the British 300,000, and the Germans 875,000. The Allied methods remained rigidly conservative while the Germans were constantly making barbaric innovations. In April 1915, it was the use of chlorine gas at Ypres. In 1916, the pattern of Allied offensives was reversed with the German assault on Verdun in February. Despite further technical innovations such as flame-throwers, phosgene gas shells, and the use of aircraft, the Germans were held at Verdun, at the cost of nearly 340,000 casualties against the French 380,000. The pattern was reasserted on 1 July 1916 with Haig's ill-fated offensive on the Somme which, in five months, advanced six miles at the cost of 419,000 British casualties, 200,000 French, and 500,000 German. Eventually, and fatefully, the Germans were to pin their hopes on destroying British trade by submarine warfare on merchant shipping on a sink-on-sight basis. The sinking of the British liner the SS *Lusitania* in May 1915 with more than one thousand fatalities including 128 Americans undermined President Wilson's isolationism and brought the United States nearer to war. In January 1917, the German High Command decided to launch unrestricted submarine warfare against all shipping in waters around Britain. This coincided with the interception of the so-called Zimmermann telegram in which Germany offered Mexico the chance to recover Texas and other territories in the south-west of the United States. On 2 April 1917, the United States declared war on Germany.

The scale of the German blunder was compounded by the fact that it brought the United States into the war just as Russia was effectively dropping out and Britain and France were seriously weakened. Strikes, food riots, and a deluge of returning wounded and deserting conscripts swamped the Russian system. The Tsarist system fell, to be replaced by a provisional government of liberals, Mensheviks, and Socialist Revolutionaries. Under Alexander Kerensky, the provisional government committed Russia to fight on in the world war. This played into the hands of Lenin's Bolsheviks and their appealing slogan of 'bread, peace and land'.

The horrors of war.
The city centre of Verdun is pulverized by artillery barrages during the attrition of 1916.

Revolutionary vanguard.
Some of the most determined and effective revolutionaries in the early days of the Russian Revolution were sailors. Here seamen from the cruiser *Aurora* fix bayonets to keep order in Petrograd.

It was a slogan which had little to do with the Bolsheviks' long-term revolutionary goals but it so captured the mood and needs of the peasantry and the peasant conscripts that it gave them a surge of popularity somewhat at odds with their real objectives. In August, General Kornilov tried to use his troops to restore order and put back the clock. He was defeated by working-class resistance and his action fatally wounded Kerensky who was perceived as his accomplice. In November, the Bolsheviks launched their own successful insurrectionary attempt and their revolution was to be the most spectacular example of how the war had fatally weakened the very system whose survival it was meant to strengthen.

With Russian troops deserting on a massive scale, the Germans were now advancing virtually unopposed. Lenin had hoped that the Russian revolutionary example would be emulated in Germany and elsewhere. When it was not, Lenin made a separate peace at Brest-Litovsk. By its terms, Germany achieved its eastern war aims, Russia losing 25 per cent of her European territory including the Ukraine

152

and Finland, 30 per cent of her population, 50 per cent of her coal and iron resources, and 30 per cent of her industry. Victorious in the East, Germany was now in a strong position, as U-boat war had seriously depleted British food supplies and the French offensive of April 1917 had broken on the rock of German defensive arrangements. In response, Haig could produce only another senseless massacre with his third Ypres offensive.

However, the British blockade was taking its toll of German domestic morale and the American presence was now to be decisive in the war. Before American aid could play its full role, the Germans might have been able to tempt the western Allies with a compromise peace suggestion for a withdrawal in the West in return for keeping their eastern conquests. This would have left them in an immensely powerful position for the future but the High Command rejected the possibility. Ludendorff gambled everything on a last offensive in the West. In doing so, he was backed by a fanatically nationalist political party called the Vaterlandspartei which advocated war to the death with the Anglo-Saxon enemy. A series of three attacks in the first half of 1918 drove back the British and French and reversed the heavily bought victories of 1917. However, despite horrendous casualties, the

Right: **Peace without honour.** In order to buy time for his beleaguered Bolshevik regime, Lenin sought to make a separate peace at Brest-Litovsk in the winter of 1917. By the terms exacted there, Germany ruthlessly achieved its eastern war aims. Russia lost great tracts of its European territory, including the Ukraine and Finland, and some its best cultivable land, iron, and coal resources, and 30 per cent of its industry. Here, Field Marshal Prince Leopold of Bavaria, the leader of the delegation of the Central Powers, sets off for a day's negotiations, 15 December 1917.

Left: **Myth-maker.** Chief-of-staff General Erich von Ludendorff (1865–1937) was a brutal but cunning operator who advocated war to the death with the Anglo-Saxon enemy. Faced with defeat in 1918, he skilfully arranged that the Kaiser would go into exile as the lone scapegoat for an entire militaristic system and that the left-liberal civilian government would sue for peace and thus carry the opprobrium of the so-called stab-in-the-back myth. He was an early supporter of Hitler. He is seen here (far right) in 1936 with General Werner von Blomberg, Hitler's Minister of War, and General Werner Freiherr von Fritsch, Commander-in-Chief of the German Army.

British and French held back the offensive until the arrival of the Americans gradually began to push back the Germans whose troops were beginning to desert.

War and Revolution

Little now remained in any country of the sense of national unity and release from social tensions which marked the outbreak of war. The victory of joyful nationalist sentiment in 1914 had marked the collapse of the Socialist International. However, in order to fight on the scale demanded, the major industrial societies had had to mobilize all their resources in a way which increased the bargaining power of the labour force. This gave something of an advantage to Britain and France whose parliamentary regimes had the flexibility to absorb the consequent changes. Nevertheless, in all countries, the labour shortages caused by conscription and carnage further strengthened the hand of trade unions. The monetary inflation and material hardship occasioned by the massive diversion of resources to the war effort also increased working-class militancy. As the costs of war bit deeper, there was sporadic disorder in Britain and France; 1917 saw attempted revolutions in Spain and Italy; under the pressure of social dislocation and impending defeat, the great empires of the East tottered. The weakest link in the capitalist chain, Russia, was severed by the Bolshevik revolution. War in 1914 had been intended to guarantee the survival and aggrandizement of the establishment in Germany and Austria-Hungary; defeat in 1918 guaranteed the collapse of the system. None the less, ruthlessness and skilful manœuvring by the right ensured that, even if the imperial system itself was doomed, Bolshevism would be bloodily defeated in Germany, Austria, and Hungary. The intensification of social polarization in the aftermath of war saw the emergence in many countries of ultra-right-wing squads which assumed the defence by violent means of the social and economic interests of the old order. Of these, the Fascists in Italy were merely the most spectacular. Moreover, in Italy, and indeed in most of Europe, the existence of the distant Bolshevik spectre ensured that even moderate socialists would be regarded as if they were potentially revolutionary communists.

A war fought to guarantee a certain kind of German-dominated stability had thus ensured a further half-century of bloody instability. The collapse of both the Austrian and Turkish empires gave rise to a host of small nationalisms. Bolshevik Russia became a beacon of hope for the left in Europe and a spectre of fear for the right. The same forces which would arise in Germany and Italy to help hold back the perceived Bolshevik threat were those with the greatest irredentist ambitions. Hungry, demoralized, and depleted by desertions, the German army was on the verge of collapse and General Ludendorff skilfully arranged that, while the Kaiser went into exile as a lone scapegoat, a left-liberal civilian government would sue for peace and thus bear the opprobrium of defeat. The new-born Weimar Republic was thus burdened with the right-wing myth that the German armies were unvanquished and that defeat was the result of a stab in the back. The new regime was also saddled with responsibility for suppressing the left-wing revolution which was sparked off by a mutiny of sailors at the Kiel naval base in November 1918. The

sailors were protesting at a last suicidal mission ordered by the High Command. With the communists in the forefront, revolution spread through Munich and Berlin. It was to be bloodily crushed by the *Freikorps*, free-booting mercenaries recruited by the socialist Minister of the Interior, Gustav Noske. Thereafter, there could be no question of socialists and communists collaborating in the struggle against the extreme right.

In different ways, divisions within the left would decide what were virtual civil wars in Germany, Hungary, and Italy after 1918. The Partito Socialista Italiano (PSI) had enjoyed a surge of power and popularity in the course of the war which drew on working-class militancy inflamed by material hardship, inflation, and the burden of battlefield casualties. The socialists were particularly strong in the rural areas of the Po valley where labour shortages brought about by mass conscription altered the balance of social power in the interests of the unions. Moreover, in the elections of November 1919, the PSI became the biggest single party with 156 out of 508 seats. However, the PSI gravely misused its power. At a local level, attempts by rural socialists to dictate working conditions and even land-use outraged landowners who, in defence of their interests, turned to Fascist squads made up of right-wing veterans, students, and the sons of landowners. At the same time, in the industrial north, major strike offensives were mistimed, coming during the postwar crisis of over production, and so were easily crushed.

Throughout this crisis period, the socialist movement was fatally split. While the doctrinaire militants pushed for extremist activism, the trade union bureaucrats and the leaders of the parliamentary party, the so-called 'minimalists',

The butcher of the Left. The German Socialist Gustav Noske (1868–1946), a woodworker-turned-journalist, was always more of a nationalist than a Marxist. Having helped control the sailors' mutiny at Kiel, in December 1918, he became *Reichswehrminister* (Minister of Defence) and turned to the freebooting mercenaries of the *Freikorps* to smash the revolutionary communists of the Spartakist League.

The peace-makers.
Georges Clemenceau, Prime Minister of France (left leaning on stick), Woodrow Wilson, President of the United States of America (centre) and David Lloyd George, the British Prime Minister (far right smiling) leave the Palace of Versailles after the formal signature of the peace treaty.

deprived them of the mass solidarity that their actions needed for success. At the same time, the party executive and its mouthpiece, the newspaper *Avanti!*, were controlled by a group known as the 'maximalists'. Intoxicated by the Bolshevik example, they pursued a set of policies which ensured the worst of all worlds. While terrifying the Italian middle classes with the revolutionary rhetoric of the dictatorship of the proletariat, the 'maximalists' guaranteed their own impotence against the backlash they provoked. Believing that revolution was inevitable, they refused to sully themselves by taking any part in what they saw as corrupt and doomed bourgeois governments. Accordingly, by depriving the system of the contribution of the largest party, they guaranteed instability and a succession of wobbly coalitions. This played into the hands of the Fascists who were thereby able to present themselves as the strong alternative to an ineffective democratic system. Even worse, by refusing to take part in government, the 'maximalists' deprived the socialist movement of any access to the levers of the state apparatus. This meant that the functionaries of key ministries, such as Interior and War, would stand back while the Fascists physically destroyed the strongholds of socialism.

Between 1920 and 1921, the Fascists moved out from the major towns in columns of trucks, often helpfully supplied by the police or the army, and conquered the agrarian provinces of central and northern Italy. The liberal establishment covertly admired the Fascists' 'restoration of order' and was confident that it could both use and contain the Fascists. Accordingly, behind-the-scenes manœuvres permitted Mussolini to come to power after a choreographed seizure of power, the 'March on Rome', in October 1922.

A Flawed Peace

The triumphs of the Bolsheviks in Russia and the Fascists in Italy set up the two poles within which both the domestic politics of each country and the international relations of inter-war Europe functioned. For that reason alone, instability could be expected over the next decades. However, the forces in Germany which had pursued policies of world domination before 1914 remained powerful and expectant. The Versailles Peace Conference did little to ensure that their

Choreography and conquest. Mussolini prepares for the March on Rome, 28 October 1922. He is seen here inspecting Black Shirts during the Naples Conference of the Fascist party held four days earlier. On Mussolini's left are Cesare Maria De Vecchi, a prominent Black Shirt leader, and Michele Bianchi, the Secretary of the Partito Fascista Italiano, two members of the so-called quadrumvirate (the others being Italo Balbo and General Emilio De Bono).

ambitions would not rise resurgent at some point in the short to middle term. One essential element in future German strength would be the existence of numerous small national groups, previously submerged in the great Turkish, Austro-Hungarian, and Russian empires, who successfully clamoured at Versailles for their independence. The plethora of new nations, together with the chaos and destruction of war, severely undermined the economic stability of the old system. The future military threat of Germany was perceived with greatest intensity by the French who believed that the decision of 1871 should be reversed and the Reich broken up into smaller units. However, both the British and the Americans favoured a lenient peace to draw the new Weimar Republic into a new stable world. Germany was both economically important and perceived as a necessary buffer against revolutionary Russia. The resulting compromise was the worst of all worlds. Germany was allowed to keep its borders. But, to appease the French, punitive financial and industrial reparations were demanded, German military capability was severely limited, the Rhineland was occupied. To a nation which had been subjected to incessant wartime propaganda guaranteeing victory, the humiliating and impoverishing clauses of the Versailles Treaty seemed not to be a just punishment for national misdemeanour but a savage and cruel *Diktat* to be shaken off as soon as possible.

Within Germany, the right had gambled everything on victory and yet, with the exception of the loss of the Kaiser, had skilfully avoided the consequences of its actions. The acceptance of the Weimar Republic was a small price to pay for survival and the stifling of revolution. Nevertheless, the German right denied that there had been any Allied victory and attributed all of the country's ills to the Social Democrats who were denounced as the 'November Criminals'. National resentment of the 'injustice' of Versailles would be a potent political force for the group fortunate enough to be able to mobilize it. The post-Versailles geopolitical situation could not have been more propitious for those Germans who wanted to complete the unfinished business of 1918. The power vacuum to the east was filled with the weak states of Austria, Hungary, Poland, Czechoslovakia, Romania, and what would eventually become Yugoslavia. They constituted little barrier against the day when an expansionist German government might begin to flex its muscles. It was an area that, in the eyes of the western powers, was fertile territory for Bolshevism. Accordingly, there would always be a covert sympathy for any German move to the east. In this sense, Germany was potentially stronger in 1919 than she had been in 1914.

In her first trial of strength with France, Germany won. The issue was German failure to meet the reparation clauses of the Versailles settlement, which were intended to pay for the deliberate destruction of the French infrastructure during the war. The French responded to German failure to pay by seizing mines and factories in the Ruhr. Encouraged by a German government ploy to print masses of paper money to prove that Germany could not pay, there was a massive inflation. Eventually, fear of total collapse in Germany impelled the British and the Americans to press the French to withdraw. The so-called Dawes Plan reduced German reparations to a level acceptable to Berlin. The French humiliation was consolidated by the Treaty of Locarno in October 1925 whereby France, Germany, and Belgium agreed to respect their mutual frontiers, which effectively prevented French freedom of action against German transgressions of the Versailles settlement.

The Failure of the Left

Throughout the inter-war period, right-wing fears of Bolshevism and left-wing hopes of a new world coalesced into an ongoing and violent struggle in many countries. Because of the existence of a 'left-wing' state in the form of the Soviet Union, the right–left polarity was not confined within national boundaries but was replicated in the international arena. What few realized was the extent to which the Soviet Union was rapidly to become more of a totalitarian nightmare than a workers' paradise. In the course of the civil war and foreign invasion, Lenin and the Bolshevik leadership were obliged to give defence of the Soviet state precedence over long-term Utopian goals. In the face of international isolation and internal economic collapse, the revolutionary instruments of workers' power, the soviets, were soon bureaucratized and a powerful secret police developed to guarantee the perpetuation of the Bolshevik state. The extent to which the Bolsheviks became a cruel and repressive minority had an element of inevitability. Lenin and the Bolsheviks perceived themselves as carrying forward the last stage of world revolution, that of the revolutionary industrial proletariat against the bourgeoisie that, in theory, had long since made its own revolution against the forces of feudalism. Unfortunately, what might have been true in Germany or Britain was not the case in backward Russia where the proletariat was a recent addition to an essentially agrarian country. It was Russia's backwardness rather than her advanced status which permitted the success of the October revolution. The world war, the revolution, the subsequent civil war, emigration, and famine had reduced the Russian population by 10 million since 1914 and halved the industrial proletariat to a mere 1,500,000.

The horrendous cost of the first years of the Russian revolution was replicated internationally in the sense that one of the more unexpected sequels to the events of 1917 was that the next two decades in Europe saw an almost uninterrupted chain of working-class defeats. Occasional heroic episodes aside, the overall trend was catastrophic. The crushing of revolution in Germany and Hungary was followed by the destruction of the organized left in Italy in a sporadic but prolonged civil war and more systematically after Mussolini's arrival in power, the establishment of dictatorships in Spain and Portugal in the 1920s, and even the defeat of the general strike in Britain. The rise of Hitler would see the annihilation of the most powerful working-class movement in western Europe and within a year the Austrian left suffered a similar fate, although there, for the first time, workers took up arms against fascism in 1934. When the Spanish Civil War broke out in 1936, it was to be only the latest and fiercest battle in a European civil war which had been under way since the Bolshevik triumph of 1917. That war had begun with Allied intervention against the fledgling Soviet Union and the savage repression of the left-wing movements in Germany, Hungary, and Italy—all part of a reaffirmation of

bourgeois Europe. There is no denying the strength of the old order or the resilience of bourgeois forces in forging new weapons against revolutionary threats. However, the successive defeats of the working class could not be attributed exclusively to the power of its enemies.

The Bolshevik experience, while perhaps providing a symbol of hope for many workers, had fatally weakened the international workers' movement. The most acrimonious divisions followed the creation in 1919 of the Communist International, its imposition of rigid policies on individual communist parties irrespective of national realities, and its blatant efforts to poach socialist militants by dint of smear campaigns against their leaders. All these factors severely diminished the capacity of European labour and the left to meet the indiscriminate rightist onslaught stimulated by 1917. Convinced of the inevitability of the collapse of capitalism, the Comintern's leaders saw Social Democrats not as possible allies against fascism but as obstacles to revolution. While the European right reacted with hysterical fear to the mere idea of the Comintern, the communists, confident that fascism was doomed along with the capitalism that spawned it, concentrated their fire on the socialists. At its Sixth Congress in 1928, the policy of 'class against class' was adopted. From it was developed the notion that the reformism of the Social Democrats would make capitalism more palatable and so divert the working class from its revolutionary mission. The socialists were therefore excoriated as 'social fascists'.

The cunning bureaucrat relishes success: Stalin's assiduous efforts to control the inner workings of the Communist Party, a task shunned by Trotsky, see him elected Secretary General at the XI Congress of the CPSU, a commanding position from which gradually to eliminate all rivals.

With the triumph of Stalin's notion of 'Socialism in One Country', world revolution had taken a back seat in Soviet calculations. Its warriors had increasingly dropped back to become the frontier guards of the 'first workers' state'. Russia's appalling economic problems combined with Stalin's instinctive insularity to ensure that he regarded the Comintern with an indifference bordering on contempt. By 1930, the leadership of the Comintern was dealing not with hypothetical prospects of future revolution but with the disturbingly real threats of fascist aggression at national and international levels. The most damning indictments of the Comintern have centred on its share of blame for the rise of Hitler apportioned because of its abusive treatment of Social Democracy. In fact, in the darkest hours for the international working class, the iron certainties of 1919 had begun to crumble. Bewilderment rather than villainy was the order of the day at Comintern headquarters, with the leadership riven by complex disputes over how best to

160

meet the fascist threat. Moreover, for all the KPD's slavish dependence on Moscow, socialist–communist hostility was based on more than Comintern-scripted insults. Apart from the memories of Noske's encouragement of *Freikorps* atrocities, there was the undeniable social reality that the respectable, well-housed, skilled workers of the SPD were bitterly resented by the young, unskilled, unemployed labourers recruited by the KPD. Indeed, KPD electoral success was greatest when its 'social fascist' line was at its most apparently absurd and irrelevant.

Italian Fascism

While the international left was in fact ripping itself asunder, the Soviet Union and its agent of world revolution, the Comintern, were perceived by the right throughout Europe as dangerous enemies properly opposed only in Italy by fascism. Ironically, the Italian fascist regime was less novel than it tried to make itself appear and was based on compromise and consensus with establishment forces. The radical, rhetorically anti-oligarchical, fascists of the early days were tamed and Mussolini relied on figures from the conservative élite. As prime minister, president of the fascist *Gran Consiglio*, Foreign Minister, Minister of the Interior,

The show commences. The climax of the skilfully orchestrated 'conquest of power' by means of the March on Rome on 28 October 1922 sees Mussolini already out of his black shirt and in ministerial garb, complete with spats. To his right can be seen the aviator hero of fascism, Italo Balbo, and to his left, Cesare Maria De Vecchi and General Emilio De Bono.

Minister for the Corporations, Minister for the Army, the Navy and the Air Force, and Commander-in-Chief of the Militia, Mussolini ('the Duce') had enormous power. The Fascist Party became an administrative machine, its power based on its position as the fount of government patronage and backed by the fascist militias, the police, and the secret political police (OVRA). Despite its ever thinner veneer of revolutionary novelty, fascism offered no challenges to the private ownership of industry or land, to the monarchy, the army, or the Catholic Church. Only the industrial working class and the radicalized peasantry of the north felt the full repressive weight of fascism as class conflict was smothered in the corporative system. The left-wing trade unions were suppressed. Wages fell to between 20 and 40 per cent of their pre-1922 levels. The basis of corporativism was the so-called Palazzo Vidoni Pact of October 1925, a deal made between the industrialists' organization, the Confindustria, and the fascist unions, the Confederazione dei Sindacati Nazionale, by which both sides recognized each other as the exclusive representative of capital and labour. Inevitably, the system worked in the near exclusive interests of industrialists who saw it as a device to control labour. It not only did that but also became a huge and cumbersome bureaucracy which provided jobs for party functionaries. The Fascist Party, militia, and corporations provided more than 100,000 jobs. This, together with skilful fascist propaganda, the totalitarian control of media, and the apparent achievement of social peace produced internal stability and political apathy, which added up to a kind of passive popularity.

Italian fascism had no real economic system. Mussolini, like General Franco in Spain, had no original ideas about economics. His anti-capitalist rhetoric was soon abandoned in favour of 'productivism' which effectively meant the acceptance of Italy's existing economic legacy. Traditionally, the Italian state had tried to boost heavy industry, at the cost of a weak consumer sector as personal income was diverted through taxation into subsidies for heavy industry. In 1925, Mussolini appointed the banker Giuseppe Volpi to run the economy, which he did by a mixture of protectionism and deflation. This was hardly distinguishable from other capitalist economies at this period. High tariff barriers to protect heavy industry (steel, shipping, armaments, chemicals, electricity) and the big landowners, or *agrari*, (especially wheat growers) created a primitive form of self-sufficient war economy or autarky. Deflation, wage-cutting, and the destruction of organized labour revealed fascism's social preferences. Stability was preferred to a vigorous domestic market economy. Many small businesses went under and there was a major concentration of capital. The most characteristic feature of fascist economics was created in 1933, the major instrument of autarky—the Istituto per la Ricostruzione Industriale—a massive state holding-company controlling investment in steel, shipping, and other heavy industries.

The Fall of the Weimar Republic

Even in Britain, the general strike of 1926 left a simmering legacy of bitterness. In Germany, the shell of Weimar legality contained a profound conflict. In Weimar

Germany, as in the Austrian Republic and the Second Republic in Spain, the forces which had hitherto monopolized the levers of political, social, and economic power lost control of the political system. Left and liberal forces would try to use this power to introduce sweeping social reforms. However, the threatened establishment forces still retained enormous social power, in the form of their domination of the systems of mass communication, and economic power, in the form of their ownership of land, industry, and the banks. They would use that power, with increasing ruthlessness in the context of economic contraction, to block the forces of reform. In the case of Germany, the destabilizing potential of this underlying conflict was exacerbated by the nature of the Weimar constitution. Because the extreme form of proportional representation gave even the tiniest groups representation in the Reichstag, a strong president had emergency law-making powers.

Although the Weimar regime survived its early difficulties between 1919 and 1923—the left-wing insurrections, Hitler's abortive 'Beer Hall Putsch' of November 1923, and inflation—social conflict remained latent within the prosperity of the mid-1920s. The Republic acquired a certain spurious respectability in the eyes of the right with the election of Field-Marshal Hindenburg as President in 1925. However, deep-seated resentments deriving from the unexpected defeat in 1918 and its consequences saw a growth in support for radical nationalist and racist groups. Hitler and the German National Socialist Workers Party appealed to a wide swathe of German society by making the Jews scapegoats for all economic and social problems while offering grandiose dreams of world domination, glory and *Lebensraum* (living space) in the east. The readiness of certain sectors of German society to listen to Hitler's skilfully projected message was increased by the Wall Street crash of October 1929 and its consequences.

By dint of war debts and subsequent credits, most of Europe was in hock to the United States. During the Great War, while the belligerents had been converting their productive capacity into weapons of destruction, other states from Spain to the United States had been expanding their industrial capacity to fill the gap. North America, Argentina, Australia, and New Zealand had been doing the same in agriculture. The burden of war debt precluded the investment which might have produced the

The mark of quality.
The endorsement of Field-Marshal Paul von Hindenburg (1847–1934) helped make Hitler acceptable to many German conservatives and to important elements in the Army High Command. He is seen here on his seventieth birthday on 2 October 1917 receiving the congratulations of veterans of the wars of unification.

economic growth that in turn might have absorbed some of the post-war crisis of overproduction. The United States refused to cancel debts and simultaneously maintained high tariffs to keep out foreign imports. After the Wall Street crash in October 1929, the process accelerated. Credit to Europe was curtailed, the German banking system collapsed, and with it much of German industry. Unemployment reached 25 per cent in Germany and the United States. World industrial production was reduced by 30 per cent and world trade by 60 per cent. Governments throughout Europe responded with draconian public spending cuts which increased the scale of depression. In Britain, cuts in unemployment benefit were

Ich bin am Ort
das größte Schwein
und laß mich nur
mit Juden ein!

The persecution begins. A street-scene in Cuxhaven in which a young woman is ridiculed by Stormtroopers because she has had a relationship with a Jewish man.

164

rendered even more urgent by the need for rearmament in a context in which the defence of Ireland, India, the Middle East, the Far East, and most of Africa was beyond the nation's economic capabilities.

In the late summer of 1930, the Weimar coalition government collapsed because its SDP members refused to cut unemployment payments in order to balance the budget. Elections were called for September and held in an atmosphere of economic crisis and nationalist fervour against the western powers who were held responsible by the radical right for the enslavement of the German people. Hitler's NSDAP gained 107 seats in the Reichstag and was second only to the SPD. As the government under Heinrich Brüning grew more unpopular, the NSDAP's support grew with the covert approval of President Hindenburg. In the elections of July 1932, the Nazis gained 230 seats. After blocking effective government, with the help of the communist KPD, Hitler finally managed to browbeat Hindenburg into making him Chancellor on 30 January 1933. Within less than a year, he was able to establish a brutal and far-reaching dictatorship, for which he secured the support of the military establishment by promises of rearmament and an aggressive foreign policy. He decreed emergency powers to curtail basic constitutional freedoms for his left-wing opponents and Jews, who were also subjected to daily terror by his brown-shirted storm troopers, the SA (*Sturmabteilungen*).

A stage-managed election at the beginning of March 1933 gave the Nazi–conservative coalition a majority which secured the Enabling Act, giving Hitler the right to rule by decree. He annihilated the socialist and communist parties, imprisoning most of their leadership cadres in concentration camps. In November 1933, a further election gave him an 88 per cent majority. To clinch the support of the army, he crushed his own militia, the SA, in the so-called 'night of the long knives' on 30 June 1934. When Hindenburg died on 2 August 1934, Hitler simply combined the powers of the Reich President and those of the Chancellor into the absolute power of the Führer. Thereafter, he presided over the ever-more frenetic efforts of his subordinates as they jostled to realize his plans for the extermination of racial enemies and for world domination. Workers were regimented into the German Labour Front, the young into the Hitler Youth. A terrifying panoply of security services was controlled by the sinister Heinrich Himmler, the head of the *Schutzstaffel* or SS.

The Popular Front

It was a cruel irony, given the success of the Nazis, that the period beginning in late 1929 with the collapse of the New York stock exchange should be hailed in communist circles as heralding the final agony of capitalism. Nevertheless, Moscow's reaction was far from one of unalloyed rejoicing. Apart from its immediate problems of the famine conditions following in the wake of forced collectivization, the USSR still needed economic and technological links with the advanced capitalist countries to further its own development. The crash of 1929 not only threatened those links but also opened the door to a hysterical capitalist lashing-out against the Soviet Union. Accordingly, the search for allies among the capitalist countries became an urgent necessity for the Kremlin. At the same time as this external context constrained the revolutionary role of the Comintern, that organization was already bitterly divided by arguments as to its best strategy. Hard-liners claimed that the communists should smash the Social Democratic heresy, make revolution, and thereby incapacitate the enemies of the motherland of socialism. Realists argued that, in the face of fascist aggression, communists should seek collaboration with other more moderate left-wing elements. Inevitably, these debates centred on Germany.

The Comintern was puzzled by Hitler's anti-capitalist rhetoric and deceived by his hostility to the same western powers who were seen to be the USSR's main enemies. Comintern thinking on Germany was also severely restricted by the identification of Social Democracy with 'social fascism'. The KPD itself was especially sectarian in its conviction that 'objectively' the SPD was a more formidable defender of capitalism than the 'doomed' Nazis. A number of factors eventually imposed a more flexible view. Growing evidence of Hitler's long-term anti-Soviet ambitions coincided with the Japanese invasion of Manchuria to persuade Moscow that France would be a better ally than Germany. At the same time, the appalling truth of what Hitler's victory meant for the workers' movement boosted spontaneous rank-and-file pressure in many countries—particularly France and Spain—for a more flexible united front policy. Accordingly, the Comintern came around belatedly to endorsing the existing movement towards unity on the left in Europe and adopting the Popular Front as its own.

The evolution towards the adoption of Popular Frontism for individual national communist parties was closely linked to the policy's international utility for the USSR. The Moscow leadership was less concerned with the advantages of a broad inter-class alliance to French or Spanish communists than with the possibility that left-leaning democratic governments might contemplate alliances with the Soviet Union against expansionist Nazism. The notion of Popular Front as espoused by the Comintern at the VII Congress in July–August 1935 was a volte-face. With little explanation and less recantation, the divisive 'social fascism' line was replaced by a strategy of class collaboration. However, that line's validity was undermined by the ultimate incompatibility between the economic aspirations of the Front's component class elements. The rank and file hoped for more radical social and economic change than Popular Front governments considered acceptable or realistic. The radicalism of the French and Spanish popular masses embarrassed Moscow. Given the wider needs of Soviet policy, it was crucial that the communists did not let revolutionism get out of hand to a point where it would alarm the French bourgeoisie or the British who had investments in Spain. Accordingly, communist moderation came to exceed that of the French and Spanish socialists.

The policy of Popular Front was effective only in France and Spain. The left in both countries was greatly affected by the events in Austria in February 1934 when the moderate SPÖ (Sozialdemokratische Partei Österreichs—Social Democratic Party of Austria) was eventually driven to violence in order to defend the constitution of the Republic against the attrition of democracy, civil liberties, and social

Facing: **The enemy:** a satirical Spanish Republican poster depicting the component elements of the Burgos Junta which directed the military rebellion in the early days of the Civil War. The boat is ironically registered at Lisbon which was the entrepôt for the rebels' international support. The passengers are a general, a cardinal, an international plutocrat, and two Moroccan mercenaries.

Los Nacionales

legislation by the right-wing Engelbert Dollfuss. In France, the left was aware of the mistakes made in Italy and Germany and thus avoided the divisions of Italian and German comrades and did not underestimate the strength of fascism. The impact of the depression had come later in France, but was still harsh, albeit less severe than in Germany, the United States, or Britain. With industrial production stagnating, a process worsened by the government's deflationary policies, unemployment and wage cuts fostered working-class militancy and the emergence of a wide range of uncoordinated ultra-right-wing groups.

The main groups on the French left were the Radicals under Edouard Daladier, the Socialist SFIO (Section Française de l'Internationale Ouvrière) under Léon Blum, and the intransigently Stalinist Communist Party, the PCF, under the leadership of a bureaucratic thug, Maurice Thorez. After previously denouncing the socialists as 'social fascists', the PCF led the move to a broad anti-fascist coalition from February 1934 onwards. After the police crushed a PCF demonstration in Paris with gratuitous violence, SFIO and PCF workers collaborated spontaneously in marches all over France. The process was accelerated by signals from Moscow, prompted by news of what was happening in Germany. Thorez, on instructions from the Comintern, put his weight behind a plan for a common front and, by June 1934, a suspicious SFIO agreed to a 'joint pact of unity of action' which was soon called Le Front Populaire. By July 1935, the Radicals had reluctantly joined the joint committee known as the Rassemblement Populaire—for a massive 14 July 1935 Bastille Day demonstration involving 500,000 people. The Comintern VII Congress in July and August 1935 approved the Popular Front strategy, a decision which was not unconnected with the signing of the Franco-Soviet Pact in May 1935.

With a moderate electoral programme, and much encouraged by the electoral victory of the Spanish Popular Front in February 1936, the French Popular Front won the elections of April 1936. However, even before the 64-year-old Léon Blum took power, a colossal spontaneous general strike broke out. In all, 2 million workers organized occupations and sit-ins and there were more strikes in one month than in the previous fifteen years. The events initially took place in an optimistic spirit of carnival with concerts in the factories. However, the communists were too concerned about the international situation to take the risk of encouraging a revolutionary situation and weakening France. On 5 June 1936, Blum took over with the communists refusing to participate in government. He resolved the strikes with the compromise known as the Matignon Agreements by which the working class received 15 per cent pay rises and compulsory collective bargaining was introduced. There was a massive increase of unionization. The number of union members at Renault plants shot from 700 (out of 33,000 workers) to 31,000 by the end of 1936. On 11 August French war industries were nationalized. As many as 133 laws in 73 days added up to an apparent threat to the established order. Like their German counterparts when faced with the social achievements of the Weimar Republic, the French employers were determined to fight back.

The strikes and the subsequent Popular Front legislation had polarized France. The mood of optimism and unity dissolved especially after the outbreak of the Spanish Civil War on 18 July. French businessmen, alarmed for the fate of their $135

Facing: **The leader canonized:** a Soviet portrait glorifying Lenin and thereby, within the norms of the personality cult, glorifying Stalin who had put enormous efforts into projecting himself as Lenin's heir.

million-worth of investments in Spain, saw the events in Spain as an opportunity to save France from her own Popular Front. Initially, Blum was inclined to help the sister regime in Spain. However, the French right-wing press portrayed his plans as irresponsible warmongering by a Jewish freemason. With both the Quai d'Orsay and Whitehall fearful that help for the Republic might tip Hitler and Mussolini into helping the Spanish rebels, Blum was pushed towards a policy of non-intervention. Blum had to face the hostility of the PCF but he remained convinced that non-intervention was in the interests of the Spanish Republic and had prevented a general European war. Like the British statesmen who took a similar view, Blum was unaware of just how far the Spanish war strengthened the German and Italian challenge to Anglo-French hegemony.

The Rome–Berlin Axis

In Italy, the crisis of the depression had undermined the carefully worked out compromises of the 1920s and once again radicalized Fascism. This took the form of a much more aggressive foreign policy. Convinced that he could fully forge a 'fascistized' nation in a war of external aggression, Mussolini believed that Italy had to break free of Anglo-French hegemony in the Mediterranean, turn it into an Italian lake, and then head for great power status in the oceans beyond. Between October 1935 and May 1936, his troops carried out the bloody conquest of Ethiopia, with the acquiescence of Anglo-French appeasement. There was little internal logic to the external aggression since it was a major drain on Italy's already stretched domestic economy and the conquered territory did not attract settlers. It had the justification only of Mussolini's craving for excitement. All this was to be even more true of Italian intervention in the Spanish Civil War. A senseless determination not to let Franco lose led Mussolini into committing ever greater resources to Spain, the social and economic costs of which began the process of the decline of the Duce's popularity. Aware that the task of breaking Anglo-French power would require the assistance of Germany, in October 1936 Mussolini clinched the so-called Rome–Berlin Axis, the symbol of his fatal friendship with Hitler, and thus began the process of his own destruction which would be completed by the Second World War.

Hitler had begun a massive programme of rearmament from the earliest moments of his rule. By a skilful combination of daring and duplicity, Hitler avoided the preventive war which might have stopped his ambitions. He had undermined France's network of eastern alliances by clinching a non-aggression pact with Poland in January 1934. A rhetoric of pacifism proved surprisingly effective, for the democracies were determined to avoid a general war at any cost. As Hitler flaunted his determination to ignore the disarmament provisions of the Versailles Treaty, Britain implicitly supported him through the Anglo-German naval agreement of June 1935 which permitted Germany a fleet one-third the size of the Royal Navy. Nothing was done when, in March 1936, he reoccupied the Rhineland and strengthened his western frontiers. The balance of power had altered in the west for France was now in a far less favourable position from which

Facing: **The Thousand Year Reich.** The tightly disciplined ranks of the German Army marching through Adolf Hitler Platz in Nuremberg under the gaze of the Führer himself. What he saw at the 1938 Nazi Party Rally did little to restrain him in his demands against Czechoslovakia when he met Chamberlain and Daladier one week later.

to attack Germany following Belgium's declaration of neutrality. This seriously diminished the value of France's defensive fortifications, the Maginot line, since, should Germany invade Belgium, France's north-eastern frontier, around which the line did not extend, would be exposed. Hitler's military expenditure dramatically outstripped that of the democracies and he soon had armed forces that he meant to use in order to secure his ambitions of *Lebensraum* and world domination. Britain and France, traumatized still by the Great War and desperate to believe that war on such a scale was a thing of the past, were unable to grasp the conclusion that Hitler's plans made a preventive war their only solution.

The Spanish Civil War

During the course of the Spanish Civil War which broke out on 18 July 1936, Hitler was to consolidate his position dramatically, seeing France weakened, and being further convinced of the cowardice of both Paris and London. The Spanish war was essentially Spanish in origin. In the first two years of the Second Republic in Spain, between 1931 and 1933, a coalition of moderate socialists and middle-class liberal republicans had attempted to carry through a programme of social reform. The success of right-wing resistance impelled the socialists to fight the November 1933 elections alone in the hope of establishing an exclusively socialist government. In a system which favoured coalitions, this handed victory to a rightist coalition. Throughout 1934, that coalition overturned the minimal social and religious reforms of 1931–33. Fearful that the right planned to establish a fascist state, socialists, anarchists, and communists rose up in the mining districts of Asturias in October 1934 only to be defeated by the army under the supervision of General Francisco Franco. It was the first battle of the Civil War. The right took its revenge in a savage repression which impelled the left to reunite in the Popular Front. In the February 1936 elections, the Popular Front won a narrow victory and immediately began to revive the reforming programme of 1931.

Alarmed by the confidence of the left, the right prepared for war. A military conspiracy was led by General Emilio Mola. The growing fascist party, Falange Española, used terror squads to create the disorder to justify the imposition of an authoritarian regime. The left's response contributed to the spiral of violence. The assassination on 13 July of the monarchist leader, José Calvo Sotelo, provided a convenient justification for the conspirators. The plotters had not foreseen a long civil war. The rising succeeded in the provincial capitals of rural Leon and Old Castile, towns like Burgos, Salamanca, and Avila, but was defeated by the workers in Madrid, Barcelona, and the industrial cities of the north. In the south, the countryside fell to the left but, in major towns such as Cadiz, Seville, and Granada, working-class resistance was savagely eliminated. The rebels controlled one-third of Spain in a huge block including Galicia, Leon, Old Castile, Aragon, and part of Extremadura and an Andalusian triangle from Huelva to Seville to Cordoba. They had the great wheat-growing areas, but the main industrial centres remained in Republican hands.

The rebels confronted unexpected initial problems. Their strongest card, the

African army, under General Francisco Franco, was blockaded in Morocco by Republican warships whose crews had mutinied against their rightist officers. Accordingly, the rebels turned abroad for help. Enticed by the possibility of causing problems for the French, Hitler and Mussolini separately decided to provide the transport aircraft which would make possible a major airlift from Morocco to Seville. Fifteen thousand men crossed in ten days and a *coup d'état* going wrong became a long and bloody civil war. The Republic, in contrast, was abandoned by the democratic powers. Inhibited by internal political divisions and by the British fear of provoking a general war, the French premier Léon Blum soon drew back from early promises to aid the Republic, which was forced to turn to the Soviet Union.

The Nationalist rebels now undertook two campaigns which dramatically improved their situation. Mola attacked the Basque province of Guipúzcoa, cutting it off from France. Meanwhile, Franco's African army advanced rapidly northwards to Madrid, leaving a horrific trail of slaughter in its wake, including the massacre at Badajoz where 2,000 prisoners were shot. On 21 September at an airfield near Salamanca, the leading rebel generals chose Franco as commander-in-chief both for obvious military reasons and to facilitate relations with Hitler and Mussolini. On the same day, he decided to divert his columns, now at the gates of Madrid, to the

south-east to relieve the besieged *alcázar* of Toledo. He thus lost an unrepeatable chance to sweep on to the capital before its defences were ready. In return, he was able to clinch his own nomination on the following day as Nationalist Head of State. Thereafter, he ruled over a tightly centralized zone. In contrast, the Republic was severely hampered by intense divisions between the communists and moderate socialists who made a priority of the war effort and the anarchists, Trotskyists, and left socialists who wanted social revolution.

Franco's delay permitted the morale of the defenders of Madrid to be boosted by the arrival of arms from the Soviet Union and the columns of volunteers known as the International Brigades. The siege of Madrid saw a heroic effort by the entire population. Despite the assistance of the crack German specialized units known as the Condor Legion, by late November 1936, Franco acknowledged the failure of his assault. His immediate response was a series of attempts to encircle the capital. At the battles of Boadilla (December 1936), Jarama (February 1937), and Guadalajara (March 1937), his forces were beaten back at enormous cost to the

Women's liberation. The rising by Spanish Army officers on 18 July 1936 was opposed principally by working-class forces in both the big cities and those rural areas where the peasantry was landless. In many places, the military coup triggered off a revolutionary impulse which saw farms and factories collectivized. It was a process in which women played a full and dangerous role. Here, some anarcho-syndicalist militiawomen defend a barricade in Barcelona in 1936.

Republic. Even after the defeat of Guadalajara, in which a large contingent of Italian troops were involved, the Nationalists held the initiative. This was demonstrated by the ease with which they captured northern Spain in the spring and summer of 1937 in a campaign backed by the terror-bombing expertise of the Condor Legion. By October, northern industry was at the service of the rebels which gave them a decisive advantage to add to their numerical superiority in terms of men, tanks, and aeroplanes.

The brutal friendship. Mussolini drew closer to Hitler in the course of the Spanish Civil War largely by dint of his determination to see Franco victorious. Here they are seen together on 29 September 1937 during the Duce's state visit to Berlin.

The assistance given to Franco by Hitler and Mussolini was not disinterested, for they knew that they were also undermining the position of the western powers, kept on the sidelines by their belief that Republican Spain was a Soviet puppet. It was hardly surprising that the activities of foreign powers would dictate both the course and the outcome of the Spanish Civil War. Much of the energy of the right in Europe during the inter-war period was devoted to trying both internationally and domestically to build barriers against both real and perceived revolutionary threats. In international terms, fear and suspicion of the Soviet Union had been a major determinant of the diplomacy of the western powers throughout the 1920s. In the context of world depression and increased working-class militancy, anti-Bolshevism became even more decisive in the 1930s. The relative tolerance shown initially by Britain and the United States to both Hitler and Mussolini in the international arena implied a tacit approval of fascist policies towards the left in general and towards communism in particular.

Only gradually had it become clear that the much admired rearrangement of the domestic power balance inside both Italy and Germany in favour of capitalism was to be followed by an effort to alter the balance of foreign competition in favour of Italy and Germany by policies of imperialist aggression. Yet, even then, the instinctive sympathy for fascism among the policy-makers of the great powers ensured that their first response would be simply to try to divert such ambitions in an anti-communist, and therefore eastwards, direction. Accordingly, the war between the Spanish left and right had wide international ramifications. The Spanish Popular Front government turned immediately for help to its French counterpart. Out of fascist solidarity and out of a desire to weaken France, the German and Italian dictators agreed to send aircraft without which the Spanish rebels would not have been able to transport their best troops for use on the Spanish mainland. Similarly, Soviet arms would play a crucial part in the defence of Madrid not just out of ideological solidarity but because Stalin did not want to see the French counterweight to Germany weakened. The British and French hoped that if non-intervention could be imposed, the Spanish war would peter out for lack of arms and ammunition. Like the French, the British government was committed to avoiding a European conflagration. British policy since 1935 had turned a blind eye to Germany's open rearmament. Now, the rearrangement of the balance of power against France would be facilitated by the policy of non-intervention.

The End of the Popular Front

Blum's difficulties over the Spanish war were a reflection of both the contradictions of his coalition and the divisions of French society. The Radicals were essentially conservative and had little interest in the Popular Front's economic programme. Blum faced the hostility of powerful economic interests: he was greeted by a major flight of capital and an investment strike. After the pay rises of Matignon, he was forced to devalue the franc by 25–35 per cent in September 1936. He was increasingly dependent on foreign loans and so under pressure to produce a balanced budget and to curtail the reform programme. The Radicals moved to the right, claiming that they were defending peasants, small businessmen, and pensioners from socialist profligacy. Blum was in the middle—trying to appease Radicals by declaring a 'pause' in reforms and shelving plans for inflation-indexing of wages, old-age pensions, and the National Unemployment Fund. This turned the left against a government which appeared impotent before the power of capital. The breach between the government and the workers came on 16 May 1937 when left-wing anti-fascist demonstrations were violently suppressed by the police, leaving seven dead and two hundred injured. Outrage that the Popular Front had spilled working-class blood erupted in a wave of national strikes. The right responded with a further flight of capital and Blum resigned on 22 June 1937.

The Popular Front experiment was over in all but name. Blum was replaced by Chautemps with a predominantly Radical cabinet dominated by an orthodox finance minister Georges Bonnet, whose policies, including a further devaluation, led to the departure of the socialists in January 1938. The major concern with security meant that by 1938 30 per cent of the budget was devoted to defence and rearmament. Chautemps was succeeded by Daladier on 12 April 1938. Daladier's government was principally concerned with foreign policy and firm economic policies—a combination of devaluation and public works, especially housing. With the enthusiastic support of industrialists, the orthodox finance minister Paul Reynaud began an assault on the 40-hour week to cut labour costs. When the unions finally responded, all they could manage was a feeble token strike whose defeat was followed by the concerted persecution of workers.

The feeble demise of the French Popular Front was not to be compared with the long heroic defeat of its Spanish counterpart. The Republicans tried to halt the Nationalists' inexorable progress by a series of offensives in 1937—at Brunete, west of Madrid, in July; at Belchite, near Zaragoza, in August, and at Teruel in December. In each case, the initial advance gained was soon contained by the superior

Nationalist forces. After defeat at Teruel, the Republicans had to retreat before a massive Nationalist offensive in the spring of 1938 through Aragon and Castellon towards the sea. The Republicans were exhausted, short of guns and ammunition and demoralized after the defeat of Teruel. That they could expect no help from the democracies was emphasized by the supine response of the latter to the German invasion of Austria on 11 March 1938 and Hitler's declaration of its annexation (*Anschluss*). By mid-April 1938, the Spanish Nationalists had reached the Mediterranean. They then attacked Valencia, only to be diverted by a spectacular Republican assault across the River Ebro in an attempt to restore contact with Catalonia. A desperate battle for the territory which had been taken lasted for over three months. Despite its strategic irrelevance, Franco was determined to smash the Republican army. By mid-November, at horrendous cost in casualties, the Republicans were pushed out of the territory captured in July. Barcelona fell on 26 January 1939; Madrid on 27 March. Over 400,000 Republicans trudged into exile. Nationalist victory was institutionalized into the Franco dictatorship. Over 1 million Spaniards spent time in prison or labour camps. In addition to the 400,000 killed in the war, there were 200,000 executions between 1939 and 1943.

The Second World War

In the course of the battle of the Ebro, Franco was deeply worried about the possible consequences of the Sudeten crisis of September 1938. After the *Anschluss*, 'Greater Germany' surrounded Czechoslovakia on three sides and Hitler ordered

Peace in our time.
Neville Chamberlain and Adolf Hitler pose during the tense discussions in the Führer's residence, the Berghof in Berchtesgaden, on the eve of the signature of the Munich Agreement. The Agreement was an act of appeasement by Chamberlain which tipped the balance of power in Hitler's favour and encouraged him to risk further conquests. To Hitler's left can be seen Paul Schmidt, his interpreter.

the Sudeten German minority to press for an autonomy which would strip Czechoslovakia of its western defences and its major industries. In the course of 1938, he turned to building up military pressure and by mid-September, to the alarm of the British and French, the Czechs were preparing to fight. Neither the German public nor the army were ready for war and Czech fortifications would have been difficult to pass. Hitler was saved from an embarrassing climb-down by Chamberlain's determination to appease him at all costs. At the Munich conference on 29–30 September 1938, Chamberlain and Daladier, encouraged from afar by Roosevelt, abandoned Czechoslovakia to Hitler. The West lost its only industrialized ally in the East and Germany boosted its industrial stock and gold reserves for future aggressions. Hitler celebrated by unleashing a violent wave of anti-Jewish pogroms. However, it was only in March 1939, when he breached the Munich agreement and annexed the rest of Czechoslovakia, that the West finally woke up to the threat.

Fascism was the extreme political weapon which emerged to fight the threat of communism. In international terms, the fascist powers were the most uninhibited enemies of the Soviet Union. To an extent the conservative democracies were marginalized, although they tried to derive benefit from that hostility. Just as the conservative establishments of Germany and Italy had been convinced that they could tame fascism and use it for their own purposes, so too Britain and France hoped to use Hitler against the Soviet Union. In its turn, the Soviet Union had tried

Chronicle of a treachery foretold. At the Munich Conference of 29–30 September 1938, the West abandoned its only industrialized ally in the East and Hitler increased his industrial power and gold reserves for future aggressions. Barely six months later, in March 1939, he breached the Munich agreement and annexed the rest of Czechoslovakia. It took sights such as these, of German armoured vehicles rolling into Prague, to alert the West to the full scale of Nazi ambitions.

175

to make allies in the democratic West against the Nazi threat. To that extent, the 1930s saw a parallel between national and international issues in the Popular Front strategy of broad class alliances within individual countries and the Soviet foreign policy aspiration of broad alliances with Britain and France against Nazi Germany. Until Hitler's entry into the Czech capital in March 1939, Britain and France pursued an ambiguous policy of support for the fascist dictators within Germany and Italy, motivated by their desire to protect their own investments, their approval of the regimes' anti-communism, and their hope of turning them eastwards.

Austria and then Spain had been examples of localized civil wars becoming part of an international pattern. When it was finally realized in London and Paris that the inevitable logic of fascist expansion would turn the fascist powers against the bourgeois powers, it was too late to make the logical leap—that the bourgeois democratic capitalist powers should ally with the Soviet Union against the fascist capitalist powers. Indeed, when Britain and France woke up sufficiently to Hitler's plans, they made the inappropriate step of making unsustainable guarantees to Poland, which was threatened by Germany, and to Romania and Greece, which

The mechanics of the holocaust. Vast resources were devoted by the Third Reich to the annihilation of East European Jews. At the goods depot of Lodz station, Polish victims are seen being herded on to trains bound for the death-camps in 1943.

were threatened by Italy. The position of the Soviet Union was now decisive. An alliance with Stalin was immensely distasteful to Chamberlain and he did little to hasten an agreement. Essentially, the West was hoping that Stalin would stiffen the guarantees to Poland and Romania and risk war with Hitler. Hitler by contrast offered a non-aggression pact and the chance to carve up eastern Europe without war. It did not take much persuasion for Stalin to agree to throw in his lot with Hitler. Once their pact was signed on 23 August 1939, there was no further obstacle to Hitler's move against Poland. In the early hours of the morning of 1 September, Germany attacked Poland. Two days later, a reluctant Chamberlain was forced, in support of the March guarantee to Poland, to issue an ultimatum and to go to war with Germany. Only Hitler's attack on the Soviet Union in June 1941 and Japan's attack on the United States in December 1941, however, brought about a circumstantial coalition capable of defeating the Third Reich.

Until that time, Hitler was able to draw on vast reserves of raw material and fuel, ranging from Scandinavian and Turkish strategic minerals to Romanian and Soviet oil. In consequence, he experienced virtually uninterrupted success. While Stalin eliminated his enemies to the east, the Germans massacred large numbers of Jews and other Poles to create *Lebensraum* for German settlers. The SS, under Heinrich Himmler, began to regiment even larger numbers into slave armies. Within Germany, Jews, gypsies, and the mentally ill began to be eliminated. During what came to be known as the phoney war, the Allies did nothing as Poland was gobbled up. Then, in April 1940, Hitler seized Norway and Denmark. On 10 May, Winston

The spoils of lightning war. German soldiers enjoy their victory in a recently conquered Paris, taking each other's photograph against the background of the Eiffel Tower.

Churchill became British war leader and Hitler invaded Holland, Belgium, and France. By 24 June, France was defeated and Hitler controlled Europe from the English Channel to central Poland and from northern Norway to the Pyrenees. His plans to invade England in the autumn of 1940 were thwarted by the RAF in the Battle of Britain and his hopes of taking control of the Mediterranean were hampered by the poor showing of Mussolini's forces. As Churchill began to woo the United States, and Lend-Lease arrangements provided a lifeline to the exhausted British economy, Hitler decided to hasten his assault on the Soviet Union.

He launched an attack on Russia, Operation Barbarossa, on 22 June 1941,

The winter war.
Hitler invaded the Soviet Union in June 1941 expecting a rapid victory. Despite the mistakes made by Stalin, the ferocity of the defence mounted by the Russian people and the harshness of the weather combined to hold the Third Reich at bay.
A German infantryman without adequate winter clothing and equipment at an observation post on the Eastern Front in January 1942.

The battle for Moscow:
Soldiers of the Red Army man an anti-aircraft gun in Moscow during the Soviet counter-offensive in early 1942.

convinced that victory would free the Japanese to attack the United States, and also create a German empire capable of defeating the British and Americans together. The advancing forces were enjoined not just to defeat the Soviet Union militarily but also to undertake sweeping 'racial measures' against the civilian population. It was assumed that the population of eastern Europe would be either exterminated or starved out of existence to make room for more German colonists. By the autumn of 1941, German forces were nearing Moscow, having massacred untold numbers of 'Jewish-Bolshevik subhumans' on the way. However, the Germans were to be bogged down as the winter took its toll. On 6 December, the tide began to turn with a Soviet counter-attack; on 7 December, Japan attacked the US fleet at Pearl Harbor and on 11 December Hitler declared war on the United States. As the war in Russia dragged on, Himmler proceeded with what was called the Final Solution, the creation of death camps in Poland whose purpose was the annihilation of European Jewry.

Spectacular Japanese advances in the first half of 1942 were finally halted at the battle of Midway in June and the Germans became enmeshed in the battle for Stalingrad. Anglo-American landings in North Africa in November 1942, Operation Torch, were the prelude to Axis defeat in that area and the invasion of Italy in July 1943. In the summer of that year, as the Soviets battered the remnants of the German army, Mussolini was overthrown and Allied navies won the Battle of the Atlantic. Nevertheless, it still required a monumental deployment of military and

The clog and the jackboot. In late September 1944, Dutch civilians in Limbricht cheer and jeer as German prisoners are marched to captivity under the vigilance of American troops.

Unity in victory.
In July 1945, while the Stars and Stripes flies alongside the Hammer and Sickle, Russian troops march on the parade ground of the headquarters of the Führer's bodyguard, the *Leibstandart Adolf Hitler* in occupied Berlin.

economic power by the Grand Alliance to push back the conquests of the Third Reich. By the spring of 1944, the Russians were driving the Germans back through Poland and towards their own frontiers. On 6 June 1944, British, American, and Canadian forces landed in Normandy. By the end of the year, it was clear that the German forces had been defeated on both the western and eastern fronts. However, Stalin delayed his drive into Germany in order to establish control over eastern Europe.

The essential underlying contradictions between the capitalist democracies and their revolutionary enemy made it inevitable that the circumstantial alliance between the Anglo-Saxon powers and the Soviet Union would begin to break up after 1943. Even before the American entry into the war, Churchill and Roosevelt had met in mid-August 1941 on a ship near Newfoundland and launched the Atlantic Charter. In it, both Britain and the United States renounced territorial aggrandizement, declared that any territorial changes coming out of the war should 'accord with the freely expressed wishes of the people concerned', and announced their commitment to free markets, freedom of the seas, and freedom from fear and want for humanity. That implied collision with Stalin's territorial ambitions and the *gulag* system over which he ruled. Stalin's ruthlessness, and his recognition of the contradictions of alliance with the bourgeois democracies, was revealed both by the Nazi–Soviet pact of August 1939 and by his wartime approaches to Hitler for a separate peace. The implicit collision would take the form of more than fifty years of Cold War in which, exhausted by its internecine struggles of the previous four decades, Europe was divided and world hegemony passed to the United States and the Soviet Union.

Between 1890 and 1914, German expansionist ambitions set off a train of events which led to war. Although capitalism survived the ordeal, the colossal social and economic dislocation of that war polarized every European country along class lines. In one country, Russia, the forces of the left were triumphant and, in consequence, the international scene was also divided in a right–left confrontation. The post-war settlement at Versailles facilitated the later resurgence of a resentful Germany. Under the leadership of Adolf Hitler, and with the covert approval of the western democracies, the Nazi regime waged class and racial war against perceived enemies both internally and externally. The internal war against communists, socialists, and Jews was replicated by external aggression against the small Slav states of eastern Europe and against Jewish–Bolshevik Russia. The enormity of the German threat finally drove the capitalist democracies and the communist Soviet Union into alliance. The costs of victory against Germany left Europe exhausted and her fate in the hands of the two new superpowers. Ironically, during the Cold War, a competition between two economic and social systems, western Europe was to know unprecedented prosperity. Kick-started by economic aid from the United States, a period of economic growth was to ensue in which many European workers were to enjoy rights and living standards, to prevent which German rulers had embarked, sixty years earlier, on the policies of 'negative integration' which had led to the 1914–45 cycle of war.

7

The Fall and Rise of the European Economy in the Twentieth Century

HAROLD
JAMES

Facing: **The first Russian Revolution:** A dour (1964) Soviet vision of the revolutionary general strike of 1905 by the brothers Alexander and Peter Alexandrovich Smolin. The stylized portrayal of mass solidarity against repressive Tsarism is deeply ambiguous. In official eyes, it had the function of validating the regime which had overthrown Tsarism. However, the implicit message was of '*plus ça change, plus c'est la même chose*' since the regime had long ago ceased to consider the needs and interests of the masses and made more thorough use of repression and violence than any Tsar.

THE economic history of Europe in this century reflects the changing position of Europe in the global economic system. Before 1914, Europe was the dynamo behind the economic development of the world. She supplied capital, goods, and services, as well as people to the other continents. The results could be appreciated by Europeans in different countries and different social positions. Some Europeans clipped coupons on bonds or equity certificates that brought them financial rewards from South American railways or Indian tea plantations or Malayan rubber. More found that they could consume tropical fruits as occasional luxuries, sold in palaces of consumption known as department stores. Some, mostly in Mediterranean Europe and in eastern Europe, received remittances sent by their emigrant relatives. For much of the European population, the early years of the century brought security and optimism about the future. The passage of time meant human progress and the increase of material rewards.

In retrospect, this Europe of the *belle époque* doubtless appeared even more charming than the reality had been. Charles de Gaulle later remembered and eulogized the secure and prosperous world of the coupon clippers, the *rentiers*, as the 'era of three per cent'. That comfortable era vanished for ever with the guns of August 1914.

The Effects of War

The subsequent economic history of Europe was moulded by the shocks of the World Wars. The First destroyed the old Europe; but only the Second made clear to Europeans how they would have to change and adapt. The response to the First World War, the desire for what was called 'a return to normalcy', proved a recipe for

disaster. It was as if the further catastrophe of the Great Depression had already been programmed on the blood-soaked fields of the Great War.

It was not just a matter of the appalling human casualties of the war (some 8.5 million deaths), or of the physical destruction, as a result of fighting, of large parts of Belgium and France, of Galicia, of parts of the former Ottoman empire. The physical damage at least could be made good relatively quickly: one of the most impressive sights of inter-war Europe was the newly reconstructed medieval city of Ypres.

Europe and the Global Economy

The war created a new pattern of financial and trading relationships. Industrial production outside Europe had increased dramatically: the textile mills of Japan and India brought the beginning of a new competition. Agricultural output in the South American plains also rose to meet the food deficits of wartime Europe. Above all, the First World War made it apparent that the United States was now the fastest growing and most powerful centre of economic growth: the location of the world's economic dynamo had shifted across the Atlantic ocean.

The role of the United States became very apparent at the political level of discussions about international economic relations because of the United States' new status as a major inter-governmental creditor. The United States had lent the money ($10.3 billion in all) which allowed France and Britain to continue fighting in the war. The British and French positions were further weakened as they had also lent money, but to the Russian government. Britain had borrowed $6.5 billion from the United States, but had lent $10.4 billion to other governments. The revolution of 1917 meant that these debts had little chance of being repaid.

Domestic Financial Problems

The war also left a legacy for domestic financial management in all the belligerents. A large part of the war had inevitably been paid through domestic borrowing, and the service of that debt almost inevitably produced unbalanced budgets. After the war, all governments faced a choice about the extent to which they would pay the war debt through deficits monetized by central banks. The consequent inflations would erode the value of claims against the government; and undermine the household finances of the coupon clippers. In the early 1920s, the west European governments chose to stabilize their budgets and reward the *rentiers*. The cost was a severe deflation, and high levels of unemployment in Britain and France.

The choice of central European governments not to stabilize quickly had its own quite disastrous consequences. Austria, Hungary, Poland, and Germany experienced first inflation and then hyper-inflation. The absence of price stability made business planning and long-term investment strategies impossible. When these countries stabilized, they required external assistance: provided in the case of Austria and Hungary by the League of Nations (in 1922 and 1923), and for Germany by an international loan consortium in association with the reparations settle-

Facing: **The British economist John Maynard Keynes** changed the way the twentieth century regarded economics. He was a harsh critic of the international economic order after the First World War, and as the British negotiator played a key part in designing a better system for the peacetime international economy after the Second World War, at the conference of Bretton Woods (July 1944).

Inset: **The legacy of the First World War** was a hyperinflation in Germany, which reached a peak in 1922 and 1923. Governments financed their deficits through the printing presses, and attempted then to blame Allied reparation demands for the depreciation of the German currency. Banknotes had to be overprinted with new figures as money lost its value: here a note for one thousand marks is corrected to one billion marks.

Fritz Lang's film
Metropolis (1927) depicted the future in terms of human servitude to giant machines in airless and dangerous underground factories, while a small élite would lead a pampered and indolent life. It offered an uncomfortable interpretation of the industrial rationalization and modernization of the 1920s.

ment of 1924 (the Dawes Plan). The hope of all participants in the stabilization arrangements was that the return of economic order would soon bring a return of confidence, and also an inflow of foreign money for reconstruction.

Short-lived Prosperity

These hopes were soon realized. In the later half of the 1920s, American investment flooded into Europe. Some of it helped European business to reorganize itself on more modern lines. The great American automobile producers acquired European firms: Ford built a plant in Cologne, General Motors acquired the Adam Opel factory.

But much of the American investment was misdirected. Europe was not ready for such an inflow. Schemes, for instance, to build a major free port on an island in the Danube near Budapest at Csepel came up against the reality that the successor states of the Austro-Hungarian empire imposed high levels of tariff. The low-price automobile producers found that the European market had not been sufficiently developed. Cars were still a luxury item, and smaller manufacturers, able to provide an expensive and individualized product, actually had a competitive advantage. Above all, a great deal of American investment took the form of bond purchases: of government or municipal authorities, which used the proceeds for the provision of municipal infrastructures, housing, roads, recreation facilities, etc., that had a high social benefit (and also brought political advantages to the governments responsible for them), but brought no immediate return.

The Great Depression

The flow of American capital dried up at the end of the 1920s, partly because of doubts about European developments and partly because returns on US investment were higher. After the crash of the New York stock market in October 1929, some flows resumed, but American investors were nervous, and after 1930 Europe obtained little capital from the United States.

By the end of the 1920s, European prospects had already deteriorated. The worsening trade situation was a major cause, but it was associated with the problems caused by financial stabilization.

The return to the gold standard was thought by most economic experts to be the best way of guaranteeing *rentiers* against expropriation, and of laying the basis for a revival of international trade. In 1925, Britain went back to gold at the pre-war parity; in 1926 France stabilized her currency. By the early 1930s, all European currencies, with the exception of Spain, had established a parity in gold.

The most important European currencies were the pound sterling and the French franc. The overvalued British exchange rate required the pursuit of deflationary monetary policies in order to prevent a run on sterling. France, which had had a sharp and painful experience of inflation before stabilization, received substantial inflows of gold after 1926, but neutralized them (i.e. did not allow the new gold reserves to be used as a basis for additional monetary creation). As a result, the system developed a deflationary bias: Britain, as a deficit country (because of the overvalued rate), was forced to contract; while France (and the United States, which also had gold inflows) did not inflate.

Faced by deflation in the major countries, the use of tariffs elsewhere was a logical response as part of a strategy of preventing the international transmission of deflation. The spread of protectionism received an additional impetus when in 1930 the United States adopted the Smoot-Hawley tariff. Other countries responded by raising tariffs, and by imposing quotas and other restrictive measures. The monetary problems of Europe had helped to produce a trading war of all against all. From the point of view of each country, the response was quite rational; but the overall result was that everyone had to pay a high price in terms of reduced output, unused capacity, and falling investment and consumption. The effects of the depression were felt until the outbreak of the Second World War, as in most countries, even though production recovered, unemployment remained at high levels.

The international depression at the end of the 1920s and the beginning of the

1930s was made more intense by two additional mechanisms. From 1925, agricultural prices on the world market had begun to fall. This development should have been predictable: the market for agricultural products is relatively inelastic, and as European production at long last recovered from the fertilizer and manpower shortages of wartime the surplus on world markets forced prices down. For many capital-importing indebted countries in central and eastern Europe (as well as in Latin America), the only way to service external debt lay in the export of agricultural products. As prices fell, the producers needed to sell more. As they sold more, prices fell still further. For instance, Hungarian wheat exports doubled in quantity between 1929 and 1932, but the proceeds from exports actually fell because of the price decline.

In addition, the development of the real economy disturbed the financial sector, which in turn provided further shocks to output. The dramatic fall in prices reduced the value of bank-held assets and made many European banks insolvent at current prices. They responded by cutting back their credits to their customers, sometimes forcing these out of business. When depositors, sometimes domestic, and sometimes foreign, realized the extent of the problem, panic developed, and withdrawals led to bank closures. European banks fell down like dominoes after the closure of the largest Vienna bank, the Creditanstalt, in May 1931. Bank collapses in Austria, then in Hungary and Germany, as well as in the United States, intensified the deflationary process. As banks tried to save themselves by calling in credits, they drove many vulnerable manufacturing enterprises to bankruptcy.

Responses to the Depression

The inter-war depression has remained the most traumatic economic event of this century. The story of the subsequent fifty years is that of the attempt of policy-makers and economists to avoid a repetition of the catastrophes of the international slump.

An immediate reaction was to blame the international economy for the problems of each country. The British economist, John Maynard Keynes, wrote a widely quoted article in 1933, whose title indicates the import of the message: 'National Self-Sufficiency'. Tariffs might stop the spread of deflation. Above all, countries should undo the link with the international monetary standard, gold. After Britain left the gold standard, in the midst of a financial panic in September 1931, the British authorities were free to determine their own monetary policy. Low interest rates in the 1930s then helped to contribute to a recovery based on a rise in consumer spending and consumer credit. It became easier to finance house purchases, and house construction, and the innovation of hire-purchase led to a boom in the sale of consumer durables: automobiles, refrigerators, radios.

On the other hand, those countries which remained longest on the gold standard, Belgium (until 1935), France, The Netherlands, and Switzerland (until 1936) suffered from continual low confidence and financial panics. The depression lasted longest in the so-called 'gold bloc'.

Germany, meanwhile, also went on a separate route to recovery. She did not for-

mally abandon the old parity of the mark against gold, but imposed such tight exchange controls that in practice she too could pursue an independent monetary policy. Lower interest rates were supplemented by large-scale public orders from the National Socialist government after 1933: first, for construction projects, the most famous of which was the creation of a network of divided highways (autobahns). But there were also party and government buildings; and increasingly important in the German recovery process was military spending. Not all the credit for the German recovery, however, should be attributed to Adolf Hitler: some of the policies that made possible a recovery, such as the adoption of a more relaxed monetary policy, and also the reduction of the German wage level, had been undertaken already before Hitler became Chancellor.

The Soviet answer to the problems that elsewhere produced the world depression was the most complete expression of the principle of autarky, or disengagement from the world economy. Stalin referred to this as building 'socialism in one country'. He reacted to falling agricultural prices and to rural unrest with the collectivization of peasant agriculture, brutally imposed after 1928, and by the forcible extraction of any farm surplus. Low levels of investment in the 1920s affected Russia as well as western Europe. The Soviet response lay in an industri-

Recovery from the depression was slow in many European countries. Workers from Jarrow, where two-thirds of the male population was unemployed, in 1936 organized a march to London to present their protest.

187

alization drive, planned on the basis of Five Year Plans. The investment could be paid for by depressing industrial and other incomes. One of the effects of collectivization was to mobilize large numbers of displaced peasants from the countryside as new recruits to the labour force. During the 1930s, some 20 million additional workers were created in this way. The new industrial workers were badly paid (real wages fell by half). They were held in order by a mixture of terror and brutality and the application of crude psychological methods, such as the campaign based on the model worker Stakhanov. Nevertheless the USSR derived a substantial propaganda advantage from the successes of large-scale industrialization; and many countries later saw the Soviet model as an attractive way of achieving an initial industrial start. Even the German Four Year Plan of 1936 was an indirect tribute to the virtues of planning and to Stalin's Five Year Plans. The price paid by Russia in the present was heavy, however, and the legacy for the future quite disastrous.

Keynesianism

The most important and influential policy prescription that followed from the depression is associated with Keynes, and calls for a policy of demand management. The cause of the depression lay in insufficient demand. Rectifying this might involve additional government expenditure, or redistributive measures to raise the incomes of those more likely to consume (in other words, lower-income groups). This prescription gave Keynesianism an egalitarian element. Keynes had already set out the practical implications of his stance before the outset of the depression, in a pamphlet written together with Hubert Henderson entitled *Can Lloyd George Do It?* In 1936, he provided a great theoretical and systematic synthesis, *The General Theory of Employment, Interest and Money* which became both an instant classic and an object of controversy.

The German and the Soviet experiments were both viewed with mixed feelings by Keynes, who recognized in military expenditure a form of demand creation, but also disapproved of both the methods and the ultimate goals of the National Socialist and communist leaderships. The country which came closest to realizing Keynes's prescription in the 1930s was Sweden, where a political alliance between the parties representing labour and farmers carried out a demand-oriented and income-raising policy. (Many of Keynes's theoretical writings had in fact already been anticipated by Swedish writers: by Knut Wicksell and his disciples.) Agreements between union and employers' organizations in 1938 (the Saltsjobaden Agreement) provided the foundation for a new social harmony.

With the benefit of hindsight, we can detect some of the Keynesian policy prescriptions as having been realized anyway in the 1930s as a product of much broader social and economic trends. One legacy of the war in every country had been a redistribution of income, and a narrowing of skill differentials. A new consuming class had been created. But for much of the inter-war period, it remained locked in conflict about wages and conditions of work. Eventually, in some countries agreements between employers and unions laid the basis for a subsequently

Adolf Hitler came to power in Germany at a time of mass unemployment, and tried to consolidate his hold on power by a large-scale work-creation programme. Here he is digging the first spadeful of earth in 1933 for the new divided highway (*Autobahn*) system in Germany as part of the 'battle for work'.

189

much more harmonious development. The most striking instance, apart from Sweden, is the Swiss pact of 1937, which transformed previously very poor labour relations into a model for other countries to follow.

The Collapse of Economic Internationalism

In time, Keynes himself came to believe that the neglect of international aspects of the economy had had disastrous implications. In the end, he and many others came to draw a very different lesson from the depression than the initial response of insulating economies as far as possible from the global context. World trade remained depressed, and few countries could manage an effective recovery in the 1930s. The considerations that propelled Keynes and others into a new advocacy of internationalism, however, were primarily political.

The economic weakness of countries in south-eastern Europe propelled them into bilateral trading arrangements with Germany, negotiated by Hitler's economics minister Hjalmar Schacht (the system so created became known to its critics as Schachtianism). These agreements were economically advantageous to Germany's smaller neighbours, in that they sold goods at higher prices than they might have done on world markets. On the other hand, the fact of these economic advantages created a form of political dependence, and offered Germany a way of drawing the surrounding states into her power orbit. The consequences of the breakdown of the world economy opened the door for states to use economic leverage to power political advantage.

International economic co-operation appeared attractive as a way of cementing an alliance against Germany. In 1936, the United States and Britain concluded a currency stabilization agreement with France (the tripartite pact) primarily for the purpose of assuring France of their political support. It brought not a return to the gold standard or to permanently fixed parities but an agreement not to engage in mutual economic warfare by using devaluations as a means to increase exports.

The Second World War

The Second World War shifted the global economic balance even more decisively than the First. Both physical destruction and loss of life in central and eastern Europe, in Russia, and in East Asia were far higher than in 1914–18; even though many economists have tried to show how the apparent physical destruction went hand in hand with increases in productive capacity. Germany's basic capacity was as high in 1945 as in 1940, despite the massive damage done to cities by bombing. But the infrastructure was in ruins, transportation had broken down, the financial system was effectively destroyed by the combination of wartime inflation and price controls. Britain had been obliged to sell her overseas assets to pay for the combat, and was a net debtor at the end of the war. The undisputed victor of the economic side of the war was the United States. American supplies under Lend-Lease had allowed Britain and the Soviet Union to continue fighting. The growth in American production finally ended the Great Depression. At the end of the

1940s, half of the world's manufactured goods were made in America. The merchant navy had constituted 17 per cent of world tonnage in 1939; at the end of the war it was 52 per cent. As *Life* magazine announced, the Second World War had produced the 'American century'.

Americans hoped to use their position as the world's pre-eminent creditor to shape the nature of the post-war settlement. After the Second World War, the United States played a much more direct and immediate role in the recasting of the world and the European economy than after the First. Although the details of the post-war economic settlement were worked out in a series of fundamentally bilateral negotiations between the United States and Britain, financial leverage always gave an advantage to the American view.

Underlying American proposals was the belief that the collapse of the international economy in the 1930s had been a major cause of war. Preserving peace in the future would require an open international system, in which currencies should be convertible and trade non-discriminatory. Time after time, American leaders, notably President Roosevelt's Secretary of State Cordell Hull, argued that only a liberal trading order could serve as an adequate foundation for the post-war order. In the course of wartime diplomacy, the United States began implementing this

At the end of Hitler's war, many German cities were in ruins (although often the damage to residential areas was much greater than to the much better-protected industrial plant). The photograph shows Freiburg in south-west Germany in 1945.

191

vision. The most difficult parts of the lengthy Anglo-American Lend-Lease negotiations concerned the commitment that the United States wished to impose on Britain to avoid 'discrimination in either the United States of America or the United Kingdom against the importation of any product originating in the other'.

Bretton Woods

At the Bretton Woods conference of July 1944, the outcome of the Anglo-American negotiations, accepted in principle by forty-four nations, was presented to the world. The vision of a liberal economic order remained; but membership in the International Monetary Fund and the World Bank imposed on surplus countries an obligation to assist development elsewhere. Currencies would be fixed in relation to each other (a system of 'fixed par values') in order to prevent the competitive devaluation which had been a feature of the breakdown of the international order in the 1930s. One clause in the IMF Articles of Agreement was viewed by the British negotiators as their greatest triumph: it gave permission to member countries to discriminate against the products of countries with 'scarce currencies' (i.e. against the products of the United States). The conference ended with a ringing endorsement of the principle of multilateralism from the US Treasury Secretary.

European Recovery

The actual course of European recovery bore only a slight relation to the mechanisms created at Bretton Woods, the International Monetary Fund and the International Bank for Reconstruction and Development (World Bank). The United States made it clear that it would never permit the dollar to be declared a

Before the June 1948 currency reform, German goods were rationed, and there were severe shortages. After the introduction of the new Deutsche Mark, shopkeepers suddenly put goods back in their shop windows.

'scarce currency'. At the same time, it insisted on the fulfilment of the pledges given at Bretton Woods to currency convertibility. But this looked impossible to most participants. In fact, the experiment of enforced convertibility of sterling in 1947 came to an end after only a few months.

Instead the United States began working on a plan for the economic revival of Europe. The European Recovery Program, or Marshall Plan, was launched by Secretary of State George Marshall in his Harvard commencement address of 5 June 1947. The United States intended to create a quite new political world in the western part of the European continent. The traditional and destructive Franco-German relationship should be replaced by a federal structure, a United States of Europe patterned after the American example. Only a combination of political strength and material satisfaction could create a society that might resist Soviet expansionism. The Organization for European Economic Co-operation (OEEC) created as part of the Marshall Plan was envisioned as a 'focal point around which closer Western European economic cohesion should be built'. It might even be

At first, many Germans blamed the occupying powers and the military authorities for higher prices after the currency reform. In Frankfurt on 14 August 1948 they attacked a jeep belonging to the US military. It was only in the longer run that the results of the currency reform proved highly popular.

The chubby-faced and cigar-smoking Dr Ludwig Erhard, German Economics Minister from 1948 to 1963, was the principal author of the currency reform and price liberalization of 1948, and came to be seen as a personification of the German economic miracle. He wrote a book with the title *Prosperity for All.*

seen as an embryonic form of a future European government, in which the United States would have a role as an 'associate member'.

The European strategy also required a revision of US policy towards Germany. The policy proposals of reagrarianizing Germany associated with the wartime US Treasury Secretary, Henry Morgenthau, or at least of greatly reducing German production (laid out as US policy in the Joint Chiefs-of-Staff directive JCS 1067), were abandoned. The German economy had been so structurally linked with her neighbours—even after the autarkic experience of the 1930s—that their recovery was impossible without a German revival. A more punitive stance was ruled out, not on moral grounds, but because of an awareness of the interconnectedness of the European economy. When France and Belgium initially insisted on high coal deliveries from Germany, the United States quickly came to the conclusion that these would reduce German performance to such an extent that the occupation authorities would need to intervene to stop widespread starvation. Already in 1945–6, when the Allied policy still aimed at punishment, the western Allies had paid some $700 million to support their zones of occupation in Germany. Making Germany pay more would in effect only force the United States to pay more for Germany. As a result, American policy towards Germany was completely different from that followed after the First World War.

In order to bring about a European recovery, Europe needed to be treated as a unit. Instead of establishing currency convertibility with the dollar, Europeans worked through a multilateral clearing system (European Payments Union) which allowed them to discriminate against imports from dollar countries. It was a version of Bretton Woods scaled down to European requirements: members committed themselves to the elimination of trade discrimination, and there was also a (rather limited) amount of credit available through the clearing union. The process of trade liberalization within Europe played a significant part in the European recovery; and in a long-term perspective this constituted the most important contribution of the EPU mechanism. Only after a sustained recovery phase did the Europeans allow a partial move to currency convertibility outside the European area (in 1958).

How much the push to European integration in the 1950s followed from an American initiative and how much it followed the self-interest of the European nation-states has sometimes been discussed by historians. In fact the debate is largely redundant: American and European interests over this issue largely coincided at this period. In particular, the key to solving both the European political and economic problem was seen as the establishment and then the institutionalization of Franco-German co-operation. One interpretation presented the wars of the European past—in 1870–1, 1914–18, and 1940—as struggles for the control and integration of Europe's coal and iron ore resources, or attempts to bring together the iron ore of Lorraine with the giant coalfields of the Ruhr. (Needless to say, this is a grotesquely oversimple analysis. Each of these European conflicts was about a great deal more.) A solution to the political problem could be accomplished by finding a way of securing economic co-operation. In addition, the process of establishing a post-war economic recovery plan in France required a reliable coal supply. The plan proposed in 1950 by the French foreign minister, Robert Schuman, for the integration of the French and German heavy industrial sectors was originally intended as a substitute for France's failure to win the battles over reparations coal. It was eventually realized in 1952, with the creation of the six-member European Coal and Steel Community (ECSC).

During the 1950s, Europe experienced an economic miracle. Rates of growth were faster than in any previous or subsequent period. German real growth of GNP amounted to 7.8 per cent in the 1950s, that of Italy 6.4 per cent, France and The Netherlands 4.5 per cent, and that of Britain 2.6 per cent. In part, the European miracle can be explained in terms of pent-up consumer demand after the depression and wartime deprivation.

But there were other uniquely favourable circumstances. The post-war recovery benefited from a ready supply both of labour and of capital. Before the Second World War, most countries in continental Europe had had large populations in rural areas, engaged in low-productivity agriculture. Any mobility would bring large gains. In Italy and France, industrial workers were recruited from the countryside. The traditional immobilism of the French countryside, a product of the system of partible inheritance written into the Code Napoleon, had been ended by a legal reform making single-heir inheritance possible. The West German economy benefited from inflows of Germans from the eastern areas allocated to the USSR and Poland at Potsdam and from the

The nylon stocking played an important part in the consumer boom of the postwar period. Here it is part of a petticoat ensemble ironically named the 'gold standard' at the Paris fashion show of 1954.

195

Sudetenland: by 1960 these 'expellees' (*Vertriebene*) represented 18 per cent of the West German population. Then in the 1950s another 3 million came to the west from the (eastern) German Democratic Republic.

The Baby Boom

The demographic upsurge (or 'baby boom') was a product of a new confidence, and added to the upswing in consumption. It reversed the long-run decline of birth rates in most western European countries since the beginning of the century. The pessimistic predictions of a rapidly shrinking population of inter-war Europe proved for the moment at least unfounded (until the widespread use of the contraceptive pill in the 1960s and its consequence for fertility brought back this interpretation). While in France the birth rate in 1935–9 had been 14.8 per thousand, it rose to 20.1 after the war in 1945–9. The German birth rate in the years immediately after the war was very low, but climbed steadily during the 1950s and reached a peak, later than in other west European countries, in the early 1960s.

The availability of a labour supply alone need not produce growth. Inter-war Europe had been torn by divisive labour conflicts. Labour and capital had seen their interests as fundamentally opposed; labour often tried to use its political muscle to extract a larger wage share, and employers reacted by making pessimistic assessments of the future and cutting back investment. The post-war miracle depended on a new approach to labour relations, in which both sides realized that they could benefit from growth. The most effective models for such co-operation had been prepared already at the end of the 1930s, in some of the smaller European countries. Both Switzerland and Sweden had had a past of highly conflictual industrial relations, but had resolved their problems at the end of the 1930s. Austrian labour relations were reformed on the basis of what was termed 'Austro-Keynesianism'. In West Germany, the same effect was achieved through the passing of the law on co-determination of 1952, which gave workers a representation on the Supervisory Boards of corporations.

The post-war miracle was characterized by a mixture of confidence but also of lingering doubts. The savings ratios of a population made nervous by the deprivations of the past decades were unusually high. Later, with greater optimism about the future, and also with the establishment of well-functioning social security systems, these ratios fell once more. The initial high savings levels generated a major domestic source of investment.

International Capital Movements

In addition, major inflows came from abroad: first the governmental assistance, through United Nations Relief and Rehabilitation, and then through the Marshall Plan. In some countries, Marshall aid played a substantial part in maintaining economic life: in Austria, for instance, in the first year of the Marshall Plan, it accounted for 14 per cent of national income; though in Germany, undoubtedly the country with the strongest and most successful recovery, this share was much less (2.9 per cent). Perhaps the quantitative significance of Marshall aid was outweighed by its qualitative effects: it allowed specific bottlenecks to be overcome. Without American machine tools in 1948 and later, the re-equipping of European industry would have been impossible. Even more basically, the supplies of food allowed workers to return to high-energy occupations such as mining and metal working: without adequate supplies of food, they were much better off conserving their energy by huddling at home. Between 1949 and 1951, four-fifths of Europe's wheat was imported from the dollar zone.

After Marshall aid ended in 1952, private American capital flows to Europe resumed. But this was a very different lending than in the 1920s, when most capital movement had taken the form of bond purchases. In the 1950s, US capital came as direct investment in European factories; it was linked to flows of technological and managerial experience. It was heaviest in science and knowledge-based industries: computers, electronics, and instruments. Innovations here brought productivity gains to a much wider range of business, and completely transformed the nature of economic activity. This was an industrial revolution—or more appropriately perhaps a knowledge revolution—at least as profound in its implications as the increase in textile output which had marked the classical industrial revolution.

New Technology

The basic breakthrough came as a result of wartime scientific research conducted in the world's leading universities and research institutions: the universities of Cambridge and Manchester in Britain, and in the United States the university of Pennsylvania (where the Moore School of Engineering produced the first complete operating electronic computer, ENIAC) and the Princeton Institute for Advanced Study, where John von Neumann developed applications for the new machines. Translating this high-level research into practical production required immense resources, which could only be supplied by large corporations working across national frontiers.

With the introduction of the IBM 360 series in 1964, affordable and powerful enough for widespread commercial use, the computerization of Europe began. It is an interesting case of the transnational or multinational character of the new high technology: the model 360/40 was developed in Britain by IBM UK, the 360/20 by IBM Deutschland. States realized very quickly that they could not afford to miss out on this technology; but

Jean **Monnet** was the author of an investment plan for the economic modernization of France, but saw that French recovery on a national basis alone was an impossibility and worked towards European economic integration, at first through the European Coal and Steel Community.

much more slowly that they could not afford to imitate it or substitute for it by themselves. The case of IBM in Europe is telling: in order to attempt to meet the potential American monopoly, France tried to support its own electronics industry. But even there it needed US help: in 1964 a very nationalistic French government was nevertheless obliged to accept a 50 per cent ownership of the French national champion, Machines Bull, by the American corporation General Electric. In 1966 as part of a Plan Calcul launched by de Gaulle, a new national champion was created, the Compagnie Internationale pour l'Informatique (CII). But the scale of investment required in high-technology branches was gigantic. France could hardly hope to spend the amounts required for technical development: the development of the 360 line cost $5 billion, or approximately the same amount spent by France between 1965 and 1970 on its nuclear force. Even on a European level, a plan to create a large multi-country corporation (named UNIDATA) in 1972, composed of the Dutch Philips, the German Siemens, and CII, broke down within four years. Technology had clearly overtaken the economic capacities of the nation-state.

Mass Consumption of Goods and Services

In another way too the 1950s marked the beginning of a new phase in economic development: the spread to Europe of a truly democratized mass consumption. The symbol of the new Europe was the automobile: from being a luxury item driven by a relatively small élite, it came within the purchasing range of average families. The Volkswagen, originally designed as the National Socialist 'People's Car', but never made in general production in Hitler's Germany, began to roll off assembly lines run by the British military occupation authorities. In West Germany, there were 515,600 private cars in use in 1950, but 4,066,000 in 1960. The architect of what became known as the economic miracle or *Wirtschaftswunder*, Ludwig Erhard, spoke of refrigerators in every house; and that dream was soon accomplished.

Economic modernization also meant the development of services. Whereas traditional industrial employment stagnated and declined, the supply and exchange of services rose as Europeans became more prosperous. Indeed the consumption of services, from advertising and banking to tourism, became as much a feature of the so-called consumer society as the purchase of goods. One of the most expensive of all services was generally taken in a socialized form. Medical services began to figure increasingly prominently as a source of expense, but usually indirectly through tax and insurance systems. The improvement of medical provision had been one of the most important reforms proposed by politicians as part of making a better world after the war.

The Americanization of European business and consumption practice in the 1950s was sometimes derided and opposed as the cocacolonization of Europe (the French populist leader Pierre Poujade made banning Coca Cola a major campaign point). In the end, Europe was as unable to do without the culture embodied by Coca Cola as without computers.

Trade Liberalization

The inflow of American capital also meant a growing availability of dollars, and an end to the dollar shortage that some economists in the late 1940s had believed to be a permanent European predicament. The balancing of international accounts made moves to trade liberalization easier. This ensured the continuation of the expansionary mechanism.

Parallel to the liberalization of exchange controls, the six European countries (Belgium, France, West Germany, Italy, Luxembourg, and The Netherlands) who had previously formed the ECSC on 25 March 1957 signed the Treaty of Rome creating a broader concept of economic co-operation, a trading area known as the European Economic Community. It came into effect at the beginning of 1958. The EEC's objectives included the progressive dismantling of internal tariffs, and the creation of a common external tariff. As a framework for liberalization, it was hugely successful. Trade within the EEC expanded. Trade within the EEC area

On 25 March 1957 in Rome the heads of state of the six members (Belgium, France, West Germany, Italy, Luxembourg, The Netherlands) of the European Coal and Steel Community signed the Treaty of Rome, creating the European Economic Community, which later evolved into the European Union.

199

grew much quicker even than world trade, which was also expanding very quickly at this time. In 1960, the six members of the EEC accounted for 22.9 per cent of world trade, and 7.9 per cent of world trade was within the EEC. In 1970, 20 per cent of world trade was inter-EEC; but the trade of the EEC with the rest of the world also expanded, indicating that the effects of the tariff area had not been primarily simply to divert trade, as some sceptics had feared. In all, 39.8 per cent of world trade involved the member countries of the EEC.

The Treaty of Rome (in Articles 104 and 105) also provided for the co-ordination of national economic policies in order to maintain equilibrium in balance of payments, a high degree of employment, and price stability. The EEC also created a mechanism to insulate its members' politically very sensitive farm populations from the effects of economic change. The Common Agricultural Policy (CAP) developed after 1962 as a way of systematizing six quite different national sets of legislation protecting agriculture. It involved a mixture of threshold prices at which import restrictions would be imposed with intervention prices intended to stabilize markets. By the end of the 1960s, EEC food prices were over double those on world markets; and they remained at this level until the 1980s. They imposed an additional cost on consumers, perhaps as much as 5 per cent of the income of poorer families. But as incomes generally rose, agrarian protection was no longer as sensitive a political issue as it had been in the late nineteenth century or in the 1920s. In the context of the EEC, it may well have been a price worth paying to prevent farmers supporting parties of political extremism. In this way, farm policy had its own role to play in creating the new European consensus.

Governments and Growth

How far was the spectacular economic performance of the 1950s a result of government policy? Governments are often eager to take responsibility for successful economic outcomes. Yet the dynamism of this period occurred in very different policy frameworks. Britain, where growth was least dynamic, had in practice committed herself to the macro-management of demand. France had an extensive planning system, relying on 'indicative' plans rather than direct controls: the most important institutional feature was the allocation of credit through organized auctions. Germany and Italy, probably because of their recent painful experiences with interventionist approaches, liberalized prices quickly and very successfully. Ludwig Erhard remained for many as an inspiring example of the benefits to be achieved through far-reaching liberalization: he was, for instance, widely regarded as the model for the reform of centrally planned economies in central Europe after 1989. But even in the centrally planned economies of central and eastern Europe, spectacular growth rates were achieved. In all cases, growth rates of over 7 per cent of net physical product were achieved. However, the rate of growth fell off significantly in the 1960s, as inefficiencies created by the planning mechanism became increasingly apparent.

The result of this brief comparison may initially suggest that there are some occasions in which circumstances are so favourable that policy plays a fundamentally subordinate role in determining the outcome. But there is also another way of reading the evidence. Liberalization had little impact on the immediate outcome: indeed, in some cases, as in Germany in 1948 at the outset of Erhard's experiment, it may have brought considerable social costs. In the long run, however, it created a better incentive structure for sustained growth.

Liberalization produced its most dramatic effects in economies that had previously been tightly controlled. The most striking instance of the benefits of liberalization and an open economy was provided by Spain. Under General Franco, Spain had implemented an autarkic planning, and suffered in the 1950s from industrial decline and accelerating inflation. At the end of the decade, after widespread urban unrest, a complete change of course took place. Spain joined the OEEC and the IMF, and dismantled her external tariffs faster than any other European country. Initially there was a major acceleration of imports; but they were financed through capital flows associated with technology transfers. Growth in the 1960s and 1970s was very fast; and the 1960s are generally reckoned to be the period of Spain's industrialization.

In the 1960s, confidence that appropriate policy could always produce the right economic response reached the point of hubris. The rates of growth achieved during the post-war recovery had been exceptional: the consequence of a catching up

The prosperity of the 1960s brought protests, and in May 1968 Parisian students launched riots while workers went on strike for higher wages.

In the 1960s, labour shortages in many west European economies led to the increased hiring of immigrant workers. The picture shows North Africans on a French construction site.

on growth that had been missed earlier. (The basic factors of production had always been available: a skilled and literate labour force; capital; and improved technology. But inappropriate institutional arrangements had made it impossible for these factors to come together.) The 1960s discovered that European growth rates, like female hemlines, could not go on rising for ever.

The response to the first signs of flagging growth involved new forms of government activism. Governments began to see the new industrial revolution (the British prime minister Harold Wilson called it the 'white hot technological revolution') in terms of state guidance. This required investment guidance and target projections. In Britain this role was to be co-ordinated by Neddy (NEDC: National Economic Development Council). Even previously liberal Germany developed new institutions, a Mifrifri (midterm financial planning) and a Mamiflex (economic policy of moderation and flexibility). In 1967 the new Great Coalition government of Christian Democrats and Social Democrats passed a Law on Stability and Growth, which adopted the basics of Keynesian macroeconomic management.

Increased levels of inflation indicated rather more than a simple problem in monetary management: they showed that the circumstances of what came retrospectively to be called the 'golden age' had changed. The long post-war boom in continental Europe had been sustained by the movement of labour from low-productivity agriculture into much higher-productivity occupations in manufacturing and services. By the middle of the 1960s, the rural source of the labour supply had been largely exhausted, and the continental European economies reached the position Britain had been in since the beginning of the century. There were no more domestic supplies of cheap labour (although foreign workers or 'guest workers' now contributed to the sustaining of the economic boom). The pace of productivity growth and income growth slowed.

The End of the Post-War Miracle?

The sustained full employment that had been the result of 'golden age' growth increased the bargaining position of labour, led to an increase in wage demands, and then to an accommodating monetary policy. Given the labour bargaining environment, any other option on the part of policy-makers would have produced higher levels of unemployment, and ended or at least challenged the social compromise on which the golden age had been founded. The labour-market encouraged a new wave of trade union militancy. In 1968, two-thirds of the French labour force was involved in strikes; in Germany 1 million workers went on strike, in Italy 4 million. The number of work days lost through strikes in Britain increased every year from 1965 to 1970. As a concession to labour, almost every European country at this time introduced legislation making redundancy harder, and thus strengthened further the position of labour and encouraged the inflationary momentum.

On an international level, the strains created by developing inflation in all major

The prototype of the Anglo-French supersonic aircraft project 'Concorde' on its maiden flight in 1969. It came to symbolize the potential for economic mobilization by governments, but also the misallocation of resources and investment funds for political reasons.

industrial countries (including the United States) helped to end the par value system. Between August 1971 (when President Nixon suspended the gold convertibility of the dollar) and 1973, when European currencies went over to a generalized floating exchange rate system, the world moved to monetary anarchy. At the same time, a general global move to increased levels of tariff and especially of non-tariff protection made the prospects for growth through trade dimmer. The immediate aftermath of the collapse of the classical Bretton Woods system, however, only accelerated inflation even further, and contributed to a spectacular boom in commodity prices. The most dramatic increases took place in the case of oil prices. In addition, at the end of 1973 Middle East oil producers used their control of the oil supply as a political weapon.

The oil shock brought a definitive end to the golden age, the high growth period of the post-war era. It made Europeans realize how vulnerable their apparent economic strength had been. A popular report produced by the Club of Rome suggested that the world had now reached 'The Limits of Growth'. The earth's mineral resources could not be exploited infinitely. In order to conserve fuel, some coun-

The quadrupling of oil prices in 1973 made economies in fuel consumption, for domestic heating but also in automobiles, an urgent necessity.

tries—The Netherlands, Germany, Switzerland—introduced car-free days. The autobahns were deserted, the most characteristic product of the post-war miracle idle.

The oil trauma also brought a new discussion of the possibility of international policy co-ordination in the face of the new challenges. The German Chancellor, Helmut Schmidt, was terrified that the economic trauma would destroy what he believed to be the very fragile political order. Italy and Britain in particular were descending into economic crisis, intractable balance of payments problems, and domestic ungovernability.

This was the background to the first world economic summit, held in Rambouillet in November 1975 in the imposing setting of an eighteenth-century château. The initiative came primarily from the French and German leaders, President Valéry Giscard d'Estaing and Chancellor Schmidt. After the meeting, the leaders of the five largest industrial countries announced that they had made 'efforts to restore greater stability in underlying economic and financial conditions in the world economy'.

Closer European Co-operation

However, faced by erratic American policy and unsure whether they could rely on the United States, the European leaders proceeded with preparations for closer European co-operation in a purely European framework. In 1978 Giscard and Schmidt prepared plans for what they envisaged as a 'zone of monetary stability in Europe' to be achieved through the European Monetary System, a system of fixed exchange rates analogous to the Bretton Woods par value system.

The first years of the system were extremely turbulent. It had barely begun working in 1979, when the world was hit by a second oil price shock. Between March 1979 and March 1983, the currencies in the EMS required seven realignments. After 1983, however, the system became much more stable. Membership in the system in 1983 helped President François Mitterrand to abandon an experiment in socialist economics and to bring the French economy on to a path of anti-inflationary convergence.

The most important relaunching of the European concept occurred in 1986, with agreement on the Single European Act. This provided a new departure in two significant respects. First, it solved a long-lasting constitutional problem as it depended on the acceptance of a new mechanism to overcome the problems of negotiation between what were now twelve member states. At a meeting of the European Council in December 1985, the Treaty of Rome was amended to allow voting by qualified majority (rather than unanimity) for measures required to create a single internal market. Secondly, the Single European Act overcame the problem of creating a single set of Community standards by extending existing national standards throughout the Community rather than imposing a common code (earlier attempts at standardization had encountered widespread ridicule). It provided for the creation of a unified internal market by the end of 1992. But it also implied a wider programme. It included a reference to an earlier statement of

1972 approving the 'objective of the progressive achievement of economic and monetary union'. The concept of a single market was also extended through a Council decision of 1988 to liberalize capital movements by 1990, and by the preparation in 1989 of the report of the Delors Committee, setting out a three-stage mechanism for monetary union. This was accepted in 1991 at the meeting of the Council in Maastricht, which prepared a treaty renaming the Community as the European Union.

Soon after Maastricht, however, the integration process began to show cracks. Danish voters initially rejected the Maastricht treaty in a referendum in 1992. The liberalization of capital markets proved to be incompatible with the working of the European Monetary System. A series of speculative movements, first against the Italian, Spanish, and British currencies, then against the French franc, effectively destroyed the European Monetary System between September 1992 and July 1993.

Deindustrialization

The debates about increased integration took place against the backdrop of fears and hopes about Europe's place in the world. Since the oil shocks of the 1970s, much of European industry had been in a chronic structural crisis. The traditional heavy industries, the veterans of the period of classical industrialization in the mid-nineteenth century—steel and coal—were the worst hit. They had been at the heart of the early European post-war efforts to obtain greater economic co-operation. They were also the industries whose future raised great political sensitivities. At first, governments were inclined to follow an approach similar to that adopted in the late 1950s and early 1960s to manage the relative decline of agriculture (which had also been a political hot potato). A European plan of 1977 (produced by the European Community's Commissioner, Etienne Davignon) to reconstruct the steel industry through a progressive reduction of productive capacity in a cartel framework also involved very costly subsidies. In the early 1980s, the United States Department of Commerce calculated that for some products the subsidy amounted to 40 per cent of the quoted price. At the same time as the taxpayer provided a significant transfer, users of steel in machine tools and other industries faced higher costs because of the cartel pricing. The steel plan meant in sum a retreat from the trade liberalization which had been the dynamic behind European industrial performance. (It was in fact also a violation of the 1952 treaty establishing the ECSC, which in Section 1, Chapter 1, had prohibited 'all agreements between undertakings that limit or control production, and the fixing of prices by any means'.)

Subsidizing heavy industry was a potentially much more expensive undertaking than dealing with agriculture. Eventually, most countries came to accept that a dramatic decline was inevitable. The number of operating coalmines in Britain fell from 958 in 1947 to 50 in 1992 (with further cuts proposed), and the number of miners from 718,000 to 43,000. The output of coal in Britain in 1946 had been 193.1 million tons, in 1970 it had fallen to 144.6 million, and in 1990 it was 93.5 million (the equivalent figures for Germany are 108.4 million, 260.6 million, and 70.2 million).

206

The fears of the 1970s and 1980s led to a Euro-pessimism which believed that it had identified a Euro-sclerosis. The impetus given by the Single European Act generated a brief Euro-phoria. The problems of the Maastricht treaty, and the belief that jobs would be lost to the formerly socialist and newly marketized economies of central Europe or to the dynamic economies of East Asia, generated a new round of scepticism and gloom.

Although after the sharp recession of 1981–2 economic growth in the 1980s was generally stronger than it had been in the 1970s, recovery created surprisingly few jobs. Unemployment at high levels appeared to have become an endemic problem.

The long coal-miners' strike of 1985 in Britain only accelerated the decline of one of the classical industries of the first industrial revolution.

Economists constantly revised upward their calculation of the non-inflationary unemployment level (the level which could only be reduced by an acceleration of inflation). Like the mass unemployment of inter-war Europe, this seemed to indicate the failure of markets. But dealing with this failure could not be tackled in the conventional way any longer. The large fiscal deficits that had built up in all European states ruled out traditional Keynesian-style approaches to the unemployment problem.

Solutions to the European Malaise

A number of different paths out of the European malaise seemed possible. European-wide co-operation of large high-technology enterprises, often with government support, brought some results. In electronics, French and Dutch and German firms co-operated to make high-capacity chips. The most striking co-operative project was the four nation (French, German, Spanish, and British) Airbus project, which began in 1970 and by the early 1990s had captured some 30 per cent of the world's market of commercial aircraft. Even in older industries such as automobiles, the creation of cross-national corporations through mergers and cross-holdings (the most significant being Volkswagen-SEAT-Skoda) repeated the process of reaping economies of scale that had already taken place within the setting of national economies.

Secondly, new impulses could be expected from a renewed liberalization, and an extension of the European Community (known after 1992 as the European Union). The long-run effects of the transformation and liberalization of central European economies after 1989 are likely to generate a considerable growth impulse. The east European revolutions of 1989 were not primarily economic in

207

Technical dynamism
produced an astonishing rate
of change in the speed with
which information could be
managed and analysed. The
mid-1960s IBM 360 computer
shown here was considerably
less powerful than cheap
personal computers available
in the late 1980s.

inspiration, but they were a reaction to severe economic failure. Attempts at
reform and partial marketization had been particularly developed in Hungary
and Poland, but in both cases they ran into constraints.

The first and most obvious was an international one. Reforms in the centrally
planned economies in the 1970s were accompanied by heavy borrowing on
international capital markets, and the borrowers became, like Mexico and Brazil,
victims of the international debt crisis of the early 1980s. The build-up of debt
made further new borrowing impossible, and its service would have required an
additional export effort. This, however, involved running into the second con-
straint: the powerful domestic obstacles to further liberalization, including effective competition and the restoration of property rights. Any change involving
increases in previously subsidized prices, or rents, or rising unemployment as
low-productivity plants were shut down, would incur immediate unpopularity,
and the rather weak regimes were unwilling to take the risk of large-scale unrest.

By 1989 the reforming countries had reached the point where further steps to 'market socialism' were no longer possible. The alternatives were retreat, or a complete liberalization accompanied by the creation of representative political institutions.

The consequences of these reforms were analogous to the past efforts and transformations of other European societies: Germany and Italy in the late 1940s, Spain at the end of the 1950s. After an initial shock, growth began. In the last decade of the century, central Europe bore witness to the effectiveness of a traditional European recipe: the combination of political and legal security as a setting for entrepreneurial initiative and a means of engendering greater prosperity for wide social groups.

Growth cannot be neatly planned and directed, any more than can society. Attempts to do either produce greater and greater problems, until the whole project breaks down in chaos. The most planned attempts in the twentieth century disintegrated most spectacularly. Because the much more moderate and limited attempt to control developments in western Europe in the 1960s and 1970s was not as totalizing, its disintegration was not as complete and its vision of neatly managed change left a substantial nostalgic appeal.

The European experience shows the importance of situating economic change within an appropriate institutional framework. It also demonstrates consistently the importance of interactions with the rest of the world: whether in permitting flows of capital, goods, or people. Development always involves change: the challenge lies in finding ways of accepting and managing change so that the consequences are not unbearably painful. After the First World War, Europe failed to meet that challenge, with terrible consequences. The European story after the Second World War was much more successful, in large part because problems of adaptation could be overcome in the context of a rapidly expanding world economy. The problems of the later period of slower growth, after 1973, are also problems of securing the continued openness of the global economic framework.

8

Warfare in Europe since 1918

The League of Nations and Disarmament

SINCE 1918 Europe has been host to the most bloody and destructive war in human history, and to the longest period of continuous peace. This is less paradoxical than it looks. The Second World War of 1939–45 was a watershed in the history of European warfare. That conflict generated weapons capable of obliterating the continent; nuclear weapons might threaten wars of unimaginable horror, but they also kept the peace. The Second World War pushed European society to its material and moral limits, and the long years of peace that followed, longer still than the 'Long Peace' that followed Napoleon's fall, reflected a profound desire never to reach the awful threshold of atomic destruction.

None of this was expected in 1918. The Great War was the 'war to end all wars', what President Wilson called the 'final war for human liberty'. The scale and ferocity of the conflict shocked European opinion. When it was over the yearning for something like perpetual peace was widespread. In June 1917 the French Chamber voted overwhelmingly in favour of a League of Nations to organize European peace. When the victorious powers, Britain, France, Italy, and the United States, met in January 1919 to decide on the terms of the peace settlement with Germany and her Allies, there was almost unanimous agreement that war should be outlawed and peace enforced. The Treaty of Versailles imposed on Germany committed all signatories to the establishment of a League of Nations to uphold what was called 'collective security', and called on all states to begin a programme of disarmament.

The League was set up in Geneva in 1920. It remained a pale shadow of the original idea. The French call for a League army to compel peace was rejected. Nor did the League include all the major states: Germany and the Soviet Union were deliberately excluded, while the United States rejected the settlement and returned to isolation. Disarmament was patchily promoted. It was possible to compel Ger-

RICHARD
OVERY

210

many to disarm. The peace settlement restricted Germany to an army of 100,000, with no general staff and no offensive weapons, no fortifications or aircraft. An Allied Control Commission oversaw the dismantling of German military facilities and the physical destruction of factories capable of producing weapons. But for the other League members disarmament was voluntary. Though Britain and France scaled down the high levels of military spending at the end of the Great War, they remained throughout the 1920s the most heavily armed states. Military reductions were a function not of moral pressure but of financial necessity. Not until the onset of the Great Slump after 1929 did pressure mount for a serious disarmament effort. In 1932 a Disarmament Conference met at Geneva to blunt once and for all any threat of European war. Little was achieved.

For Europe's armed forces the 1920s were lean times. They faced shrinking military budgets and popular pacifism. The collapse of the Russian, German, and Habsburg empires undermined the special position enjoyed by the military in authoritarian, monarchical states. Finally the Great War itself compromised the traditional role of European armed forces. In 1914 they had expected a brief conflict, won in decisive encounters between the forces to hand. The war turned into a conflict of vast mass armies, and the mobilization of whole societies, soldier and civilian alike. General Ludendorff, the mastermind behind Germany's war effort between 1916 and 1918, christened the new kind of warfare 'total war', for it called on the material, moral, and psychological resources of the whole nation. Such a war could only be prosecuted in co-operation with civilian authorities and with the goodwill of the civil population. From the experience of 1914–18 it seemed that war was no longer the monopoly of the armed forces, and indeed could not be adequately fought by relying only on the professional military.

Preparing for Total War

The concept of total war transformed military thinking after 1918. The idea of national mobilization, of a blurred distinction between the soldier at the front and the workers and engineers at home, turned whole communities into objects of war. During the Great War the Allied blockade of Germany was directed primarily at the civilian population who felt its privations; the onset of long-range bombing of cities in 1917 and 1918 established the inglorious precedent that civilian installations and civilian morale could be regarded as legitimate targets for attack. The vital role of the economy in providing the sinews of mass, industrialized warfare hastened the development of a clear concept of economic warfare, directed against the trade and production of the enemy state. One lesson stood out above all others from the recent war. It was manifestly imperative to prepare well in advance for the prospect of another total war, or be caught on the hop. When the German defence minister, Wilhelm Groener, outlined the future course of German military policy in 1926 his basic premiss was the need 'to organize the entire strength of the people for fighting and working'.

No development better exemplified the new view of warfare than the development of military air power. From humble beginnings in 1914, the air weapon by the

In the 1930s Hitler's Germany was perceived as the greatest threat to peace. Here at the annual Party rally in Nuremberg in 1936, Germany's air force, publicly proclaimed only a year before, stages a fly-past of medium-bombers.

end of the Great War had advanced beyond recognition. In 1918 the Allies established an Independent Air Force whose object was to fly deep into Germany to attack its industrial cities and undermine the morale of the German population, the direct forerunner of the vast Combined Bomber Offensive in the Second World War. During the 1920s the bombing threat assumed fantastic proportions. In 1921 the Italian General, Giulio Douhet, published *The Command of the Air* in which he outlined the probable course of the next war. He argued that aircraft would be the deciding factor because they could not be effectively stopped, and could inflict in a matter of days a 'knock-out blow' against the terrified population centres of the enemy. Though professional soldiers remained sceptical of the claim, the fear of a sudden annihilating assault from the sky dominated popular strategic debate from the 1920s down to the city-busting fears of the 1960s.

Douhet's thesis posed a direct threat to Europe's armies and navies, for if air power really could deliver the *coup de grâce*, the old services were redundant. To prevent this reality the army and navy kept close control over the development of air power, tying it as firmly as possible to the strategic role of assisting surface forces. Even here redundancy threatened. Aircraft proved a more effective way of obtaining reconnaissance than the cavalry scouting party, while the application of air power to naval warfare (which made only slow headway in Europe) made the naval vessel an easy and expensive target. In practice, navies everywhere resisted

212

this encroachment. Even by 1939 Germany and Italy had no aircraft carriers, France only one, and Britain had carriers, but no developed doctrine for their use.

Aircraft made most strides with army co-operation. The weapons developed during the Great War—fighter aircraft, tanks, machine-guns, and radio—transformed the traditional European army. Though horse soldiers accepted the fact with an ill grace, the days of cavalry were numbered. Nor could infantry continue to hold the battleground unprotected by aircraft and unassisted by tanks and armoured vehicles. The issue that the Great War had not resolved was how the new battle forces should be organized. There emerged two major schools of thought. On the one hand, the Great War appeared to confirm the superiority of defence over offence, and encouraged the view that fixed fortifications and a carefully prepared battlefield could blunt any attack, even by tanks. Massed artillery, machineguns, and anti-tank weapons, supported where necessary by small mobile formations, parcelled out to the defending infantry, was thought sufficient to hold any enemy at bay and wear down his resistance. The most famous expression of this view was the broad line of fortifications built along the French eastern border, which bore the name of the French war minister, André Maginot, who set up the project in 1929. But the practice was repeated in Czechoslovakia, Italy, Belgium, and, later, in rearmed Germany. It was generally held in the 1920s that tanks in

Tunnel vision. Deep underground, French troops were transported by train through the Maginot Line fortifications. The Line was a response to the bleak trench warfare of the Great War in which the balance on the battlefield shifted to the defence.

their existing technical form were too vulnerable to be used in concentrated attacks. Almost all armies used tanks simply as mobile artillery to support the infantry.

The contrary view was regarded by most military men after 1918 as dangerously radical. Drawing on the lessons of limited tank warfare in the last year of the Great War, some military thinkers began to argue that the only way to free warfare from the trench stalemate was to restore both mobility and offensive power to the land army; and this could be done only by concentrating tanks and armoured vehicles in a powerful mailed fist, designed to pierce and destroy the enemy front. In Britain these ideas were vigorously promoted by, among others, Captain Basil Liddell Hart and Major-General J. F. C. Fuller, but little came of it. In France the conservative elements in the army leadership distrusted mechanization as they disliked other elements of encroaching modernity. Only in Germany did the idea of concentrated armoured warfare make much headway. Forced by disarmament to think of ways of maximizing the striking power of limited armed forces, and anxious to avoid another trench-based war, German military leaders explored in the 1920s the possibility of using tanks in mass. Since the use of tanks was outlawed, they shared their views with Red Army officers at secret training sites set up in the Soviet Union. Both sides were impressed by the results. In the Soviet Union the energetic young Chief of Army Staff, Mikhail Tukhachevsky, set about transforming Soviet forces by creating a powerful core of tanks, motor vehicles, and aircraft designed to inflict an annihilating blow on the enemy, but both Tukhachevsky and the plans for tank/air attack fell foul of Stalin, and were purged in 1937. Only in Germany, with the development of fast tanks and dive-bombing battlefield aircraft in the mid-1930s, did the concept of the armoured punch survive.

There was more at stake in these arguments than honest differences over strategy. The revolution in military technology and the management of mass armies required more professional, highly trained armed forces. Soldiers and sailors with scientific education or technical experience were needed to cope with the new weaponry. Skilled workers and mechanics were needed to service and maintain vehicles and aircraft in the field. Though traditional soldiers might deplore what one of them called the 'Garage Army', there was no disguising the change in the social composition and outlook of Europe's armed forces. In the Soviet Union the change was dramatic; the old Imperial Army was broken up and replaced by the Red Army, run in the main by men who had been NCOs or junior officers in the war. Soviet leaders stressed the need for military modernization to match the more general process of modernizing Russian life. In the 1920s Soviet soldiers paraded on May Day on bicycles; ten years later Stalin watched a stream of tanks, lorries, and motor-cycles pass in front of him, certainly the largest, and among the most modern armed forces in the world. Elsewhere the transformation was slower and patchy. In Germany the engineering officers in the navy won parity with the combat officers, but remained the butt of sneers and disdain. In the German airforce, created in defiance of the Versailles settlement in 1935, ex-cavalry officers rubbed shoulders with professional airmen and technocrats in an uneasy alliance. In France the foremost champion of professionalization was the young

Facing: **While most of Europe** was suffering from unemployment and depression, the Soviet Union launched a radical industrialization drive, the Five Year Plan. This initiative was a propaganda triumph, although production targets were not fulfilled and there were significant quality deteriorations. It convinced many outsiders for at least a generation that socialist economics could work where the market had failed.

214

Charles de Gaulle, whose book *Vers l'armée de métier*, published in 1933, was excoriated by military traditionalists, who feared that a merely functional view of military life would destroy the social prestige and political conservatism of French forces. The tension that existed in every military establishment between gentlemen and players, amateurs and professionals, reflected the wider resistance in European society against the impact of the industrial, managerial age.

Rearmament

During the 1930s many of these issues came sharply into focus. The collapse of international co-operation during the Slump, and the drift towards exaggerated nationalism that economic crisis provoked, ushered in a new wave of international tension and rearmament. At the centre lay Germany, ruled from 1933 by Adolf Hitler's popular nationalist movement the NSDAP, committed to overturning the Versailles settlement, and asserting German hegemony, violently if necessary, in continental Europe. But Germany was not the only player. The Soviet Union began a massive programme of industrial and military modernization in the late 1920s, and by the mid-1930s had laid the foundation for the military superpower that dominated the international order down to the 1980s. Soviet rearmament encouraged Japan and Germany to convert their economies in the late 1930s to an emphasis on 'strategic' industries and high levels of military production. When British airmen planned a new generation of heavy bombers in 1936, they were designed not only to reach Germany but to fly to the industrial regions of the western Soviet Union and the oil of the Caucasus. The twin threats of reviving Germany and a heavily armed USSR were enough to stampede the rest of Europe. Britain and France began to rearm in 1934, and accelerated the programmes in 1936. Mussolini's Italy rearmed from the early 1930s, and the Italian economy by the end of the decade was dominated by war preparation. The world trade in arms doubled between 1932 and 1937. In 1935 the major powers produced some 10,000 military aircraft between them, mostly low-powered biplanes. In 1939 they produced 42,000, mostly fast new monoplanes.

The arms race fuelled the very disequilibrium it was supposed to alleviate. The popular anti-war sentiment of the 1920s gradually gave way to the reluctant recognition that major war was once again a serious possibility. Few welcomed this prospect, even in Germany, whose ambitions in central and eastern Europe did more than anything to dissolve the existing international order. The concept of total war came home to roost. Governments everywhere were forced to recognize that they ran unacceptable risks unless they prepared for all-out war. Military advice, based on the experience of the Great War, emphasized economic preparation and plans for national mobilization. In Germany Hitler launched in 1936 a Four Year Plan whose object was to transform the German economy so that Germany could be supplied by the 1940s with the military hardware necessary to become a European superpower. By 1939 two-thirds of all industrial investment went into war-related industries, one-quarter of the industrial workforce was employed on war orders, and the armed forces were completing national registers

In the Second World War women were mobilized for war work in every fighting state. The woman aircraft worker shown here was one of over seven million working women in Britain, 45 per cent of all those women aged between fifteen and sixty. In Germany the proportion was over 50 per cent, in the USSR even higher.

215

of labour and industrial resources in order to convert the civilian economy to war tasks smoothly and rapidly. Military spending reached 23 per cent of the national product; at the height of the Cold War in the 1960s the figure was only 5 per cent. In Britain and France plans for total mobilization were well advanced by 1939, and current military spending absorbed half the government's budget. The view that war between great states could be won only by the fullest exertion of national energies became a self-fulfilling prophecy.

The decade of rearmament presented the armed forces with all kinds of problems. During the 1920s military technology changed very slowly; much of it was left over from the Great War. In the 1930s the scientific threshold suddenly accelerated, spurred on by the urgent search for new means of military protection. So rapid were the technical strides that countries with poor resources and a small science community were left behind. Even for resource-rich states the unstable scientific frontier presented a bewildering array of projects from which the most militarily useful had to be selected. At the beginning of the decade aircraft were flimsy biplanes of limited range and carrying power. By 1939 German aircraft designers were working on bomber aircraft to fly to New York with a ton of bombs;

By the late 1930s armoured forces were accepted by the military establishment of every great power. France possessed the heaviest and best-equipped tanks in Europe on the eve of war. The Char B-1 took part in the Bastille Day Parade in 1938 in Paris.

rocket research was well advanced; and in Germany and Britain the first jet engines were being developed. More significant in the long term was the work done in theoretical physics to pave the way for the first atomic weapons. On the ground, developments were just as marked. In 1930 tanks were slow and light, often little more than glorified armoured cars. By 1939 the new generation of heavy, fast tanks with improved armour and fire-power were in place, supported by an array of self-propelled guns, armoured carriers, and specialized military vehicles. Radio, too, made rapid strides. In 1935 the first primitive radar sets were developed. By the outbreak of war Britain was defended by a chain of radar warning stations, and radar was installed in ships. Radio was used to guide aircraft to distant targets, and radio interception became the key element in building up an intelligence picture of enemy intentions and strengths. Refined and improved, these were the weapons that dominated military strategy for the rest of the century.

The Onset of War

Rapid technical change made it more difficult still to decide on a fixed strategy. In the end strategic options owed a great deal to the experience of the last war. When British and French planners sat down in the spring of 1939 to draw up a common

Between the two world wars the Soviet Union established the largest army in the world. Soviet military might was displayed each year in mass parades through Moscow. Here in November 1922 Lenin reviewed a march-past to mark the fifth anniversary of the Bolshevik Revolution.

217

war plan they opted for a war of attrition and blockade, such as had brought them victory in 1918. They eschewed the established conventions of war, the concentration of all military forces on the destruction of the enemy forces, in favour of an indirect strategy, using naval strength to isolate Germany from the world market, bombing to wear down domestic morale and economic power, and the Maginot line as an unbreachable rampart against which German armies would hurl themselves until, weakened by the blood-letting and undermined economically, the western Allies would kick in the German door. This was almost exactly the position in the summer of 1918, without the trenches, and it promised a slow if remorseless victory, with low losses. The outlook in Germany and the Soviet Union was quite different, for both states had suffered defeat because of declining economic strength and crumbling morale; both feared attrition war, even if the long land frontiers in the east had permitted the construction of an effective defensive wall. The military in both states continued to follow Clausewitz: force against force, in pursuit of the decisive battle. For this the German strategy of the mailed fist, the hard core of tanks and aircraft, was essential. It was what Ludendorff needed when Germany launched the last abortive offensive in the spring of 1918. National mobilization was to provide the means lacking in the Great War to strike a blow of annihilating power.

In 1939 Britain and France had had enough. Hitler's determination to revive German power and transcend the limitations imposed in 1919 threatened the fundamental interests and security of the British and French empires. When Hitler refused to abandon further expansion in eastern Europe, in the belief that Britain and France were too weak and divided to obstruct him, he provoked in both states a wave of patriotic indignation and urgent military preparation. When he threatened Poland in August 1939, after months of escalating tension, Britain and France were braced for war. Within two days of the German invasion of Poland on 1 September Britain and France declared war. The two contrasting strategies were unleashed: German armies and air forces smashed Polish resistance in two weeks with a vast pincer movement spearheaded by armoured divisions, supported by waves of bombing aircraft; Britain and France sat on the Maginot line, and set in motion the slow wheels of blockade.

It is tempting to argue that, with the current state of military technology, German choices were the right ones. Of course, in the end Germany was defeated by the very battlefield strategies she had pioneered in the early years of war, though attrition warfare, particularly bombing, played its part. But in the opening campaigns German forces were unstoppable. They confounded all those predictions that modern weapons favoured the defence, and indeed offensive operations always prevailed, even against the fixed fortifications of the Maginot line, or the Atlantic Wall, or, in 1945, Germany's own *Westwall* built to keep the Allies out in 1939. The rapid armoured thrust, backed up by motorized infantry and large tactical air forces, defeated The Netherlands, Belgium, France, and the British army in May and June of 1940. So successful was the modern battle of annihilation (*Vernichtungsschlacht*) that in the summer of 1940 Hitler began to plan a great blow against the Soviet Union using the same battle plan on a vast scale. Ever since the

1920s Hitler had harboured vague plans to carve out a new Germanic empire from the Eurasian heartland. Here was to be found *Lebensraum* for German settlers, and vast economic resources in what became known as the 'Great Economic Area' to provide Germany with the sinews of superpower status. In June 1941 Hitler unleashed Operation Barbarossa against an unprepared Soviet state. In a matter of weeks Soviet forces were close to defeat, destroyed in a series of devastating blows based on the pattern practised so successfully in Poland. Only early mud and snow, and exceptionally heavy losses inflicted by determined Soviet resistance, prevented German victory by the end of 1941. As it was, Hitler felt confident enough that Soviet strength had been expended to declare war on the United States following the Japanese attack on Pearl Harbor in December.

Stalingrad was regarded at the time, and since, as the turning-point of the Second World War. It was the first major defeat for Hitler's armies, achieved at appalling cost to both sides. The city was fought for building by building; the factory district was the scene of old-fashioned hand-to-hand fighting.

The following summer German forces once again drove deep into Soviet territory searching for final victory. Though the Red Army in the south was pushed back to the Volga at Stalingrad and to the very foothills of the Caucasus Mountains, the rest of the Soviet front held. In the south German armies conquered large areas of steppe but could not pin down their enemy to a decisive engagement. When the Red Army finally stood to fight, it was at Stalingrad, where German mobile tactics were much less effective, and where the winter weather and long supply lines weakened German fighting power. In November carefully garnered reserves were hurled at the taut German front, using tanks and aircraft as the German forces did. Stalingrad was encircled and the German forces there forced to surrender. Slowly the Red Army learned to adopt the technology and tactics of the enemy. Tank and air forces were strengthened and organized into tank armies and air fleets. Better radio communications and radio intelligence transformed battlefield performance and knowledge of enemy movements. When German forces renewed the offensive in the summer of 1943 either side of the town of Kursk they were faced with a Soviet force that made the most of up-to-date equipment and better training, and fought with a ferocious patriotism. German assaults were blunted, and then the architect of Soviet revival, Georgii Zhukov, ordered a series of heavy armoured thrusts that broke the German front.

Total War

In the months between November 1942 and July 1943 the Red Army broke the back of the German war effort. Though German forces fought well in retreat, it was

Facing: **The Allied invasion of France** on 6 June 1944 was the largest combined-arms operation ever mounted. Over 4,000 ships, supported by 12,000 aircraft, carried the first 5 divisions in the attack wave. Sea power and air power were vital to the success of D-Day.

German leaders placed great hopes in the submarine blockade of Britain. By 1943 the application of air power, radar, and effective intelligence eliminated the submarine threat. Low's cartoon from July 1943 highlights the dangers faced by submariners. Out of 39,000 German U-boat sailors, 28,000 died.

retreat none the less. The Soviet armed forces developed the strategy of 'deep battle', heavy frontal assault on the enemy line with tanks and aircraft and rockets, backed up with large reserves and a solid base of supply. Though Soviet air forces toyed with the idea of bombing German cities, they abandoned it in favour of the destruction of the enemy armed forces, which remained the target of first priority. The German and Soviet armies fought wars on the classical principles of combat.

Not so the two western Allies. For much of the war Britain had little realistic prospect of defeating Germany on land. Instead Britain adopted a more indirect strategy: containing German and Italian forces in the Mediterranean, while the British navy imposed a blockade and protected the flow of American supplies to Britain, and the Royal Air Force bombed German cities in the hope of wearing down German economic power and the resistance of the population. There were Americans who also hoped to avoid a bloody land battle and high losses by concentrating on air and sea power, Roosevelt among them. The United States air forces joined the bombing offensive in 1943 with the aim of crippling the German home economy and the flow of war supplies. Yet it was impossible in the end to avoid the strategy of force confronting force. The bombing offensive almost ground to a halt in the face of effective German resistance in the winter of 1943 and was only resumed seriously when long-range fighters were introduced to fight the enemy air force. During 1944 the bombing of Germany depended on prior victory over the German air force. The Atlantic shipping lanes faced disastrous losses in 1942 and 1943 until the two Allied navies decided to fight the submarine directly rather than try to sail round it. In two months, April and May 1943, the German submarine offensive was fought to a standstill with long-range aircraft, escort carriers, and advanced radar detection equipment.

During 1943 the British came reluctantly to accept the argument that there was little choice but to fight the German army too, face to face. Stalin constantly harried his western Allies to produce the 'Second Front' to relieve Soviet forces. Neither bombing nor the Mediterranean strategy promised to defeat the German army in the short term. When Stalin met Churchill and Roosevelt at Teheran in November 1943 he extracted from them the promise that in the spring of 1944 their forces would invade north-western France and take the war to Hitler. They finally did so on 6 June 1944, in an operation of extraordinary complexity and high risk. It

"OUR U-BOATS WILL BE REDESIGNED"—*BERLIN*

was only possible as a genuinely combined operation. Its purpose was to land a large army in France, but naval power was needed to ship and supply it, and air power was recruited to bomb bridges and railways and to keep the German air force neutralized. Even with the advantage of surprise and overwhelming fire-power from air and sea the bridgehead remained vulnerable. German resistance was finally worn down by August and a long retreat began westwards and eastwards into the Reich. Germany finally surrendered on 8 May 1945.

The Second World War was everything expected from the lessons of the First. It was a total war from the start. The sheer expense and complexity of modern weaponry made exceptional demands on the economy; so too did the global scale of the war, which forced the creation of armed forces on a scale unimaginable even half a century before. The major European powers devoted two-thirds of their industrial output to war, and more than half the national product. Women were brought in to replace men. By 1945 over half the German workforce was female; in Britain over one-third. In Germany and the Soviet Union women kept peasant agriculture going as the men were recruited to fight. Economic effort on this scale reflected the harsh and uncompromising nature of the conflict. Each side saw the war as a struggle for survival, democracy against fascism, fascism against communism, race against race. The fundamental stakes in the contest were used to justify measures of extraordinary desperation and brutality. The assumption that civilians were now both instruments and victims of war became the norm. Throughout German-occupied Europe, Jewish communities were first forced into ghettoes and camps, and then, from the summer of 1941, systematically exterminated. Hitler and his racist companions argued that the war had been fomented by Jewish intrigue and that a state of war existed between German and Jew that legitimized genocide. Other 'lesser races', Poles, Russians, Serbs, suffered indiscriminate victimization and killings. Across Europe an active resistance to the German occupation developed, and for five years a shadow war of civilian terrorist and German police and military forces ran alongside the conventional conflict. The result of the war directed against civilians was loss of life on an unprecedented scale. In Russia civilian losses totalled at least 7 million; in Poland almost 6 million, many of them Jews; in Yugoslavia 1.7 million. German civilian losses were 2.3 million, only slightly less than the number of German soldiers who died.

A large number of German civilian dead were the victims of bombing. Though Douhet's vision of the knock-out blow from the air never materialized, neither side scrupled to attack targets which involved civilian deaths. British strategy for much of the war was based on the view that bombing was the one means of destroying German war capability. Unable to hit precise targets because of enemy defences and poor navigation aids, British Bomber Command switched in 1942 to attacks on industrial centres by night. In July 1943 the attack on Hamburg produced the first firestorm—a heat of such intensity that everything was destroyed in the path of the fire. The American Eighth Air Force joined the attack on Germany during 1943 with daylight attacks on key industrial targets, though in practice even 'precise' attacks produced wide civilian damage. During 1944 the bombing diverted over half the German fighter aircraft and absorbed one-third of

heavy gun, optical, and electronic equipment production. During 1944 German oil supplies were reduced to a fraction, while the planned output of aircraft and tanks was cut by more than one-third. These losses constituted a severe limitation on the fighting power of German forces, already stretched taut. On the home front bombing caused widespread demoralization and disruption. Air attacks killed an estimated 600,000 Germans, and destroyed or damaged 90 per cent of the residential housing in Germany's major cities.

The ruins of the German city of Dresden came to symbolize the horror of bombing civilian targets. Allied bombing killed 600,000 Germans and destroyed or damaged 90 per cent of the buildings in the centre of Germany's major cities.

The Nuclear Age

Racial violence and civilian bombing blurred irreversibly the distinction between combatant and non-combatant. Both relied on the increasing application of science. German chemists developed the Zyklon-B gas that was used to kill racial victims sent to the extermination camps; British and American scientists perfected navigation aids and radar equipment that allowed bombers to reach and destroy their targets with increasing precision, while the bomb itself became a larger and more sophisticated weapon. The Second World War completed the process begun in 1914–18 of turning war from a labour-intensive to a capital-intensive activity,

223

By the end of the war long-range missiles heralded a new strategic age. The German A-4 rocket (the V2) carried only a small payload and was very inaccurate, but it was the direct ancestor of the generation of inter-continental missiles developed in the 1960s.

reliant on very expensive, scientifically advanced weaponry in a constant, fluctuating process of technical advance. Two projects illustrated the change: the development of rocket missiles at the German research establishment at Peenemünde, and the Anglo-American atomic weapons programme at Los Alamos, New Mexico. Both research programmes were the fruit of modern Big Science, requiring huge research teams and enormous public funding. Both were intended to push the technical frontier forward beyond the grasp of the enemy; both were weapons of indiscriminate mass destruction, pushing warfare to new ethical, as well as technical, thresholds. Both were used, but, of the two, atomic weapons were the greater threat. German rockets, the V2s, carried an insignificant payload and were very inaccurate in attacks on London in 1944. The atomic bombs dropped in August 1945 on Hiroshima and Nagasaki revealed an awesome scientific power, and, at a stroke, altered the nature of modern strategy.

The advent of nuclear weapons made possible a new kind of total war. The Second World War was 'total' in the sense that it was fought by whole communities under conditions of gruelling attrition. Nuclear war promised total annihilation in a matter of hours. Destruction on this scale did not require massive armies and air forces, but small numbers of bombs and missiles. National mobilization, the hallmark of the two world wars, was redundant. By the time soldiers and workers were mobilized, their country would be, in the words of an American airman in 1955, 'a smoking, radiating ruin'.

This was a prospect bleaker than anything in 1918. But it was not yet a reality. There was a great deal of wild talk about the nuclear age, but there were many soldiers and statesmen—Stalin included—who thought that nuclear weapons meant no serious breach with the military past. The technology was in its infancy and adolescence for years. Soviet military leaders sought a nuclear capability to match American achievements, but until the late 1950s relied largely on conventional forces for defence. Only one other European state, Britain, remained in the nuclear club. The British developed their own bomb by 1952, but had so few warheads and delivery aircraft that it remained a feeble threat. In practice, the cost of researching and establishing and operating large nuclear forces was simply beyond the economic means of smaller European states. Britain's rocket, *Blue Streak*, was cancelled in 1960. When the French President, the 1930s champion of a professional armed force, Charles de Gaulle, agreed in principle to the establishment of a French nuclear capability in the 1960s, it took fifteen years for a force to emerge, and it possessed a tiny fraction of the nuclear fire-power of the United States and the Soviet Union. Though other European states had nuclear weapons stationed on their soil, none became a nuclear power in its own right.

As the new technology matured, so the temptation to put nuclear weapons at the forefront of military strategy became irresistible. The driving force could be found in the post-war international settlement. Following the defeat of Germany, relations between the wartime allies deteriorated sharply. The western states feared the spread of communism and the massive military power that defeated Hitler's armies, which now lay athwart eastern Europe. Soviet leaders wanted to avoid any repetition of 1941 by establishing a solid security system in the areas liberated by their armies. In 1949 the states of western Europe allied with the United States and Canada in the North Atlantic Treaty Organization, an alliance aimed at preventing Soviet advance into Europe. For Europe it was a vital lifeline, for it kept open the military commitment to Europe that the United States made during the war, though it made their war-weary territories the potential battlefield between the two new superpowers. Military collaboration between NATO partners remained a constant feature of the European security system. In May 1955 the Soviet Union signed a pact of mutual assistance—the so-called Warsaw Pact— with the communist states of eastern Europe which committed the signatories to pooling efforts to organize the defence of the Soviet bloc. Europe was divided into two armed camps, dominated by the interests of the two major states involved. The Soviet Union provided four-fifths of the costs of Warsaw Pact defence, the United States almost two-thirds of the costs involved in NATO. As the two sides solidified, their strategy became more and more simplistic. Neither side relished the prospect of nuclear war. The object of strategy was no longer to prepare for war, but to possess sufficient force to prevent the enemy from risking war. It was a strategy that relied on deterrence. To be credible both sides developed nuclear arsenals of exceptional destructive power, and tried to create in the potential aggressor the strong conviction that this power really would be used in a crisis. With the development in the 1960s of inter-continental ballistic missiles, multiple warheads, and thermo-nuclear bombs, the prospect of what American strategists called Mutual Assured Destruction was mutually assured.

Though Germany developed the rocket, the atomic bomb that might have won Hitler the war was years from completion by German scientists. Development by an Anglo-American team during the war produced a bomb only after the war in Europe was over. But it was evident by August 1945 that the nature of warfare had been radically altered.

"BABY PLAY WITH NICE BALL?"

225

Return to Conventional Warfare

The development of an unstable nuclear confrontation had the salutary effect of turning Europeans back towards conventional warfare. The military in the Soviet bloc always emphasized the importance of maintaining large armed forces along their wide European frontier, primed for offensive operations. Soviet military thinking remained, despite the advent of nuclear weapons, dominated by the harsh lessons of the Second World War: the primacy of the land offensive; concentration of armoured and air forces; a deep battlefield and extensive reserves. It was knowledge of the great disparity of conventional forces between NATO and the Warsaw Pact that encouraged a reassessment of strategy in the 1960s. But there were many other causes. European leaders came to doubt that the nuclear threat was very credible. It was inconceivable that either side would use the weapons and risk the obliteration of their entire social fabric. Rather than put the system to the test, European statesmen argued that the risk of nuclear escalation should be reduced by building up Europe's conventional forces in order to provide an alternative means of defence. The prospect could never be ruled out that the United States might abandon Europe, or use Europe as the nuclear battlefield. Either way, conventional defence promised a safer and more believable deterrent. There were also political pressures. The traditional armed forces faced virtual extinction with the use of rocket-borne nuclear weapons. The renewed emphasis on conventional warfare ensured their survival and re-equipment. Public opinion was far from unanimous on any of these issues, but there existed throughout western Europe a vocal, well-organized lobby hostile to all nuclear weapons, but less resistant to the old-fashioned bomb and shell.

When NATO altered its strategy in December 1967 to one of 'flexible response' on a spectrum from conventional defence to all-out nuclear attack, the framework was set for the expansion of the conventional alternative. The model remained the Second World War. The emphasis on flexible air power, on large tanks and motorized infantry, on radar and scientific surveillance, all in use by 1945, was retained and elaborated. The technology was refined to achieve a much higher level of precision and increased destructive power—indeed modern artillery and fighter-bombers could wield nuclear

Facing: **The advent of nuclear weapons** provoked a widespread peace movement throughout Europe. Protesters gathered in Trafalgar Square in London before the annual march to Aldermaston, the British nuclear weapons research centre.

In the 1960s, governments in Europe developed civil defence programmes to cope with a nuclear conflict. The film *The War Game* (1965) showed how little could be done to prevent devastation. The dramatic reconstruction of a nuclear explosion helped to fuel the often violent anti-war demonstrations of the late 1960s.

warheads—but it was substantially the same. The idea of the mobile punch, delivered by armoured divisions, backed up by aircraft, self-propelled artillery, and mobile troop carriers was adopted across Europe; the traditional infantry, even the remnants of cavalry still in use in 1945, disappeared for good. At sea the aircraft carrier and the submarine kept alive Europe's exiguous naval power. In the air, fast fighters and fighter-bombers, for tactical warfare on or just behind the battle line, were developed rather than large bombers, whose place was gradually taken by rockets.

The central purpose of NATO's conventional forces was to block any Soviet advance on what was known as the Central Front, the long Iron Curtain frontier from the Baltic to the Austrian frontier. This was not a natural defensive barrier. On the Warsaw Pact side there stood in the 1980s over 50 divisions, 16,000 tanks, 26,000 fighting vehicles, and 4,000 combat aircraft. During the 1970s and 1980s NATO deployed a large multinational force, smaller in numbers, but allegedly superior in quality of equipment and in training. There were only half the number of divisions, tanks, and aircraft, and less than half the number of artillery pieces. Worse still, NATO forces had no very clear idea of how to defend the front if they were faced with a surprise assault. To make the conventional deterrent work,

NATO forces were compelled again to look to nuclear weapons. A new generation of short-range battlefield nuclear weapons—the cruise missile, the neutron bomb, the nuclear artillery shell—were adopted to strengthen the other theatre forces. To satisfy German fears that Warsaw Pact armies would use western Germany as the ground of combat, and repeat the devastation of 1944–5, the NATO forces were deployed in a posture of 'forward defence', which left a thin, heavily defended front line with few reserves, and the very great risk that within hours all the NATO nuclear weapons stationed there might be captured by a quick Soviet incursion.

Conventional or nuclear, war was no longer regarded as a test of national mobilization. Soviet planners worked on the contingency of a quick strike; their enemies feared that Soviet bloc forces could reach the Atlantic in a week. A nuclear exchange might be over in a day. But it was not just the increased mobility and destructiveness of modern weaponry that made short wars likely. Modern weapons were far too expensive and technically complex to reproduce quickly. Most European states could not afford a high level of mobilization or military readiness. A modern fighter in the 1980s cost forty times the small monoplanes of 1940. For the cost of a heavy bomber, General Eisenhower remarked in 1953, a state could build thirty schools or two fully equipped hospitals. Under these circumstances it was impossible to plan the rapid conversion of the civilian economy to mass produce sophisticated armaments. Instead, the emphasis shifted to the quality of weapons rather than their quantity. It was the same story with manpower. Large conscript armies were no longer necessary if they could not be supplied with weapons. The evolution of highly trained professional armed forces, with a high level of technical and managerial skill, begun in the inter-war years, was completed in the age of missiles. Soldiers were no longer cannon-fodder, but highly specialized military workers, not easily substituted by hastily trained civilians. The prospect of a short war with the weapons and trained men to hand turned the wheel full circle, back to the situation before 1914, when war was the job of warriors, not of the civil population.

In the late 1980s the Cold War confrontation in Europe ended with the collapse of communist power throughout the Soviet bloc. For almost fifty years peace had been maintained between the major states of the continent. The obvious conclusion was that deterrence worked; fear of the unimaginable consequences of a nuclear confrontation imposed a mutual rationality. War was kept to the periphery. Britain and France fought small wars in their overseas empires in the 1950s; the Soviet Union became involved in war in Afghanistan in the late 1970s. Beyond that, violence was confined to civil conflicts. Most Europeans in the 1990s had had no experience of war beyond the television screen. Deterrence may explain this outcome. But there are other causes. After the terrible destruction and inhumanity of the war of 1939–45 no European government, east or west, relished the prospect of another. Mutual self-restraint sustained the long peace, as it had done under the Metternich System after 1815. The Second World War, not the First, was the war to end all wars, for the moment.

European Society in the Twentieth Century

9

Introduction

As the nineteenth century drew to a close, the belief that Europe was the centre of the civilized world was virtually unquestioned. European cultural influence, European imperialism, and the migrations of millions of Europeans had spread European society around the globe. When, for example, towards the end of the nineteenth century, Brazilians (of European extraction) planned the rebuilding of Rio de Janeiro, their model was not drawn from the New World; it was Paris. Paris was the epitome of European civilization and the model of what a city should be; European civilization obviously was the only civilization worth emulating. So emulate the Brazilians did. Parisian avenues were reproduced in Rio; French building styles were copied; French public parks were reproduced. When, in 1904, work was begun on Rio's Haussmann-inspired boulevard, its 'showcase of civilization' the Avenida Central, one of the city's literati, Olavo Blanc, could assert:

A few days ago, the picks, intoning a jubilant hymn, began the work of the Avenida Central's construction, knocking down the first condemned houses. . . . With what happiness they sang, the regenerating picks! And how the souls of those who were there understood well what the picks were saying, in their unceasing rhythmic clamor, celebrating the victory of hygiene, of good taste, and of art. (Quoted in Jeffrey D. Needell, *A Tropical Belle Epoque: Elite Culture and Society in Turn-of-the-Century Rio de Janeiro* (Cambridge, Cambridge University Press, 1987), 48.)

When the élites of Rio sought models of 'hygiene, of good taste, and of art', it was to Europe that they looked.

They were not alone. Across the New World, the Old World provided the model.

RICHARD
BESSEL

231

Europe provided the images of civilized society towards which civilized people strove. Structures whose architectural inspiration was the École des Beaux-Arts, Greek temples, and Italian monuments multiplied. For example, Springfield, Massachusetts, could boast two classic Greek temples (the City Hall and the Municipal Auditorium) separated by a copy, in white marble, of Venice's Campanile; and the citizens of Nashville, Tennessee, could admire their own full-scale replica of the Parthenon. At the beginning of the twentieth century it was the society of the Old World which provided the model for the society of the New.

As we approach the end of the twentieth century, the opposite seems true. Now the New World appears to provide the model for the Old. Whereas, at the beginning of the century, it was Paris which supplied the model for modernity and urbanity in cities such as Rio, towards its end the relationship appears to have been reversed: near Paris the glass towers of La Défense appear to be an American transplant, and between London and Birmingham Britain's boldest new city, Milton Keynes, looks like an attempt to copy Brasilia. Furthermore, if anyone outside Europe were still keen to ape European society and European culture, it is far from

232

clear just what they might attempt to copy. European society and European culture have become so fragmented and diffuse, and at the same time so greatly influenced by extra-European impulses that it no longer is certain to what these terms refer.

It is not the intention here to repackage the cliché that European society suddenly has been swamped by American culture—with MacDonalds becoming a feature of European cities from Dublin to Moscow and with Euro-Disney bringing Donald Duck and Goofy to shake hands with the European masses. Americanization is hardly new to Europe. During the inter-war years American influence was already widely felt in Europe; Coca Cola had already invaded the continent, and even in Nazi Germany the most popular film star of the 1930s was Clark Gable. Nevertheless, there has been an important shift in focus. No longer are American public buildings modelled on European ones; as the century nears its end, it appears increasingly that Europe's cities are modelled on those in North America.

'Clark Gable's Romantic Path' in the Third Reich: the heart-throb of Nazi Germany. An advertisement for the December 1937 issue of the cheap monthly periodical, *True Stories*.

How are we to explain the extraordinary, and changed, relationship between European society and extra-European societies during the twentieth century? A number of developments played a part. First, Europe's position at the centre of the world economy was deeply damaged by the First World War. Economic leadership moved from the Old World to the New; after 1918 the world centre of economic gravity shifted from London to New York; and the First World War, the Russian Revolution, and Russia's civil war made Europe a much poorer place after 1918 than it had been before 1914. Secondly, after the violence and destruction of the Great War, European civilization appeared tarnished and no longer necessarily offered a terribly desirable model. Thirdly, the extraordinary emigration from Europe of the nineteenth and early twentieth centuries was sharply reduced.

The history of European migration offers a good example of how European society and its relationship with the world beyond Europe changed during the twentieth century. During the century before the First World War nearly 50 million people emigrated to North and South America, most of them Europeans; this constituted the greatest migration of human beings the world had ever seen, and it more or less came to a

Clark Gables abenteuerlicher Weg

und viele andere fesselnde Beiträge finden Sie in dem reichhaltigen und interessanten Dezemberheft WAHRE GESCHICHTEN. Die Wahren Geschichten sind für 50 Pfennig überall zu haben!

stop during the inter-war years. The reasons are not hard to find: the end, as a consequence of the Great War, of the great economic boom which had set in during the 1890s; the restrictions to immigration put into place by the United States during the 1920s, with a quota system which shut out large numbers of potential migrants from southern and eastern Europe; and the deep depression of the 1930s which removed the demand for labour in countries which previously had accepted large numbers of people. This cutting off of European migration to the wider world was followed, during the 1940s, by forced mass movements of European populations *within* Europe: the terrible deportations carried out by the Nazis in their attempt to construct a racial 'new order'; the mass deportations carried out in the Soviet Union under Stalin; and the mass expulsions (for example, of more than 9 million Germans from East Prussia, Pomerania, Silesia, the Sudetenland, and elsewhere in eastern Europe) which followed the Second World War as it

The changing face of Europe. Migrant workers gather in the main railway station in Stuttgart during the 1970s.

was decided—in stark contrast to the case after 1918—to create ethnic boundaries through ethnic deportations. By 1945, European society had become, in large measure, a society of refugees.

The Cold War, and the almost insurmountable state frontiers to which it gave rise, put a temporary halt to east-to-west migration within Europe. Immediately after the war, Europe continued to export considerable numbers of people: between 1946 and 1960, roughly half a million people left the continent annually. However, western Europe, which benefited from extraordinary economic growth and was temporarily cut off from its traditional sources of immigrants, then became a goal for migrants from other continents: from Africa and Asia, and from the Caribbean. With the transition from a period of low unemployment, which lasted roughly to the mid-1970s, to one of high unemployment in western Europe—subsequently joined by eastern European countries emerging into the cold economic winds of capitalism—this changed again. Western employers ceased recruiting foreign labour, but migrants from poorer countries continued to seek a better life in western Europe and immigrant communities continued to grow. Whereas at the beginning of the century Europeans, like European society, were items for export, towards the end of the century Europe became a major goal of poor migrants from elsewhere. Consequently, European society at the end of the century includes millions of people whose backgrounds and cultures are African and Asian. No longer is Europe colonizing the world, with its people and with its culture; now, at the end of the twentieth century, it is the former colonizers who are being colonized.

European society always has been in flux, fragmented and diverse, and during the twentieth century it became more fragmented and diverse than ever. But it is not enough simply to observe that European society has become diverse and that the idea of European society no longer possesses the coherence or attraction which it appeared to possess when the century began. It also is necessary to appreciate the general trends which have characterized and linked European societies during the twentieth century—what Europe has had in common as well as what has divided her.

Population

Many more people live in Europe in the late twentieth century than did at its beginning. Particularly in eastern and southern Europe, populations increased substantially during the century. However, probably the most striking demographic development in Europe during the twentieth century has not been population growth but the decline in fertility which, with varying speeds, has affected just about all the nations of the continent. During the nineteenth century, Europe contained some of the fastest growing populations in the world; during the twentieth, it came to contain those growing most slowly. This presents a fascinating paradox in the changing social mores of Europeans during the twentieth century: that increases in public preoccupation with sex have been accompanied by declines in child-bearing. Increasingly, sex in twentieth-century European

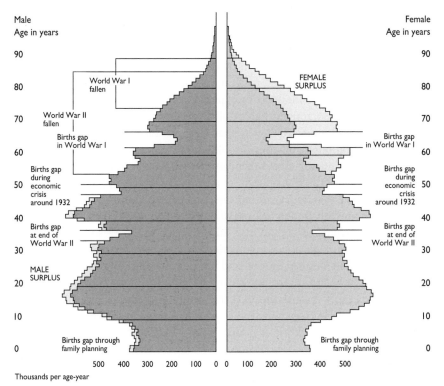

Male
Age in years

90

80

World War I
fallen

World War II
fallen

Births gap
in World War I

70

60

Births gap
during
economic
crisis
around 1932

50

40

Births gap
at end of
World War II

30

MALE
SURPLUS

20

10

0

Births gap through
family planning

500 400 300 200 100   0

Thousands per age-year

FEMALE
SURPLUS

Female
Age in years

90

80

Births gap
in World War I

70

60

Births gap
during
economic
crisis
around 1932

50

40

Births gap
at end of
World War II

30

20

10

0

Births gap through
family planning

0 100 200 300 400 500

The human consequences of war, economic crisis, and contraception. This population pyramid shows the West German population at the end of 1981, clearly revealing the effects of the two world wars, the depression of the early 1930s, and the spread of effective contraception in the 1960s and 1970s.

societies was disconnected from reproduction; instead, as birth rates plummeted and sexuality became more public and explicit, it came to be regarded as a leisure pursuit and an advertising ploy.

Declines in population growth were accompanied by an upsurge of concern about the size and health of the population and interest in eugenics, the 'science' of race improvement by judicious mating. Concern to reverse declines in population growth, and to improve the health of the human stock arose across the continent—from Fascist Italy and Weimar and Nazi Germany to Stalinist Russia and Romania under Ceausescu. States actively intervened to reverse falling birth rates, with various programmes ranging from the French *assistance familiale* designed to provide financial incentives for producing a large family and financial payments upon marriage, to Romanian bans on the means of fertility control and medical inspections to prevent women from resorting to abortion.

Across Europe profound changes in demographic structures unfolded in the twentieth century. Declines in fertility, reductions in family size (as a smaller proportion of couples had more than two children), later marriage (especially in northern and western Europe), and considerably increased life expectancy resulting from improvements in nutrition and medical care, have led to profound changes in the structures of population across the continent. European societies during the last quarter of the twentieth century contained smaller proportions of children and young people and larger proportions of the elderly than they had

236

during the early decades of the century. Remarkably, perhaps, the two world wars which ravaged Europe had no great effect on these long-term demographic trends. Once the post-war baby booms had run their course, long-term trends towards smaller families resumed. Consequently, as the century nears its end societies across Europe contain ageing populations, a smaller proportion of which are children and young people in work, and a larger and larger proportion of which are pensioners.

These demographic changes greatly altered popular perspectives and expectations. European women (very few of whom now die in childbirth and for whom child-bearing no longer necessarily occupies so large a proportion of their adult lives) increasingly entered the paid labour-market during their middle years. Across the continent, rates of infant mortality and death in childbirth declined steeply (although there have been tragic recent reverses, particularly in eastern Europe). By the second half of the twentieth century, most European parents could expect that their children would survive the first year; few European children were cut down by infectious diseases; and infectious diseases ceased to pose the threat to adult Europeans which they had in the nineteenth century. Two examples may serve for many: polio ceased to haunt Europeans with the spectre of a lifetime of paralysis after inoculation became widespread from the 1950s; and tuberculosis, which had cast a terrible shadow across the lives of millions of Europeans, became a rarity in many countries of the continent once they recovered from the effects of the Second World War (although the spread of AIDS and poverty may make it more common again). Whereas tuberculosis may be characterized as the fatal disease of the nineteenth century, the fatal disease of the twentieth century has been cancer.

The position of the elderly too has changed profoundly. At the outset of the century there were few pensioners. People who reached the grand old age of 65 usually had to keep working. Now almost all Europeans expect to receive pensions when they are elderly, and a major proportion of public expenditure in European countries has gone to provide state pensions for the increasingly large proportion of the population which is retired. Retirement has become a common expectation of Europeans as they reach their sixties, and many more of them now reach their sixties and seventies than was the case one hundred years ago.

Finally, it is worth noting that the nuclear family is a phenomenon of a specific time and place: of the developed world during the twentieth century. The self-contained family unit consisting solely of parents and children probably only became widespread in Europe during the middle decades of the twentieth century. During the previous decades, poverty, the absence of social services (such as the provision of old people's homes), and high death rates made such a family unit rather rare; during the final decades of the twentieth century, at least in the more advanced states of western Europe, liberalization of divorce laws and concomitant increases in divorce, together with steep rises in the numbers of children born out of wedlock, have led to huge increases in the number of single-parent households. The nuclear family, far from embodying an eternal moral truth, may be only a fleeting social form which enjoyed popularity during a short period between the demographic revolution of the late nineteenth and early twentieth centuries on the one hand and the late twentieth century 'divorce revolution' (to use the phrase of Lawrence Stone) on the other.

Labour

The work which most Europeans do in the late twentieth century is quite different from that which their ancestors did at its beginning. Although the world's most industrialized regions were located in Europe at the outset of the century, the continent also contained largely rural societies and agriculture was the sector of the economy which provided livelihoods to the largest number of people. This was the case not only in the less developed societies of southern and eastern Europe—of Spain, Portugal, Romania, Russia—but of northern and western Europe as well. When the century opened the majority of France's population still lived in communities with fewer than 2,000 inhabitants; Denmark and Sweden were largely rural; and more than twice as many Germans were employed in agriculture as in heavy industry. Times changed: in France, for example, while there still were roughly 4 million independent farmers in 1945, by the beginning of the 1980s there were only 1.5 million.

While the proportion of the population earning a living from agriculture declined steeply across Europe—east and west—during the twentieth century, this was not necessarily accompanied by a corresponding rise in the proportion employed in industry. The beginning of the century, as we now can see with the benefit of hindsight, was the high-water mark of classic industrialization, and the economic difficulties of the inter-war period stemmed in part from a decline in old heavy industries (iron, steel, coalmining, shipbuilding) which has continued to the present. In the more developed economies the numbers of people employed in coalmining, steel-making, and shipbuilding have fallen sharply; eastern Europe lagged behind in this regard, as socialist industrialization involved the planned growth of yesterday's industries, but the phenomenal collapse of eastern European industry and corresponding increases in unemployment after 1989 indicate that eastern Europe is rapidly catching up with the west in this respect at least.

Where employment clearly has increased is elsewhere: in white-collar work, services, state employment, medical care, and social welfare. With the possible exception of services, this general trend occurred in the now defunct socialist systems of eastern Europe as well as the capitalist economies in the western half of the continent; indeed, the socialist systems of eastern Europe spawned state bureaucracies which provided employment for huge numbers of people. The growth in white-collar and service-sector employment paralleled a tremendous increase in the number of women working outside the home. While the largest single source of employment for single women outside their own homes—domestic service—virtually disappeared in Europe, there has been a huge increase in the number of *married* women working, particularly during the second half of the century. Here too developments in the formerly socialist half of the continent paralleled (in a more extreme form) those in the western half, as female participation rates in the labour-market came to exceed 90 per cent. Virtually all women between the ages of 18 and 60 had to work outside the home under 'real-existing socialism'; virtually none was able to remain a 'mere' housewife.

Where there has been employment there also has been unemployment. Looked at from a long-term perspective, at least in those European countries which have a largely uninterrupted history of market economics, European labour-markets have been characterized by four main periods during the twentieth century: (1) a period of relatively low unemployment until the end of the First World War; (2) a period of high unemployment during the inter-war period; (3) a period of low unemployment from the Second World War until roughly the mid-1970s; and (4) a period of relatively high unemployment since the mid-1970s. Each of these has affected not only the material conditions and daily lives of millions of people in Europe; each also has shaped hopes and expectations. During the inter-war period Europeans often looked back with longing to the imagined normality of the pre-1914 world; Europeans emerging from the Second World War were haunted by the spectre of the economic crises which followed the First and the savage depression and mass unemployment of the 1930s and their possible repetition; in the last quarter of the century Europeans routinely expected politicians somehow to reconstitute the 'full employment' of the 1950s and 1960s.

Incomes and Living Standards

There can be little doubt that real incomes and living standards rose in most of Europe during the twentieth century, although many Europeans suffered terrible poverty as a consequence of war, inflation, and economic depression. While hundreds of millions of Europeans are better housed, better clothed, and better nourished at the end of the twentieth century than were their forebears at its beginning, the road to improvement has been extremely bumpy and many Europeans have fallen by the wayside.

The greatest improvements were experienced by inhabitants of western Europe during the decades after the Second World War. After the stagnation which characterized most European economies during the inter-war years and the destruction caused by the Second World War, during the 1950s and 1960s western Europe benefited from the greatest economic boom the world has ever known. Real incomes rose substantially, and the proportion of income spent on basics (in particular food) declined as expenditure on what previously had been considered luxuries (private motor vehicles, washing machines, holidays, and tourism) increased. Consequently, these luxuries no longer were the exclusive property of the upper and middle classes. In the eastern half of the continent a stunted parallel development occurred. There too real incomes rose, although from a lower base and within a framework of shortages and artificial prices which made many items of consumer expenditure (private cars, for example) effectively beyond the reach of most people.

The rise in real incomes in Europe during the twentieth century was accompanied by the squeezing of income differentials. That is to say, at the beginning of the century the incomes of the European bourgeoisie were far higher relative to working-class incomes than in the last decades of the century. This reduction of income differentials has had considerable consequences: for example, the virtual disappearance of domestic service as an employer of single women (only partly compensated for by the employment of *au pairs*), and the recent growth of do-it-yourself in the realm of house repairs. In the late twentieth century Europe's middle classes expect to cook and clean for themselves, and many are prepared to hang their own wallpaper and plumb their own sinks, tasks which few of their counterparts earlier in the century would probably have considered doing for themselves. This change has been paralleled by the introduction into the home of so-called 'labour-saving devices'. At the beginning of the twentieth century, cooking and cleaning—without the benefits of electric refrigeration, power vacuum cleaners, or gas central heating—involved much more heavy work than in recent decades; the demise of relatively cheap labour has been compensated for to some extent by a technological revolution in the home.

In socialist eastern Europe after the Second World War a far more extreme version of income levelling occurred, as 'workers' states' (the primary employers) depressed professional salaries relative to workers' wages. One consequence of the levelling of incomes and living standards in socialist eastern Europe was that the distinction between 'working-class' and 'middle-class' neighbourhoods largely disappeared; the levelling of incomes, extremely low subsidized rents, the extreme shortage of housing, and the virtual monopoly of its distribution in the hands of state authorities meant that almost all people, except for the political élite, were in the same boat—or housing estate.

The squeezing of income differentials in capitalist systems was due not only to trade union pressure and legislation to protect wage-earners, but also to inflation. Indeed, rapid inflation affected the lives of almost all Europeans since the First World War. While during much of the nineteenth century (except, for example, during the Napoleonic wars) Europeans enjoyed fairly stable prices, the twentieth century has been a century of inflation. European societies experienced some of the worst inflations the world has ever seen (in Germany, Austria, Poland, and Russia after the First World War; in Hungary after the Second World War; in Poland, Ukraine, and Russia after the collapse of Marxist-Leninist socialism); no European country, not even Switzerland, escaped completely. Consequently, price and price–wage relationships have shifted and personal and corporate savings periodically have been ravaged. The accumulated private capital of generations has at times been wiped out in various countries across Europe, leaving people more dependent upon the state for welfare and for investment.

Despite inflation, there can be no denying that hundreds of millions of Europeans became far wealthier towards the end of the twentieth century than their great-grandparents were as the century began. During the twentieth century, most European societies left a domestic economy of self-sufficiency behind; despite savage economic crises and terrible wars, nearly three decades of almost uninterrupted economic growth after the Second World War brought mass consumer society to tens of millions of western Europeans. This was true not only for the affluent countries of northern and western Europe but also, to a lesser extent, for southern and eastern Europe as well. Indeed, one reason for the destabilization of eastern European socialist regimes during the 1980s was that their populations had come to expect the fruits of a consumer society which the state-socialist regimes were unable to deliver. In western Europe, in particular, people increasingly came to regard themselves as consumers (rather than as producers), with their self-identity shaped to a considerable degree by what make of car they drove, what kind of furniture and decor they chose for their homes, what sort of holiday they took. No longer did Europeans simply purchase margarine: they bought Flora or Rama.

Town and Country

Enormous changes in how Europeans lived their lives during the twentieth century resulted from the decline in numbers employed in agriculture. The nineteenth century may be seen as the century of European industrialization, with railways spreading their tentacles across the continent and the landscapes of great industrial regions such as Lancashire, Upper Silesia, and the Ruhr becoming filled with textile mills, pit-heads, and iron smelters. Nevertheless, as we have seen, at the outset of the twentieth century the single most important source of livelihood across Europe was agriculture—not just in the predominantly rural countries (Russia, Portugal, Spain, southern Italy, Greece, Romania, Bulgaria) which comprised so much of Europe but even in the great industrial powerhouse of Germany. It is worth remembering, therefore, that the confident European society which provided the model for civilization at the beginning of the twentieth century was far removed from the societies in which most Europeans lived. At the beginning of the century most Europeans lived in communities which revolved around the parish pump, not the factory or the opera house.

As the proportion of European populations living on and from the land declined, the relative economic (and social and cultural) importance of the countryside diminished. The exploitation of green-field sites in capitalist western Europe and the industrialization of previously rural regions in socialist eastern Europe provided new employment possibilities to populations which previously had had to rely essentially upon agriculture for a living. In western Europe increasing numbers of people living in rural villages came to earn their livelihoods in towns and to commute daily to offices or factories. Urban lifestyles became the norm, even for Europeans not living in urban areas—but who, like their city cousins, became connected to the wider world first via radio and telephone, then via television and satellite dish.

Nevertheless, the diminished importance of the countryside to European society does not mean that the twentieth century has been the century of European urbanization—at least in so far as western Europe is concerned. The nineteenth century was the century of classic urbanization in Europe. The urbanization of the twentieth century has been different: first, the cities of western Europe which had

become the great metropolises of the world by the end of the nineteenth century—London, Paris, Berlin—have not grown appreciably since the First World War; urban growth has been of the periphery and suburbs, rather than inner London, historic Paris within the Périphérique motorway, or Berlin as defined before the creation of Greater Berlin in 1920. Secondly, the greatest urban growth in Europe has been in the east, not the west: in Moscow, Kiev, Bucharest, Warsaw; not London, Amsterdam, Hamburg, Paris. There the introduction of socialist planned economies and forced industrialization led to enormous urban growth, in many cases built on the rubble left behind by war—the civil war in Russia and the Second World War. Thirdly, there has been a trend towards increased residential persistence: Europeans became less likely to move home. In western Europe, this has been due partly to increased owner occupation; in socialist eastern Europe, it resulted from the state regulation of a housing market characterized by extreme shortage. Fourthly, the face of much of Europe was scarred by a Second World War which generally affected the towns more than the countryside, as cities from Stalingrad to Rotterdam were reduced to rubble. Finally, the rapid (re-)building of European cities led to the construction of massive high-rise housing developments, which buried the distinctiveness of individual European cities under the projects of planners and tonnes of concrete.

The changes outlined above, together with the replacement of horse-powered transport by motor-driven transport, also altered the relationship of most Europeans to animals. At the beginning of the twentieth century, before the spread of the internal combustion engine and with agriculture still the largest single source of employment, contact with animals was a regular and essential part of everyday life for most Europeans. They met them on their streets, kept them in their back gardens, rode them, and slaughtered them. Relatively few Europeans—at least in the northern and western parts of the continent—now keep animals in their back gardens, milk cows, drive horses or oxen; today for most Europeans regular contact with animals is limited to caring for domestic pets.

Travel and Leisure

Europeans became far more mobile in the course of the twentieth century. At the beginning of the century, most people's principal everyday means of transport was their own feet. Since the Second World War, however, the private motor vehicle has become the most important mode of transport for tens of millions of Europeans. In France, for example, whereas in 1938 there was one private motor vehicle for 20.8 inhabitants, by 1980 this ratio stood at one car for every 2.9 inhabitants; in the Netherlands the ratio fell from 90.9 to 3.1 during the same period, in Switzerland from 55.5 to 2.8, and in Italy from 125 to 3.2. Not even the erstwhile socialist societies of eastern Europe (with the exception of Albania) completely escaped private motorization during the 1970s and 1980s, as clones of Fiat cars were churned out in their hundreds of thousands from Russian and Polish factories.

Although it is now common to bemoan the effects of the motor car upon the environment, private motor-vehicle transport has been liberating for millions of

Facing: **Where is this?** Can you tell what European country these housing developments are in?

Main picture: Parisian suburb, France. *Inset*: Hoyerswerda, in eastern Germany; Halifax, UK; and Marseilles, France.

243

people. Rural inhabitants with their own motor transport could travel easily to town; the countryside became accessible to motorized urban dwellers to an extent never before experienced; the geography of employment, commerce, and leisure altered once people no longer were limited as to where they could work and shop by how far they could walk or by the routes offered by public transport operators.

Europe gave the world its first motor vehicles (those of Gottfried Daimler in Stuttgart and Karl Benz in Mannheim in 1885) and its first motorways (the German autobahn network). Nevertheless, pictures of clover-leaf motorway intersections and of suburban motorists now are associated more with twentieth-century America than with Europe. It was in the United States that levels of economic well-being allowed the first mass motorization during the second and third decades of the century; and it was in the United States that the massive interstate highway building programme brought motorways to the masses. Europe lagged behind. In western Europe—despite the building of the German autobahn network during the second half of the 1930s—mass motorization did not come about until after the Second World War.

Europe's answer to Henry Ford's 'Model T'. The 'Strength-through-Joy' car, which became the best-selling car of all time and the first car for millions of Europeans: the Volkswagen Beetle.

VOLKSWAGEN

Rêve d'hier... Réalité d'aujourd'hui

This motorization might be regarded as evidence of an Americanization of European society. In fact, it is more a sign that in recent decades the population at least of western Europe achieved levels of personal wealth similar to those enjoyed by the majority of United States citizens. While the result is not necessarily American, it is not necessarily European either. The transport revolution of the twentieth century eroded that self-confident European urban culture which had served as a model in so much of the rest of the world. While a hundred years ago the Paris Opéra may have been an object to be copied, it cannot really be said that the Paris Périphérique provides a model for anything. Birmingham's Spaghetti Junction is neither a copy of an American road nor a distinctive European approach to traffic flows; it is just another motorway junction, much like motorway junctions in Los Angeles, Frankfurt, Tokyo, and Rio.

Improved mobility meant not just getting to work or to the shopping mall more swiftly. It also allowed a phenome-

The open road.
A passenger's view of Europe's
first motorway network, the
Reichsautobahn, in the
mid-1930s. The autobahn did
not fill up with cars until after
the Second World War.

nal growth of tourism. At the beginning of the century, tourism was reserved for
the wealthy. During the twentieth century millions of Europeans came to expect a
holiday, often involving foreign travel, almost as a matter of right. The most phenomenal growth of the European tourist industry occurred after the 1960s—
another reflection of the achievement of high levels of personal wealth (at least in
northern and western Europe), as well as of cheap air travel. However, the beginnings of modern mass tourism in Europe can be traced to the inter-war period—
with the growth of Butlins in Britain, the *dopolavoro* in Fascist Italy, and the Nazi
Kraft durch Freude organization. Although their achievements fell somewhat
short of their propaganda, these programmes consciously extended mass leisure
activities to Europeans who never before had enjoyed tourist travel, but whose
children and grandchildren came to expect it.

The mass tourism of late twentieth-century Europe had a number of important
characteristics. First, it was a consequence of the extension of lengthy paid holidays to the great mass of full-time employees. Secondly, it became international:
it no longer is exceptional for Europeans to hold passports for foreign travel; in
striking contrast with the tourism of the 1930s, the tourism of the 1980s commonly
involved travel across national frontiers. This meant that millions of western
Europeans were exposed to countries, languages, and cultures other than their
own—even if this contact frequently was limited to enjoying fish and chips or
bratwurst on the Costa del Sol rather than in Leeds or Nuremberg. Thirdly, the
tourism boom in western Europe had its parallels in socialist eastern Europe.
Although socialist tourism tended to be heavily subsidized, low-quality group
travel organized through the state-regimented trade unions and offering very limited opportunity for international travel, Europeans in the socialist east also came
to expect annual holidays and travel. At the same time, the inadequacies of travel

for eastern Europeans—restrictions on international travel especially to the West, the lack of convertible currency, the difficulties facing anyone who preferred individual travel to organized group activities—helped to undermine the socialist regimes in the eyes of their populations. The inhabitants of Dresden and Prague wanted the same leisure and travel opportunities which their cousins in Düsseldorf and Vienna enjoyed.

State and Society

At the beginning of the twentieth century the contact which most Europeans had with the state was, compared with today, rather limited. Men were conscripted into national armies; businesses faced increasing regulation; urban police and rural gendarmes enforced order; and criminals and the destitute sometimes landed in prison or the poor house. However, few Europeans carried identity documents issued by the state, the state's tax demands were by present-day standards very modest, and almost no one expected that the state would or should provide for them if they fell ill or became disabled or pay pensions if and when they became old. The social dimension of state provision was conspicuous largely by its absence.

By the last third of the century, this had changed profoundly. Where once an extended family may have been expected to care for the elderly or incapacitated, Europeans came to look to the state for aid. Women's economic dependence upon men was replaced to some extent by economic dependence upon the state. Millions of parents received state child benefit; millions of Europeans collected state unemployment benefit; vast social service organizations were created and armies of social workers employed by European states; millions of Europeans dwelt in state-built (and often state-subsidized) housing; health care was administered through state-run or state-supervised health insurance schemes.

While the origins of modern social welfare may be traced to the late nineteenth century, and in particular to Bismarck's introduction of social insurance in Germany during the 1880s, its expansion has been a largely twentieth-century affair. The world wars, which saw increased state regulation and intervention in almost all aspects of social life, left millions of invalids, widows, and orphans in their wake and thus created the demand for an enormous extension of state welfare provision. This trend was furthered by the advent of political systems with totalitarian claims to run society, and rising expectations that the state has a duty to provide for its citizens. Then the great western European economic boom, which lasted almost without interruption from the Second World War until the late 1960s, provided the resources for a seemingly open-ended expansion of welfare provision (for example, the linking of state pensions to the cost of living, beginning in West Germany in 1957). Even more comprehensively, if less effectively, the socialist regimes of eastern Europe expanded the role of the state in welfare provision. Vast subsidies were channelled into child care (to enable women to work in economies which were extremely labour intensive), into keeping down prices for basic foodstuffs, into organized leisure pursuits, and into cheap subsidized housing. While

Is this Europe? Well, yes . . . This is Paris of the 1980s—rather different from the image which inspired imitation at the beginning of the century—with the small-scale reproduction of the Statue of Liberty on the Seine dwarfed by a high-rise hotel, and with the Pont de Grenelle suitably decked out with American flags.

Left: **The changing face of Europe**. A Senegalese worker harvests tomatoes near Naples in the early 1990s.

Is this Europe? Yes, again. New corporate headquarters at La Défense, Paris.

this experiment proved resoundingly unsuccessful, as the collapse of eastern Europe's economies after 1989 exposed the often dire state of actual welfare provision and levels of investment, the general development paralleled what occurred elsewhere in Europe.

The extension of state welfare during the twentieth century arose from strong ideological motives. It spelled 'progress'; it allowed the state's administrative control over the peoples of Europe to increase; and it was guided by what may be described as therapeutic intentions. That is to say, European states designed interventionist programmes to combat social practices which allegedly undermined the health of society. Images of a healthy society guided attempts by state institutions across Europe to intervene in the lives of their subjects and to shape social developments—whether these attempts were in the form of the relatively benign technocratic urges of Swedish social democracy, Francoist myths of a healthy moral Spain, a socialist society which was supposed to have created Soviet man, or the horrific racialist Utopia which the Nazis aimed to achieve through the extermination of human beings of allegedly lesser worth. European interventionist states became, in their various ways, the self-appointed doctors of European societies.

Education

A central element of the state's role in European societies has been the provision of formal education. By the late nineteenth century most European states had made schooling legally compulsory; and at the outset of the twentieth century the countries of northern and western Europe contained the world's most literate and best-educated populations. The inhabitants of the Netherlands, Germany, and Scandinavia already had achieved virtually complete literacy by the end of the nineteenth century. However, southern and eastern Europeans lagged behind. At the turn of the century only about one-fifth of the Russian population was literate, and only about one-tenth of the female rural population could read and write. Before the First World War, in neither Italy nor in Spain did half the children in the age-group 5–14 actually attend school. And on the eve of the First World War only about one-third of the adult population of Portugal, Spain, Greece, Romania, and Bulgaria could read and write. This altered in the course of the twentieth century, as (in this regard at least) the south and east of Europe caught up with the north and west. Adults in present-day Spain and Italy are largely literate, as are those in eastern Europe.

The extension of formal education and mass literacy campaigns were among the most successful programmes of the erstwhile socialist states of eastern Europe. Of course, political control was a motive here, nowhere more so than in the Soviet Union under Stalin. While Stalin's *History of the Communist Party of the Soviet Union/Bolsheviks. Short Course* may have been neither a literary masterpiece nor a model of historical accuracy, it was a book presented to millions of newly literate people. As the century nears its end and many of the achievements of socialism in eastern Europe reveal themselves to have been of dubious value, the educational campaigns which put almost all of eastern Europe's children in schools and taught almost all of eastern Europe's people to read and write may be Marxist-Leninist socialism's lasting positive achievement.

Of course, the expansion of educational provision (and of the state's role in it) was not just a matter of primary schools and basic literacy. Much more striking has been the expansion in the provision of secondary, technical, and higher education across Europe. At the beginning of the century, only a small minority of children remained in secondary education beyond the school-leaving age, even in the relatively advanced countries of northern and western Europe. Higher education was for the few, and almost all of those few were men. In 1910 in no country in Europe were more than 2 per cent of people aged between 20 and 24 in higher education; and generally only about one-tenth of these were women. During the second half of the century higher education became a huge industry across Europe, employing hundreds of thousands of people and teaching millions of students. Higher education ceased to be something to which only a tiny proportion of the population could aspire; instead, it came to be regarded as a passport to a growing number of well-paid jobs in increasingly meritocratic societies in which academic qualifications and expertise—measured in certificates, diplomas, and degrees—were seen as absolutely necessary.

Communications

Literacy promotes reading. Or does it? It is a paradox of the social history of twentieth-century Europe that the establishment of near universal literacy has been paralleled by a diminution of the literary standards of mass-market newspapers and a vast increase of readily available pornography. The main reason for the change, however, is less that standards have fallen than that the nature of communications has changed. Europeans, like most inhabitants of the developed world, receive their news of the world almost instantly, via radio and television. This, indeed, is one of the great social changes of the twentieth century: people can be aware much more quickly of momentous political events far away than were their forebears at the beginning of the century.

Compare how Europeans learned of the outbreak and course of the First World War, of the Second World War, and of more recent conflicts—say, the Gulf war of 1991 or the civil wars in the former Yugoslavia. When the First World War broke out, most Europeans found out about these momentous events from newspapers or from publicly displayed pronouncements; their news of developments on the battlefield, in so far as it did not come by word of mouth, came from the printed media—often days after the event.

At the outbreak of the Second World War in Europe things were very different. The main source of current news was the radio, and one could hear war being declared as it happened; newsreels provided images of what had occurred during the previous week. More recently, television became the main and instant source of news and entertainment. European television viewers watched Baghdad being bombed as it happened, and graphic pictures of the miseries inflicted on the pop-

ulation of Sarajevo were presented in their living-rooms on the day they occurred (often courtesy of an American television news network). This is a far cry from the way in which news spread of the assassination of the Archduke Franz Ferdinand in Sarajevo nearly eight decades previously.

The history of the communications and media revolution is not one of benign progress, devoid of political content. During the twentieth century, European states attempted to control the media as never before. As means of communications improved and developed, so did the concern of government to control and censor. Censorship was, of course, nothing new. However, the extent and brutality of attempts to control the communications media have been unprecedented. The spread of radio coincided both with the great inter-war depression (during which radio receivers were one of the few items of consumer expenditure to increase) and with the dictatorships of Mussolini, Hitler, and Stalin. As microphones were installed in the piazza and radios came into millions of homes, European dictatorships with totalitarian claims to control the whole of society sought to eliminate all dissenting voices in the public sphere. Yet we should not assume that such developments were the exclusive preserve of dictatorships: the model for George Orwell's Ministry of Truth in his *1984* was not in Berlin or Moscow, but the wartime Ministry of Information in London.

The spread of communications media has involved not just hundreds of mil-

What did they think they were cheering?
This is probably the most famous photograph of cheering crowds in the summer of 1914, taken by Heinrich Hoffmann of the Munich Odeonsplatz on 2 August 1914, the day war was declared. By chance, the young Adolf Hitler (holding a hat, near the centre of the photo) was photographed here by Hoffmann, who later became the Nazi leader's court photographer.

lions of Europeans becoming listeners to radio, and later viewers of television in the privacy of their own homes. Perhaps even more important in changing how Europeans lead their everyday lives has been the growth of private telecommunications. At the turn of the century businesses and government offices in the more developed parts of the continent were able to communicate with one another by telephone, although messages still tended to be sent via messengers or the post; private telephones were limited to the well off, and long-distance and international communication was extremely difficult by more recent standards. However, with the increase in prosperity enjoyed by western Europeans during the second half of the century came a boom in private telephone usage. Millions of homes were connected to national (and international) telephone networks; telecommunications beyond the local area became progressively easier, to the point where dialling a number in another country differed little from dialling a number across town. Hundreds of millions of Europeans were put into instant contact with people outside of their own localities.

In this, first northern and western Europe and later (and less thoroughly) south-

Two views of radio in Nazi Germany: The familiar propaganda image ('All Germany listens to the Führer with the people's receiver'); and advertising aimed at the better off who wanted to tune in to America.

ern and eastern Europe essentially followed an American lead, treading a path down which the inhabitants of the United States had already passed. In yet another sphere, revolutionary change in the ways European societies functioned during the twentieth century meant essentially that Europe was following trends established elsewhere. This did not necessarily mean that European societies were becoming Americanized (although Europeans may frequently have regarded this as so), but that the same things were changing the ways in which Europeans lived as had changed Americans' lives.

God and Science

Whether most Europeans consciously subscribed to it or not, the societies in which they have lived during the twentieth century increasingly have taken as their point of orientation not God but science. Europeans may, if asked, have continued to proclaim a personal belief in the existence of God, but they came to lead their everyday lives largely without reference to an extra-worldly authority. The twentieth century saw the completion of what Max Weber described as the 'de-mystification of the world', a world in which phenomena apparently can be explained with reference to the laws of science. Nevertheless, new obstacles have formed to an unambiguous, optimistic belief in science, a faith in improvement through technology. Certainly during the twentieth century the fruits of scientific discovery and progress were widely disseminated: medical advances and professional medical care were extended to European populations; the majority of Europeans came to enjoy the benefits of clean water supply and efficient waste-disposal systems; electricity entered millions of homes, as electricity grids were developed and electricity supply extended into the European countryside from Brittany to the Urals; new energy supplies brought adequate heating into millions of European homes. However, after the horrors unleashed by Europeans in two world wars and countless other conflicts, campaigns of mass murder, deep economic crises, the collapse of 'scientific socialism', the threat of nuclear terror, and the spectre of Chernobyl, it has become rather more difficult for Europeans to put their faith in science.

Against this background processes of secularization were felt across Europe. This had a number of manifestations: declines in church attendance, reductions in state-provided religious education, a tendency towards civil rather than religious marriage ceremonies, the effective disestablishment of Churches in most European countries, and a declining influence of Church teachings in such matters as divorce and abortion. Of course, these trends have been neither universal nor uncontested, as the recent growth of evangelical Christian Churches and the heated reactions to reforms in the Catholic Church and the Church of England testify—to say nothing of the bitter conflicts among differing religious groups in Northern Ireland or the former Yugoslavia. Yet there can be little doubt that formal religion came to occupy a rather less secure place in the lives of most Europeans towards the end of the century than it had done at the beginning.

It is not just religious teaching and religious influence which has altered in Euro-

A monument to a vanished European society. This is all that remains of the Jewish community of Breslau (today's Polish city of Wroclaw). The picture shows the main German-Jewish cemetery of Breslau as it looked in the mid-1980s, in which (among others) Ferdinand Lasalle was buried.

pean societies. The position of Europe as religious focus changed profoundly during the twentieth century. Most of the major religions which had their centres in Europe at the outset of the century experienced profound dislocations. Russian Orthodoxy spent decades cowering before a regime which preached earthly progress, materialism, and militant atheism. The classic centres of Jewish culture in central and eastern Europe were wiped out by the Nazis, and whereas the overwhelming majority of the world's Jews lived in Europe at the beginning of the century the major centres of world Jewry lie outside Europe as the century nears its end—in Israel and the United States. The majority of the world's Catholics no longer are Europeans, putting the Italian and European domination of the Church of Rome into question. And as the twentieth century nears its end, the fastest growing religion in what once was the centre of Christendom is Islam.

Conclusion

European societies have undergone many revolutions during the twentieth century. They have been rocked by political revolutions, which led to the destruction of old élites which ruled much of the continent at the outset of the century, and which were followed by the establishment of totalitarian systems of unparalleled

252

brutality. They have been engulfed in world wars which produced mass violence and mass bereavement. They have witnessed economic revolutions—not only the failed attempts to impose socialist planned economies but also the advent of a prosperity (at least in western Europe) which had no precedent and which spread far beyond the narrow stratum of the rich. They have experienced demographic revolutions, as Europe came to house the world's oldest and slowest growing populations. They have experienced cultural revolutions, as modernist culture has shown both the extent and limits of its potential. At the same time, however, Europe has lost its unique position in the world. Post-revolutionary, post-postwar, post-modern Europe no longer can be regarded as being in the economic, politi-

The modern face of religious belief in Europe. The new Milton Keynes mosque, the centre of a thriving Islamic community in Britain's newest new town.

cal, or cultural vanguard. As a consequence of the developments outlined above, Europe has emerged much like the rest of the developed world. Simultaneously, the myopic self-confidence and concept of Europe which were in place at the outset of the twentieth century have been shattered—through the horrors of war, revolution, mass violence, and totalitarianism, and by massive economic and social changes.

While it is tempting to discuss the history of western and eastern Europe in separate categories—the one developed, the other backward; the one capitalist, the other socialist for much of the century—to retrace the iron curtain here would be inappropriate. For if there has been such a thing as European society, then eastern Europe has been as much a part of it as western Europe. Virtually all the trends and developments discussed above were played out in eastern as well as in western Europe, and the socialist experiment which was imposed upon eastern Europe reflected many of the same desires which motivated Europeans in the western half of the continent. This is not to assert that there necessarily is a thing such as a single coherent European society. There have been many European societies, not all of whose members are Europeans and not all of whose locations are in Europe.

The European society which provided a model for the rest of the world at the outset of the twentieth century was the society of only a small minority of Europeans: of the London, Berlin, or Paris bourgeoisie, not of the Bulgarian or Andalucian peasantry. At the end of the twentieth century European society no longer provides a model for anything in particular. At the same time, European society has become both more fragmented and more embracing of the peoples of Europe. As Europe became more urban, European urban society lost its apparent coherence and paradigmatic quality. As Europe reflected more the social and cultural influences of peoples from beyond the European continent, it simultaneously became less a model for the rest of the world. At the beginning of the twentieth century, a combination of advanced economic development, imperialism, and cultural myopia allowed European society to become a model for the rest of the world; at the end of the twentieth century a democratization of culture and society has meant that there no longer is a coherent idea of European society which necessarily provides a model for others. As the rest of the world has caught up with Europe, Europe has become like the rest of the world and European society as a coherent idea has evaporated.

From Modernism to Post-modernism

10

A HISTORY of aesthetic modernism in Europe written in the middle of the twentieth century might have gone something like this: rebelling against inherited aesthetic forms, impatient with the conventional values of bourgeois society, and dismayed by the spread of vulgarized mass culture, an international band of creative artists coalesced in the waning years of the nineteenth century into a militant avant-garde dedicated to the radical transformation of the cultural *status quo*. Assuming a defiantly adversarial position *vis-à-vis* the dominant traditions of their various fields, its members sought to create an art that would be purely of their time, ruthlessly 'modern' in the root sense of 'recently, just now' from the Latin *modo*. In so doing, they extended the boundaries of what had hitherto been considered art, often scandalizing a conservative public resistant to their innovations in form and offended by their inclusion of previously tabooed subject-matter.

Although in part anticipated by certain tendencies in the romantic movement of the early nineteenth century and prepared by the art-for-art's-sake aestheticism that followed, a self-conscious modernism can be said to have emerged only with writers such as the French poet Charles Baudelaire (1821–67) in the mid-century and painters such as the impressionists, who began to exhibit in the 1860s and 1870s. By the turn of the century, when the languorous nostalgia of the decadent *fin de siècle* had finally been left behind, modernism began to proliferate throughout all artistic fields into competing movements of artists vying for the honour of being the most *avant* of all the *gardes*.[1]

Indeed, one of the most striking characteristics of modernism, setting it apart from previous cultural formations such as romanticism, realism, or naturalism, was its fragmentation into a bewildering succession of distinct submovements. Even a partial list conveys the energy of its invention: post-impressionism, symbolism, cubism, vorticism, imagism, acmeism, neo-plasticism, De Stijl (the Style),

MARTIN
JAY

255

orphism, fauvism, futurism, constructivism, purism, Dadaism, expressionism, surrealism, and the Neue Sachlichkeit (the New Objectivity). The general term 'modernism', first used in the 1890s by the Nicaraguan writer Rubén Darío (1867–1916) to distinguish Latin American from Spanish literature, only became widely accepted to embrace all of these -isms in the 1920s. Although certain modernist artists—for example, the novelists James Joyce (1882–1941) and Marcel Proust (1871–1922)—resisted the discipline of a collective movement, many others—such as the poets André Breton (1896–1966) and Filippo Marinetti (1876–1944)—eagerly organized their followers into close-knit bands of like-minded militants in the struggle for cultural power. While each group may have only enjoyed a relatively brief moment at the cutting edge, and some were stronger in certain countries than others (for example, expressionism in Germany, surrealism in France, futurism in Italy and Russia), the cumulative effects of their efforts finally told. Albeit still met with anger and incomprehension by certain traditionally oriented segments of the larger public, the modernists managed to gain a wide measure of acceptance in the wake of the First World War, which did so much to topple—or at least threaten—the already fragile pieties of bourgeois culture. As one wag later put it, the war may not have made the world safe for democracy, but it certainly made it safe for the avant-garde. The French poet Paul Verlaine's (1844–96) famous

256

injunction to 'twist the neck' of the nineteenth-century's tired rhetoric—visual and musical as well as literary—now found a ready audience. Although denounced by inter-war totalitarian political movements of the left and right, which preferred 'healthier' pseudo-realist or neo-classical alternatives, modernism inexorably became the dominant cultural force in much of western Europe and North America, indeed throughout a great deal of the world. What significantly became known as 'the international style' in architecture meant the triumph of high-rise modern towers of steel, concrete, and glass in city after city around the globe. The first museum devoted entirely to modern art was founded in 1929 in New York; others soon followed. By the end of the Second World War, high modernism had become so successful that its works successfully competed with those of the old masters in the market-place for artistic commodities and its once scandalous texts achieved canonical status on the required reading lists of college courses everywhere.

In a mid-century historical narrative of aesthetic modernism's hard-won triumph, its complicated relationship to the general trends of European history would have merited extended comment. For not only did the modernists frequently choose their subject-matter from the everyday life of a Europe rapidly undergoing the larger socioeconomic transformations soon to be called 'modernization', but they also emulated the experimental method that had provided so many remarkable results in the natural sciences. Even if they scornfully rejected

Hitler and Goebbels viewing the Exhibition of Degenerate Art, Munich, 1937. Drawing on a well-established anxiety about alleged cultural *cum* biological 'degeneracy', the Nazis mockingly exhibited the work of many avant-garde artists in Munich in 1937. They invidiously contrasted it with the 'healthy' heroic realism of 'authentic' German art, a style curiously akin to the socialist realism then being produced by artists in the Soviet Union.

Peter Behrens,
AEG Turbine Factory, Berlin,
1908–9. Built for a giant
electrical firm, this remarkable
structure balanced architectural innovations—an exposed
steel frame on its long façade
and walls of windows—with a
traditional faceted gable roof
and heavy stone, banded
corners to produce an
integrated temple to modern
technology and industrial
might.

the positivist mentality that often accompanied nineteenth-century scientific
enquiry, they drew sustenance from the newer models of science, such as Ein-
steinian relativism and Freudian psychoanalysis, and from the most advanced
philosophies, those of Friedrich Nietzsche (1844–1900), Ernst Mach (1838–1916),
Henri Bergson (1859–1941), and the later existentialists of the twentieth century,
such as Martin Heidegger (1889–1926) and Jean-Paul Sartre (1905–80). Most modernists felt at home in the metropolitan whirl that had compelled earlier artists to
seek solace in rural simplicity or natural beauty; cities like Paris, Vienna, Berlin,
Milan, and Munich became the enabling contexts of their creativity. Many modernists were also fascinated by the rapid development of advanced technologies,
which helped expand the possibilities of perceptual experience and facilitate the
radical 'derangement of the senses' sought by poets like Arthur Rimbaud (1854–
91). In certain cases, most notably the Italian and Russian futurists, unbridled enthusiasm for the radically new led to what their detractors disparagingly called
'modernolatry'.

The attitude of many modernists towards certain non-cultural aspects of modernization was, to be sure, often deeply ambivalent. Their frequently explicit
élitism meant a contempt not only for conventional 'high' art, but also for the
debased kitsch they identified with most 'low' art as well. Reproducing the characteristic nineteenth-century bohemian disdain for the commodification of
beauty and the soulless alienation of modern mass society, many modernists were

258

deeply disillusioned by liberal democracy and drawn to radical solutions, both on the right and the left, to the cultural and political crisis of their day. Some, like the poets T. S. Eliot (1888–1965), Ezra Pound (1885–1974), and Wyndham Lewis (1884–1957), flirted with fascism; others among the expressionists and surrealists were drawn to the extreme left, as were many constructivists and futurists in the new Soviet Union. Even the most seemingly nihilist and destructive of the movements, Dadaism, ultimately made common cause in Weimar Germany with revolutionary Marxism and turned its efforts towards fighting fascism. The apocalyptic mood that often accompanied the modernists' violent dismantling of traditional culture led many to expect some sort of future redemption, understood in almost religious terms, once the job of demolition was complete.

And yet, in a mid-twentieth-century account of modernism, such extra-aesthetic expectations would likely have been considered somewhat of an embarrassment, evidence of the birth-pangs of an aesthetic movement that ultimately transcended its origins. For the dominant narrative of that time generally saw the modernist project as a process of progressive purification. That is, modernism was understood to foster what might

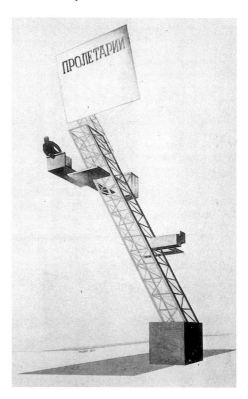

Lazar (El) Lissitzky, *Lenin Tribune,* 1920. The constructivist Lissitzky combined a familiar image of Lenin exhorting the masses with a crane-like contraption suggesting modern technology. Shortly after he completed this drawing, he went into exile in Holland and Germany, where his ideas of a machine aesthetic found a new audience.

Giacomo Balla, *Dog on a Leash,* 1912. Inspired in part by the stop-action chrono-photography of Eadweard Muybridge and Etienne-Jules Marey, the Italian futurist Balla sought to capture the movement of a toy-like pet and his half-visible mistress as they skitter with comical effect across the static canvas.

be called the differentiation of the purely aesthetic from other realms of human endeavour, such as ethics, politics, religion, or economics. As such, it was seen as the heir to the nineteenth-century art-for-art's-sake ethos, which resisted the subordination of the aesthetic to external functional ends.

Evidence for this attitude would have been found in the modernist disdain for evolutionary, progressive, or dialectical development—the chronologies of historical time—in favour of a temporality of pure presence. What the critic Roger Shattuck called the modernist 'art of stillness' meant replacing an aesthetic of transitions with one of juxtapositions, classically expressed in the comte de Lautréamont's (1846–70) oft-cited image of 'an umbrella and a sewing machine on a dissecting table', which provided inspiration to the symbolists and the surrealists alike. Imagist poets like Pound sought to banish abstract, conceptual language

Vladimir Tatlin, *Model of the Monument to the Third International,* 1920. Designed when avant-garde artists like the constructivist Tatlin could still align themselves with the Bolshevik Revolution, this combined kinetic sculpture, radio tower, and functioning building was to dwarf the Eiffel Tower in height and serve as a monument to internationalism and technology. Rejected as impractical and utopian by the Soviets, who soon spurned modernism in general, it was never actually built.

and find the means to register that intensely immediate experience of the here and now celebrated by Bergson and the English critic T. E. Hulme (1883–1917). The montage techniques of Russian film-makers like Sergei Eisenstein (1898–1948) and novelists like the American John Dos Passos (1896–1970) expressed what was often called the modernist 'spatialization of form'. Pound's *Cantos* or Eliot's *Wasteland* abandoned normal syntactic development for the juxtaposition of seemingly discordant word-groups, fragments often explicitly extracted from other texts, to produce an effect of detemporalization.

An equally ahistorical fascination with cyclical time, the temporality of eternal myth, betrayed the frequent modernist desire to lift art above the meaningless course of everyday life, to achieve what became known as 'absolute art'. Emblematic of this quest was the symbolist poetry of Stéphane Mallarmé (1842–98), who sought a language that no longer functioned as a medium of mundane communication, but which mysteriously evoked a higher truth beyond experience, calling up, in his celebrated phrase, 'flowers absent from all bouquets'.

John Heartfield, *Millions Stand behind Me: The Meaning of the Hitler Salute*, photomontage, 16 October 1932. The radical politics and innovative montages of Berlin Dada combined to produce powerful satirical images. One of the most striking was John Heartfield's refunctioning of the populist Nazi slogan 'millions stand behind me' to mock Hitler's dependence on funding from big business.

The Modernist Apotheosis of Purified Form

In general, modernists saw aesthetic form as independent of, and more important than, content; they gave the medium of representation or expression priority over what was represented or expressed. Or more precisely, form and the media of representation were themselves understood to be the content of the work, which was treated as a self-contained sign system of its own. In such modernist dramas as Luigi Pirandello's *Six Characters in Search of an Author* (1921), the fictional nature of theatricality and the audience's complicity in its illusion is what the play is about. Accordingly, much of the critical discourse surrounding modernism— most notably that of the Russian formalists and the American New Critics— stressed an immanent analysis of works in isolation from their generative context, personal as well as social. Although residues of romantic expressivist aesthetics could be found in occasional accounts of the putative debts creations owed to their creators' lives, by and large modernist works were understood as self-contained artefacts, whose aesthetic value was irreducible to anything beyond

261

their own internal dynamics. As Eliot put it, 'the progress of the artist is a continual self-sacrifice, a continual extinction of personality. Poetry is not the turning loose of emotions but an escape from emotion, not the expression of personality but the escape from personality'.

It was precisely its heightened reflexivity, tolerance of ambiguity, and ironic self-consciousness about its technical means of production that set modernism apart from the other, more traditional art that continued to be produced by its less innovative competitors (and that also allowed modernism to invent its own subterranean counter-tradition of reflexive forebears, such as Lawrence Sterne, the author of the eighteenth-century anti-novel *Tristram Shandy*, or Gustave Flaubert, who famously claimed that he wanted to write 'a book about nothing'). Even when surrealists such as Breton sought to unleash the forces of the unconscious or objective chance by such techniques as automatic writing, the apparently incoherent results could more easily be justified by invoking formalist than substantive criteria.

Following this logic of aesthetic purification, the retrospective narrative of international-style architecture, as it was written at mid-century, often repressed the socially Utopian aims of certain of its founders in the Weimar Republic's

Walter Gropius,
Bauhaus, Dessau, 1925–6. Forced to move for political reasons from Weimar to Dessau, the Bauhaus relocated in a new building designed by their director Walter Gropius. Among the first proponents of what later became known as 'the international style', they introduced reinforced concrete floor slabs, supporting columns set back from the façade and walls of sheer, uninterrupted glass.

Umberto Boccioni, *The City Rises* (*above*), 1910–11. Depicted by the Italian Futurist Boccioni, the modern city becomes a whirl-wind of movement, force, and raw power. Workers and their draft-horses merge together in a frenzy of excitement, producing an urban landscape pulsing with the energy of animal life.

Modernist sculpture of the kind exemplified by Brancusi (*left*) is best understood as a process of abstraction, which left behind both the site-specificity of traditional sculpture, its location in a monumental or architectural context, and its representational function. Although what remained approached pure form, the stubborn materiality of its embodiment, shown here in the mirroring effects of the polished bronze, resisted total etherialization.

Bauhaus School, stressing instead the clarity of unadorned geometrical form. Although at times such forms were justified as following the function of the building, at other times purely optical values—clarity, simplicity, transparency—prevailed. Similarly, the history of modernist painting was often construed in terms of the progressive abstraction of pure shape, colour, and texture from the mimetic, anecdotal, or even emotional referent outside of the canvas. Significantly, the flat grid became emblematic of a new anti-perspectivalism, which decried the illusionist intentions of traditional painting. Modernist sculpture could likewise be defended in terms of abstraction, not only from representational subject-matter (typically the human form), but also from the culturally meaningful site in which monuments were normally placed (churches, palaces, public squares, etc.). The modernist appropriation of art from so-called primitive sources, typically African or Oceanic, was also understood to mean appreciating their formal qualities or colouristic intensity apart from their ritual or religious-use value. Modernist music, especially that associated with the so-called Second Vienna School led by Arnold Schoenberg (1874–1951), was likewise understood to follow imperatives internal to musical form following the crisis of tonality, and, in so doing, to scorn the need to caress the ear of the listener or arouse his or her emotional associations. Even the most seemingly referential and mimetic of visual phenomena, the photograph, could be raised to the level of high art and defended in modernist terms of formal beauty, as a pure image sufficient unto itself and produced as much by the skilled hand of an artist as by the mechanical process of the camera.

Although some modernists continued the mixed media tradition inspired by the nineteenth-century composer Richard Wagner's idea of the *Gesamtkunstwerk*—a celebrated example is the 1917 Sergei Diaghilev (1872–1929) production of the ballet *Parade*, on which Igor Stravinsky (1882–1971), Erik Satie (1866–1925), Jean Cocteau (1889–1963), and Pablo Picasso (1881–1971) collaborated—many tried to eliminate the influence of one medium on another, seeking to isolate the 'essential' characteristics of each. Critics such as the American Clement Greenberg (1909–94) were influential in turning the doctrine of self-referential purification into a new orthodoxy, which a later generation of commentators would claim tyrannized the art world during the middle of the century.

For many modernists, differentiation and purification meant highlighting not only formal properties, but also the materiality of the media through which form was conveyed. Not the illusion of a mimetically reproduced external scene viewed

The Death of Dresden by Wilhelm Lachnit (*facing*). The bombing raid which killed so many civilians and destroyed one of Europe's most beautiful cities at a time when the end of the war was imminent raised some awkward questions about the morality of Allied strategy which have never been given an adequate answer.

Piet Mondrian, *Painting I (Composition in White and Black)*, 1926. Exemplifying the modernist search for economy of means and purity of form, Mondrian experimented with variations on grids, eccentrically situated in differently shaped frames. Was the result a self-enclosed work or a fragment of a larger, perhaps infinite pattern extending out into the world?

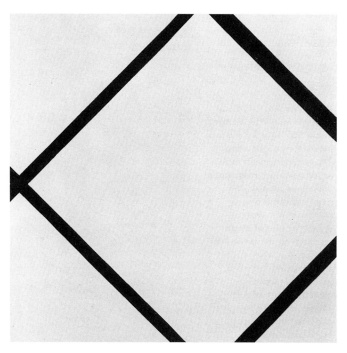

through a transparent 'window', but the actual paint on a two-dimensional canvas or even the glued scraps of already marked paper in a collage or photomontage was their main concern. Not the historical or natural references of a building's ornamented façade, but rather the steel, glass, or concrete out of which the building was composed became paramount. Not the sentiments expressed or events described in a poem, but instead the evocative sound of the words or the sight of their shape on the page often gained pride of place.

What the Russian formalist critics led by Viktor Shklovsky (1893–1984) famously called 'ostranenie' (making strange or baring the device) meant exposing the deceptive techniques used by traditional art to hide its means of production and

Pablo Picasso, *Still Life with Violin and Fruit,* 1913. Collage means both a pasting and two people living together illicitly. The pasted fragments of an actual newspaper, their letters themselves conveying fragments of meaning, juxtaposed with charcoal drawing or painted shapes, resist turning the canvas into a transparent window. They also destabilize figure and ground and mock the modernist fetish of pure visuality, thus allowing some critics to see them as proto-post-modernist.

264

occlude the traces of its raw materials. In fact, as the Austrian architect Adolf Loos's (1870–1933) oft-cited claim that 'ornamentation is a crime' shows, modernism often saw itself—with no small measure of moral self-righteousness—as a quest for authenticity and honesty in aesthetic terms. Its rejection of received historical models was thus defended as a refusal to play the hypocritical game of obeying authorities whose legitimacy had been exhausted.

Purification of form and material thus meant that modernist works often sought the condition of absolute self-referentiality and utter disinterestedness that aesthetic theoreticians since the eighteenth century had con-

Adolf Loos, Steiner House, Vienna, 1910. Two years after his anti-decorative manifesto *Ornament and Crime*, Loos designed the first of a series of houses in Vienna built according to a *Raumplan* (spatial plan) with unadorned façades and windows. Inside, however, the Steiner house still made use of timbered beams and wooden panelling, traditional antidotes to the anti-ornamental severity soon embraced by full-blown modernism.

tended was the ultimate goal of all art. One implication of this quest was an explicit disdain for the traditional expectation that art should not only elevate, but also be a vehicle of sublimated sensual pleasure for its beholder. As Schoenberg contemptuously told a Hollywood producer who wanted to employ his talents for the movies, 'I don't write lovely music'. Reflecting this disdain for mere pleasure, the aesthetic discourse that developed along with modernism eschewed a stress on ineffable sensibility, refined taste, or the virtues of connoisseurship in favour of rigorous attention to the theoretical issues raised by artistic experimentation.

Such self-abnegating austerity did not, however, always define the modernists' self-understanding or completely dominate the mid-century account of their project. For like many artists before them, the modernists often sought to heal cultural wounds as well as to explore the limits of their media. Although, in certain moods, they merely gave voice to the anxiety and confusion produced by the crisis of traditional cultural vocabularies, in others, they proposed an antidote to that crisis through a kind of aesthetic fiat, which would construct a new symbolic order out of entirely modern materials. The etymological meaning of symbol—from the Greek *symballein*, to throw together—was retained in their hope that a renewed vision would restore the wholeness that somehow had been lost, successfully retelling, as Pound famously put it, the collective 'tale of the tribe'. In fact, in their most optimistic (or self-inflated) moments, modernists arrogated to themselves the role of filling the gap left behind by the collapse of traditional religion, providing a new spirituality of the senses to reverse what the sociologist Max Weber had followed Friedrich Schiller in calling 'the disenchantment of the world'. The defamiliarization sought by ruthlessly baring the device and honestly showing the materials of artistic production was not always understood as an end in itself, but rather as a means to break through the dry crust of convention and allow something authentic and fresh to shine through. Rimbaud's celebrated equation of the poet with seer struck a chord among artists who saw themselves as the vehicles of a new sacralization.

Joseph Beuys, *The End of the Twentieth Century,* 1983/5. Beuys's apocalyptic vision evoked both the fate of Germany in 1945 and the threat of nuclear holocaust. Although the Christian symbols of regeneration and hope for the renewal of humankind's link with primal nature evident elsewhere in his work are absent from this installation, the words 'the silence of Marcel Duchamp is overrated' indicate a belief that art can still make a difference.

In our imagined mid-century history of modernism, this quest for re-enchantment—stripped of its more problematic political manifestations—might well have been closely identified with the search for human freedom. That is, modernism's defiance of conventional norms, its valorization of individual or (small) group creativity, and its internationalist ethos of an art transcending national frontiers could become emblematic of the notion of freedom as it was most frequently posited in the liberal democracies of the West during that period. When the centre of gravity of modernism shifted after the Second World War from Europe to America, where the lobbies of modernist skyscrapers were filled by abstract expressionist canvases, the mobilization of this linkage for Cold War purposes was intensified still further. The triumphant struggle of modernists to liberate themselves from the weight of oppressive cultural traditions and defy the attempts of the authoritarian state to impose new controls on their creativity, as well as the image of the modernist artwork as an entirely autonomous whole, easily lent themselves to such self-aggrandizing allegorization. In this way, aesthetic

266

modernism at mid-century, precisely because of its alleged detachment from concrete social and political practice, came to be taken by many as the appropriate cultural expression of a much larger project of human emancipation.

The Crisis of High Modernism

It continued to be so construed, however, only until the challenge of its putative post-modernist successor in the last third of the century. For with the slow but inexorable emergence of a new cultural mood—or to borrow the term of one of that mood's loudest champions, Jean-François Lyotard (1924–), a new 'condition'—the modernists' heroic narrative of liberation from the dead hand of the past, based on formal and material purification and experimental freedom, came itself under increased scrutiny. Although not universally discredited, the mid-century version of the triumph of modernism began to seem commercially self-serving, politically suspect, and theoretically flawed in many important ways. What had once seemed innovative, critical, and subversive now appeared tired, affirmative, and complicitous with the very establishment it once tried to undermine.

As the twentieth century neared its end, however, no alternative master narrative emerged to displace it. Indeed, the very possibility of such a totalizing and teleological story was one of the casualties of the new mood. The very ambiguity of its name indicated this loss. From one perspective, *post*-modernism suggested a chronological reading as the cultural movement that supplanted a modernism no longer at the cutting edge of innovation. As such, it invited comparison with other recent 'post' categorizations, such as *post-histoire*, post-structuralism, post-Marxism, and post-industrial society. But, paradoxically, it also acknowledged its parasitic debt to the modernism still in its name (and still often in its practice). For how, after all, was it possible to get entirely beyond the 'recently, just now' at the root of the word modern? The oxymoronic quality of the term post-modernism might be thus understood as expressing a radical challenge to coherent, uniform temporality (a challenge that is neatly encapsulated in the fact that perhaps the earliest use of the term post-modern appeared in remarks the English painter John Watkins Chapman made about impressionism in 1870!).

In adopting so paradoxical a label, post-modernism might be said to have merely brought to the surface modernism's own contradictory affirmations of mythic repetition, atemporal immediacy (the art of stillness), and futurist redemption. For this and other reasons, post-modernism thus initially seemed to many—and still does to some—as little more than the latest modernist movement, the most recent ploy of the avant-garde to establish its credentials at the cutting edge. But, by the 1980s, it came increasingly to be understood as providing a fundamental challenge to many of the most fundamental assumptions of the modernist project, assumptions which were unquestioned in our idealized mid-century version of its history.

To compound the paradox, it was also soon appreciated that one of the first sources of that challenge emerged from within aesthetic modernism itself, at least once it was understood that its history could support a different narrative from the one described above. The epochal shift in that historiography is nicely illustrated by the difference between two highly influential books with virtually the same title: the Italian critic Renato Poggioli's *Teoria dell'arte d'avanguardia* of 1962 and *Theorie der Avantgarde* of 1974 by the German critic Peter Bürger (translated respectively as *The Theory of the Avant-Garde* and *Theory of the Avant-garde*). Whereas the terms modernism and the avant-garde were employed by Poggioli as virtual synonyms, it became possible by the time Bürger was writing to distinguish between them, at least in ideal-typical terms. The discriminating marker was their attitude towards the differentiation of the aesthetic realm from the rest of the social whole. Whereas modernists like Joyce, Mallarmé, Schoenberg, or Pollock could be identified by their withdrawal into the alleged autonomy of art, confining their innovations to the discrete work or the genre, members of the avant-garde could be equated with those who questioned the very institution of art as a separate realm unto itself. Thus movements like Dadaism, futurism, and surrealism could now be understood as having sought, in large measure, to break down the barrier between art and life, thus dedifferentiating the aesthetic from the other spheres of modern culture and society. Their frequent, if often unsuccessful, alliances with radical political movements could now be interpreted less as embarrassing episodes on the road to a purer and less compromised art, and more like valiant efforts to reinvigorate life by imbuing it with the redemptive energies that the modernists had sought to unleash only within art itself. The defamiliariz-

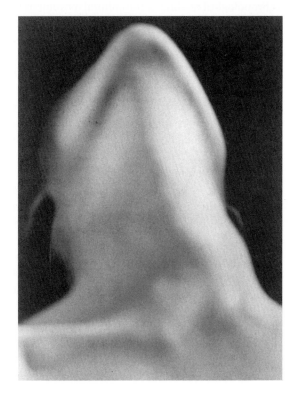

Man Ray, *Anatomies, c.*1930. Surrealist photography often produced uncanny effects that undercut the notion of pure form. By rotating the head of his subject so that the result suggests another part of the male anatomy, Man Ray evoked what the surrealist Georges Bataille called the *informe*, a concept of formlessness subsequently appropriated by post-modernist theorists.

ing techniques of militant artists such as the German playwright Bertolt Brecht (1898–1956) could be appreciated as attempts less to renew tired aesthetic forms or rediscover a lost language of authenticity than to inspire critical reflection and political praxis in the audiences whose consciousness was meant to be raised by them.

Once isolated figures such as the French artist Marcel Duchamp (1887–1963), who mockingly rejected traditional and modernist painting alike, could now be understood as presenting a profound challenge to the very possibility of purified visual experience. The self-consciously 'anti-retinal' quality of Duchamp's later work, its denial of formal beauty, anticipated the visually impoverished, discursively constituted conceptual art that provided a transition to post-modernism in the 1960s. His so-called 'readymades' ironically bestowed the aura of the aesthetic on objects from everyday life such as urinals or bicycle wheels, which were not formally beautiful or the product of unusual skill. In so doing, they undercut the assumption that high art, modernist or otherwise, was the expression of creative genius—an assumption that had survived the modernist assault on expressivity—and challenged the institutional settings—museums, the art market, state-sponsored academies, the community of critics—in which that genius was acknowledged. The *Mona Lisa* adorned with a moustache and naughtily retitled *L.H.O.O.Q.* (which sounds like the French words for 'she has a hot ass') would never be the same.

Post-modernism and the Virtues of Pollution

Post-modernism, broadly speaking, thus meant a turning away from the ethic of purification and differentiation in high modernism, and an embracing of the contrary impulse in the avant-garde. This reversal was evident, *inter alia*, in the return of figuration into its no longer abstract painting, an appreciation of the referential rather than merely formal or symbolic dimension of its photography, and the conflation of fiction and non-fiction in its literature. Rather than seeking stylistic refinement, post-modernists fused together different, even conflicting styles to create visual palimpsests, reminiscent of the carnivalesque confusion of rhetorical codes the ancient Greek Cynics had called Menippean satire. But unlike modernist champions of radical intertexuality, such as Joyce, post-modernists rejected the goal of an aesthetic sublimation of the seemingly random and unintelligible results. Countering the austere Bauhaus slogan of Ludwig Mies van der Rohe (1886–1969), 'less is more', post-modernists such as the American architect Robert Venturi (1925–) puckishly claimed instead that 'less is a bore'.

Whereas modernism sought to privilege form over content, the medium over the substance of what was expressed, post-modernism saw the hesitant return of what had been banished, often, to be sure, placed in quotation marks to undermine its foundational status. Or it came to appreciate what the dissident surrealist Georges Bataille (1897–1962) had called *informe*, the heterogeneous formlessness that sabotaged all attempts to contain excess and suppress noise. Surrealist photographers such as Man Ray were now celebrated for having pre-

Marcel Duchamp, *Fountain* (readymade), 1917. By being signed 'R. Mutt', one of Duchamp's many pseudonyms, this common urinal was turned into an 'art object' by the fiat of the artist rather than through any intrinsic aesthetic qualities of its own. Duchamp's readymades were deliberate provocations to the institution of art and the ideology of originality, whose full implications were not realized until the advent of post-modernism.

sented the human form in images of undecidable meaning. German artists such as Georg Baselitz (1938–) and A. R. Penck (1939–) were recognized for having revived the disfiguring excesses of pre-abstract expressionism. Others such as Joseph Beuys (1921–86) and Anselm Kiefer (1945–) were lauded for leaving behind the transcendental internationalism of high modernism in favour of more nationally inflected natural and historical themes.

Similarly, post-modernist architecture rejected the geometric purity and authenticity of materials of international-style buildings; form need not follow function, historical citation ceased being a sin, and ornament lost its criminal status. It was no longer progressive, post-modern architects contended, to generate abstract models of built form indifferent to the specific natural, historical, and cultural contexts in which they were inserted. The isotropic, repetitive space of international-style buildings needed to be supplemented by new spatial variations that harkened back to the baroque at its most dazzling. Likewise, post-modern sculpture, moving beyond the minimalism and conceptualism of the 1960s, rediscovered the importance of specific sites and the temporality of creation and decay; artists such as the Bulgarian Christo (1935–) wrapped historical buildings and features of the natural landscape in ways that extended the already diffuse definition of sculptural form.

The post-modernist rediscovery of the (non-modernist) avant-garde assault on the institution of art did, however, self-consciously jettison one essential dimension of most earlier avant-garde movements: their redemptive hopes for a revitalization of the fragmented social totality. That is, whereas movements like the Bauhaus, surrealism, and futurism had wanted to revivify life through the realization of artistic values—to aestheticize existence, we might say, by overcoming the reified differentiations of bourgeois society—most post-modernists lost faith in the possibility of such a project, whose failure they claimed was now self-evident. The constructivist spirit was supplanted by that of deconstruction, which replaced both differentiation and dedifferentiation by what its most celebrated spokesman Jacques Derrida (1930–) called *différance*, a neologism implying endless deferral as well as unbridgeable difference. Yearnings for plenitudinous order and the revival of totalized meaning, the post-modernists scoffed, were exercises in nostalgia for a golden past that never really existed. Although they sought to level oppositions, it was thus not in the triumphalist spirit of the Hegelian or Hegelian-Marxist *Aufhebung* (sublation) of contradictions, a spirit which had often tacitly infused the avant-garde. According to a leading champion of post-

270

modernist architecture, the American Charles Jencks, the end of such hopes can even be symbolically dated. On 15 July 1972, when the Pruit-Igoe housing project in St Louis, Missouri, was ignominiously dynamited, the goal of providing humanizing mass housing through what the French modernist architect Le Corbusier (1887–1965) had called 'machines for living' was definitively laid to rest.

Indeed, the very image of an avant-garde preparing the way for a broad-based revitalized culture was rejected by post-modernists as complicitous with a totalizing and teleological meta-narrative, whose élitist political implications were inherently problematic. The widespread repudiation in the late twentieth century of political vanguards claiming to represent the interests of the whole, a repudiation exemplified by the débâcle of Leninism, was extended to cultural vanguards as well. They too were damned for arrogating to themselves the right to condemn present values and tastes as ideological in the name of a putatively superior future. The age of what the French theorist Michel Foucault (1926–1984) called the 'universal intellectual' with his—specific gender intended—search for synoptic meta-

Anselm Kiefer, *Shulamite*, 1983. Turning the Nazi discourse of degenerate art on its head, Kiefer implies that German society has itself been sick. The tone of his dark, brooding, often apocalyptic work recalls German expressionism, but the subject-matter reflects more recent events. Here the ominous vaults covering tracks leading to a fire suggest the fate of Jewish women, eponymously indicated by the title of the painting, during the Third Reich.

271

Le Corbusier (Charles-Edouard Jeanneret), Villa Savoye, Poissy, 1927–31. According to Le Corbusier's 'purist' text *Five Points of a New Architecture* (1925), the 'syntax' of a modern house should be based on columns elevating the mass off the ground, the separation of load-bearing columns from walls, a free façade, a long horizontal, sliding window, and a roof garden. The resulting 'machine for living' proudly displayed the modern materials out of which it was constructed.

theories was now over; in its place was the 'local intellectual' content to remain within the modest limits of what the Italian philosopher Gianni Vattimo (1936–) dubbed 'weak thought'.

Thus, for post-modernists, such avant-garde techniques as baring the device or defamiliarization could no longer be placed in the service of exploding ideological mystifications through exposing the 'real workings' of cultural signification, which would in turn inspire radical political praxis. Instead, they were redirected at demonstrating that in culture there were nothing but devices 'all the way down', nothing but artifice, rhetoric, and contrivance. The goal of full transparency was unattainable; indeed the priority of the visual over the other senses, which had been tacitly maintained in the modernist fetish of formal clarity, should be overturned.

Although the institution of art lost its special status as a realm apart from the other spheres of a differentiated modernity, its reintegration brought with it no Utopian pay-off. If life were to be aestheticized, theoreticians like Lyotard insisted,

the aesthetics involved was that of the sublime rather than the beautiful, an aesthetics of absence, unrepresentability, and even terror, rather than formal purity, sensual presence, and organic order. In the place of the romantic and modernist symbol, the concrete embodiment of an abstract idea or fragment of a latent whole, post-modernists put a process of infinite allegorization with no expectation of final closure or plenitudinous meaning. Simulacra, Jean Baudrillard (1929–) insisted, have no originals to which they refer; images must therefore be set adrift from their putative referents. Rejecting both synchronic, spatialized time and the smoothly meaningful flow of narrative, post-modernists also embraced multiple and heterogeneous temporalities that never cohered into a single story, and endorsed as well the endless circulation of signifiers that refused to adhere to a definitive signified. As a result, they denied the possibility of unmediated authenticity, complete subjective autonomy, or non-ideological consciousness—a conclusion that tied them to late nineteenth-century 'decadent' writers like Oscar Wilde (1854–1900), whose playful, ironic defence of mendacity the deadly serious modernists thought they had somehow transcended.

At times, post-modernism, in fact, seemed hostile to all emancipatory projects, even those with more modest, non-redemptive goals. Emerging to prominence after the failures of the counter-cultural cum new leftist politics of the 1960s, it was taken by some to be an expression of a dangerous, new cynicism, a turn towards uncritical inwardness, or an acceptance of the shallow consumer society cultured Europeans had long identified with meretricious America. In Germany, in particular, where the memory of past counter-Enlightenment and anti-modernist movements was particularly raw, the wholesale repudiation of what the second-generation Frankfurt School theorist Jürgen Habermas (1929–) called the 'uncompleted project of modernity' appeared especially ominous. Other critics darkly warned against post-modernism's nihilistic and anti-humanist implications—and in so doing unwittingly repeated the same charges made against many of the early modernists almost a century before.

What, for example, in the 1960s became known as 'pop art' was attacked for recycling mass-produced commercial images with no attempt to purify them of their origins in the economic market-place or undermine their unapologetically pleasure-giving function. Whereas the efforts in the mid-1950s of the British Independent Group led by Richard Hamilton (1922–) to incorporate such images had caused little negative comment, those of the more successful American Andy Warhol a decade later were often greeted with dismay by the embattled defenders of the last high modernist movement, abstract expressionism. Warhol, moreover, achieved global notoriety for turning himself into a product: the artist as shallow celebrity rather than creative genius, who churned out mechanical reproductions without originals in a studio he significantly dubbed 'the factory'.

Indeed, the very distinction between art and commodity, which had been a staple of western aesthetics ever since the romantics, was now gleefully abandoned in ways that outraged purists, both aesthetic and political. Although a vague residue of the apocalyptic mood surrounding early modernism still often accompanied its successor, it was an apocalypse without the expectation of a revelation after the destruction of the old order. History returned to post-modernism, it was often remarked, but in the form of a helter-skelter pastiche of older styles rather than in that of a faith in the historical process as a story of potential emancipation. History as *post-histoire*, a term first popularized after the Second World War by conservatives unhappy with its outcome, meant the ironizing of all such plots of meaningful development.

It would, however, be misleading, its defenders responded, to infer that all artists and critics who identified themselves with post-modernism shared the same quietist or cynical politics. In certain ways the adversarial, subversive spirit of high modernism was not entirely lost, they pointed out, even if it was now directed against some of modernism's own most sacred shibboleths. A salient example was the deliberate blurring of the very boundary between high—whether traditional or modernist—and low art. Modernism itself, to be sure, had often drawn on the popular and even mass culture surrounding it; fragments of newspapers, retail catalogues, advertisements, even music-hall reviews found their way into cubist collages and Dada poetry, and the noises of the city informed the music of composers such as Edgar Varèse (1883–1965) and Luigi Russolo (1885–1947). But whereas modernists generally sought the elevation of low into high through a process of aesthetic sublimation, hoping for the redemption of elements from everyday life through artistic transfiguration, post-modernists questioned the very hierarchy on which such an outcome might be based. It was possible, they defiantly argued in the words of Venturi and his collaborators Denise Scott-Brown and Steven Izenour, to 'learn from Las Vegas', the very epitome of mass-culture vulgarity. A post-modernist novel like Umberto Eco's *The Name of the Rose* could thus combine esoteric metaphysical and linguistic conundrums and subtle accounts of medieval theology with a plot that provided all the painlessly accessible rewards of a detective thriller.

The unapologetic mimesis or recycling—if now in quotation marks—of what had earlier been dismissed as kitsch also challenged the very distinction between 'authentic' genuine and 'fraudulent' copy, which had been so important a pillar of the differentiated and sacralized institution of art. In literary terms, the distinction between citation and original text was blurred, as everything became a second-order quotation without a first-order referent. Even the distinction between natural body and artificial prosthesis was called into question by the post-modern fascination with cyborgs, body piercing, the paintings of Francis Bacon (1909–1992) (which turned human bodies into animal meat), and the transformational magic of computer 'morphing'.

What the German Marxist critic Walter Benjamin (1892–1940) had famously called the cultish 'aura' surrounding unique artworks was deliberately effaced in post-modernism, as ephemeral, dematerialized 'installations' or 'performances', like those of the Austrian Hermann Nitzsch (1938–), replaced objects made for the ages. New technologies like television allowed video artists to augment the decline of the aura already begun by such earlier innovations as the cinema and phonograph. Some post-modernists, rejecting the cynical example of Warhol, worked to thwart the transformation of art into commodity, which modernism, for all its dis-

Facing: **In 1971 Bacon** redid an earlier painting because a museum was slow to lend the original for an exhibition of his work. This casual historical citation typifies the post-modernist recirculation of past images. Less gruesome than the first, the new version still expresses Bacon's dark musings on the interchangeability of flesh and meat, life and machine automation.

taste for bourgeois values, had clearly failed to undermine (indeed, as the tens of millions spent on canvases by a Van Gogh or Monet show, it had the very opposite effect). What became known as 'auto-destructive art', first developed by anti-artists such as Gustav Metzger (1926–) and Jean Tingueley (1925–) in the 1960s, mocked the goal of timeless works of art. Equally challenged was the privileged site of the museum as the repository of such works, whose most idealized form was to be found in André Malraux's (1901–70) post-Second World War notion of a photographic super 'museum without walls'. Politically motivated critics such as the German Hans Haacke (1936–) stressed the increasing financial dependency of museums on corporate sponsorship.

The populist defence of such a demolition of hierarchy did not, however, always convince its critics, who variously worried about the erosion of cultural standards, the schizophrenic literalization of signifiers blocking access to meaningful signification, and the ideological aestheticization of daily life. Post-modernism, they charged, was uncomfortably close to craven capitulation before what the French situationist Guy Debord (1931–1994) had castigated as the mystifying 'society of the spectacle'. Its eclectic pluralism and self-indulgent playfulness was an example of what another radical critic Herbert Marcuse (1898–1979) had called 'repressive desublimation'.

Hans Haacke,
MetroMobiltan, 1985.
Extending the avant-garde critique of the institution of art, Haacke has probed the material bases of the current art world by exposing the links between museums, galleries, and their corporate patrons. His exposés of the museum industry, here directed against the Metropolitan in New York, show that post-modernism need not be inherently apolitical.

Feminism, Multiculturalism, and Post-modern Inclusivity

Even its critics had to acknowledge, however, that post-modernism's inclusive rather than exclusive aesthetic had opened certain new possibilities that modernism had shunned. One of the most significant concerned the addressing of gender issues in a more complex way than was evident in the heyday of modernism. During the late nineteenth century, mass society had been often figured as a woman—irrational, out of control, lacking in higher cultural values—by crowd psychologists such as Gustave Le Bon (1841–1931), literary critics such as Hippolyte Taine (1828–93), and novelists such as Émile Zola (1840–1902). Not surprisingly, mass culture also came to have similar associations, which allowed it to be invidiously compared with the virile spirituality of the élite modernists. For all their subversive intentions, many modernists remained wedded to traditional misogynist notions of women as culturally inferior and somehow complicitous with a mass culture that was regressive, engulfing, and debased. Whereas men were cultural producers, able to embark on a lonely quest for artistic redemption, women were understood to be consumers of such cultural kitsch as sentimental fiction, cynically devised to console them for their inferior status. Even when they renewed the nineteenth-century bohemian challenge to bourgeois mores and glorified free sexual expression, modernists such as the English novelist D. H. Lawrence (1885–1930) and avant-garde movements such as surrealism perpetuated many conventional attitudes towards the object of (male) desire.

Post-modernism, which emerged at a time when powerful feminist critiques of these assumptions were impossible to ignore, lost its taste not only for master narratives, but also for narratives of male masters. Often parodically appropriating the dominant culture's image of women, such post-modern feminists as the Americans Cindy Sherman (1954–) and Barbara Kruger (1945–) self-consciously sought to undermine the hegemony of what was darkly called the 'male gaze'. Theoretically inspired by the Nietzschean and post-structuralist critique of centred subjectivity in the name of heterological difference that initially came into prominence in post-1968 France, they developed practices that contested the modernist demand for authenticity and presence. Defiantly valorizing the traditionally feminine (and often gay) tactics of masquerade, cross-dressing, and posing, which had been negatively valued by mainstream modernists (although adopted by heterodox figures such as Duchamp), they raised parody, dissimulation, camp, and mimesis to the level of cultural norm.

Post-modern inclusiveness also entailed the incorporation of the work done by so-called post-colonial artists, some of whom lived in the former possessions of the European powers, others of whom were now hybridized citizens of the 'mother countries'. The 'magical realism' evident in the work of Latin American novelists such as Gabriel Garcia Marquez (1928–) was also developed by post-colonial Europeans such as the Pakistani-born Salman Rushdie (1947–), whose most notorious work, *The Satanic Verses*, affronted not only western modernist sensibilities, but also the non-western and anti-modernist sensibilities of the Islamic world that he had thought—as it turned out in vain—he had left behind to come to England. The post-modern fascination with alterity, difference, and the non-identical reflected the new realities of an increasingly multicultural Europe struggling to accommodate its new 'impurity', adjusting to the long-awaited 'decline of the West', and hoping to forge politically effective, post-Marxist 'rainbow coalitions' of disparate groups.

Because post-modernism self-consciously sought to break down the barriers between the aesthetic and its other, such considerations as gender, ethnicity, and multiculturalism inevitably entered the rapidly expanding theoretical discussion surrounding it. Attempts were also made to link it with the larger, non-cultural processes of modernization (or post-modernization). As had been the case with modernism, the impact of new technologies—then, aeroplanes, cinema, and the radio, now computers, fibre optics, and video—was credited with revolutionizing the cultural 'imaginary' of the day. 'Virtual reality', 'simulacrum', and a host of words cloned from the Greek *kybernan* (to steer), such as 'cyborg', 'cyberspace', and 'cyberpunk', all became catchwords of the critical discourse that both reflected on and stimulated the changes in artistic production.

For those less interested in what one commentator called the 'mode of information' than the more traditional mode of production, post-modernism could be understood to express in some complex way developments in late capitalism. One analyst, the English geographer David Harvey, sought to tie it to the transition from an economy based on centralized, large-scale 'Fordist' accumulation to one grounded in a more flexible and fluid alternative that involved, *inter alia*, the radical decoupling of the financial system from real production and the rapid, if ephemeral, dispersion of capital flows. Another, the American literary critic Fredric Jameson, linked it to the virtual completion of the modernization process, which meant the ubiquity of market relations and the loss of any palpable resistance in the form of a classical proletariat.

However post-modernism as a cultural condition was construed, however its origins were explained in terms of larger social, technological, or economic forces, however its political imperatives were understood, one implication of its arrival could not be denied: its radical disruption of the triumphalist mid-century narrative of modernism described above. It is, of course, still too early to write a final balance sheet on post-modernism itself; indeed, such an outcome may well be permanently thwarted, if the post-modernist insistence on multiple narratives, heterogeneous subject positions, and the impossibility of totalizing perspectives survives its own heyday. We remain, in any case, still too much in the middle of this uncertainly defined, internally contested, and discursively exfoliating cultural paradigm to imagine what will come next. What can be called the uncompleted project of post-modernity has, it seems, still to run its course.

Facing: **Richard Hamilton,** *Just What is it that Makes Today's Homes So Different, So Appealing?*, 1956. A leading member of the British Independent Group, Hamilton sought to include hitherto denigrated examples of kitsch in his work. Accepting rather than resisting the pleasure produced by mass consumption, his collages foreshadowed the pop art subversion of the modernist distinction between High and Low in the 1960s.

[1] The cultural appropriation of this originally military term (which meant an army's fore-guard) can be traced back as far as the 17th-cent. Quarrel of the Ancients and the Moderns, but its 19th-cent. use dates from the Utopian socialist Saint-Simon. It came into common usage, however, only in France in the 1870s. As its later version as Leninist vanguard theory shows, it often gained political as well as aesthetic acceptations.

11

Europe Divided and Reunited

1945–1995

'ANYONE under the age of fifty grew up—or was born into—a world glaciated into its Cold War form,' wrote the British historian and peace activist E. P. Thompson in 1987. 'It must seem like an immutable fact of geography that the continent of Europe is divided into two blocs which are struck into postures of "deterrence" for evermore.' Two years later, however, the eastern bloc had dissolved, by the end of 1990 Germany was reunified, and on 31 December 1991 the Soviet Union itself ceased to exist. Why did the barriers seem so permanent? Why, in the end, did they fall so quickly?

Europe between the Superpowers

In the summer of 1945 the old Europe was in ruins. Literally. In the shell of Hitler's Chancellery building his marble-topped desk lay shattered in pieces, surrounded by a litter of Iron Crosses and once-secret documents. Like Berlin, the cities of Cologne, Hamburg, Dresden—in fact most of urban Germany—had been ravaged by bombing and fire. It was the same story across the continent. Paris, Rome, and Prague had been spared but they were the exceptions. The great Habsburg monuments of Budapest and Vienna had largely disappeared; commercial centres from Rotterdam to Piraeus had become rubble; vital arteries like the Rhine and the Danube were blocked by sunken ships and demolished bridges. Destruction brought disease in its wake. War and occupation left the 1 million people of Naples ravaged by typhus and VD on a scale reminiscent of the great plagues of the seventeenth century. And recovery promised to be painfully slow. France, whose 'liberation' had occurred rapidly in 1944, faced the post-Nazi era with railways paralysed, bridges destroyed, and coal production at half its pre-war levels. Even

Facing: **Prague's false spring**. The liberalization of communist rule in Czechoslovakia in 1968 raised hopes of a new era. But it also threatened Soviet control over Eastern Europe and the Red Army soon took control. People power could not tame the Russian tanks for long.

Facing, below: **The French Exocet missile,** shown here at the Paris Air Show at le Bourget, has brought missile warfare to a new level of sophistication. Almost impossible to detect and intercept, the Exocet can achieve the accuracy and destructive power together that conventional bombing lacked.

DAVID
REYNOLDS

Britain, spared German occupation, lost a quarter of her national wealth and became the world's leading debtor. Hitler had failed, but, true to his promise, he had brought Europe down with him.

Victors in this terrible conflict were the United States and the Soviet Union, the two 'superpowers'—a word coined specially at the end of the war. The price they paid for victory was not the same. America had been neither bombed nor occupied and had lost only 300,000 dead (about 0.25 per cent of the population). In fact, the war boom had pulled the country out of depression to produce half the world's industrial output by 1945. Across Europe gum-chewing GIs in their ubiquitous jeeps became symbols of American wealth and technology. In August 1945 the mushroom clouds over Hiroshima and Nagasaki dramatized America's status as the world's first (and, until 1949, only) nuclear power.

The Soviet Union, by contrast, had been a battleground for three years and had borne the brunt of the struggle against the German army. Authoritative estimates of Soviet dead during the war have now reached at least 28 million—over 14 per cent of the pre-war population. Yet the extent of Soviet losses were not known at the time. What struck the rest of the world were images of Soviet power—the hammer and sickle hanging over the ruined Reichstag, Stalin's face adorning a huge hoarding on the Unter den Linden, and the cascade of Nazi standards tossed at his feet during the Victory Parade in Red Square (a deliberate replay of Tsar Alexan-

The shell of the Mosaic Hall of Hitler's Chancellery in May 1945. Designed by Albert Speer as one of the great monuments of the Thousand Year Reich.

der's triumph over Napoleon). The Red Army had vanquished the German *Wehrmacht* and now occupied eastern Europe, much as America and her junior partners, Britain and France, garrisoned the west.

For the superpowers it seemed a triumph of ideals as well as might. Twice in thirty years the great powers and so-called 'civilized' countries of Europe had fought with unparalleled horror and brutality. Eight million and now 50 million had died. The follies of nationalism seemed particularly evident to Americans, citizens of a federal country the size of a continent. For Congressmen and GIs alike a visit to Europe in 1945, with its ruined cities and wretched people, confirmed their sense of American moral as well as military superiority. But the most shocking images of 1945 were those of the Nazi concentration camps. The Allied leaders and publics had not known (or had ignored) their full horror during the war; afterwards the systematic, genocidal character of German racism became appallingly evident. Slavs, gypsies, the mentally ill, above all the Jews had been exploited, tortured, and executed with ruthless ingenuity. Names like Belsen and Auschwitz became household words, and shocked Allied generals forced local Germans to visit the camps and see for themselves the human costs of Aryan race purity.

German civilians from Weimar are brought by US military police to view the horrors perpetrated in nearby Buchenwald concentration camp.

Virtually all of European Jewry, some 6 million people, had been exterminated. The death camps seemed to sum up the moral bankruptcy of Europe.

Post-war Europe therefore became an arena of contending ideologies as well as powers. Undoubtedly American liberty and largesse had a widespread appeal. In 1945–6 American relief aid was already making its mark in Germany and Italy. Yet the discrediting of fascism led initially to a widespread swing to the left. One cannot grasp the strength and tenacity of communism in post-war Europe unless this is appreciated. Suspicions of American plutocracy and philistinism remained strong among European élites, especially in France, while the communists benefited both politically and morally from their prominent role in wartime resistance movements, notably in France and Italy. The years 1945–6 saw communists in coalition in France, Italy, and Belgium, and socialist governments mounted ambitious programmes of welfarism and nationalization in Britain and Scandinavia. In eastern Europe, too, socialist, communist, and agrarian parties formed coalition governments in the mid-1940s and agreed on the need to eliminate large landowners and bring heavy industry under state control, for example in eastern Germany and Hungary.

Yet in 1945 Cold War Europe had not yet taken shape. Under Presidents Roosevelt and Truman, the American policy, despite growing suspicion, was to work with the Soviets, and there was a strong inclination to disengage from Europe. 'Bring the boys home; don't be a Santa Claus; don't be pushed around,' as Under-Secretary of State Dean Acheson summed up the mood at the end of 1945. Stalin, for his part, was determined to guarantee Russia's security and to advance her influence through a strong position in east-central Europe. Yet he was not bent on unlimited expansion. He left Greece, for instance, under Britain's aegis, as agreed with Churchill in 1944, and he certainly did not want confrontation with the West to disturb his priority of post-war reconstruction. It is likely, of course, that two strong powers, competing in a vacuum and motivated by rival ideologies, would eventually have come up against each other. But what caused relations to deteriorate rapidly was their dispute over the post-war settlement. Eastern Europe was not the main problem: the Americans conceded Soviet influence in Poland, Bulgaria, and Romania in 1945, though the lack of democracy was regarded as sinister. The European cold war really took shape as another struggle for mastery of Germany.

To the Russians, German recovery posed a military threat; to the Americans it was an economic necessity if Europe was to be prosperous again. In 1945–6 the Russians stripped German industry to rebuild their own economy and blocked moves for economic recovery, while the United States and British governments tired of feeding Germany at the expense of their own taxpayers—'paying reparations to Germany', as the British Chancellor of the Exchequer Hugh Dalton put it. After European production plummeted in the harsh winter of early 1947 and Allied diplomats reached deadlock in a month of discussions in Moscow in April, the Americans decided to act. On 5 June 1947 Secretary of State George C. Marshall promised American funding for a European recovery programme, if the Europeans came up with a joint package. Quickly British and French leaders convened meetings in Paris and the outlines of a plan were then thrashed out with the Americans, though it was not until March 1948 that the European Recovery Program (better known as the Marshall Plan) completed its passage through Congress.

Equally important was the Soviet reaction. The Russians sent an eighty-strong delegation to Paris, and east European countries like Czechoslovakia and Poland expressed keen interest. But Stalin saw the American offer as a challenge to his sphere of influence. He warned the Czechs and others against participating and withdrew the Soviet delegation.

WARNING! CONSTRUCTION: A street sign is used to remind West Germans that things are improving thanks to the Marshall Plan.

'The Air Bridge'. Children in West Berlin watch as an American transport plane lands with vital supplies during the Soviet blockade of 1948–9.

That autumn he declared ideological war on western capitalism, creating Cominform (the Communist Information Bureau) to orchestrate foreign communist parties and replacing the coalitionist strategy in France and Italy with strikes intended to bring down the governments. In the east, Soviet influence now became Soviet domination. The coup in Czechoslovakia in February 1948 (a country previously independent but friendly to the USSR) was followed by the Stalinization of much of the region. All but communists were proscribed, those independent of Moscow were purged, agriculture and heavy industry were brought under state control, and civil and political liberties systematically abolished. In March 1946 Winston Churchill had talked of an 'iron curtain' descending from the Baltic to the Adriatic, but it was in 1947–8, with the Marshall Plan and Stalin's response, that the barriers really came down.

The Americans pressed ahead with the rehabilitation of western Germany, including plans for a new federal state. Fearful of this trend, Stalin tried to warn off them (and the Germans) in June 1948 by imposing a blockade of Berlin, where all the Allied powers maintained zones in a city deep within Soviet-controlled territory. Instead of backing down, the Americans and British sustained Berliners through the winter by a hazardous airlift, and eventually Stalin was obliged to desist in May 1949. It was a major political and propaganda defeat. Not only had he been outfaced in a trial of strength, he had also lost the moral battle. The Czech coup and the Berlin crisis did much to damage the Soviet image in Europe, even in France where the communist party was still picking up about a quarter of the vote in elections. Equally important, well-advertised Marshall aid was winning hearts and minds. Between 1948 and 1951 the United States put into western Europe about $13 billion; during the same period the Soviet *took out* roughly the same amount from their part of the continent.

In the autumn of 1949 two new German states came into existence—the Federal Republic in the west and the German Democratic Republic (GDR) in the old Soviet zone. The four-power presence in Berlin remained a potential flashpoint. Over the next few years the two superpower blocs gradually became armed camps. Again, this was not intended but was a process of action and reaction on both sides. In April 1949, after months of negotiation, the United States, Canada, and ten west European countries signed the North Atlantic Treaty. Henceforth, an attack on one would be an attack on all. This was the first time the once-isolationist United States had made a peacetime alliance—some commentators called it a modern American Revolution. Yet the North Atlantic Treaty Organization was initially a loose defence pact and not a military alliance. What 'put the "O" into NATO' (in American diplomat Averell Harriman's phrase) was Stalin's second great error of the post-1945 period—the Korean war.

When Stalin sanctioned the North Korean attack on the South in June 1950, he assumed that America would be indifferent. Instead he precipitated a full-scale conflict in Korea and also a massive war scare in Europe. The Americans committed four United States combat divisions to Europe—the beginnings of a substan-

The open hand of Uncle Sam. US military police distribute food to Munich orphans in 1950.

tial military presence—and pressed the rest of NATO to increase their own conventional forces. Above all, they demanded German rearmament as the price for their own increased involvement. Reconciling that with the fears of their allies, especially France, took four years. But in May 1955 the Federal Republic became a member of NATO and the Soviet satellites were organized into the Warsaw Pact. Exactly a decade after Nazi Germany had surrendered, the division of Europe was complete.

America's Europe

The eclipse of war-torn Europe by the ideology and power of America and Russia largely explains the division of the continent in the decade after 1945. But the durability of that division owes much to the way that it suited Europeans and helped solve some of their problems.

NATO's principal function was to deter possible Soviet aggression by the threat of American nuclear retaliation. By the late 1950s this encompassed battlefield as well as strategic nuclear weapons, long-range missiles as well as bombs dropped from aircraft. But NATO protected all members against attack from any quarter and, for many Europeans, Germany remained a real threat. As the contemporary joke had it, NATO's role was to keep the Russians out, the Americans in, and the Germans down.

No western country feared German revival more than France. Its leaders had initially tried to restrict German recovery. When the Americans and British won out, in 1950 the French developed an alternative strategy, masterminded by Jean Monnet—if you can't beat them, join them. This was most evident in the European Coal and Steel Community, which came into existence in 1952. These industries were crucial for European economic recovery; they were also vital to national warmaking potential. By placing them under an international authority, 'the Six' (France, West Germany, Italy, Belgium, The Netherlands, and Luxembourg) were abridging national sovereignty in the interests of prosperity and security. They were also motivated by the strong federalist sentiments of the time, after the war had exposed the ruinous cost of national rivalries. Indeed the three small members of the Six had already formed their own Benelux customs union in 1948. Nevertheless, the Coal and Steel Community was as much a diplomatic strategem as an idealistic vision, with the 'German question' at its heart.

This helps us understand the subsequent chequered history of European integration. The Benelux countries, particularly Belgium, were the most ardently federalist in the mid-1950s, and they helped push the Six towards the European Economic Community which came into existence on 1 January 1958. For Germany and Italy, Europe's pariah nations, integration was a way of recovering international status and influence. But it was France which had most success in shaping the EEC around her national interests. Anxious to avoid a repeat of the French crisis over German rearmament, the other five allowed France preferential treatment for her colonies and a Common Agricultural Policy that suited the interests of her small and inefficient peasant farmers, a powerful political constituency. In 1963

French president Charles de Gaulle (1958–69) vetoed Britain's belated application to join the Six, on the grounds that she was not yet truly European in her outlook. Equally important, though not stated publicly, was the fear that Britain would weaken France's influence: a case of two cocks rather than one in the hen-house, as a chauvinistic French diplomat observed. De Gaulle also diverted the Community's evolution away from Monnet's federalist goals. In 1965 he blocked the development of majority voting, arguing that the EEC should be a *Europe des patries* and not a supranational state.

The EEC nevertheless proved a remarkable success. Its first decade saw the creation of a common market with all internal tariffs abolished and a single external tariff established against outsiders. At the heart of the new Community was a remarkable *entente* between France and Germany. For Konrad Adenauer, Federal Chancellor from 1949 to 1963, friendship with France was as great a priority as the containment of communism. Although his economics minister, Ludwig Erhard, had advocated a less protectionist economic grouping—akin to the free trade area originally proposed by Britain—Adenauer believed that politics took priority over

French president Charles de Gaulle and German chancellor Konrad Adenauer amid enthusiastic crowds in Bonn, September 1963. Placards call for a united, federal Europe.

287

economics. German acceptance of the EEC on French terms was essential to reconciling the two old enemies. De Gaulle and Adenauer hit it off personally and in January 1963 they solemnized the new special relationship in a Franco-German friendship treaty.

The Community was therefore, in part, an answer to Europe's vexed 'German question'. And within this new framework of co-operation Germany's economic strength, no longer a threat, could be used for the benefit of her neighbours. In the 1950s the West German economic miracle transformed the country's place in the world economy. By 1960 it accounted for one-fifth of world trade in manufactured goods, surpassing Britain economically and acting as the powerhouse of the Six.

What also made German recovery both possible and potent, apart from the political settlement created by the EEC, was the fact that the Americans had assumed much of the burden of western Europe's defence. Their commitment to NATO guaranteed France and her neighbours against Russia (and also Germany). In addition, it meant that full-scale German rearmament, with all the fears that this would evoke, was not necessary. Germany was only allowed conventional forces, committed to NATO, and forswore nuclear weapons. Without the American guarantee, the issue of Germany as a nuclear power could not have been avoided, given the size of the Warsaw Pact.

The American commitment to Europe offered other benefits to western European states. By freeing them from prime responsibility for the security of the West, it allowed France and Britain to mount a rearguard defence of their colonial empires. Both had suffered as a result of the war: the French lost Lebanon and Syria in 1946, the British relinquished India in 1947. But the French fought a long and bitter war to hold Indochina from 1946 to 1954. And as soon as this ended in failure, they began another struggle to keep control in Algeria against nationalist rebels and French settlers, which lasted until de Gaulle conceded independence in 1962. For a decade and a half, therefore, most of the French army was committed outside Europe in colonial wars. Although Britain's imperial retreat was less bloody, the country's main energies were also employed imperially throughout the 1950s, and this was one reason why she was slow to take seriously the EEC. The British position in countries such as Malaya and Egypt was regarded as so important economically that substantial defence commitments were maintained. The effort to keep control of the Suez Canal led to the disastrous Anglo-French attack on Egypt in October 1956, whose failure did much to show the world the limits of their power.

Dwight D. Eisenhower, NATO's first Supreme Commander and then United States President (1953–61), had always hoped that the American commitment to NATO would be a temporary expedient to help the Europeans bounce back. But by the end of the 1950s the springboard seemed to have become a crutch. Moreover, it was an increasingly expensive crutch for the Americans. In 1945 the United States, as the world's leading economy with massive financial reserves, could afford the costs of containment—paying for aid and troops in sensitive countries abroad. By 1960 the world economy was more in balance, with the recovery of Germany and Japan. America's share of world production had shrunk from a half to a quarter, her holding of world gold reserves from 70 per cent to 50 per cent. Eisenhower and his successors, John F. Kennedy (1961–3) and Lyndon B. Johnson (1963–9), pressed Europeans, particularly Germany, to contribute to the costs of their own defence. They also came to view the EEC, originally welcomed in Washington, as a trading rival.

On the European side, feelings grew that the original Atlantic contract was now out of date. Some Germans, for instance, resented the continued American occupation. The vast and deliberately visible American presence in cities such as Heidelberg or Kaiserslautern began to seem offensive. There was also debate in the early 1960s about Germany joining the nuclear 'club'. But France, once again, went furthest with her protests. De Gaulle believed that the Alliance had become an instrument of American domination. He also felt that incidents such as the Cuban missile crisis of 1962—when the world waited impotently, under threat of nuclear war, for the superpowers to resolve their confrontation—showed the folly of Europe relying on the volatile United States. By 1960 France, like Britain, had become a nuclear power and de Gaulle gradually extracted France from NATO's integrated command, evicting US troops and headquarters in 1966.

This rupture was not total. France remained a signatory to the North Atlantic Treaty, prompting charges that she was enjoying the benefits of NATO *à la carte* rather than paying for the full menu. And fears that the French would adopt a stance of neutrality between east and west evaporated with de Gaulle's resignation in 1969. Although the transatlantic contract was under increasing strain in both Europe and America by the end of the 1960s, it still seemed mutually beneficial.

The Soviet Bloc

Even in regimented eastern Europe the 1950s and 1960s saw a moderation of superpower hegemony. The main stimulus was the death of Stalin in March 1953. His worst excesses were curbed by his successors—particularly Nikita Khrushchev, party secretary from 1953 to 1964, who denounced Stalinism and its personality cult in a sensational speech to the party conference in 1956. At home Khrushchev made some efforts to reform agriculture, increase production of consumer goods, and promote rule by law instead of secret police. But the process of destalinization had more effect in eastern Europe. There the new course was expressed in the doctrine that there were now 'many roads to socialism'.

The most spectacular example was Yugoslavia. A creation of Serbian imperialism in the First World War, this polyglot state was held together after 1945 by a federal constitution and (until his death in 1980) by the leadership of Josip Broz Tito (son of a Croatian father and Slovene mother). Tito's revolution had owed little to the Red Army, and his communists were in complete control by the end of 1945. Tito's imperialist ambitions in the Balkans led to ostracization by Moscow in 1948, whereupon he followed his own distinctive course. In foreign policy he was a pioneer of the so-called 'non-aligned movement', exploiting both sides in the Cold War. At home he repudiated Stalinism and went farthest of all the eastern bloc countries along the road of economic devolution and self-management.

Yugoslavia was unique, however. Other Balkan dictators adopted a more independent foreign policy while remaining grimly Stalinist at home. In Albania Enver Hoxha (1945–85) and his nepotistic party shunned the West but took Chinese aid after Beijing broke with Moscow in the late 1950s. Romania, particularly under Nikolai Ceausescu (1965–89), adroitly played the same game while also opening up trade with the West. For both leaders, Moscow's attempt to keep them as Russian economic colonies was the main reason for breaking away from the USSR. But Ceausescu was careful to remain within the Warsaw Pact (as was Hoxha until 1968), and communist rule in both countries remained unchallenged and repressive. Moscow therefore did not feel threatened, particularly since the Balkans were of peripheral interest.

Comrades again. Soviet leaders Nikolai Bulganin and Nikita Khrushchev patch up their differences with Marshal Tito of Yugoslavia in Belgrade in June 1955.

The heart of the Soviet bloc was east-central Europe—the axis of German aggression in the past and now the border with NATO's Central Front. Here deviation in foreign policy was unacceptable, as the Hungarians found in October 1956 when they tried to withdraw from the Warsaw Pact and their revolution was suppressed by Soviet troops. On the other hand, these were some of the most advanced industrial areas of the eastern bloc, particularly the GDR and the Czech lands, and pressures for economic liberalization

The head of a tyrant. A 25-foot-high bronze statue of Stalin stood in front of the City Park in Budapest until toppled by demonstrators on 23 October 1956. It was gradually dismembered and the head ended up near the National Theatre surmounted by a road sign: 'Dead End'.

were particularly strong. The pattern, in consequence, was domestic reform but diplomatic conformity (the complete opposite of Romania and Albania). Janos Kadar led Hungary farthest along the path blazed by Tito, sensitive to the causes of the rising of 1956. Kadarism allowed individual local enterprises freedom, within the overall economic plan, to set their own wage and price levels in response to profits. In Poland, where there was also unrest in 1956, Wladislaw Gomulka stopped the process of agricultural collectivization, leaving some 80 per cent of the land in private hands.

Even the Soviet bloc, therefore, was no monolith but accommodated itself to local circumstances. In a deeper sense, too, an element of consent was involved in communist rule. Throughout eastern Europe the ideological fervour of the immediate post-war era had still not been entirely extinguished. Moreover, the general public were beneficiaries as well as victims of 'people's democracy'. Mass industrialization and the collectivization of agriculture entailed huge social and environmental costs, but they also wrought a social revolution. In twenty years after 1950 the majority of eastern Europeans (outside the Balkans) was transformed from peasant farmers into urban industrial workers. Housing remained poor and consumer goods scarce, but the provision of free education, basic health care, and (outside Yugoslavia) full employment were all signs that the lot of the average person had markedly improved under communism. This was an important source of political cohesion in the 1950s and 1960s.

That said, it remains true that communist rule rested ultimately on force. The most striking example was East Germany. It was the most industrialized country of the eastern bloc, with the highest living standards. The regime of Walter Ulbricht had worked hard to create a sense of East German national consciousness, using sport as one of its main weapons. Huge amounts of money (and steroids) were pumped into athletic stars and at the Munich Olympics of 1972 the GDR won twenty gold medals—trailing only the USSR and the United States. Yet this remained an artificial state, and the appeal of its neighbour was enhanced by the accessibility of West German TV in most of the GDR. Denied true democracy, East Germans voted with their feet. In the 1950s the GDR was the only Soviet bloc country to decline in population, from 19 million to 17 million, as people slipped through the unchecked exits into west Berlin and thence to the Federal Republic.

Faced with this haemorrhage of personnel (much of it skilled), Ulbricht finally persuaded Moscow to seal off the city and begin the Berlin Wall on 13 August 1961. Eleven days later Günter Litfin, aged 24, scaled the wall and swam the River Spree, only to be shot down as he climbed on to the West Berlin bank. A simple stone memorial was erected to 'the first victim of the Wall'. It was a stark reminder that 'freedom', though a cliché of the Cold War, was not an empty slogan.

Coexistence and Stagnation, 1968–1981

By 1968, some two decades after Europe was divided, the Cold War had lost much of its ideological intensity. The post-war generation in East and West had seen in their own lifetimes how communism or capitalism had provided undreamt-of

A new French revolution?
Demonstrators fill the
Champs Elysées in May 1968.

prosperity. Their children, however, had no such experience. For them the -isms were systems, and increasingly depressing ones at that. In the East the hallmark of dissent was growing political cynicism at the corruption of the party establishments. In the West students protested openly at the conformism and consumerism of their elders, adopting populist forms of Marxism and heroes such as Che Guevara and Mao Tse-tung in repudiation of both American capitalism and Soviet communism. Most of these protests were short lived yet they spawned small but notorious terrorist groups, notably the Red Army Faction in Germany and the Red Brigades in Italy, who were responsible for a spate of robberies and kidnappings before their suppression in the late 1970s. Although degenerating into nihilism, these terrorists, like the student movements from which they sprang, were reacting against the Americanized capitalism of 1960s Europe.

Nothing did more to tarnish America's international reputation than the war in Vietnam. The spectacle of endless bombings of the North, played out nightly on

Facing: **Across the divide:
Berlin.** West Berliners shout
to relatives and friends over
the Wall, October 1961.

293

Facing: **'Bliss was it in that dawn to be alive'**. The 1989 revolution in eastern Europe aroused euphoria reminiscent of France two centuries before. Its most potent symbol was the dismantling of the Berlin Wall in November 1989. Here joyful Berliners celebrate their new freedom and unity in front of the Brandenburg Gate.

TV screens, was a propaganda disaster for the United States. Vietnam served as a shorthand for all the iniquities of military–industrial capitalism, no more so than in Paris in May 1968, where the student uprising set off protests that nearly toppled de Gaulle. The analogue of Vietnam in the East was the Soviet invasion of Czechoslovakia in August 1968. Communism there had remained highly centralized, provoking growing opposition both from liberals and from the Slovak minority. The reformist government of Alexander Dubcek (a Slovak) ushered in the so-called 'Prague spring'—a source of alarm throughout the Soviet bloc. Dubcek allowed other political parties to organize and launched inquiries into the past record of Stalinism. There was talk that Czechoslovakia would leave the Warsaw Pact. On 20 August the Soviet tanks rolled in, though it took Moscow months to construct a pliant alternative government. The Soviet right to intervene as guardian of 'socialist internationalism' was stated in what became known in the West as 'the Brezhnev Doctrine'.

By the late 1960s the two blocs seemed to be facts of life. The Cold War no longer threatened to become hot war but had frozen solid. The shorthand for this process was *détente*, meaning a relaxation of tension. The superpowers' main motive for *détente* was to control the arms race, which not only consumed a substantial por-

Alexander Dubcek, reformist leader of Czechoslovakia until reined in by Moscow, visits a Prague factory in September 1968.

294

The planned economies of eastern and central Europe laid a primary emphasis on heavy industry. In addition, state-owned enterprise was less easily subjected to environmental controls than privately owned businesses in market economies. The result was an environmental catastrophe, which left very high clean-up costs after the end of communism. The picture shows a state-owned chemical works at Espenhahn in the German Democratic Republic.

tion of their budgets but had also brought the world close to nuclear disaster over Cuba in 1962. In May 1972 President Richard M. Nixon flew to Moscow—the first visit there by an American leader—and signed the SALT 1 arms limitation treaty. Although only a limited, temporary measure, it appeared to herald a new attitude on both sides.

Détente also had a German dimen- sion. Adenauer and the Christian Democrats had worked for ultimate reunification, but the socialists, led by Willy Brandt, a former mayor of West Berlin, believed it was time to face the reality of division and reach a *modus vivendi* with the East. Brandt, Chancellor from 1969 to 1974, never abandoned the goal of reunification—his motto was 'two states, one nation'—but his period in office saw the *de facto* recognition of the GDR and acceptance of the post-war border with Poland. A four-power treaty on Berlin regularized Allied access to this former flashpoint and allowed greater opportunities for visits to and fro by Berliners. The corner-stone of *détente* was the Helsinki agreement of 1975. In return for Soviet bloc commitments on human rights, the West acknowledged the post-war frontiers of Europe as 'invio- lable' and not to be changed by force. Thirty years after Hitler the division of Europe seemed immutable.

Détente: Soviet leader Leonid Brezhnev and American president Richard Nixon during their Moscow summit, May 1972.

Unlike NATO and the Warsaw Pact, the EEC became more dynamic after the demise of de Gaulle. Its relaunch at the Hague summit of December 1969 led to closer foreign policy co-ordination and a commitment to monetary union by 1980. This further integration was part of the agenda for deepening the Community. The other great aim was widening. Britain's long-delayed entry became possible once de Gaulle had left the stage. Together with Denmark and Ireland, she joined the Community in January 1973, turning the Six into the Nine. By 1977 serious negotia- tions were under way with Greece, Spain, and Portugal.

The motives for this second enlargement remind us again of the Cold War con- text of European integration. These three poor, Mediterranean countries were very different from the industrialized core of the EEC and posed huge problems of assimilation. The pressures for their inclusion were frankly political. Spain and Portugal had been stagnant backwaters of authoritarian dictatorship since before the war. But the Portuguese revolution of April 1974 and the death of General Fran- cisco Franco in November 1975 ushered in new democracies. Greece had been semi-democratic until 1967 but thereafter a repressive military junta held power until November 1974. In the mid-1970s, therefore, all three countries were strug- gling to establish democracies, and their admission to the EEC was intended to consolidate that process. Greece joined in 1981, but French fears about agricultural competition delayed the admission of Spain and Portugal until 1986.

By the 1980s the European Community rivalled the superpowers in population and resources. Yet the two aims of deepening and widening seemed increasingly incompatible. Except for southern Italy, the original Six had much in common, with long-standing economic and cultural links. The assimilation of Britain, with her small agricultural sector and continued interest in global trade, proved extremely hard, and much of the Community's energy in the decade after 1973 was taken up with arguments about the size of the British budget contribution. Absorbing the backward Mediterranean states was also problematic, requiring a substantial transfer of resources to bring their levels of development closer to that of northern Europe. With enlargement so difficult, the deeper integration of the Community, envisaged at The Hague in 1969, took second place. There was greater co-operation in foreign policy but a limited attempt at monetary co-ordination collapsed in the mid-1970s.

At the root of the EEC's problems was the end of the long post-war boom. For two decades from the late 1940s western Europe's economies had grown steadily and almost without interruption, in a quite unprecedented period of prosperity. The Cold War had contributed to this, through the American security umbrella and also the profitability of what became known as the military–industrial complex. Europeans had become used to growth: indeed social stability was predicated on the expectation of rising living standards and generous welfare and medical provision. Similarly, the success of the EEC in its first decade or so had owed much to the post-war boom, and the absence of growth greatly complicated the process of enlargement. Just as such lengthy growth was unprecedented, so too was the bizarre mix of economic stagnation and soaring inflation ('stagflation') that followed. Underlying the confusion were fundamental changes in the world economy, notably the huge rise in oil prices after the Arab–Israeli war of 1973 and the new industrial challenge from Asia, led by Japan.

Economic crisis therefore threatened the foundations of political stability. This threat was even more apparent in the eastern bloc. By the 1960s the gains of forced modernization had been achieved, and its problems were all too apparent. Soviet-style communism, in historian Charles Maier's phrase, was a 'heavy-metal' ideology. Its core was smokestack industries under state direction. Production was geared to central planning targets, with little attention to profitability and efficiency, even in more westernized economies such as Yugoslavia. By the 1970s these industries were grossly uncompetitive in world terms and their unrestricted growth had created appalling pollution. Economic reform in the wake of the Prague spring was mere tinkering, and the corrupt neo-Stalinist leaderships ruled over increasingly sullen populations. What helped keep the Soviet bloc going, ironically, was *détente*. Its great attraction, not least for the Soviets, was the possibility of western trade and credits. West Germany's loans and markets became vital to the economies of her eastern neighbours. But *détente* proved a virus as much as a blood transfusion. The West's price at Helsinki in 1975 was a Soviet bloc commitment to human rights and to procedures for their monitoring. In order to maintain the economic benefits of *détente*, communist regimes had to accept the political price of small-scale dissidence. Despite police harassment, groups like Charter 77 in Czechoslovakia and the Evangelical Church in the GDR chipped away at the legitimacy of their respective regimes. They were to prove the nuclei of eventual political opposition.

Nowhere was the double-edged character of *détente* more evident than in Poland. Under Eduard Gierek, Poland was one of the world's fastest growing economies in the early 1970s. But its 'little economic miracle' was the result of massive imports of industrial equipment from the West, financed not by Polish exports but western credits. The result was the largest foreign debt in eastern Europe, which could only be serviced through raising prices and squeezing living standards.

Mounting Polish resentment found powerful institutional expression in what was about the least Stalinized country of eastern Europe. Most of the population was Catholic and the Church drew additional strength from its championship of Polish nationalism against Russia and from the election of a Polish cardinal as Pope John Paul II in 1978. Also distinctive was the organized militancy of the Baltic shipyard workers. In August 1980 they secured the right to an independent trade union, Solidarity. Under the leadership of Lech Walesa this became a potent political force. The retirement of Gierek failed to defuse the crisis and in December 1981, with communist monopoly of power threatened and fears of Soviet military intervention, the Polish leadership imposed martial law. Solidarity was suppressed, the

Polish pope John Paul II at a huge open-air mass in Gdansk in June 1979.

Polish 'Solidarity' leader **Lech Walesa** addresses a protest meeting at the Gdansk shipyard in 1980. The pictures of the Pope and the Virgin Mary are reminders of the importance of the Catholic Church in Polish nationalism and anti-communism.

party purged, and a tenuous order restored. The year 1981, like 1956 and 1968, was a reminder that Soviet power was what ultimately held the eastern bloc together.

From the 'New Cold War' to the End of the Soviet Empire, 1981–1989

The Polish crisis signalled the end of *détente*. Already under strain for other reasons, notably the Soviet invasion of Afghanistan in December 1979, it was now repudiated by the West. Loans ended, debts soared, and the socio-economic pressures in eastern Europe mounted. The Soviet Union was forced to increase economic aid to Poland and her neighbours, further increasing the pressures on its own ossified economy.

Equally alarming for the Soviets was the 'new Cold War' with the United States. Modernization of Warsaw Pact nuclear weapons in the 1970s had prompted a new NATO deployment of Pershing and Cruise missiles in western Europe. In the short run this led to a revival of anti-American peace movements in Britain, West Germany, and The Netherlands, while the Soviets broke off all arms control negotiations in 1983. Nevertheless, NATO successfully deployed the missiles and the Soviets were further alarmed by President Ronald Reagan's Strategic Defense Initiative (SDI). The USSR had only been able to hold its own to date by devoting perhaps one-fifth of GDP to defence, but the cost of its military–industrial complex was backwardness in every other sector of the economy. 'Star Wars' (as SDI

298

became known) threatened Moscow with a new, high-technology twist to the arms race, already spiralling out of control.

By the mid-1980s the Soviet Union faced a major crisis. The increasingly senile Leonid Brezhnev, Khrushchev's successor from 1964, had presided over what became known as the 'era of stagnation'. With typical Russian black humour, one joke imagined recent Soviet leaders in a train that had broken down out in the steppes. 'Flog the driver,' Stalin ordered. But nothing happened. 'Rehabilitate the driver,' cried Khrushchev, to no avail. Then pudgy Brezhnev drew the curtains of the compartment, smiled his hooded smile, and said: 'Let's just pretend the train is moving.'

After Brezhnev died in 1982, the Soviet communist party chose two more ailing septuagenarians (Yuri Andropov and Konstantin Chernenko) who expired in quick succession. It then made a generational leap and appointed the 54-year-old Mikhail Gorbachev as party secretary in March 1985. Under his dynamic leadership the Soviet Union reopened dialogue with the United States and totally changed its nuclear policy. In December 1987 Gorbachev and Reagan signed a historic agreement to remove all intermediate-range nuclear missiles, not only in Europe but world-wide. This was the first time the superpowers had actually agreed to reduce their nuclear arsenals. 'Gorby' became a folk hero in the West.

But Gorbachev wanted reform, not revolution. He was a communist functionary trying to make the system work by more radical means. The economy was his priority. He wished to control the arms race so as to reduce its crushing financial burden and facilitate economic modernization through western help. But he was persuaded that political liberalization (*glasnost* or openness) was essential to the process of reconstruction (*perestroika*). In the event, the former succeeded while the latter failed. As the economy collapsed, freedom to protest grew. Reconstruction became deconstruction.

In eastern Europe the result was revolution. Gorbachev had hoped that liberalization throughout the Soviet bloc would create a new framework for economic co-operation, thereby strengthening Russian influence. But his public backing for *perestroika* and *glasnost* in the Soviet satellites only served to shake their neo-Stalinist regimes to the foundations. When Gorbachev visited Prague in April 1987, one of his aides, Gennadi Gerasimov, was asked what was the difference between Gorbachev and Dubcek. 'Nineteen years,' was the reply. Even the political élites privately acknowledged the need for reform. Certainly they were not ready to use brute force to maintain the old order.

By 1989 the situation had become critical.

Gorbymania: In Prague in April 1987 Soviet leader Mikhail Gorbachev greets joyful crowds for whom he had become the symbol of reform. Behind him hard-line Czech president Gustav Husak tries to look cheerful.

In Poland and Hungary the combination of economic crisis and political opposition was most advanced. In the former, Solidarity was relegalized and it swept the board in elections in June. In Hungary, too, a multiparty system was authorized and border controls abandoned. This permitted a new haemorrhage of citizens from the GDR, exiting via Hungary to Austria and West Germany. When Gorbachev visited Berlin in October 1989 for the GDR's fortieth anniversary celebrations, he was openly critical of the Honecker government's failure to reform. It was also made clear that, unlike 1968, the USSR would not intervene with force. Gerasimov said that the 'Brezhnev Doctrine' had been replaced by the 'Sinatra Doctrine'. 'You know the Frank Sinatra song, "I did it my way"?' he asked. 'Well, Hungary and Poland are doing it their way.'

By November 1989 powerful opposition groups had emerged in the GDR and Czechoslovakia—New Forum and Civic Forum. A new government in the GDR tried belated liberalization but its decision to end border controls only led to a massive flood of East Berliners into the western part of the city on the night of 9 November. Within days the Wall—the most forbidding symbol of Europe's division—was being pulled down. By the end of the year communist rule had col-

Exodus: On their way to the promised land, East German refugees who have reached Prague line up for buses on the next stage of their journey to West Germany in the summer of 1989.

300

lapsed in the GDR and Czechoslovakia. The flood-tide swept on, even into the Balkans, where Stalinism had been more deeply rooted. In November Bulgarian dictator Todor Zhivkov resigned after forty-five years in power. Romania's Christmas present was the summary trial and execution of Nikolai Ceausescu and his wife.

From start to finish, the whole drama of liberation had been played out on the television screens of Europe and the world. Indeed, TV images had been a revolutionary force in themselves, inspiring acts of emulation. Thanks largely to Gorbachev the Cold War was over, but so was the Soviet bloc. The thaw had become an avalanche.

'The Rebirth of History'

1989 was as momentous a year in European history as 1789. Like the would-be reformers of the *ancien régime*, Gorbachev had sown the wind and reaped the whirlwind. Without the controlled border East Germany was not viable and on 3 October 1990 Germany was united again. In the Soviet Union the failure of *perestroika* and the

Nikolai Ceausescu's grave in a secluded corner of Bucharest's Ghensea cemetery, falsely identified as that of a colonel in the Army reserve.

success of *glasnost* undermined both the basis of communist power in the republics and also the dominance over them by Moscow. Fighting a rearguard action on both fronts Gorbachev was nearly toppled by a conservative coup in August 1991, which he survived only with his authority in shreds. At the end of 1991 the Soviet Union ceased to exist and was replaced by a loose Commonwealth of Independent States, each riven by economic crisis and political confusion.

The Cold War had ended with the collapse of one of the blocs and one of the protagonists. As the dust settled, two institutions of Cold-War western Europe remained more or less intact—NATO and the EC. NATO had lost its fundamental rationale with the collapse of the Warsaw Pact, and Allied forces in Germany were substantially reduced. But the alliance structure, especially America's leadership role, clearly constituted one important pillar of stability for the future. Like NATO, the European Community was a deeply flawed institution, as the collapse of its Monetary System in 1992–3 reminded the world. But by 1993 the member states had fulfilled the Single European Act of 1985, designed to abolish all economic barriers between them, including those on the movement of labour and capital. And the spate of membership applications indicated that the Community was seen as the economic heart of Europe after the Cold War. The most advanced of the applicants—Austria, Finland, and Sweden—joined in January 1995. The Twelve became Fifteen, comprising some 370 million people—roughly the same population as the United States and Japan combined. Former communist states pressed for admission or association, as did those from the Mediterranean and North Africa.

After 1989 it seemed meaningful once again to talk about Europe as a single entity. The polarized language of East and West had always been misleading. Turkey, for instance, was a member of NATO, yet this backward, largely Islamic country could hardly be considered western in the sense of France or Germany. As for eastern Europe, this had lumped together countries like Bulgaria (Slavic, predominantly Orthodox, with strong links to Russia) and Hungary (non-Slavic, mainly Catholic, self-defined 'bastion of the West' against Russians and Turks). Above all, central Europe had disappeared down the bipolar chasm, wrenching Hungary and the Czech lands away from their historic links with Germany and leaving Austria frozen in neutrality between East and West.

Yet the end of these historically artificial blocs did not signal unity. Economic backwardness and environmental pollution in the East would take years to overcome. The strain of reunification on Germany's finances was enormous. Establishing civil society on the western model was also difficult in former police states with few democratic traditions. In the Balkans the communists remained strong and were often able to rebuild their power in modified form. In other words, Europe was still divided, albeit less brutally, by her history, and communism was one legacy that would be hard to throw off. As the Balkan case also suggested, older patterns became visible again, such as the divide between Catholic and Orthodox Europes—the latter being economically more backward—or even between Christian Europe and Balkan extremities such as Albania and Bosnia where the Ottoman, Islamic imprint had been much deeper.

Such distinctions were far from precise, but they served as indicators of what became known as the 'rebirth of history'. Past movements, frozen by the Cold War, were now on the move again. This was most evident in the case of nationalism. The demand that separate nations should form separate states had proved one of the most potent battle-cries of nineteenth-century Europe. In the twentieth century its resonance was world-wide. Yet nationalism was a problematic concept. In only a few western European countries, notably France, was there congruence between state and nation. Eastern Europe after the demise of the Ottoman and Habsburg empires had been a patchwork of multinational states, with a dominant majority (such as the Czechs) presiding over more or less oppressed minorities. The Cold War had largely frozen these ethnic conflicts; after its thaw struggle resumed. At the end of 1992 Czechoslovakia managed to split in two peacefully. But Yugoslavia's break-up proved appallingly bloody.

In Tito's early years, the federal structure of Yugoslavia (six republics and two autonomous provinces) had been carefully modulated by the central communist party to hold the Serbs in check and to balance the other ethnic groups. But economic devolution and political liberalization had gradually weakened the authority of the centre. The 1974 constitution confirmed the result—what veteran Yugoslav communist Milovan Djilas called eight little party states with eight small, competing economies. Thus, even before his death in 1980, Tito had helped undermine his own creation. His successors had little interest except in cultivat-

ing ethnic support within their own republics. The most egregious was Slobodan Milosevic, the Serbian leader from 1987, and the nationalism fostered by him provoked a backlash from other ethnic groups. In this struggle, history was not so much reborn as reconstructed. In 1989 Serbs focused on Kosovo, site of their celebrated battle six hundred years before against the Turks, and now dominated by the Muslim Albanians. Similarly, Croat agitation aroused Serbian memories of the atrocities committed by the Croatian fascists, the Ustasi, against them in 1941–5. Thus, history became a convenient tool of ethnic politicians as the federation broke apart. The secession of Slovenia in 1991 proved relatively bloodless, since this was an ethnically distinct republic. By 1992 Croatia had also won independence, although leaving the Serbs with one-third of the territory. But in Bosnia—where Muslims formed 44 per cent of the population, Serbs 31 per cent, and Croats 17 per cent—the declaration of independence in March 1992 resulted in a ruinous war from which the Muslims were the real losers as the other two groups carved up the territory.

Even in more coherent western Europe, nationalism remained strong. The European Community had been partly an attempt to control and channel German nationalism. Federalist sentiment, though widespread, was often an instrument of national policy, as in Gaullist France. Some countries, such as Britain and Denmark, had joined the Community largely for economic reasons and were not enthusiastic about the larger project of political integration. And, at work within most nation-states, were erosive regionalist tendencies. In Italy, which dated from the 1860s as a unified nation, the political structures of the state lacked authority. In Spain, the south still bears the imprint of its long Muslim occupation, while, in

Past as present: Kosovo. Stirred up by Slobodan Milosevic, Orthodox Serbs commemorate the 600th anniversary of their devastating defeat by the Muslim Turks on 28 June 1389 at the grimly named battle of *Kosovo Polje* (field of black birds).

303

Across the divide: Mostar.
The capital of Herzegovina
took its name from this old
bridge (*stari most*) over the
River Neretva built by the
Turks in the 1560s. Linking
the Croat west bank of the
city with the Muslim east
bank, it came to symbolize the
ideal of Bosnian ethnic amity
until destroyed by Croat
shells on 9 November 1993.

the north, Catalonia and particularly the Basque country have been allowed substantial political autonomy. Another apparently ancient nation-state, the United Kingdom of Great Britain and Northern Ireland, is also an uneasy historical accretion, with Northern Ireland struggling to bridge its sectarian divide and Scotland vocal in demands for devolution or even independence. Although renamed the European Union in November 1993, the Community remained fragmented, both among and within the member states. And its failure to intervene effectively in Yugoslavia, or even maintain a consistent policy, was a reminder of how far it was from constituting a security organization.

The political map of Europe after the Cold War was therefore complicated, even chaotic. It would take years to overcome the manifold legacies of communist rule in the East, ranging from democratic inexperience to environmental pollution. Although large supranational entities such as NATO and the EC offered some promise as forces of stability, internal arguments reduced their ability to confront the forces of nationalism and regionalism which threatened to fragment the continent, particularly in the Balkans and the old Soviet Union. In the Cold War, Europe's division had been a source of stability as well as oppression; after 1989, unification brought confusion and not just liberation. To a degree unimaginable to Bismarck, Europe in the 1990s was more than a geographical expression. But, no less than in the days of Bonaparte or Hitler, European unity remained an idea and not a reality. And reality was the product of history.

304

Further Reading

1. Revolutions from Above and Below: European Politics from the French Revolution to the First World War

General

GILDEA, ROBERT, *Barricades and Borders: Europe, 1800–1914* (Oxford, 1987).
ROBERTS, J. M., *Europe, 1880–1945* (2nd edn., London, 1989).
SPERBER, JONATHAN, *The European Revolutions, 1848–1851* (Cambridge, 1994).

International Relations

BRIDGE, F. R., and BULLEN, ROGER, *The Great Powers and the European States System, 1815–1914* (London, 1980).
SCHROEDER, PAUL W., *The Transformation of European Politics, 1763–1848* (Oxford, 1994).
TAYLOR, A. J. P., *The Struggle for Mastery in Europe, 1848–1918* (Oxford, 1954).

France

DOYLE, WILLIAM, *The Oxford History of the French Revolution* (Oxford, 1989).
ELLIS, GEOFFREY, *The Napoleonic Empire* (London, 1990).
FURET, FRANÇOIS, *Revolutionary France, 1770–1880* (Oxford, 1992).
MCMILLAN, JAMES F., *Napoleon III* (London, 1991).
MAYEUR, J. M., and RÉBERIOUX, M., *The Third Republic from its Origins to the Great War, 1871–1914* (Cambridge, 1984).
SCHAMA, SIMON, *Citizens* (New York, 1989).

Germany

CRAIG, GORDON A., *Germany, 1866–1945* (Oxford, 1978).
PFLANZE, OTTO, *Bismarck and the Development of Germany*, 3 vols. (Princeton, 1963, 1990).
SCHULZE, HAGEN, *The Course of German Nationalism: From Frederick the Great to Bismarck 1763–1867* (Cambridge, 1991).
SHEEHAN, JAMES J., *German History, 1770–1866* (Oxford, 1990).
WEHLER, HANS-ULRICH, *The German Empire, 1871–1918* (Leamington Spa, 1985).

The Habsburg Empire

BRIDGE, F. R., *From Sadowa to Sarajevo: The Foreign Policy of Austria-Hungary, 1866–1914* (London, 1972).
MAY, ARTHUR J., *The Habsburg Monarchy, 1867–1914* (Cambridge, Mass., 1965).
SKED, ALAN, *The Decline and Fall of the Habsburg Empire, 1815–1918* (London, 1989).
TAYLOR, A. J. P., *The Habsburg Monarchy, 1809–1918* (London, 1951).

Russia

ASCHER, A., *The Revolution of 1905* (Stanford, Calif., 1993).
PIPES, RICHARD, *Russia under the Old Regime* (London, 1974).

SETON-WATSON, H., *The Russian Empire, 1801–1917* (Oxford, 1967).

VENTURI, FRANCO, *Roots of Revolution: A History of the Populist and Socialist Movements in Nineteenth Century Russia* (London, 1960).

WESTWOOD, J. N., *Endurance and Endeavour: Russian History, 1812–1992* (4th edn., Oxford, 1993).

Italy

BEALES, DEREK, *The Risorgimento and the Unification of Italy* (London, 1971).

HEARDER, HARRY, *Italy in the Age of the Risorgimento, 1790–1870* (London, 1983).

MACK SMITH, DENIS, *The Making of Italy, 1796–1870* (London, 1968).

—— *Mazzini* (New Haven, 1994).

SETON-WATSON, C., *Italy from Liberalism to Fascism, 1870–1925* (London, 1967).

Great Britain

BEALES, DEREK, *From Castlereagh to Gladstone, 1815–85* (London, 1969).

BOURNE, K., *The Foreign Policy of Victorian England, 1830–1902* (Oxford, 1970).

GASH, NORMAN, *Aristocracy and People, 1815–65* (London, 1979).

PARRY, JONATHAN, *The Rise and Fall of Liberal Government in Victorian Britain* (New Haven, 1993).

SHANNON, RICHARD, *The Crisis of Imperialism, 1865–1915* (London, 1974).

The Origins of the First World War

BERGHAHN, VOLKER, *Germany and the Approach of War in 1914* (London, 1973).

FISCHER, FRITZ, *Germany's War Aims in the First World War* (London, 1967).

LIEVEN, D. C. B., *Russia and the Origins of the First World War* (London, 1983).

STONE, NORMAN, *Europe Transformed, 1878–1919* (London, 1983).

WILLIAMSON, SAMUEL R., *Austria-Hungary and the Origins of the First World War* (London, 1991).

2. The Industrialization of Modern Europe, 1750–1914

BÖHME, H., *An Introduction to the Economic and Social History of Germany* (Oxford, 1979).

BRUCK, W. F., *The Social and Economic History of Germany, 1888–1939* (New York, 1962).

CAMERON, R. E., (ed.), *Essays in French Economic History* (Homewood, Ill., 1970). This is a most useful collection of essays.

CRAFTS, N. R. F., *The Industrial Revolution and British Economic Growth* (Oxford, 1985). This exceptionally influential book epitomizes the currently fashionable view of the 'slow British Industrial Revolution'.

CRISP, O., *Studies in the Russian Economy before 1914* (London, 1976).

CROUZET, F., 'England and France in the Eighteenth Century: A Comparative Analysis of Two Economic Growths', in R. M. Hartwell (ed.), *The Causes of the Industrial Revolution in England* (London, 1967). A pioneering study which reveals how closely pre-Revolutionary France came to rivalling the capabilities of the world's first industrial nation.

—— 'Wars, Blockade and Economic Change in Europe, 1792–1815', *Journal of Economic History*, 24 (1964).

DHONDT, J., and BRUWIER, M., 'The Low Countries, 1700–1914' in C. M. Cipolla (ed.), *The*

Fontana Economic History of Europe, iv: *The Emergence of Industrial Societies* (London, 1978), Pt. I. In general, the Fontana series is a useful and wide-ranging companion for the industrial history of most continental states.

ELBAUM, E., and LAZONICK, W., (eds.), *The Decline of the British Economy* (Oxford, 1986). A powerful explanation of the 'British problem' in terms of deficiencies in institutional systems.

FISCHER, F., *War of Illusions: German Policies from 1911 to 1914* (London, 1975), 517–22. This work famously revealed the importance of economic objectives among German war aims.

GATTRELL, P., *The Development of the Tsarist Economy, 1850–1917* (London, 1986).

GERSCHENKRON, A., *Economic Backwardness in Historical Perspective* (Cambridge, Mass., 1962). This set of essays comprises one of the masterworks in comparative economic history. An essential conceptual tool.

GOOD, R., 'Stagnation and Take-Off in Austria, 1873–1913', *Economic History Review*, 27 (1974).

GREGORY, P., 'Economic Growth and Structural Change in Tsarist Russia: A Case of Modern Economic Growth?', *Soviet Studies*, 23 (1972).

HAUSER, H., *Germany's Commercial Grip on the World* (London, 1917). A powerful, near-contemporary perspective on Germany's pre-1914 development.

KITCHEN, M., *The Political Economy of Germany, 1815–1914* (London, 1978).

LANDES, D. S., 'The Old Bank, and the New: The Financial Revolution of the Nineteenth Century', in F. Crouzet *et al.* (eds.), *Essays in European Economic History* (London, 1969); see also his exceptional hymn to technological change in the growth process, *The Unbound Prometheus* (Cambridge, 1969).

LAUE, T. H. VON, *Why Lenin, Why Stalin?* (New York, 1964). This author also produced a celebrated treatment of early Russian industrialization, *Sergei Witte and the Industrialization of Russia* (New York, 1963), very much in the heroic vein.

McKAY, J. P., *Pioneers for Profit* (Chicago, 1970). An altogether cooler assessment than von Laue.

POLLARD, S., *Peaceful Conquest* (Oxford, 1981). Important argument for the transnational nature of the industrialization process.

POUNDS, N., 'Economic Growth in Germany', in H. G. J. Aitken (ed.), *The State and Economic Growth* (New York, 1959).

ROSTOW, W. W., *The Stages of Economic Growth* (Cambridge, 1960).

—— (ed.), *The Economics of the Take-Off into Self-Sustained Growth* (London, 1963). These works define key stages in the debate over the necessary preconditions for, and essential characteristics of, the industrial 'take-off'.

RUDOLPH, R., *Finance and Industrialization in Austria-Hungary* (Cambridge, 1976).

STEARNS, P. N., *The Industrial Revolution in World History* (Boulder, Col., 1993).

SUPPLE, B. E., 'The State and the Industrial Revolution', in C. Cipolla (ed.), *The Fontana Economic History of Europe*, iii: *The Industrial Revolution* (London, 1973). A useful, and rare, attempt to define what the interventionist 'state' in economic affairs actually consists of.

TIPTON, F. B., 'National Consensus in German Economic History', *Central European History*, 7 (1974).

—— *Regional Variations in the Industrial Development of Germany during the Nineteenth Century* (Middleton, Conn., 1976) features a theme of major importance.

TREBILCOCK, C., ' "Spin-off" in British Economic History', *Economic History Review*, 22 (1969).

—— 'British Armaments and European Industrialization', *Economic History Review*, 26 (1973). The link between the demanding requirements and precise technology of armament manufacture and advances in engineering or metallurgy of wide civilian application is a pervasive feature of economic history in the 18th, 19th, and 20th centuries.

TREBILCOCK, C., *The Industrialization of the Continental Powers* (London, 1981).

3. Military Modernization, 1789–1918

General

BEST, GEOFFREY, *War and Society in Revolutionary Europe, 1770–1870* (London, 1982).
BOND, BRIAN, *War and Society in Europe, 1870–1970* (London, 1983).
GOOCH, JOHN, *Armies in Europe* (London, 1979).
HOWARD, MICHAEL, *War in European History* (Oxford, 1976).
MCNEILL, WILLIAM H., *The Pursuit of Power* (Oxford, 1983).
PARET, PETER (ed.), *Makers of Modern Strategy from Machiavelli to the Nuclear Age* (Oxford, 1986).
STRACHAN, HEW, *European Armies and the Conduct of War* (London, 1983).

Naval Warfare

BAXTER, J. P., *The Introduction of the Ironclad Warship* (Cambridge, Mass., 1933).
BRODIE, BERNARD, *Sea Power in the Machine Age* (Princeton, 1941).
HERWIG, HOLGER, *'Luxury' Fleet: The Imperial German Navy, 1888–1918* (London, 1980).
KENNEDY, PAUL, *The Rise and Fall of British Naval Mastery* (London, 1976).
MARDER, A. J., *From the Dreadnought to Scapa Flow: The Royal Navy in the Fisher Era, 1904–1919*, 5 vols. (London, 1961–70).

Period Studies

BERTAUD, JEAN-PAUL, *The Army of the French Revolution: From Citizen-Soldiers to Instrument of Power* (Princeton, 1988).
BIDWELL, SHELFORD, and GRAHAM, DOMINICK, *Fire-Power: British Army Weapons and Theories of War, 1904–1945* (London, 1982).
CHANDLER, DAVID G., *The Campaigns of Napoleon* (London, 1966).
CLAUSEWITZ, CARL VON, *On War*, ed. and transl. Michael Howard and Peter Paret (Princeton, 1976).
CRAIG, GORDON A., *The Battle of Königgrätz* (London, 1965).
FULLER, WILLIAM C., Jr., *Strategy and Power in Russia, 1600–1914* (New York, 1992).
HORNE, ALISTAIR, *The Price of Glory: Verdun 1916* (London, 1963).
HOWARD, MICHAEL, *The Franco-Prussian War: The German Invasion of France, 1870–1871* (London, 1961).
MILLET, ALLAN R., and MURRAY, WILLIAMSON (eds.), *Military Effectiveness*, i: *The First World War* (Boston, 1988).
PARET, PETER, *Yorck and the Era of Prussian Reform, 1807–1815* (Princeton, 1966).
ROTHENBERG, GUNTHER E., *The Art of Warfare in the Age of Napoleon* (London, 1977).
SHOWALTER, DENNIS E., *Railroads and Rifles: Soldiers, Technology and the Unification of Germany* (Hamden, Conn., 1975).
STONE, NORMAN, *The Eastern Front, 1914–1917* (London, 1975).
TRAVERS, TIM, *The Killing Ground: The British Army, the Western Front and the Emergence of Modern Warfare, 1900–1918* (London, 1987).

4. From Orders to Classes: European Society in the Nineteenth Century

BAINES, D., *Emigration from Europe, 1815–1930* (London, 1991). A brief, stimulating introduction.

BLACKBOURN, D., and EVANS, R. J. (eds.), *The German Bourgeoisie: Essays on the Social History of the German Middle Class from the Late Eighteenth Century to the Early Twentieth Century* (London, 1991). Immensely lucid and informative, and based on recent German research; the first chapter a superb summary of issues.

BREUILLY, J., *Labour and Liberalism in Nineteenth-Century Europe: Essays in Comparative History* (Manchester, 1992). A salutary warning from the author that comparative history must study what is genuinely comparable.

BUSH, M. L. (ed.), *Social Order and Social Classes in Europe since 1500* (London, 1992). A comprehensive selection of incisive essays.

CROSSICK, G., and HAUPT, H.-G., *Shopkeepers and Master-Artisans in Nineteenth-Century Europe* (London, 1986). An invaluable starter on a complex subject.

EVANS, E., *The Forging of the Modern State: Early Industrial Britain, 1783–1870* (London, 1983). Excellent—the most clear, no-nonsense exposition of the subject with a really useful bibliography.

EVANS, R. J., *Death in Hamburg: Society and Politics in the Cholera Years, 1830–1910* (Harmondsworth, 1987). Detailed, but worth investigating.

FOSTER, J., *Class Struggle and the Industrial Revolution* (London, 1974). A pioneering study of the emergence of a labour aristocracy in Oldham, Northampton, and South Shields.

HOWARTH, J., and CERNY, P. G., *Élites in France: Origins, Reproduction and Power* (London, 1981). Fascinating insights.

KIRK, N., *The Growth of Working Class Reformism in Mid-Victorian England* (London, 1985). Explores in a sensible well-rounded manner how radicalism gave way to reformism.

LIEVEN, D., *Aristocracy in Europe, 1815–1914* (London, 1992). A wide-ranging comparative survey.

LYNCH, K. A., *Family, Class and Ideology in Early Industrial France: Social Policy and the Working-Class Family, 1825–1848* (Madison, Wis., 1988). An innovative investigation, well worth reading.

MAGRAW, R., *History of the French Working Class*, 2 vols. (London, 1992). A supremely useful synthesis—Magraw has read everything!

MORRIS, R. J., *Class and Class Consciousness in the Industrial Revolution, 1780–1850* (London, 1979). A succinct demand for the study of class to be grounded in people, not theory.

NOIRIEL, G., *Workers in French Society in the Nineteenth and Twentieth Centuries* (1986; trans. New York, 1990). A thoroughly workmanlike, refreshingly empirical approach with a very useful bibliography.

PERKIN, H., *The Origins of Modern English Society, 1780–1880* (London, 1972). The subject is clearly and forcefully defined and explored.

PERROT, M., *Histoire de la vie privée*, iv: *De la révolution à la grande guerre*, ed. P. Aries and G. Duby (Paris, 1987). A feast of revealing illustrations of all aspects of social history.

PILBEAM, P., *The Middle Classes in Europe 1789–1914: France, Germany, Italy and Russia* (London, 1990). A comparative investigation of the social, economic, and political interests of the middle classes.

PRICE, R. D., *Social History of Nineteenth-Century France* (London, 1987). The thematic structure is effective—an excellent basic work.

RAEFF, M., *Understanding Imperial Russia: State and Society in the Ancien Régime* (New York, 1984). A lucid introduction.

RIEBER, A. J., *Merchants and Entrepreneurs in Imperial Russia* (Chapel Hill, NC, 1991). An excellent example of an increasing number of English-language investigations into the pre-Revolutionary middle class.

SEWELL, W. H., *Work and Revolution in France: The Language of Labour from the Old Régime to 1848* (Cambridge, 1980). A firmly stated case for the importance of traditional structures in the labour movement.

SHUBERT, A., *A Social History of Modern Spain* (London, 1990). An indispensable work of reference.

STEDMAN JONES, G., *Language of Class: Studies in English Working-Class History, 1832–1982* (Cambridge, 1983).

STEVENSON, J., *Popular Disturbances in England, 1700–1870* (London, 1979). Briskly and effectively argued.

THOMPSON, E. P., *The Making of the English Working Class* (London, 1963). A classic which is hard to put down.

TRANTER, N. L., *Population and Society, 1750–1940* (London, 1985). A work which lucidly illustrates the interconnected factors in demographic change.

WOOLF, S., *A History of Italy, 1700–1860: The Social Constraints of Political Change* (London, 1979). A unique study in the English language—not to be missed.

WRIGLEY, E. A., *People, Cities and Wealth: The Transformation of Traditional Society* (Oxford, 1987). A splendid source of information.

5. The Commercialization and Sacralization of European Culture in the Nineteenth Century

CHARLTON, D. G. (ed.), *The French Romantics*, 2 vols. (Cambridge, 1984). Excellent essays covering all aspects of French romanticism.

CLARK, KENNETH, *The Romantic Rebellion: Romantic Versus Classical Art* (London, 1973). Urbane lectures.

CLARK, T. J., *The Painting of Modern Life: Paris in the Art of Manet and his Followers* (London, 1985). Full of original if controversial insights.

DEATHRIDGE, J., and DAHLHAUS, C., *The New Grove Wagner* (London, 1984). The best introduction.

EHRLICH, CYRIL, *The Music Profession in Britain since the Eighteenth Century: A Social History* (Oxford, 1985). Deserves to become a classic of social history.

EINSTEIN, A., *Music in the Romantic Era* (London, 1951). Still the best survey.

FORSYTH, MICHAEL, *Buildings for Music: The Architect, the Musician, and the Listener from the Seventeenth Century to the Present Day* (Cambridge, Mass., 1985).

HABERMAS, JÜRGEN, *The Structural Transformation of the Public Sphere: An Inquiry into a Category of Bourgeois Society* (Cambridge, 1989). Difficult but repays perseverance.

HAMILTON, GEORGE HEARD, *The Art and Architecture of Russia* (Harmondsworth, 1975).

HANSON, ALICE, *Musical Life in Biedermeier Vienna* (Cambridge, 1985). An illuminating blend of musical and social history.

HAUSER, ARNOLD, *The Social History of Art*, ii (London, 1962). Still useful despite its primitive Marxist conceptual framework.

HEMMINGS, F. W. J., *Culture and Society in France, 1789–1848* (Leicester, 1987).

—— *The Theatre Industry in Nineteenth Century France* (Cambridge, 1993).

HITCHCOCK, HENRY-RUSSELL, *Architecture: Nineteenth and Twentieth Centuries* (Harmondsworth, 1977). Comprehensive.

HOLLIER, DENIS (ed.), *A New History of French Literature* (Cambridge, Mass., 1989). Oddly organized but effective.

HONOUR, HUGH, *Neo-Classicism* (Harmondsworth, 1968). Best on the visual arts.

—— *Romanticism* (Harmondsworth, 1979). Again best on the visual arts.

KENNEDY, EMMET, *A Cultural History of the French Revolution* (New Haven and London, 1989). Rather bland.

KIMBELL, DAVID, *Italian Opera* (Cambridge, 1991). Illuminating about all aspects of Italian culture.

LOESSER, ARTHUR, *Men, Women and Pianos: A Social History* (London, 1955). A minor masterpiece.

MENHENNET, A., *The Romantic Movement* (London, 1981). Deals only with German literature.

MOSER, CHARLES A. (ed.), *The Cambridge History of Russian Literature* (Cambridge, 1989). The best introduction.

NIPPERDEY, THOMAS, 'In Search of Identity: Romantic Nationalism', in J. C. Eade (ed.), *Romantic Nationalism in Europe* (Canberra, 1983). Applies modernization theory to the romantic movement with interesting results.

—— *The Rise of the Arts in Modern Society* (London, 1990). A short but stimulating lecture.

NOCHLIN, LINDA, *Realism* (London, 1971).

NORMAN, GERALDINE, *Biedermeier Painting* (London, 1987). Rescues a neglected and underrated era.

OZOUF, MONA, *Festivals and the French Revolution* (Cambridge, Mass., 1988). The argument is conveniently summarized by Lynn Hunt in her foreword.

PESTELLI, GIORGIO, *The Age of Mozart and Beethoven* (Cambridge, 1984).

RINGER, ALEXANDER (ed.), *Man and Music: The Early Romantic Period* (London, 1990). An excellent collection of articles.

ROGERS, PAT (ed.), *The Oxford Illustrated History of English Literature* (Oxford, 1987). A first-rate team of contributors.

ROSENBLUM, ROBERT, and JANSON, H. W., *Art of the Nineteenth Century: Painting and Sculpture* (London, 1984). Penetrating as well as comprehensive.

ROSSELLI, JOHN, *Music and Musicians in Nineteenth Century Italy* (London, 1991). Informative and highly entertaining.

SADIE, STANLEY (ed.), *The New Grove Dictionary of Music and Musicians*, 20 vols. (1980). Simply indispensable.

SAMSON, JIM (ed.), *Man and Music: The Late Romantic Era from the mid-Nineteenth Century to World War I* (London, 1991).

SCHORSKE, CARL E., *Fin de siècle Vienna: Politics and Culture* (Cambridge, 1961).

VAUGHAN, WILLIAM, *German Romantic Painting* (New Haven, 1980).

WEBER, EUGEN, *France, fin de siècle* (Cambridge, Mass., 1986). A brilliant *tour de force*.

6. The Great Civil War: European Politics, 1914–1945

ABRAHAM, DAVID, *The Collapse of the Weimar Republic: Political Economy and Crisis* (2nd edn., New York, 1986). An immensely stimulating marxisant interpretation which sparked off an acerbic controversy, particularly with Turner (see below)

ACTON, EDWARD, *Re-thinking the Russian Revolution* (London, 1990). A lively and thoughtful survey of recent controversies.

BESSEL, RICHARD, *Germany after the First World War* (Oxford, 1993). A path-breaking examination of the political traumas suffered in the wake of defeat.

BOYCE, ROBERT, and ROBERTSON, ESMONDE M. (eds.), *Paths to War: New Essays on the Origins of the Second World War* (London, 1989). A collection of stimulating essays, with a commendably sane introduction.

BULLOCK, ALAN, *Hitler: A Study in Tyranny* (2nd edn., Harmondsworth, 1962). Remains the classic biography.

CARR, E. H., *The Twilight of Comintern, 1930–1935* (London, 1982). Illuminates the internal divisions and weaknesses of international communism.

CARR, RAYMOND, *The Spanish Tragedy* (London, 1977). A strikingly elegant and perceptive essay on every aspect of the Spanish Civil War.

CARR, WILLIAM, *Arms, Autarky and Aggression: A Study in German Foreign Policy, 1933–1939* (London, 1972). A concise and intelligent interpretation of the escalation of German ambitions.

DEUTSCHER, ISAAC, *Stalin: A Political Biography* (2nd edn., Oxford, 1967). An unsurpassed masterpiece of critical interpretation.

—— *The Unfinished Revolution: Russia, 1917–1967* (Oxford, 1967). A startlingly compelling interpretation of why Stalin was inevitable.

GEARY, DICK, *European Labour Protest, 1848–1939* (London, 1981). A trenchantly argued and richly learned comparative account.

GRAHAM, HELEN, and PRESTON, PAUL (eds.), *The Popular Front in Europe* (London, 1986). An accessible survey which goes far beyond the usual Franco-Spanish perspective on the Popular Front.

GRAND, ALEXANDER DE, *Italian Fascism: Its Origins and Development* (Lincoln, Neb., 1982). A masterpiece of lucid synthesis.

JACKSON, JULIAN, *The Politics of Depression in France, 1932–1936* (Cambridge, 1985). A clear and sensible analysis of the economic difficulties underlying French politics in the 1930s.

—— *The Popular Front in France: Defending Democracy, 1934–1938* (Cambridge, 1988). A comprehensive survey which coolly debunks many myths about the period.

JAMES, HAROLD, *The German Slump: Politics and Economics, 1924–1936* (Oxford, 1986). A powerfully argued, if somewhat technical, analysis of the conflicting economic problems afflicting Germany in this period.

KERSHAW, IAN, *Hitler* (London, 1991). A compelling and original interpretation of the nature of Hitler's charismatic rule.

—— *The Nazi Dictatorship: Problems and Perspectives of Interpretation* (3rd edn., London, 1993). Disentangles the most complex issues with authority and clarity.

KINDLEBERGER, CHARLES P., *The World in Depression, 1929–1939* (London, 1973). A standard, but quite technical, account of the underlying instability of the inter-war monetary system.

LUEBBERT, GREGORY M., *Liberalism, Fascism or Social Democracy: Social Classes and the Political Origins of Regimes in Interwar Europe* (New York, 1991). A complex but rewarding comparative analysis.

LYTTLETON, ADRIAN, *The Seizure of Power: Fascism in Italy, 1919–1929* (London, 1973). A highly detailed and incisively intelligent account.

MCMILLAN, JAMES F., *Twentieth Century France: Politics and Society 1898–1991* (London, 1992). A wide-ranging and well-written survey.

MACK SMITH, DENIS, *Italy: A Modern History* (2nd edn., Ann Arbor, 1969). A powerfully argued and illuminating interpretation from a liberal perspective.

—— *Mussolini's Roman Empire* (London, 1976). A tightly argued exposé of the inconsistencies and irresponsibility of Mussolini's foreign policy.

—— *Mussolini: A Biography* (London, 1982). An important and readable work marred only by a tendency to play up Mussolini's buffoonery.

MAIER, CHARLES S., *Recasting Bourgeois Europe: Stabilization in France, Germany, and Italy in the Decade after World War I* (Princeton, 1975). An impressively original comparative study of responses to the dislocation caused by the First World War.

MAYER, ARNO J., *Dynamics of Counterrevolution in Europe, 1870–1956: An Analytical Framework* (New York, 1971). A brilliantly argumentative reinterpretation of authoritarianism and fascism.

—— *Politics and Diplomacy of Peacemaking: Containment and Counterrevolution at Versailles, 1918–1919* (London, 1967). These two volumes argue the case for the incursion of class divisions into international politics.

MEDVEDEV, ROY, *Let History Judge: The Origins and Consequences of Stalinism* (New York, 1971). A disturbing denunciation of Stalinism from a Russian Marxist.

OVERY, RICHARD, with Andrew Wheatcroft, *The Road to War* (London, 1989). A wide-ranging and stimulating survey.

PEUKERT, DETLEV J. K., *Inside Nazi Germany: Conformity, Opposition and Racism in Everyday Life* (Harmondsworth, 1989). A provocatively original interpretation.

—— *The Weimar Republic: The Crisis of Classical Modernity* (Harmondsworth, 1993). A brilliant, if occasionally abstract, essay by one of German's most original historians.

PRESTON, PAUL, *The Coming of The Spanish Civil War* (2nd edn., London, 1994). A study of the interrelationship between social conflict and national politics in the breakdown of democracy.

—— *Franco: A Biography* (London, 1993). A study of the banality of evil which none the less shows that Franco was not just a sphinx without a riddle.

—— *The Spanish Civil War* (London, 1986). A provocative and lavishly illustrated interpretative essay.

SETON-WATSON, CHRISTOPHER, *Italy from Liberalism to Fascism* (London, 1967). A massively comprehensive and urbanely written work.

STEVENSON, DAVID, *The First World War in International Politics* (Oxford, 1989). A thorough and judicious weighing of war aims and peace aims and of the mistakes of politicians as well as soldiers.

TURNER, HENRY ASHBY, Jr., *German Big Business and the Rise of Hitler* (New York, 1985). A massively researched, densely detailed, yet fascinatingly controversial account of the hostility of industry to the Weimar Republic.

WATT, DONALD CAMERON, *How War Came: The Immediate Origins of the Second World War, 1938–1939* (London, 1989). A vividly written and authoritative panoramic view.

7. The Fall and Rise of the European Economy in the Twentieth Century

JAMES, HAROLD, *International Monetary Cooperation Since Bretton Woods* (Washington, DC, 1995).

KINDLEBERGER, CHARLES P., *The World in Depression, 1929–1939* (Berkeley and Los Angeles, 1986).

LEWIS, W. ARTHUR, *Economic Survey, 1919–1939* (London, 1953).

The Limits to Growth: A Report for the Club of Rome's Project on the Predicament of Mankind (Washington, DC, 1972).

MADDISON, ANGUS, *Phases of Capitalist Development* (Oxford, 1982).

MILWARD, ALAN S., *War, Economy and Society, 1939–1945* (London, 1977).

—— *The Reconstruction of Western Europe, 1945–1951* (Berkeley and Los Angeles, 1984).

—— (with George Brennan and Federico Romero), *The European Rescue of the Nation-State* (London, 1992).

SKIDELSKY, ROBERT, *John Maynard Keynes: The Economist as Saviour* (London, 1992).

VAN DER WEE, HERMAN, *Prosperity and Upheaval: The World Economy, 1945–1980* (Berkeley and Los Angeles, 1986).

VAN DORMAEL, ARMAND, *Bretton Woods: Birth of a Monetary System* (New York, 1978).

8. Warfare in Europe since 1918

BERGHAHN, V. (ed.), *Germany in the Age of Total War* (Oxford, 1981).

BIALER, U., *The Shadow of the Bomber: The Fear of Air Attack and British Politics, 1932–1939* (London, 1980). First-rate introduction to the issues of a moral and political nature raised by air power.

CEADEL, M., *Pacifism in Britain, 1914–1945* (Oxford, 1981). A valuable case-study of the strong anti-war feeling in Europe after the First World War.

DEIST, W., *The Wehrmacht and German Rearmament* (London, 1981). One of the best detailed surveys of 1930s' rearmament.

ERICKSON, J., *The Road to Stalingrad* (London, 1975).

—— *The Road to Berlin* (London, 1983). A classic study of the eastern front in the Second World War.

FARINGDEN, H., *Confrontation: The Strategic Geography of NATO and the Warsaw Pact* (London, 1986). An indispensable study of the defence posture of East and West during the later stages of the Cold War.

FREEDMAN, L., *Britain and Nuclear Weapons* (London, 1980). One of the best surveys of a European nuclear force.

GLANTZ, D. M., *The Military Strategy of the Soviet Union: A History* (London, 1992). A thorough survey of Soviet military thinking and force development from the Revolution to the 1980s.

HARDESTY, V., *Red Phoenix: The Rise of Soviet Air Power* (London, 1982). A thorough and original survey of Soviet air power.

HOWARD, M., BIRKE, A., and AHMANN, R. (eds.), *The Quest for Stability: Problems of West European Security, 1918–1957* (Oxford, 1993).

KIMBALL, W., REYNOLDS, D., and CHUBARIAN, A. (eds.), *Allies at War: The Soviet, American and British Experience, 1939–1945* (New York, 1994).

MARDO, R. DI, *Mechanized Juggernaut or Military Anachronism: Horses and the German Army in World War II* (London, 1991). A remarkable study which convincingly demolishes the myths of German technical power in the Second World War.

MARTIN, L., *Arms and Strategy: An International Survey of Modern Defence* (London, 1973). The standard work on the Cold War era.

MENDL, W., *Deterrence and Persuasion: French Nuclear Armament in the Context of National Policy* (London, 1970).

MILLETT, A. R., and MURRAY, W. (eds.), *Military Effectiveness, 1914–1945*, 3 vols. (London, 1988).

NORTHEDGE, F. S., *The League of Nations: Its Life and Times* (Leicester, 1986). The best and most up-to-date assessment of the League and its problems.

ORGILL, D., *The Tank: Studies in the Development and Use of a Weapon* (London, 1970).

OVERY, R. J., *The Air War, 1939–1945* (London, 1980).

PARKER, R. A. C., *Struggle for Survival: The History of the Second World War* (Oxford, 1989). The best general survey of the conflict.

ROSEN, B. R., *The Sources of Military Doctrine: France, Britain and Germany between the Wars* (Ithaca, NY, 1984).

ROSKILL, S., *The Navy at War, 1939–1945* (London, 1960). The best single-volume study of Europe's major sea power in the Second World War.

THAYER, G., *The War Business: The International Trade in Armaments* (New York, 1969). The classic study of the modern arms trade.

WRIGHT, G., *The Ordeal of Total War* (New York, 1968). An excellent one-volume survey that has stood the test of time well.

YOUNG, R. J., *In Command of France: French Foreign Policy and Military Planning, 1933–1940* (Cambridge, Mass., 1978).

9. European Society in the Twentieth Century

ALDCROFT, DEREK, *The European Economy, 1914–1980* (London, 1980). Basic text on the economic background.

AMBROSIUS, GEROLD, *A Social and Economic History of Twentieth-Century Europe* (Cambridge, Mass., 1989). Clear and comprehensive.

BOCK, GISELA, and THANE, PAT (eds.), *Maternity and Gender Politics: Women and the Rise of the European Welfare States* (London, 1991). An important collection of essays on a vital theme.

CASTLES, STEPHEN, and KOSACK, GODULA, *Immigrant Workers and Class Structure in Western Europe* (Oxford, 1985).

CHANT, COLIN (ed.), *Science, Technology and Everyday Life, 1870–1950* (London, 1989).

CIPOLLA, CARLO (ed.), *The Fontana Economic History of Europe: The Twentieth Century* (London, 1976).

CRAMPTON, RICHARD J., *Eastern Europe in the Twentieth Century* (London, 1994).

CROSS, GARY, *Time and Money: The Making of Consumer Culture* (London, 1993). Focuses on the United States as well as France and Britain during the inter-war years.

GILBERT, FELIX, and LARGE, DAVID CLAY, *The End of the European Era: 1890 to the Present* (4th edn., London, 1991). First published in 1970, focusing mainly on political developments.

HARVIE, CHRISTOPHER, *The Rise of Regional Europe* (London, 1994). By taking regions, rather than nation-states, as the focus, challenges how we view European society and politics.

HAYES, PAUL (ed.), *Themes in Modern European History, 1890–1945* (London, 1994).

HOBSBAWM, ERIC, *The Age of Extremes: The Short Twentieth Century, 1914–1991* (London, 1994). Brilliant survey by the master, who has seen it all and has retained his faith in Marxism.

KAELBLE, HARTMUT, *A Social History of Western Europe, 1880–1980* (Dublin, 1990).

LANDES, DAVID S., *The Unbound Prometheus: Technological Change and Industrial Development in Western Europe from 1750 to the Present* (Cambridge, 1969). A classic text.

LEWIS, JANE (ed.), *Women and Social Policies in Europe* (Aldershot, 1993). An important collection of essays on women's position in family and employment; the focus is contemporary, but contains much historical background.

NOIN, DANIEL, and WOODS, ROBERT (eds.), *The Changing Population of Europe* (Oxford, 1993).

POLLARD, SIDNEY, *Peaceful Conquest: The Industrialisation of Europe, 1760–1970* (Oxford, 1981).

SHELLY, MONICA and WINCH, MARGARET (eds.), *Aspects of European Cultural Diversity* (Milton Keynes, 1993). See especially the stimulating essay by Wolfgang Kaschuba on 'Everyday Culture'.

STEARNS, PETER N., *European Society in Upheaval: Social History since 1750* (London, 1975).

THOMPSON, PAUL, *Our Common History: The Transformation of Europe* (London, 1982). Fascinating insights, based on oral testimony, on a variety of topics.

TIPTON, FRANK B., and ALDRICH, ROBERT, *An Economic and Social History of Europe, 1890–1939* (Basingstoke, 1987).

—— and—— *An Economic and Social History of Europe from 1939 to the Present* (Basingstoke, 1987).

10. From Modernism to Post-modernism

ARAC, JONATHAN (ed.), *Postmodernism and Politics* (Minneapolis, 1986). Important essays on the political implications of post-modernism.

BERGER, JOHN, *The Moment of Cubism and Other Essays* (New York, 1969). Insightful Marxist reading of visual modernism.

BERMAN, MARSHALL, *All That is Solid Melts Into Air: The Experience of Modernity* (New York, 1982). A lively consideration of the links between modernization and aesthetic modernism.

BEST, STEVEN, and KELLNER, DOUGLAS, *Postmodern Theory: Critical Interrogations* (New York, 1991). Useful general account of current debates.

BRADBURY, MALCOLM, and McFARLANE, JAMES (eds.), *Modernism: 1890–1930* (New York, 1978). Helpful essays on the cities, movements, and personalities of modernism.

BÜRGER, PETER, *Theory of the Avant-Garde*, trans. Michael Shaw (Minneapolis, 1984). An indispensable theoretical account of the differences between modernism and the avant-garde.

BURGIN, VICTOR, *The End of Art Theory: Criticism and Postmodernity* (Atlantic Highlands, NJ, 1986). Thoughtful reflections of a post-modernist artist and critic.

CALINESCU, MATEI, *Five Faces of Modernity: Modernism, Avant-Garde, Decadence, Kitsch, Postmodernism* (Durham, NC, 1987). Careful historical analyses of the major concepts in its subtitle.

CHIPP, HERSCHEL B. (ed.), *Theories of Modern Art* (Berkeley and Los Angeles, 1970). A wide-ranging collection of documents from the heyday of modernism.

CLARK, T. J., *The Painting of Modern Life: Paris in the Art of Manet and his Followers* (Princeton, 1984). A controversial reading of impressionism and its relations to the modern world.

FOSTER, HAL (ed.), *The Anti-Aesthetic: Essays on Postmodern Culture* (Seattle, 1983). Fundamental essays in the debate over post-modernism.

FRAMPTON, KENNETH, *Modern Architecture: A Critical History* (London, 1985). A magisterial history of modernist architecture.

GOLDWATER, ROBERT, *Primitivism in Modern Art* (Cambridge, Mass., 1986). An important account of a central theme in early modernism.

GREENBERG, CLEMENT, *Art and Culture: Critical Essays* (Boston, 1961). Classic essays by the leading theoretician of visual modernism.

GUILBAUT, SERGE, *How New York Stole the Idea of Modern Art: Abstract Expressionism, Freedom, and the Cold War*, trans. Arthur Goldhammer (Chicago, 1983). Iconoclastic critique of the relationship between art and politics.

HABERMAS, JÜRGEN, *The Philosophical Discourse of Modernity*, trans. Frederick Lawrence (Cambridge, Mass., 1987). Powerful defence of one version of the modern project against its post-modern critics.

HARVEY, DAVID, *The Condition of Postmodernity: An Enquiry into the Origins of Cultural Change* (Oxford, 1989). Shrewd Marxist analysis of the sources of post-modernity.

HASSAN, IHAB, *The Postmodern Turn: Essays in Postmodern Theory and Culture* (Columbus, Oh., 1987). Imaginative attempt to illustrate and defend post-modernism.

HOESTEREY, INGEBORG (ed.), *Zeitgeist in Babel: The Postmodernist Controversy* (Bloomington, Ind., 1991). Many of the most important contributions to the international debate over post-modernism.

HOWE, IRVING (ed.), *The Idea of the Modern in Art and Literature* (New York, 1967). An older collection of classic commentaries.

HUGHES, ROBERT, *The Shock of the New* (New York, 1981). A lively and influential reading of modernist developments.

HUYSSEN, ANDREAS, *After the Great Divide: Modernism, Mass Culture, Postmodernism* (Bloomington, Ind., 1986). Excellent essays on the implications for modernism and post-modernism of mass culture.

JAMESON, FREDRIC, *Postmodernism, Or, The Cultural Logic of Late Capitalism* (Durham, NC, 1991). An ambitious Marxist reading of the links between post-modernism and the totality of relations in contemporary capitalism.

JENCKS, CHARLES, *The Language of Post-Modern Architecture* (New York, 1984). A spirited defence of post-modern trends in architecture.

KAPLAN, E. ANN (ed.), *Postmodernism and its Discontents: Theories, Practices* (London, 1988). Essays on a wide range of themes in post-modernist theory and practice.

KARL, FREDERICK R., *Modern and Modernism: The Sovereignty of the Artist, 1885–1925* (New York, 1985). Traditional account of modernism, resisting the novelty of the post-modern.

KENNER, HUGH, *The Pound Era* (Berkeley, and Los Angeles, 1971). A classic analysis of Anglo-American high modernist literature.

KOSTELANETZ, RICHARD (ed.), *The Avant-Garde Tradition in Literature* (Buffalo, 1982). A useful collection of seminal texts, especially concerning poetry.

KRAUSS, ROSALIND E., *Passages in Modern Sculpture* (New York, 1977). A subtle account of recent trends in sculpture and its successors.

—— *The Originality of the Avant-Garde and Other Modernist Myths* (Cambridge, Mass., 1985). An important critique of the high modernist consensus.

—— *The Optical Unconscious* (Cambridge, Mass., 1993). Provocative essays against Greenberg and other defenders of modernist notions of pure opticality.

KROKER, ARTHUR, and COOK, DAVID, *The Postmodern Scene* (New York, 1986). Devotees of the scene celebrate its implications.

LEVIN, HARRY, *Memories of the Moderns* (New York, 1980). Personal and theoretical accounts of classic modernists.

LUNN, EUGENE, *Marxism and Modernism: An Historical Study of Lukacs, Brecht, Benjamin and Adorno* (Berkeley and Los Angeles, 1982). A helpful survey of the ways in which avant-garde art and radical politics intersected in the 20th century.

LYOTARD, JEAN-FRANÇOIS, *The Postmodern Condition*, trans. Geoff Bennington and Brian Massumi (Minneapolis, 1984). A crucial defence of post-modernity as the end of grand narratives.

McGOWAN, JOHN, *Postmodernism and Its Critics* (Ithaca, NY, 1991). A useful overview of recent debates.

MITCHELL, DONALD, *The Language of Modern Music* (New York, 1970). A clear presentation of the issues in 20th-century music.

ORTEGA Y GASSET, JOSÉ, *The Dehumanization of Art*, trans. Helene Weyl (Princeton, 1968). A classic critique of modernism's alleged anti-humanism.

OWENS, CRAIG, *Beyond Recognition: Representation, Power, and Culture*, ed. Scott Bryson, Barbara Kruger, Lynne Tilman, and Jane Weinstock (Berkeley and Los

Angeles, 1992). A politically charged defence of recent cultural trends, especially sensitive to issues of gender.

POGGIOLI, RENATO, *The Theory of the Avant-garde*, trans. Gerald Fitzgerald (Cambridge, Mass., 1968). An influential account of the underlying assumptions of modernism; a foil for Peter Bürger's later account.

QUINONES, RICARDO, *Mapping Literary Modernism: Time and Development* (Princeton, 1985). A useful overview.

ROGOFF, IRIT (ed.), *The Divided Heritage: Themes and Problems in German Modernism* (Cambridge, 1991). Disparate essays on visual arts in 20th-century Germany.

SCHWARTZ, SANFORD, *The Matrix of Modernism: Pound, Eliot, and Early Twentieth-Century Thought* (Princeton, 1985). A thoughtful exploration of the philosophical issues in modernist poetry.

SHATTUCK, ROGER, *The Banquet Years: The Origins of the Avant-Garde in France, 1885 to World War I* (New York, 1968). A wonderfully written evocation of *belle époque* Paris seen through four of its most innovative artists.

SPENDER, STEPHEN, *The Struggle of the Modern* (London, 1963). A still useful statement about modernist poetics.

VATTIMO, GIANNI, *The End of Modernity* (Oxford, 1985). A defence of 'weak thought' in the post-modern era.

WALLIS, BRIAN (ed.), *Art after Modernism: Rethinking Representation* (New York, 1984). Important essays on shifts in the visual arts.

WILSON, EDMUND, *Axel's Castle: A Study in the Imaginative Literature of 1870–1930* (London, 1961). A classic analysis of the importance of symbolism for early modernist authors.

WOLLEN, PETER, *Raiding the Icebox: Reflections on Twentieth-Century Culture* (London, 1993). Lively investigations of a variety of themes from Russian ballet to situationism.

11. Europe Divided and Reunited, 1945–1995

General

WEGS, J. ROBERT, *Europe since 1945: A Concise History* (3rd edn., London, 1991). A wide coverage, including economics, society, and culture.

YOUNG, JOHN W., *Cold War Europe, 1945–1989: A Political History* (London, 1991).

The Cold War

ELLWOOD, DAVID W., *Rebuilding Europe: Western Europe, America and Postwar Recovery* (London, 1992). A useful introduction to the Atlantic economic nexus, 1945–61.

GROSSER, ALFRED, *The Western Alliance: European–American Relations since 1945* (London, 1980). Particularly strong on France and Germany and also on cultural relations.

KAPLAN, LAWRENCE S., *NATO and the United States: The Enduring Alliance* (2nd edn., New York, 1994). The American angle.

LOTH, WILFRIED, *The Division of the World, 1941–1955* (London, 1988). A good overview of Cold War origins, from a German viewpoint.

NOGEE, JOSEPH L., and DONALDSON, ROBERT L., *Soviet Foreign Policy since World War II* (3rd edn., London, 1991). An informed survey.

REYNOLDS, DAVID (ed.), *The Origins of the Cold War in Europe: International Perspectives* (London, 1994). Essays summing up recent scholarship on the United States, Russia, Britain, France, Germany, Italy, Benelux, and Scandinavia.

Western Europe

BARK, DENNIS L., and GRESS, DAVID R., *A History of West Germany*, 2 vols. (2nd edn., Oxford, 1993). Comprehensive and up to date. Written from a pro-Adenauer perspective.

GEORGE, STEPHEN, *An Awkward Partner: Britain in the European Community* (Oxford, 1990). The problems of adaptation, from Heath to Thatcher.

GINSBORG, PAUL, *A History of Contemporary Italy: Society and Politics, 1943–1988* (London, 1990). Lively and informative on both the themes of the subtitle.

HANLEY, D. L., KERR, A. P., and WAITES, N. H., *Contemporary France: Politics and Society since 1945* (2nd edn., London, 1984). The main focus is political, but there is also discussion of foreign policy and education.

PADGETT, STEPHEN, and PATERSON, WILLIAM E., *A History of Social Democracy in Postwar Europe* (London, 1991). The rise and decline of one of western Europe's most influential post-war ideologies.

URWIN, DEREK W., *The Community of Europe: A History of European Integration since 1945* (London, 1991). A lucid survey of the European Community's evolution.

The Soviet Bloc

JELAVICH, BARBARA, *History of the Balkans*, ii: *Twentieth Century* (Cambridge, 1983). Includes the Second World War, the Soviet bloc, Yugoslavia, and Greece.

LEWIS, PAUL, *Central Europe since 1945* (London, 1994). The focus is on East Germany, Czechoslovakia, Hungary, and Poland.

SCHÖPFLIN, GEORGE, *Politics in Eastern Europe, 1945–1992* (London, 1993). A perceptive narrative.

SWAIN, GEOFFREY, and SWAIN, NIGEL, *Eastern Europe since 1945* (London, 1993). Strong on national variations and on economics.

The End of the Cold War and After

ASH, TIMOTHY GARTON, *In Europe's Name: Germany and the Divided Continent* (London, 1993). A detailed and fascinating analysis of Ostpolitik from the 1970s to reunification.

DAWISHA, KAREN, *Eastern Europe, Gorbachev, and Reform: The Great Challenge* (2nd edn., Cambridge, 1990). Interesting both for its subject-matter and for its interpretation, being written and revised as the 'challenge' unfolded.

GLENNY, MISHA, *The Rebirth of History: Eastern Europe in the Age of Democracy* (London, 1990). A nation-by-nation study of the 1989 revolutions by an experienced journalist.

—— *The Fall of Yugoslavia: The Third Balkan War* (2nd edn., London, 1993). A vivid account, taking the story to mid-1993.

HOGAN, MICHAEL (ed.), *The End of the Cold War: Its Meaning and Implications* (Cambridge, 1992). Short reflective pieces by a variety of international scholars.

JARAUSCH, KONRAD A., *The Rush to German Unity* (Oxford, 1994). A richly detailed account of events, 1989 to 1991.

Chronology

1789	5 May	Estates-General convene at Versailles
	17 June	Estates-General declares itself to be the 'National Assembly'
	14 July	storming of the Bastille
	5–6 October	the 'October Days'—Louis XVI and the Estates-General are removed to Paris
1790	12 July	Civil Constitution of the Clergy
1791	13 April	Pope Pius VI condemns the Civil Constitution of the Clergy
	20 June	the 'flight to Varennes'—Louis XVI tries unsuccessfully to escape from France
	1 October	National Constituent Assembly makes way for the National Legislative Assembly
1792	20 April	National Assembly declares war on Austria
	25 April	guillotine used for first time
	13 June	Prussia declares war on France
	10 August	monarchy overthrown
	2–6 September	September massacres in Paris
	20 September	Prussian invasion force defeated at the battle of Valmy
	6 November	Austrians defeated at Jemappes and Belgium conquered
1793	21 January	execution of Louis XVI
	1 February	war declared on Britain and the Dutch Republic
	7 March	war declared on Spain
	11 March	counter-revolutionary rising in the Vendée begins
	18 March	Austrians defeat the French at Neerwinden and reconquer Belgium
	6 April	Committee of Public Safety created
	2 June	Girondin regime falls
	autumn	French armies go back on the offensive in Belgium
	16 October	Marie Antoinette executed
1794	26 June	French defeat Austrians at Fleurus and expel them from Belgium
	27–8 July	fall of Robespierre (*coup d'état* of 8–9 Thermidor)
1795	January	French conquer the Dutch Republic and turn it into a satellite–'the Batavian Republic'
	5 April	treaty of Basle, by which Prussia leaves the war
	22 July	treaty of Basle, by which Spain leaves the war
	1 October	Belgium annexed to France
1796	April	General Bonaparte invades Italy, defeats the Piedmontese and the Austrians
1797	18 April	preliminary peace of Léoben between France and Austria
	29 June	Austrian territory in northern Italy turned into a satellite state (the 'Cisalpine Republic')

	18 October	peace of Campo Formio between Austria and France
1798	May	revolt in Ireland
	19 May	General Bonaparte leads an expedition to conquer Egypt
	1 August	British fleet under Admiral Nelson destroys Bonaparte's fleet at the battle of Aboukir Bay
1799	March	war between France and Austria resumes; Russia enters the war on the side of Austria; French are expelled from Italy
	8 October	Bonaparte returns from Egypt
	9–10 November	Bonaparte overthrows the Directory
1800	14 June	Bonaparte defeats the Austrians at battle of Marengo
	1 August	Act of Union between Britain and Ireland becomes law
	3 December	Moreau defeats the Austrians at Hohenlinden
1801	9 February	peace of Lunéville between France and Austria
	14 March	William Pitt resigns as prime minister over George III's refusal to allow Catholic emancipation
	16 July	Bonaparte signs a Concordat with the Papacy
1802	27 March	peace of Amiens between Britain and France
1803	18 May	war between Britain and France resumes
1804	18 May	General Bonaparte assumes imperial title as Napoleon I
1805	August	the third coalition consisting of Britain, Austria, Russia, and Sweden is formed against France; war resumes on the continent
	20 October	Austrian army capitulates at Ulm
	21 October	battle of Trafalgar
	2 December	battle of Austerlitz; Napoleon inflicts a crushing defeat on an Austro-Russian army
	26 December	peace of Pressburg ends war between Austria and France
1806	23 January	death of William Pitt
	30 March	Napoleon makes his brother Joseph king of Naples
	5 June	Napoleon makes his brother Louis king of the Netherlands
	12 July	Napoleon reorganizes Germany as the 'Confederation of the Rhine'
	6 August	end of the Holy Roman Empire
	8 October	Prussia declares war on France
	14 October	Prussian armies routed at the dual battle of Jena and Auerstedt
	21 November	Napoleon introduces the 'Continental System'
1807	25 March	slave trade abolished in all British possessions
	9 July	treaty of Tilsit ends the continental war
	December	Napoleon orders invasion of Spain
1808	2 May	rising against French in Madrid
	6 June	Napoleon makes his brother Joseph king of Spain
	August	British send an expeditionary force to Spain
1809	April	war resumes between France and Austria
	21 May	Austrians defeat Napoleon at Aspern
	6 July	Napoleon defeats Austrians at Wagram
	14 October	treaty of Schönbrunn ends war between France and Austria
1810	9 July	Napoleon annexes the Netherlands to France

	10 December	Napoleon annexes north-western coast of Germany
1811	March	Luddite riots in Britain
1812	24 June	Napoleon begins invasion of Russia
	12 August	duke of Wellington captures Madrid
	7 September	Napoleon fights the indecisive battle of Borodino and enters Moscow a week later
	18 October	retreat from Moscow begins
	13 December	remnants of Napoleon's army leave Russia
1813	28 February	treaty of Kalisch between Prussia and Russia
	21 June	Wellington defeats French at Vittoria, prompting King Joseph to flee to France
	12 August	Austria declares war on France
	16–19 October	Napoleon is defeated at the battle of Leipzig and loses control of Germany
	31 December	Prussian army under Blücher begins the invasion of France
1814	12 March	Wellington captures Bordeaux
	31 March	Allied armies enter Paris
	6 April	Napoleon abdicates and is exiled to Elba
	30 May	first treaty of Paris gives France the frontiers of 1792
	1 November	Congress of Vienna opens (lasts until 8 June 1815)
1815	1 March	Napoleon returns from Elba
	18 June	Napoleon is defeated at Waterloo by the British and the Prussians
	26 September	Austria, Russia, and Prussia form the 'Holy Alliance'
	20 November	second treaty of Paris reduces France to frontiers of 1789
1817	October	Wartburg festival to celebrate 300th anniversary of the Reformation—and to protest against political conditions in Germany
1819	16 August	'Peterloo Massacre' at Manchester
	November	'Carlsbad decrees' impose strict censorship and other restrictions on personal liberty in Germany
1820	29 January	death of George III
1820–1		revolt in the kingdom of Naples suppressed by Austrian troops
1821		revolt in Greece against Turkish rule
1823		Daniel O'Connell forms Catholic Association of Ireland
1824	24 April	death of Byron at Missolonghi
1825		'Decembrist revolt' in Russia following death of Alexander I
1827		Britain, Russia, and France recognize Greek independence
1829	April	Roman Catholic Relief Act and Irish Catholic Emancipation Act passed in Britain
1830	27 July	revolution in France; Charles X abdicates; Louis Philippe, duke of Orleans is proclaimed king
	25 August	Belgians revolt against Dutch rule
	September	revolt in some German principalities extracts political concessions
	29 November	revolt in Poland against Russian rule
	30 December	Belgian independence is recognized

1832	4 June	Great Reform Bill passes the House of Lords
		Greek independence recognized
		Mazzini founds 'Young Italy'
1834	1 August	slavery is abolished in all British possessions
1836		Chartist movement in Britain begins
1837	20 June	accession of Queen Victoria
1845		Great Famine begins in'Ireland
1846	23 May	repeal of the Corn Laws
1848	22 February	Louis Philippe abdicates; a republic is proclaimed
	13 March	riots in Vienna; Metternich resigns
	18 March	street-fighting in Berlin; army evacuates; parliament convened; ministry containing liberals appointed
	18 March	Austrians evacuate Milan
	22 March	Venetian Republic proclaimed
	31 March	provisional all-German parliament (*Vorparlament*) meets at Frankfurt
	18 May	full Frankfurt parliament opens
	17 June	Czech revolt suppressed
	22 July	Austrian army commanded by General Radetzky defeats the Piedmontese at Custozza
	22–26 June	'June Days' in Paris; General Cavaignac suppresses radical revolt
	26 August	armistice of Malmö signed by Prussia and Denmark
	5 September	Frankfurt parliament votes against accepting the armistice; 16 September votes to accept it
	27 October	the Frankfurt parliament opts for a future Germany which will include all states of the German Confederation (*Grossdeutschland*)—i.e. including Austria with Bohemia and Moravia—with only 90 deputies voting against
	31 October	General Prince Windischgrätz reoccupies Vienna
	9 November	General von Wrangel reoccupies Berlin
	2 December	Ferdinand I of Austria abdicates, is succeeded by Franz Joseph I
	5 December	Prussian parliament is dissolved and a new constitution is imposed from above
	10 December	Louis Napoleon Bonaparte elected president of the French Republic by a large majority
1849	4 March	a 'neo-absolutist' constitution is imposed on the Habsburg empire
	23 March	Austrians defeat Piedmontese at Novara
	27 March	the Frankfurt parliament opts for a *Kleindeutschland*—i.e. excluding any part of the Habsburg empire—by 267 to 263. 28 March they vote 290 to 248 to offer the post of hereditary German emperor to Frederick William IV, who rejects it on 3 April
	June–August	Hungary is reconquered by Austrian and Russian armies
	28 August	Venice surrenders to the Austrians
1851	2 December	Louis Napoleon carries out *coup d'état*
1852		Cavour becomes prime minister of Piedmont
	2 December	Louis Napoleon proclaimed Emperor Napoleon III
1853		Crimean war begins

1856	25 February	peace of Paris ends the Crimean war
1858		Sinn Fein founded in Ireland
	20 July	Cavour and Napoleon III sign agreement of Plombières
1859	29 April	Austrian army invades Piedmont
	3 May	France declares war on Austria
	4 June	Austrians defeated at Magenta
	24 June	Austrians defeated at Solferino
	11 July	peace of Villafranca
1860	5 May	Garibaldi and his 'Thousand' sail for Sicily
	22 August	Garibaldi invades the Italian mainland
	26 October	Victor Emmanuel II of Sardinia-Piedmont proclaimed king of Italy
1861		emancipation of serfs in Russia
1862	22 September	Bismarck becomes prime minister of Prussia
1863		revolt in Poland against Russian rule
1864	January	Austria and Prussia go to war against Denmark over Schleswig-Holstein
	30 October	peace of Vienna; Denmark cedes Schleswig-Holstein to Austria and Prussia
1866	April	war between Austria and Prussia
	3 July	Prussia defeats Austria at the battle of Königgrätz (Sadowa) Venice ceded to Italy by Austria
1868	28 February	Disraeli becomes prime minister for the first time
	9 December	Gladstone becomes prime minister for the first time
1870	19 July	France declares war on Prussia
	19 August	French army besieged at Metz
	2 September	French defeated at Sedan; Napoleon III is taken prisoner
	4 September	republic proclaimed in France
	20 September	Italian forces enter Rome
1871	18 January	William I of Prussia proclaimed German emperor
	28 January	Paris capitulates
	18 March	rising of the Paris Commune
	10 May	peace of Frankfurt; France cedes Alsace and Lorraine to Germany
	28 May	end of the Paris Commune
	July	Kulturkampf begins in Germany
1877–8		war between Russia and Turkey
1878		Congress of Berlin sorts out the Eastern Question for the time being
1881		assassination of Tsar Alexander II
	16 August	Irish Land Act
1882		Germany, Austria-Hungary, and Italy form the Triple Alliance
1887	1 October	General Boulanger attempts a *coup d'état* in France
1890	17 March	Bismarck is forced to resign
1893	13 January	Independent Labour Party founded in Britain
1894	January	France and Russia sign defensive alliance
	15 October	Dreyfus affair begins in France
1897		Germany begins to build a major battle fleet
1898	July	'Fashoda incident'—confrontation between Britain and France in the Sudan

1899	19 September	Dreyfus pardoned
	October	Boer war begins
1900	27 February	British Labour Party founded
1901	22 January	death of Queen Victoria
1904	8 April	*entente cordiale* between Britain and France
		war between Russia and Japan begins
1905	22 January	'Bloody Sunday' in St Petersburg
	February	first Moroccan crisis
	17 October	Nicholas II promises a constitution and an elected parliament
1907	August	Britain and Russia sign a convention
1908	October	Austria-Hungary annexes Bosnia-Herzegovina
1911	July	second Moroccan crisis
1912		Social Democratic Party becomes the largest party in the German parliament
	October	first Balkan war
1913		second and third Balkan wars
1914	28 June	assassination of the Archduke Franz Ferdinand at Sarajevo
	24 July	Russia threatens war if Austria-Hungary attacks Serbia
	25 July	Austria-Hungary mobilizes against Serbia
	30 July	Russia begins general mobilization
	1 August	Germany declares war on Russia
	3 August	Germany declares war on France and invades Belgium
	4 August	Britain declares war on Germany
	5 August	Austria-Hungary declares war on Russia
	25–30 August	German army commanded by Hindenburg routs invading Russian army at Tannenberg
	5–14 September	German invasion of France is halted at the battle of the Marne
	27 September	Russians invade Hungary
1915	February	Russians are defeated decisively by Germans at the battle of the Masurian Lakes
	22 April	Anglo-French forces land at Gallipoli
	May	Russians defeated by Austrians and Germans in Galicia
	23 May	Italy declares war on Germany and Austria-Hungary
1916	February	battle of Verdun begins
	23 April	Easter rising in Dublin
	June	Brusilov offensive begins in the east
	31 May	battle of Jutland
	July	battle of the Somme begins
	September	strikes and mutinies in Russia
1917	February	revolution in Russia; Nicholas II abdicates
	6 April	United States enters war against Germany
	16 April	Lenin arrives in Petrograd
	May	mutinies in French army
	26 June	American forces land in France
	October	Bolshevik *coup d'état* in Russia
	November	Balfour Declaration on Palestine
	5 December	Germany and Russia sign armistice at Brest-Litovsk
1918	8 January	President Wilson's 'Fourteen Points'
	3 March	peace of Brest-Litovsk

	21 March	Germans begin spring offensive on the western front
	July	German offensive halted on the Marne
	16 July	Russian imperial family murdered by Bolsheviks
	10 November	Kaiser Wilhelm II flees to the Netherlands; Emperor Charles of Austria-Hungary abdicates
	11 November	Germany signs armistice at Compiègne
1919	21 January	proclamation of the Irish Free State
	29 June	Treaty of Versailles signed
1920	23 December	Poland invades the Ukraine
1921	March	Lenin introduces the New Economic Policy
	6 December	Anglo-Irish treaty establishes the Irish Free State
1922	March	Stalin becomes general secretary of the communist party of the USSR
	16 April	Treaty of Rapallo between Russia and Germany
1923	11 January	French occupation of the Ruhr
	8–9 November	Hitler's abortive 'beer-hall' putsch in Munich
	14 December	Primo de Rivera establishes a dictatorship in Spain
1924	21 January	death of Lenin
1925	26 April	Hindenburg elected president of Germany
	16 October	Locarno pact
1926	May	general strike in Britain
	19 October	Trotsky expelled from the Politburo
1929	January	Trotsky exiled
	5 June	first Labour government in Britain
	29 October	Wall Street crash
1930	September	Hitler's National Socialist Workers Party becomes second strongest party in the German parliament
	28 December	Primo de Rivera resigns
1931	14 April	Alfonso XIII abdicates and Spain becomes a republic
1932	July	Nazis become strongest party in the German parliament
1933	30 January	Hitler becomes Chancellor of Germany
	27 February	Following Reichstag fire, civil liberties are abolished in Germany
	23 March	the Enabling Law gives Hitler dictatorial powers
1934	30 June	Hitler eliminates several thousand opponents, including the leader of the SA, Ernst Röhm
	December	purges begin in USSR
1935	16 March	Hitler repudiates disarmament clauses of the Versailles treaty
	October	Italy invades Abyssinia
1936	16 February	Popular Front wins a majority in Spanish elections
	7 March	Germans reoccupy the demilitarized Rhineland
	3 May	Popular Front wins a majority in French general election
	17 July	Spanish Civil War begins
	26 October	Axis Rome–Berlin formed
	18 November	Italy and Germany recognize Franco as legitimate ruler of Spain; France decides on policy of non-intervention in Spanish Civil War
	10 December	abdication of Edward VIII
1937	26 April	German Condor Legion destroys the town of Guernica in Spain

1938	11 March	*Anschluss* of Austria to Germany
	30 September	Munich agreement gives the Sudetenland to Germany
	9–10 November	*Kristallnacht*—widespread anti-Jewish rioting in Germany
1939	February	final collapse of Republican resistance in the Spanish Civil War
	15 March	Germans occupy rest of Czechoslovakia
	7 April	Italy invades Albania
	23 August	Molotov–Ribbentrop pact
	1 September	Germany invades Poland
	3 September	Britain and France declare war on Germany
	17 September	Russians invade Poland
	30 November	Russo-Finnish war begins
1940	March	Russo-Finnish war ends
	9 April	Germans invade Norway and Denmark
	10 May	Germans invade the Netherlands
	10 May	Churchill becomes prime minister
	12 May	Germans invade France
	29 May	British begin evacuation at Dunkirk
	June	Russians occupy the Baltic states
	10 June	Italy declares war on France
	14 June	Germans enter Paris
	18 June	de Gaulle's call for continued French resistance
	22 June	French sign armistice with Germany at Compiègne
	July–September	Battle of Britain
	14 September	Hitler orders postponement of invasion of Britain
	December	Italians defeated in North Africa
1941	February	German army sent to assist Italians in North Africa
	April	Germans begin conquest of Yugoslavia and Greece
	20 May	Germans capture Crete
	22 June	Germans invade Russia
	11 August	Roosevelt and Churchill agree on the Atlantic Charter
	8 September	Germans begin siege of Leningrad
	November	German forces advance to within 20 miles of Moscow
	5 December	Russian counter-offensive begins
	7 December	Japanese bomb Pearl Harbor
	11 December	Hitler declares war on United States
1942	15 February	Singapore surrenders to the Japanese
	4 November	British victory at El Alamein
	8 November	Anglo-American landings in North Africa
1943	31 January	German army surrenders at Stalingrad
	May	Axis forces in North Africa surrender
	July	Soviet victory at Kursk
	10 July	Allies invade Sicily
	3 September	Italy surrenders
	November	Roosevelt, Churchill, and Stalin meet at Teheran
1944	22 January	Allies land at Anzio
	27 January	siege of Leningrad ends
	June	Soviet summer offensive begins
	4 June	Rome falls to Allies
	6 June	D-Day: Allied landings begin in Normandy

	1 July	Bretton Woods meeting
	20 July	attempt to assassinate Hitler fails
	1 August	Warsaw rising
	17 August	Russians cross German frontier
	21 August	Dumbarton Oaks conference begins
	25 August	liberation of Paris
	16 December	Battle of the Bulge begins in the Ardennes
1945	4 February	Roosevelt, Churchill, and Stalin meet at Yalta
	13 February	Allied bombing of Dresden
	13 April	Russians reach Vienna
	20 April	Russians reach Berlin
	28 April	Mussolini executed by partisans
	30 April	Hitler commits suicide
	2 May	fall of Berlin
	8 May	end of the war in Europe
	5 June	Allied Control Commission set up to administer Germany
	July	Stalin, Truman, and Churchill meet at Potsdam
	27 July	Churchill replaced by Attlee as prime minister after Labour victory in the general election
	6–9 August	atomic bombs dropped on Hiroshima and Nagasaki
	14 August	Japan surrenders
1946	6 March	Churchill's Iron Curtain speech at Fulton, Missouri
	May	Italy becomes a republic
	October	Fourth Republic established in France
	6 November	National Health Act in Britain
1947	12 March	Truman doctrine speech
	June	partition of India announced
	5 June	Marshall Plan proposed
1948	March	American Congress adopts the Marshall Plan
	April	Organisation for European Economic Co-operation (OEEC) set up
	May	Communist take-over in Czechoslovakia completed; state of Israel created
	June	Yugoslavia expelled from Cominform
	June	Berlin airlift begins
1949	April	North Atlantic Treaty signed
	May	Berlin blockade ends
	May	Communists take power in Hungary
	23 August	NATO created
	September	Federal Republic of Germany established
	October	German Democratic Republic established
1950	May	Schuman Plan unveiled
	6 June	Korean war begins
1951	18 April	Treaty of Paris establishes a 'common market' in coal and steel for the Benelux countries, France, Italy, and Germany—the Six
1952	October	Britain becomes a nuclear power
1953	5 March	death of Stalin
	June	risings in East Germany suppressed
	September	Khrushchev becomes first secretary of the communist party

1954	May	French forces defeated at Dien Bien Phu in Indo-China
1955	May	Germany joins NATO
1956	July–November	Suez crisis
	October	abortive Hungarian revolution begins
1957	25 March	Treaty of Rome; the European Economic Community (EEC) comes into existence
1958	May	Algerian crisis
	1 June	General de Gaulle returns as prime minister
	December	General de Gaulle elected president of the Fifth French Republic (formally created 1 January 1959)
1959	November	European Free Trade Association (EFTA) established
1960	February	France becomes a nuclear power
1961	August	construction of the Berlin wall
	October	Stalin's body removed from the mausoleum in Red Square
1962	October	Cuban missile crisis
1963	14 January	de Gaulle vetoes British membership of the EEC
	22 January	Franco-German treaty
	October	Adenauer retires as Chancellor of West Germany
1964	October	Brezhnev replaces Khrushchev as first secretary
	October	Labour government in Great Britain
1966	January	de Gaulle vetoes EEC majority voting
	February	de Gaulle announces French withdrawal from NATO
1967	June	Arab-Israeli Six Day war
1968	May	violent student unrest in France
	August	Warsaw Pact forces invade Czechoslovakia
1969	April	de Gaulle resigns
	August	British troops sent to Northern Ireland
	October	Willy Brandt becomes German Chancellor
1972	May	Strategic Arms Limitation Treaty (SALT) signed in Moscow
1973	January	Britain, Ireland, and Denmark join EEC
	October	Arab-Israeli Yom Kippur war, followed by oil crisis
1974	May	Helmut Schmidt becomes German Chancellor
1975	August	Helsinki agreement on security and human rights
1975	April	Political pluralism returns to Portugal
	20 November	death of Franco; restoration of the monarchy in Spain
1977	June	Brezhnev becomes president of the USSR
1978	16 October	election of John Paul II, first non-Italian pope for 400 years
1979	3 May	Margaret Thatcher becomes prime minister following Conservative victory
	June	Pope John Paul II visits Poland; first direct elections to the European parliament
	December	Russian army invades Afghanistan
1980	May	death of Tito
	September	Solidarity formed in Gdansk under leadership of Lech Walesa
1981	January	Greece joins EEC
	December	martial law declared in Poland
1982	April	Falklands war
	October	Helmut Kohl becomes German Chancellor

	November	death of Brezhnev; Andropov becomes first secretary
1984	February	death of Andropov; Chernenko becomes first secretary
1985	June	death of Chernenko; Gorbachev becomes first secretary, *Glasnost* and *Perestroika* programmes launched
1986	January	Spain and Portugal join EEC
	26 April	Chernobyl nuclear disaster
1987	December	Intermediate Nuclear Forces Treaty signed in Washington between United States and USSR
1988	May	USSR announces withdrawal from Afghanistan
1989	January	Political pluralism returns to Hungary
	March	Political pluralism returns to Poland; Solidarity is made legal
	June	free elections in Poland give a landslide to Solidarity
	September	Hungary opens border to Austria; thousands of East Germans flee to the West
	October	Erich Honecker replaced as president of East Germany by Egon Krenz
	November	political pluralism returns to East Germany; Berlin wall opened
		Politburo in Czechoslovakia resigns
	December	Cold War declared over by Presidents Bush and Gorbachev at a summit in Malta; Ceaucescu regime in Romania overthrown; political pluralism returns to Bulgaria
1990	29 January	Polish communist party dissolved
	February–March	communist party of USSR votes for return of pluralism; independence of Lithuania proclaimed; general election in East Germany returns a large majority in favour of unification
	29 May	Boris Yeltsin elected chairman of the Russian Supreme Soviet and thus president of the Russian SFSR
	July	economic unification of the two Germanies
	12 July	Yeltsin renounces membership of the communist party
	16 July	agreement between West Germany and USSR on reunification of Germany and withdrawal of Soviet forces
	3 October	reunification of Germany
	22 November	resignation of Margaret Thatcher
	9 December	Lech Walesa elected president of Poland
1991	January	Gulf war begins
	25 February	dissolution of the Warsaw Pact
	March	Latvia and Estonia vote for independence; Gulf war ends
	May	civil war in Yugoslavia begins
	June	Croatia declares independence
	August	failure of attempted *coup d'état* in Moscow; independence of Baltic states recognized; communist party of the USSR dissolved
	24 August	Gorbachev resigns as general secretary
	December	Commonwealth of Independent States set up to replace now defunct USSR
1992	January	Yugoslavia dissolves

	1 February	agreement between Bush and Yeltsin formally ends the Cold War
1993	1 January	Czechoslovakia divides into separate Czech and Slovakian republics
	November	European Community renamed European Union
1995	1 January	Austria, Finland, and Sweden join the European Union

Maps

Europe in 1789

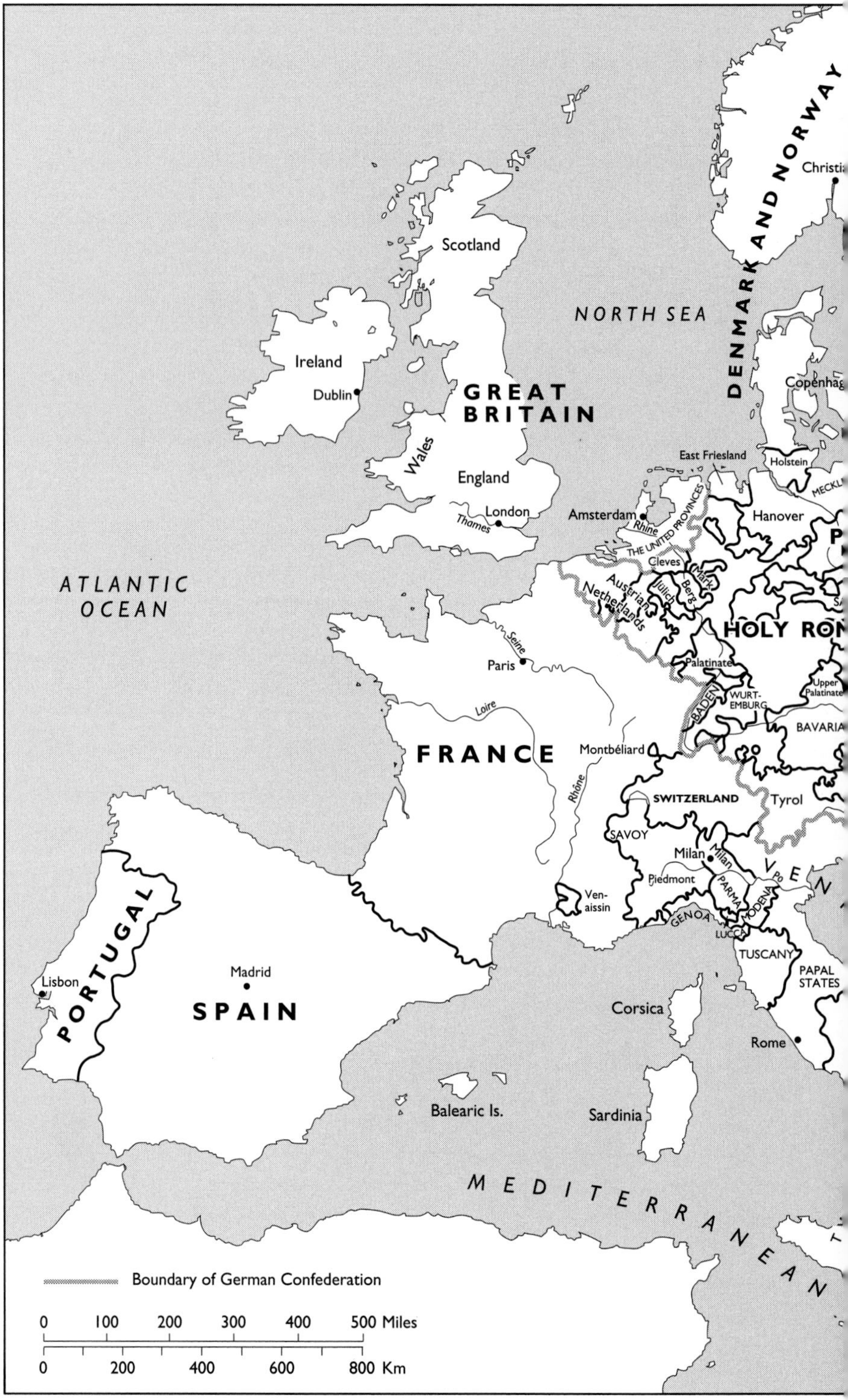

ATLANTIC
OCEAN

NORTH SEA

DENMARK AND NORWAY

Christia

Copenha

Scotland

Ireland

Dublin

GREAT
BRITAIN

Wales

England

London

Thames

Amsterdam

Rhine

THE UNITED PROVINCES

Cleves

East Friesland

Holstein

MECKL

Hanover

P

Austrian
Netherlands

Julich

Berg

HOLY RO

Seine

Paris

Palatinate

Upper
Palatinate

WURT-
EMBURG

BADEN

BAVARIA

Loire

FRANCE

Montbéliard

Rhône

SWITZERLAND

Tyrol

SAVOY

Milan

Milan

VEN

Piedmont

PARMA

Ven-
aissin

GENOA

MODENA

LUCCA

PORTUGAL

Madrid

TUSCANY

PAPAL
STATES

Lisbon

SPAIN

Corsica

Rome

Balearic Is.

Sardinia

MEDITERRANEAN

Boundary of German Confederation

| 0 | 100 | 200 | 300 | 400 | 500 Miles |

| 0 | 200 | 400 | 600 | 800 Km |

DEN.

Finland

● Helsinki   ● St Petersburg

● Stockholm

BALTIC SEA

Gothland

Riga

Dvina

Moscow

RUSSIA

Neman   Vilnius
●

P R U S S I A

omerania Danzig
●

Desna

Vistula

Warsaw
●

P O L A N D

IRE

Oder

Galicia and
Lodomeria

Dnieper

mia
Moravia
ria

THE HABSBURG
MONARCHY

Dniester

Moldavia

Buda● ●Pest

H u n g a r y

Tran-
sylvania

nia   Slavonia

B a n a t

BLACK SEA

Bosnia   Belgrade
●

Bucharest
●

Wallachia

Servia

Danube

O T T O M A N

ntic Sea   RAGUSA

● Sofia

Constantinople
●

E M P I R E

Aegean
Sea

Morea   Athens
●

E A

Candia

Cyprus

335

Europe in 1815

NORWAY

Christi

NORTH SEA

DENMA
Copenha

SCOTLAND

IRELAND

Dublin

UNITED
KINGDOM

WALES

ENGLAND

London

Thames

Amsterdam

HANOVER

UNITED NETHERLANDS

WEST
PHALIA

SAXO

Brussels

LUX

R

P

Rhine

ATLANTIC
OCEAN

Seine

Paris

BAVARIA

BADEN

WURTTEM-
BERG

Danube

Loire

FRANCE

Rhône

SWITZERLAND

SAVOY

Milan

LOMBARDY-VENETI

PORTUGAL

Madrid

SPAIN

MONACO

ANDORRA

PIEDMONT

PARMA

MOD

Po

SARDINIA

LUCCA

TUSCANY

SAN
MAR

PAPAL
STATE

Lisbon

Corsica

Rome

Balearic Is.

Sardinia

MEDITERRANEAN

K. O

Boundary of German Confederation

| 0 | 100 | 200 | 300 | 400 | 500 Miles |

| 0 | 200 | 400 | 600 | 800 Km |

336

DEN

Helsinki •
• St Petersburg

• Stockholm

BALTIC SEA

Gotland

• Riga

Dvina

RUSSIA

• Moscow

RANIA
Danzig •
I   A
EAST PRUSSIA

Neman   Vilnius
•

POLAND
Warsaw •

SIA

Vistula   *Oder*

REP. OF
KRAKOW
Krakow •

Dnieper

RAVIA

Vienna

THE HABSBURG
EMPIRE

Buda • Pest

Dniester

MOLDAVIA

HUNGARY

Belgrade •

WALLACHIA
Bucharest •

BLACK SEA

BOSNIA

SERBIA

Danube

OTTOMAN

BULGARIA

MONTE-
NEGRO   • Sofia

ntic Sea

ALBANIA

THRACE
Constantinople •

MACEDONIA

EMPIRE

*Aegean
Sea*

Athens •

MOREA

E A

Crete

Rhodes

Cyprus

Europe in 1914

NORWAY

Christ[...]

NORTH SEA

DENMAR[...]

Copenha[...]

SCOTLAND

Rosyth

IRELAND

Dublin

UNITED
KINGDOM

SCHLESWIG Kiel
HOLSTEIN
Kiel
canal

WALES

ENGLAND

London

Amsterdam

NETHERLANDS

GERMA[...]

Thames

Portsmouth

Brussels

ATLANTIC
OCEAN

BELGIUM

HESSE-NASSAU

Rhine

LUX.

HESSE

SA[...]K

Seine

ALSACE-
LORRAINE

BADEN

WÜRTTEM-
BERG

BAVARIA

Paris

Danube

Loire

FRANCE

Rhine

SWITZERLAND

LIECHTEN-
STEIN

Milan

PORTUGAL

MONACO

SAN
MARINO

ITA[...]

Lisbon

Madrid

ANDORRA

Corsica

Rome

SPAIN

Rhône

Balearic Is.

Sardinia

MEDITERRANEAN

Sic[...]

| 0 | 100 | 200 | 300 | 400 | 500 Miles |

| 0 | 200 | 400 | 600 | 800 Km |

338

EN

Helsinki

St Petersburg

Stockholm

ESTONIA

LATVIA

Riga

Moscow

Dvina

BALTIC SEA

LITHUANIA

Neman

Vilnius

Danzig

RUSSIA

I A

POSEN

Vistula

Warsaw

PIRE

Oder

POLAND

Dnieper

ORAVIA

Dniester

enna

STRO-HUNGARIAN

MONARCHY

Budapest

MOLDAVIA

HUNGARY

TRANSYLVANIA

Crimea

ROMANIA

OSNIA

Belgrade

ROMANIA

arajevo

WALLACHIA

Bucharest

HERZE-
GOVINIA

SERBIA

Danube

BLACK SEA

TIA

MONTE-
NEGRO

BULGARIA

Sofia

tic Sea

ALBANIA

Constantinople

Tirana

OTTOMAN EMPIRE

GREECE

Aegean
Sea

Athens

E A

Crete

Rhodes

Cyprus

NORWAY

NORTH SEA

Os

DENMA
Copenha

SCOTLAND

N.
IRELAND

IRISH
FREE
STATE• Dublin

UNITED KINGDOM OF
GREAT BRITAIN AND
NORTHERN IRELAND

WALES

ENGLAND

Thames
London

Amsterdam •

NETHERLANDS

Brussels
BELGIUM

G   E   R

LUX.

Rhine

ATLANTIC
OCEAN

Seine

Paris •

FRANCE

Loire

Danube

Rhine

SWITZERLAND

LIECHTEN-
STEIN

A

• Milan

Po

PORTUGAL

Madrid

ANDORRA

SAN O
MARINO

ITA

Lisbon
•

SPAIN

Corsica

Rome •

Balearic Is

Sardinia

M E D I T E R R A N E A N

Sie

0	100	200	300	400	500 Miles
0	200	400	600	800 Km	

Europe after 1945

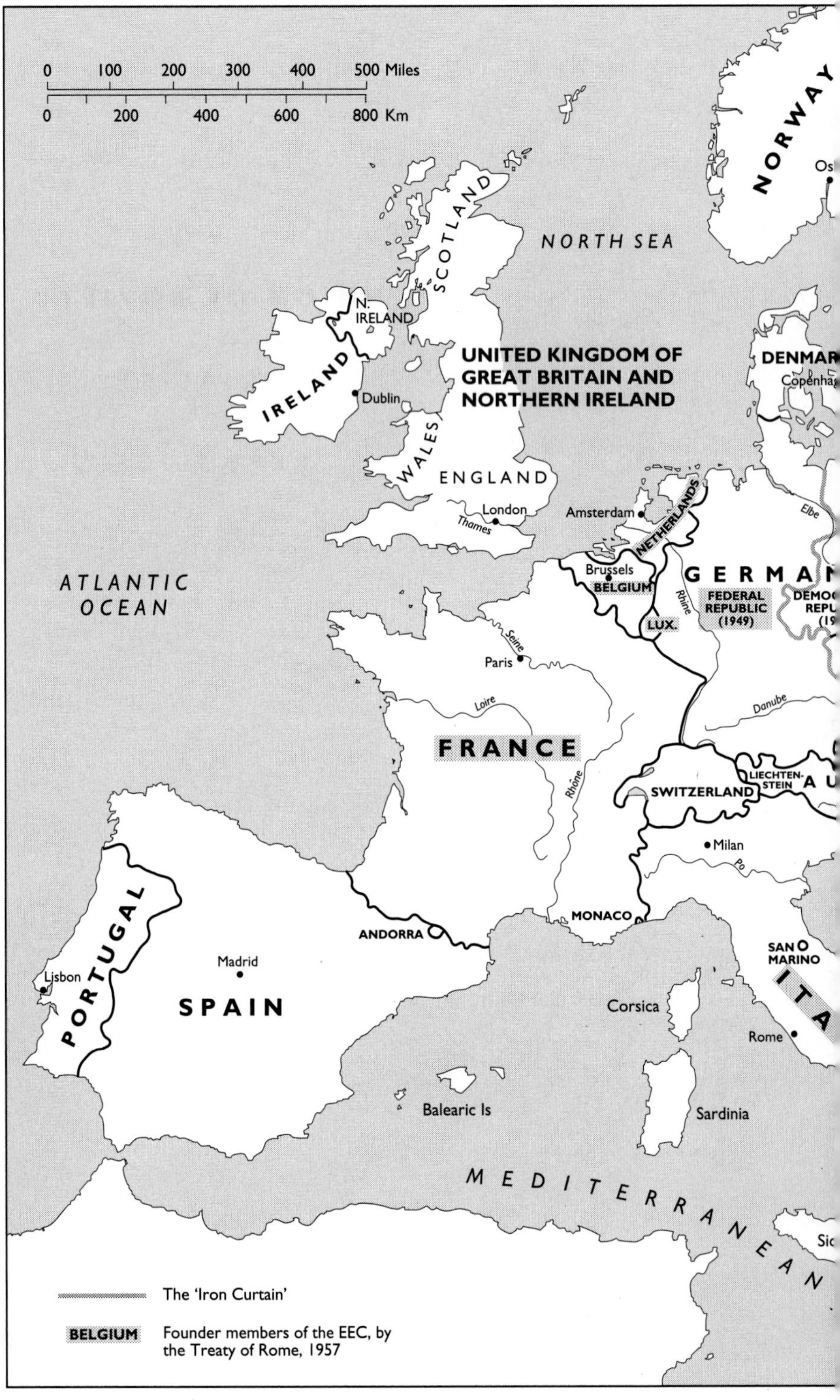

Scale:
0 100 200 300 400 500 Miles
0 200 400 600 800 Km

NORWAY

Os[...]

NORTH SEA

SCOTLAND

N. IRELAND

IRELAND

Dublin

DENMAR[...]
Copenha[...]

UNITED KINGDOM OF
GREAT BRITAIN AND
NORTHERN IRELAND

WALES

ENGLAND

London
Thames

Amsterdam

NETHERLANDS

GERMA[...]

Brussels
BELGIUM

Elbe

ATLANTIC
OCEAN

LUX.

FEDERAL
REPUBLIC
(1949)

DEMO[...]
REPL[...]
(19[...]

Paris

Seine

Rhine

Loire

Danube

FRANCE

Rhône

LIECHTEN-
STEIN

A U[...]

SWITZERLAND

Milan

Po

PORTUGAL

ANDORRA

MONACO

SAN O
MARINO

ITA[...]

Madrid

Corsica

Lisbon

SPAIN

Rome

Balearic Is

Sardinia

MEDITERRANEAN

Sic[...]

━━━━━ The 'Iron Curtain'

BELGIUM Founder members of the EEC, by
the Treaty of Rome, 1957

FINLAND

Helsinki
Leningrad

Stockholm
Tallinn

ESTONIA

EDEN

Gotland

BALTIC SEA

Riga
LATVIA

Dvina

UNION OF SOVIET

Moscow

SOCIALIST

REPUBLICS

LITHUANIA

Neman
Vilnius

Gdansk

POLAND

Vistula
Warsaw

Oder

Dnieper

CHOSLOVAKIA

na

Dniester

Budapest

HUNGARY

RUMANIA

YUGOSLAVIA

Belgrade
Bucharest

BLACK SEA

Danube

BULGARIA

Sofia

tic Sea

ALBANIA

Tirana

Istanbul

GREECE

Aegean
Sea

TURKEY

E A

Athens

Rhodes

Crete

Cyprus

Europe in 1995

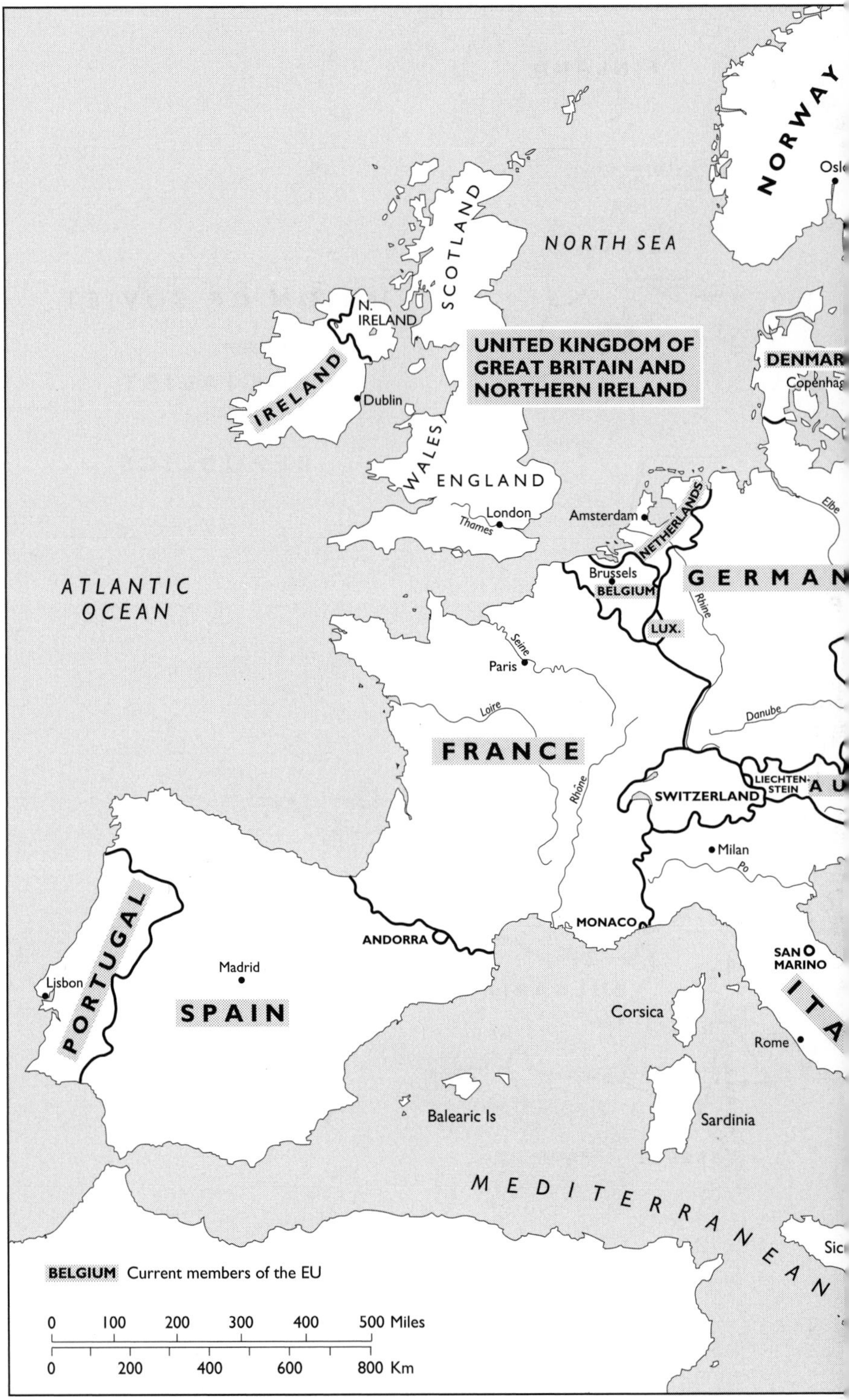

NORWAY

Oslo

NORTH SEA

SCOTLAND

N. IRELAND

IRELAND

Dublin

WALES

ENGLAND

London

Thames

UNITED KINGDOM OF
GREAT BRITAIN AND
NORTHERN IRELAND

DENMARK

Copenhagen

Amsterdam

NETHERLANDS

GERMANY

Elbe

ATLANTIC
OCEAN

Brussels

BELGIUM

LUX.

Rhine

Seine

Paris

Loire

Danube

FRANCE

Rhône

SWITZERLAND

LIECHTEN-
STEIN

AU

Milan

Po

PORTUGAL

Lisbon

Madrid

SPAIN

ANDORRA

MONACO

SAN
MARINO

ITA

Corsica

Rome

Balearic Is

Sardinia

MEDITERRANEAN

Sic

BELGIUM Current members of the EU

| 0 | 100 | 200 | 300 | 400 | 500 Miles |

| 0 | 200 | 400 | 600 | 800 Km |

Acknowledgement of Sources

The editors and publishers wish to thank the following who have kindly given permission to reproduce the illustrations on the following pages:

13 Private Collection; 17 Bulloz; 18 Giraudon; 20 E. T. Archiv; 23 Musée Carnavalet, Paris; 24 Lauros-Giraudon; 27 Bildarchiv Preussischer Kulturbesitz; 28 Private Collection; 29 AKG Berlin; 30 (top) AKG Berlin, (bottom) Mansell Collection; 31 Mansell Collection; 32 (top) Bildarchiv Preussischer Kulturbesitz, (bottom) Popperfoto; 33 The Ulster Museum, Belfast; 34 National Library, Sofia; 36 L'Illustration; 38 Prague Parliament House, Prague; 41 Hulton Picture Co.; 42 Mary Evans Picture Library; 43 (top) Mary Evans Picture Library, (bottom) Popperfoto; 45 Mary Evans Picture Library; 47 SCCR (Society for Cultural Relations with USSR); 48 Novosti; 49 Hulton Picture Co.; 50 Bildarchiv Preussischer Kulturbesitz; 51 AKG London; 56 IMech.E (Institute of Mechanical Engineers); 58 Hulton Picture Co.; 60 Hulton Picture Co.; 61 Bildarchiv Preussischer Kulturbesitz; 62 Hulton Picture Co.; 64 Novosti; 65 Novosti; 66 David King; 67 SCCR (Society for Cultural Relations with USSR); 68 David King; 70 (top) Hulton Picture Co., (bottom) AKG Berlin; 71 Range/Bettman; 72 (top) Popperfoto, (bottom) Hulton Picture Co.; 73 AKG Berlin; 74 AKG Berlin; 76 AKG Berlin; 77 © Her Majesty Queen Elizabeth II. Photo: Royal Collection Enterprises; 83 Hulton Picture Co.; 84 Hulton Picture Co.; 85 AKG Berlin; 87 Hulton Picture Co.; 89 Hulton Picture Co.; 90 Hulton Picture Co.; 91 Hulton Picture Co.; 92 AKG Berlin; 93 Hulton Picture Co.; 96 Sotheby's, London; 97 AKG Berlin; 98 (top) Hulton Picture Co., (bottom) AKG Berlin; 99 AKG Berlin; 101 Hulton Picture Co.; 102 AKG Berlin; 103 Hulton Picture Co.; 106 Illustrated London News Picture Library; 108 Bridgeman Art Library; 110 AKG Berlin; 111 (top) AKG Berlin, (bottom) AKG Berlin; 112 (top) AKG Berlin, (bottom) Illustrated London News; 113 Dr Pamela Pilbeam (bottom) Musée Carnavalet, Paris. Photo: Giraudon; 114 (top) AKG Berlin, (bottom) Dr Pamela Pilbeam; 115 AKG Berlin; 117 Mansell Collection; 120–1 Musée Carnavalet, Paris. Photo: Giraudon; 123 AKG London; 125 Markisches Museum, Berlin; 127 National Gallery, Berlin. Photo: Bridgeman Art Library; 128 Weltliche und Geistliche Schatzkammer, Vienna; 129 Museen der Stadt Wien; 130 AKG London; 131 AKG London; 132 © Roger-Viollet; 133 City of Edinburgh Museums & Art Galleries. Photo: Bridgeman Art Library; 136 Novosti; 137 Illustrated London News Picture Library; 138 Private Collection; 139 Private Collection; 141 British Library; 143 Range/Bettman; 144 Staatliche Kunstsammlungen, Dresden. Photo: Bridgeman Art Library 145 National Trust Photographic Library; 146 Ali Meyer; 149 AKG London; 151 AKG Berlin; 152 Range; 153 (top) AKG London, (bottom) AKG London; 155 AKG London; 156 AKG London; 157 AKG London; 160 Collection Astier/Magnum; 161 AKG London; 163 AKG London; 164 AKG London; 169 Range/Bettman/UPI; 171 Robert Capa/Magnum; 172 Range/Bettman; 174 AKG London; 175 AKG London; 176 AKG London; 177 Range/Bettman/UPI; 178 (top) AKG London, (bottom) AKG London; 179 Range/Bettman; 180 Range/Bettman/UPI; 184 British Film Institute; 187 Popperfoto; 188 AKG London; 191 Magnum; 192 AKG Berlin; 193 Popperfoto; 194 Popperfoto; 195 Popperfoto; 197 Hulton Picture Co.; 199 Popperfoto; 201 © Roger-Viollet; 202 Magnum; 203 Popperfoto; 204 Gilles Peress/Magnum; 207 Popperfoto; 208 IBM; 212 AKG London; 213 Roger-Viollet. © Harlingue-Viollet; 216 © Roger-Viollet; 217 AKG London; 219 Magnum; 220 Evening Standard, Solo Syndication & Literary Agency. Photo: Centre for the Study of Cartoons and Caricature, University of Kent, Canterbury; 221 Magnum; 223 AKG London; 224 Popperfoto; 225 Evening Standard, Solo Syndication & Literary Agency. Photo: Centre for the Study of Cartoons and Caricature, University of Kent,

Canterbury; **226** Philip Jones Griffiths/Magnum; **227** British Film Institute; **228** Popperfoto; **229** Popperfoto; **232** Lima Library, the Catholic University of America; **233** Staatsbibliothek, Berlin; **234** Jean Mohr, Geneva; **242** (main picture) B. Barbey/Magnum, insets: (top) Gilles Peress/Magnum, (middle) Martin Parr/Magnum, (bottom) Aurora; **244** Volkswagen, Germany; **245** Staatsarchiv Freiburg. Photo: Willy Pragher/Generallandesarchiv Karlsruhe; **249** Bilderdienst Süddeutscherverlag; **250** (left) Bundesarchiv Koblenz, (right) Bildarchiv Preussischer Kulturbesitz; **252** AKG London; **253** C. Metcalfe Photography; **256** Bildarchiv Preussischer Kulturbesitz; **257** Ullstein Bilderdienst; **258** AKG London; **259** (top) David King, (bottom) Albright Knox Art Gallery, Buffalo, NY, bequest of A. Gonger Goodyear and gift of George F. Goodyear; **260** Museum of Modern Art, New York; **261** © DACS 1996. Photo: David King; **262** AKG London; **263** © 1995 ABC/Mondrian Estate/Holtzman Trust. Licensed by IPL. Photo: Museum of Modern Art, New York; **264** © DACS 1996. Photo: Philadelphia Museum of Art, A.E. Gallatin Collection; **265** Architectural Association; **266** AKG London; **268** © Man Ray Trust/ADAGP, Paris/DACS, London 1996. Photo: Museum of Modern Art, New York, gift of James Thrall Soby; **270** © ADAGP, Paris & DACS, London 1996. Photo: AKG London; **271** Saatchi Collection, London; **272** Tim Benton; **275** Museum Ludwig, Cologne; **276** © DACS, London. John Weber Gallery, New York; **280** AKG London; **281** Magnum; **282** Hulton Picture Co.; **283** AKG Berlin; **284** AKG Berlin; **285** AKG Berlin; **287** AKG Berlin; **290** (top) Hulton Picture Co., (bottom) David King; **292** AKG Berlin; **293** Magnum; **294** Hulton Picture Co.; **295** Frank Spooner/Gamma; **297** Topham Picture Library; **298** Jean Gaumy/Magnum; **299** Frank Spooner/Gamma; **300** Frank Spooner/Gamma; **301** Associated Press/Topham; **303** Frank Spooner/Gamma; **304** Frank Spooner/Gamma.

In a few instances we have been unable to trace the copyright holder prior to publication. If notified the publishers will be pleased to amend the acknowledgements in any future edition.

Picture research by Gill Metcalfe.

Index

Tipton, F. B. 46
Tirpitz, Alfred von 89
Tito, Marshal 289–91, 302
Tocqueville, Alexis de 13, 25, 107
Toledo 171
Tolstoy, Count Leo Nikolayevich 134
total war 211, 215, 222
Toul 86
tourism 8, 198, 239, 243, 245–6
towns 120
trade unions 31, 109–10, 118, 148, 154–5, 162, 167, 189, 203
Trafalgar, battle of (1805) 76
transport 8
Transylvania 25–6, 31, 33, 35
Trentino 36
Trieste 34
Tristan, Flora 109
Trollope, Anthony 133–4
Trotsky, Leon 160, 171
Truman, Harry S. 283
Tse-Tung, Mao 293
Tsushima, battle of (1905) 76, 89
Tukhachevsky, Mikhail 214
Turkey 3, 139
  in NATO 302
  Ottoman empire 11, 14, 21–2, 27, 29, 34, 36, 71, 154, 158, 183
  and Serbs 303–4
  in World War I 71
  and World War II 177
Turpin de Crisse 77
Tyneside 52
typewriter 45

Ukraine 35, 152–3, 240
Ulbricht, Walter 291
unemployment 103, 165, 173, 183, 187, 207, 208, 235, 238, 239
underground railways 45
United Kingdom, see Great Britain
United Provinces, see Netherlands
urbanization 8, 97, 103, 116, 120, 133, 241–2
USA 6, 7, 73, 77, 205, 206, 227, 291, 302
  Civil War 82
  and communications 251
  corporations 56
  in Depression 167
  and fascism 172
  and industrialization 42, 44, 190–1
  inflation in 204
  investment in Europe 184, 197, 205
  merchant navy 191
  and migrants 97, 234
  military presence in Europe 285–6
  modernism in 266

and NATO 225, 288, 296
and 'new Cold War' 298
and new technology 197
piano industry 126
and post-World War II revival 191–2, 194, 280, 282
and stabilization of French currency 190
as superpower 148, 181, 183, 191, 225, 280
and transport revolution 244
Wall Street crash 163, 186
in World War I 37, 150–1, 153–4, 158, 183
in World War II 177, 179, 190–2, 220
USSR 6–7, 9–10, 195, 217, 304
  agriculture 66, 74, 103, 187, 238, 241
  collectivization 187–9
  and détente 296–7
  emergence of 37
  and fascism 175
  and industrialization 187–9
  inflation 240
  League of Nations, exclusion from 210
  military modernization 214, 215, 227
  modernism in 259
  and 'new Cold War' 298–9
  and Popular Front 166
  post-World War I 159–60, 166, 172
  post-World War II 279–80, 283, 286
  Soviet bloc 289–91, 296
  as superpower 148, 181, 215, 279–80, 286, 289–91
  in World War I 151–3
  in World War II 177–9, 180, 218–19, 222, 227
  See also Russia

vaccination 95, 106, 237
Valhalla 142
Valmy, battle of (1792) 69
Van Gogh, Vincent 147, 276
Varèse, Edgar 274
Vatican 131
Vattimo, Gianni 272
Vecchi, Cesare Maria de 161
Venice 28, 29, 134
Venturi, Robert 269
Verdi, Giuseppe 140
Verdun 70, 86, 150–1
Verdun, battle of (1916) 85
Verlaine, Paul 8, 256
Versailles, palace of 120
Versailles settlement (1919) 6, 38, 156–9, 181, 210
Verviers 42
Vickers 72
Victor Emmanuel II 143
Victoria, Queen 129